"Many 'weeknight' cookbooks claim to deliver on quickness and ease, but *Nights and Weekends* is the first book I've ever seen to actually live up to the promise. In Nights, de Boschnek cuts corners in the smartest ways possible to deliver recipes that, both literally and practically, show you how quick a delicious meal can be made. In Weekends, she switches things up with party-style plating and lavish-feeling dishes that make eating feel celebratory."

—BEN MIMS, AUTHOR OF *CRUMBS*

"Alexis is the friend you always look forward to visiting because she constantly finds a way to make every meal feel special. Her cookbook encourages home cooks to do more of that: to celebrate every day of the week with approachable, flavor-packed, and highly rewarding recipes. Whether you're searching for casual dinners for busy weeknights or crowd-pleasing meals for your next weekend gathering, this cookbook has it all."

—CAROLINA GELEN, *NEW YORK TIMES* BESTSELLING AUTHOR OF *PASS THE PLATE*

"Alexis's kind soul, infectious passion for all things delicious, and hard-earned kitchen knowledge are on full display in the luscious pages of her new book. Her simple, seasonally inspired food is beautiful without being pretentious, achievable without feeling pedestrian, and hits that perfect balance between healthful and exciting, which is exactly how I want to eat all the time."

—CHRISTINA CHAEY, WRITER AND RECIPE DEVELOPER

Nights and Weekends

ALEXIS DE BOSCHNEK

Nights and Weekends

RECIPES THAT MAKE THE MOST OF YOUR TIME

Photographs by Christian Harder

U

UNION
SQUARE
& CO.

NEW YORK

U
UNION
SQUARE
& CO.
NEW YORK

UNION SQUARE & CO. and the distinctive Union Square & Co. logo are trademarks of Sterling Publishing Co., Inc.

Union Square & Co., LLC, is a subsidiary of Sterling Publishing Co., Inc.

Text © 2025 Alexis deBoschnek
Photographs © 2025 Christian Harder

All rights reserved. No part of this publication may be reproduced, stored in a retrieval system, or transmitted in any form or by any means (including electronic, mechanical, photocopying, recording, or otherwise) without prior written permission from the publisher.

ISBN 978-1-4549-5498-9
ISBN 978-1-4549-5499-6 (e-book)

For information about custom editions, special sales, and premium purchases, please contact specialsales@unionsquareandco.com.

Printed in China

10 9 8 7 6 5 4 3 2 1

unionsquareandco.com

Editor: Caitlin Leffel
Designer: Renée Bollier
Photographer: Christian Harder
Food Stylist: Rebekah Peppler
Prop Stylist: Rebecca Bartoshesky
Project Editor: Ivy McFadden
Production Manager: Terence Campo
Copy Editor: Ana Deboo

*For Ryan,
my favorite person to eat with,
every day*

NIGHTS

Pasta

- 19 Crab Pasta with Pistachios and Olives
- 20 Not-Your-Mom's Pasta Salad
- 23 Pasta with Brown Butter Wilted Greens and Walnuts
- 24 Tomato Sauce with Pancetta, White Beans, and Rosemary
- 27 One-Pot Gnocchi Ragù
- 28 Stovetop Mac and Cheese
- 31 Crispy Gnocchi Caprese
- 32 Udon Noodles with Peanut Sauce
- 35 Orzo with Leeks, Olives, and Golden Raisins
- 36 Pasta with Bacon, Peas, Sour Cream, and Dill
- 39 Creamy Green Pasta

Soups and Stews

- 43 Lemon Chicken Soup for Whatever Ails You
- 44 Chickpea Curry
- 47 Spring Vegetable Soup with Dumplings and Dill
- 48 Roasted Tomato and Red Pepper Soup
- 51 Split Pea Soup with Bacon and Croutons
- 52 Pasta e Ceci
- 55 White Turkey Chili
- 56 Salmon, Potato, and Corn Chowder
- 59 Zucchini Soup
- 60 Red Coconut Curry with Tofu
- 63 Creamy Cauliflower Soup with Chile Crisp

Vegetable Mains, Sides, and Salads

- 67 Couscous and Chickpea Salad
- 68 Socca with Arugula Salad
- 71 Mushroom and Pea Toast
- 72 Roasted Broccoli and Crispy Chickpeas with Tahini Dressing
- 75 One-Pot Rice and Beans
- 76 Summer Squash Casserole with Buttery Ritz Crackers
- 79 Tofu in Miso Butter Sauce with Corn
- 80 Kale Salad with Roasted Grapes
- 83 Marinated White Beans and Artichokes
- 84 Everything Bagel Tomato Panzanella
- 87 Brussels Sprout Salad with Hazelnuts and Feta
- 88 Cheesy Potato and Pinto Bean Tacos
- 91 Artichokes with Herb Aioli
- 92 Tofu with Scallion Garlic Ginger Oil
- 95 Sweet Potatoes with Miso Sesame Butter
- 96 Roasted Broccolini and Banana Peppers over Ricotta
- 99 Mushroom Larb
- 100 Chopped Chicory Salad
- 103 Roasted Cauliflower, Chickpeas, and Sweet Potatoes with Spiced Yogurt
- 104 Cheesy Potato Tart
- 107 Halloumi Fattoush
- 108 Big Green Seedy Salad

Meat

- 113 Skirt Steak with Scallion Butter and Slaw
- 114 Chicken Thighs in Creamy Paprika Sauce
- 117 Turkey and Butternut Squash Bowl
- 118 Rotisserie Chicken Salad with Snap Peas and Dilly Ranch
- 121 Spiced Lamb Flatbreads
- 122 Sheet-Pan Sausage with Corn, Peach, and Cucumber Salad
- 125 Polenta with Saucy Sausage and Tomatoes
- 126 Couscous with Merguez, Broccoli, and Halloumi
- 129 Pork Tenderloin with Pineapple and Peppers
- 130 Grilled Chicken Sandwiches
- 133 Pork Chops au Poivre
- 134 Turkey Meatballs with Puttanesca Sauce

Fish

- 139 Chile Crisp Salmon with Quick Pickle Salad
- 140 Cod in Green Sauce
- 143 Saucy Shrimp with Beans and Greens
- 144 Potato Salad with Pesto, Smoked Fish, and Asparagus
- 147 Roasted Tomatoes, Artichokes, and Leeks with Sardines
- 148 Shrimp Salad with Horseradish Aioli Dressing

CONTENTS

151 Baked Halibut with Pesto Rosso
152 Hot Butter Garlic Shrimp
155 Conserva Plate

WEEKENDS

Snacks

163 Salmon Ceviche with Cucumber and Tajín
164 Caramelized Shallot Dip
166 Marinated Olives in Citrus and Spices
167 Jammy Eggs with Mayo and Chile Oil
169 Soy-Blistered Shishitos
170 Hot Cheesy Crab Dip
173 Fire Crackers
174 Everything Bagel Spice Cheese Ball
177 Cornmeal Fried Okra with Special Sauce
178 Antipasti Skewers
181 Gochujang Almond Butter Dip

Brunch

185 Cacio e Pepe Popovers
186 Prosciutto and Brie Frittata
189 Pear and Pecan Baked Oatmeal
190 Stone Fruit Salad
193 Buttermilk Ginger Scones
194 Savory Breakfast Bowl
197 French Onion Soup Strata
198 Sticky Rolls with Pistachios and Caramel
202 Olive Oil Banana Bread with Chocolate Chunks
205 Sour Cream Waffles

Dinner

209 Crêpes with Mushrooms and Gremolata
210 Rib Eyes with a Party Wedge Salad
213 Braised Chicken Thighs with Prunes and Lemons
214 Butternut Squash and Ricotta Lasagna
217 Whole Roasted Spiced Cauliflower with Herby Yogurt Sauce
218 Soy-Braised Cumin Lamb
221 Tofu Schnitzel with Braised Cabbage
223 Slow-Roasted Salmon with Grapefruit and Crispy Shallots
226 French Market Chicken with Schmaltzy Potatoes
229 Shrimp Boil with Garlicky Old Bay Butter
230 Curried Chicken and Cauliflower Phyllo Pie
233 Vinegary Pot Roast with Parsnips and Carrots
235 Tomato Pie with Buttermilk Biscuit Crust
238 Greekish Whole Fish

Dessert

243 Strawberry Rhubarb Cake
244 Classic Lemon Bars
247 Grilled Peaches with Cardamom Honey Whipped Cream
248 Chocolate Frosting and Yellow Sour Cream Birthday Cake
251 Party Pavlova
253 Maggie's Brown Butter Apple Crumble
256 Gingersnap Cookies
259 Spumoni
260 Tahini Chocolate Cheesecake Bars
263 Dark Chocolate Mousse with Mascarpone Whipped Cream
264 Sticky Toffee Pudding

Introduction 9
Acknowledgments 267
Index 268

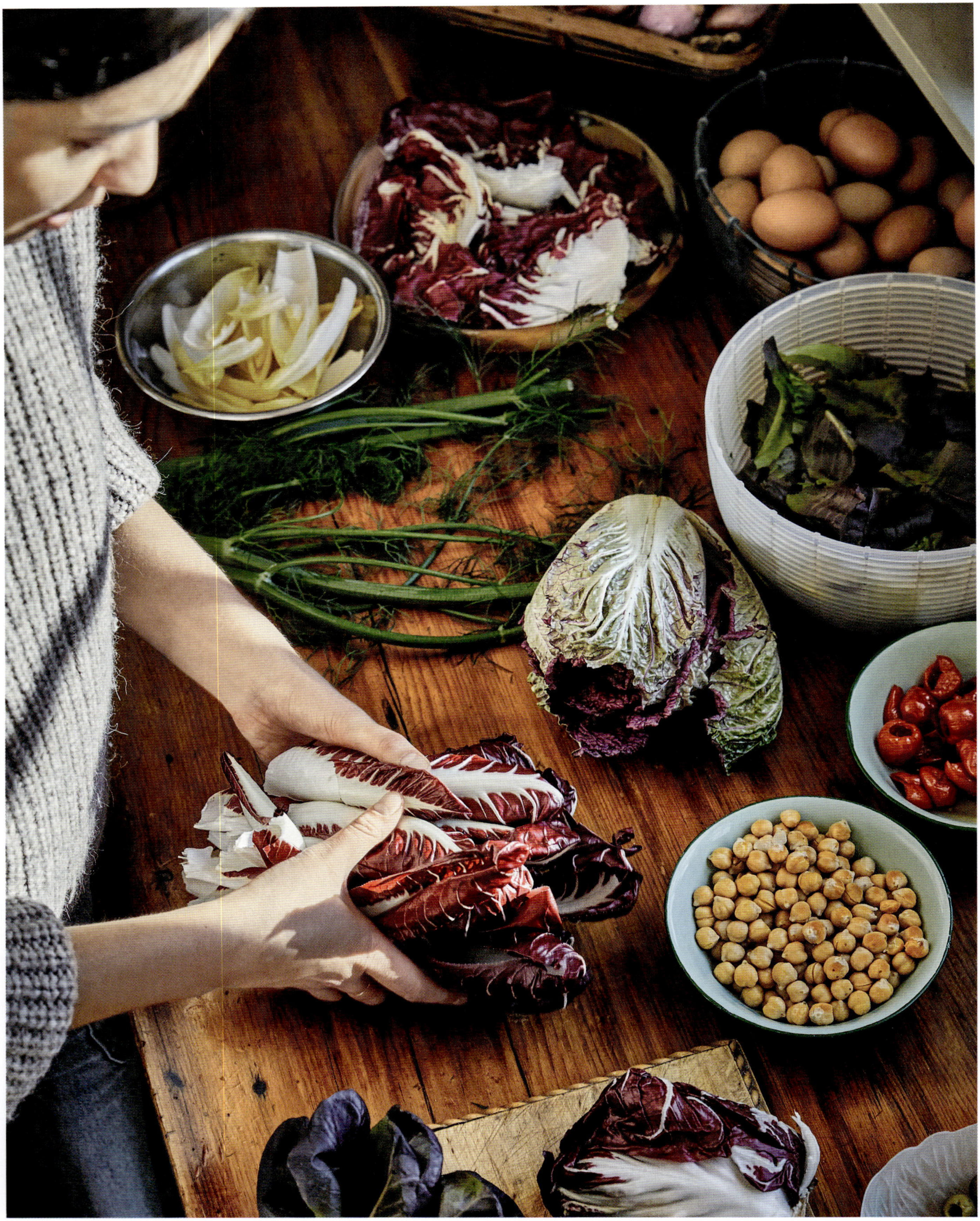

Introduction

There's an assumption when you've made cooking your livelihood that every meal involves hours in the kitchen, tinkering away on meticulously written recipes, each involving multiple dishes, ingredients, and techniques. You might imagine someone in this position would spend leisurely afternoons pondering what produce is begging to be picked from the market, or that putting together a menu for a week of eating might be an effortless endeavor.

To some extent, there's an element to this vision that's true. I do dream of afternoons spent making a double-crust pie teeming with fruit from the market or braising a hunk of meat that'll inevitably perfume the whole house. I have a knack for planning and keep a well-stocked pantry and feel the most comfortable drifting across the kitchen. As much as I love eating, so much of the joy for me has been in the process of cooking.

But then there's work to do, chores to tend to, errands to run, and suddenly it's six p.m. and I'm peering into the fridge wondering what to make for dinner. After unexpectedly being thrust into a full-time caretaker role, along with tending to the animals on our farm and maintaining my own career (and, and, and), the prospect of figuring out what to make for dinner felt more daunting than ever. I wasn't thinking about how I'd slowly roast a chicken over potatoes until they became creamy and tender, or how I might try making homemade pasta and cut it by hand (just for fun!). I just needed to get dinner on the table, and quickly.

In this season of caretaking, cooking was less about passion and more about utility. So often weeknight cooking can feel like pantry roulette where you're spinning the wheel on the same six recipes in your back pocket. No matter how long you wait for that lightning bolt of inspiration to

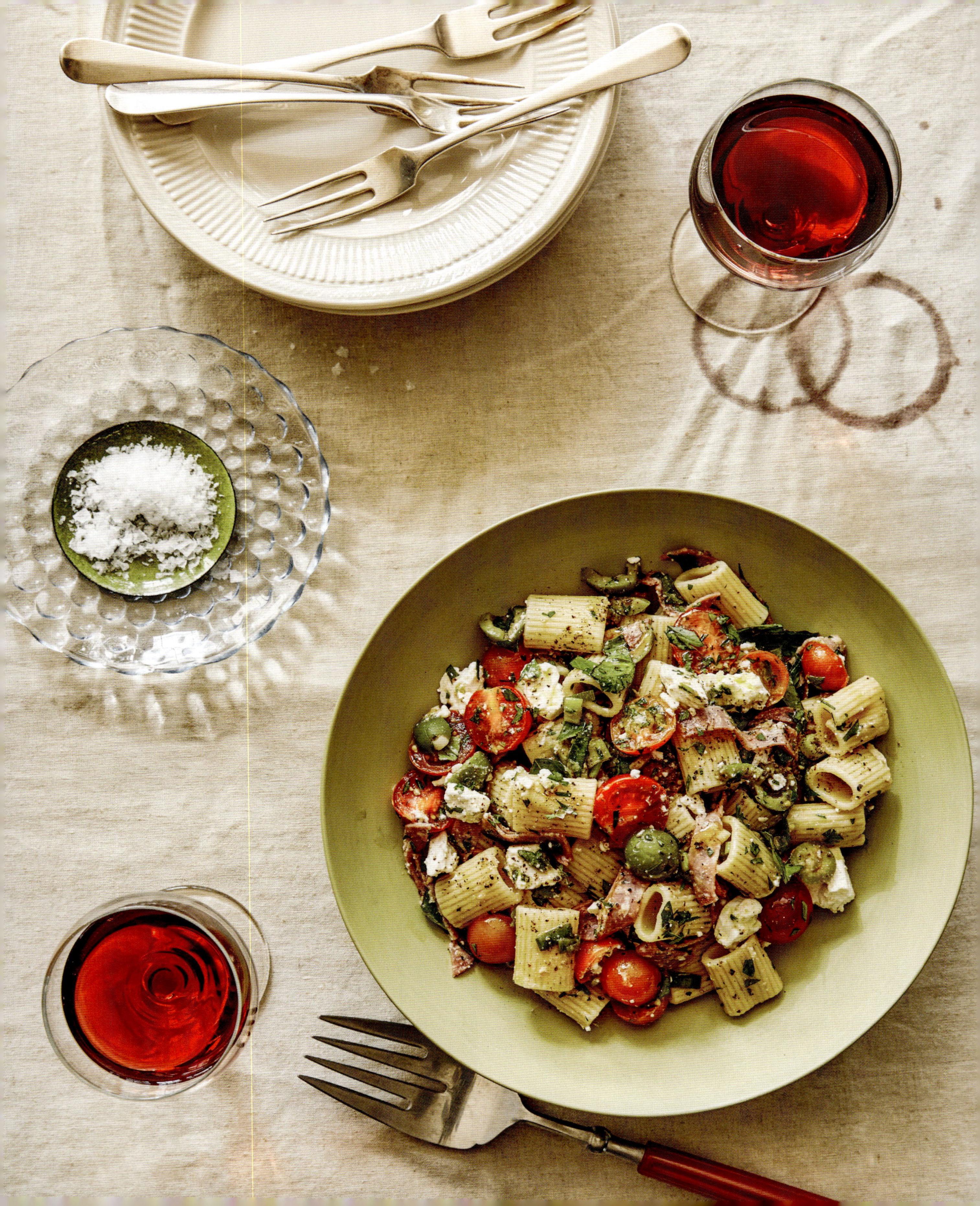

strike, after a long day, it feels almost impossible to land on anything worth getting excited about. There's nothing like staring at your pantry for the fifteenth time that night to make you start scrolling through delivery apps again. This plight is hardly unique. Nearly everyone I know is under the same type of pressure in their day-to-day life.

For the last decade, and even in my first book, my whole ethos has been about trying to encourage people to get in the kitchen in any capacity, with the hope they'll eventually share my passion for the process. While that will always be true, this moment in time shifted my perspective to the simple question of how can I help people get dinner on the table? I love an aspirational recipe, but to really get people cooking, I knew recipes needed to be accessible, come together quickly, and most important, taste delicious. After all this effort, maybe the best way to share my love for cooking is just to make it feel like something attainable.

While I still love making long, arduous recipes, those meals are typically reserved for special occasions or dinner parties on the weekend. If you're like me, you want a quick pasta on a Tuesday, but are still leaving room for the potential of rib eyes and a martini on a Saturday. This is the space where *Nights and Weekends* was born. Low-effort, high-reward recipes to take you through the week.

This book is organized into two primary sections—dishes to cook on busy weeknights and meals to make when you've got more time on your hands. Two-thirds of the recipes fall into the weeknight dinner category, with chapters including pasta, soups and stews, meat, fish, and tons of vegetarian options. Think about pastas that sneak in a ton of greens (page 23), cheesy bean and potato tacos (page 88), and hot butter garlic shrimp (page 152) that ensure dinner is on the table in under ten minutes. The Nights section is all about dinner, because let's be real, who's making dessert on a Wednesday?

The remaining third of the recipes are for dishes you might make when you have a little more time on your hands, like a vegetarian lasagna with layers of silky butternut squash puree and ricotta (page 214), braised chicken thighs studded with prunes and charred lemons (page 213), or sticky rolls topped with pistachios and caramel (page 198). The Weekends section is broken down by occasion and meal type rather than category of food.

I've made it a mission to create recipes that are easy to follow, no matter what night they fall on. The recipes in the weekend section don't mean they're harder, just a bit more involved than something you'd want to make after work. There are a few recipes that even toe the line, like the Greekish fish (page 238), which is painfully easy to prepare, but I know it might take a Saturday night to coax out the enthusiasm to try cooking a whole fish.

I'm a passionate omnivore, but like so many, I'm trying to incorporate more vegetarian meals into my rotation. I'm a firm believer in eating less meat and fish and taking where these proteins are being sourced more into consideration. Because of this, over half the recipes in *Nights and Weekends* are vegetarian or vegan, and many more can be swapped out to be so.

Nights and Weekends is first and foremost about getting dinner on the table, but my hope is that it inspires you throughout the week, no matter what day it is.

NIGHTS

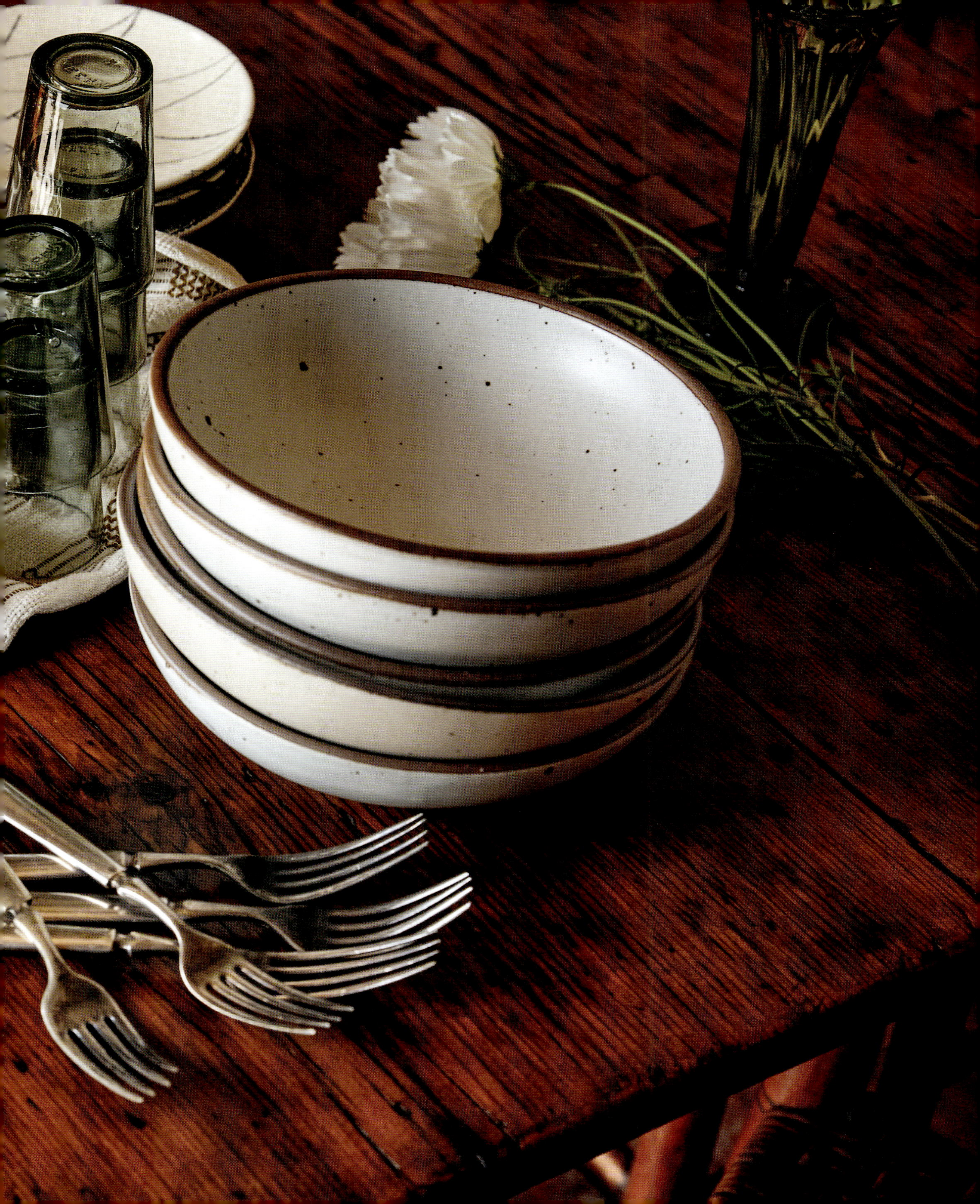

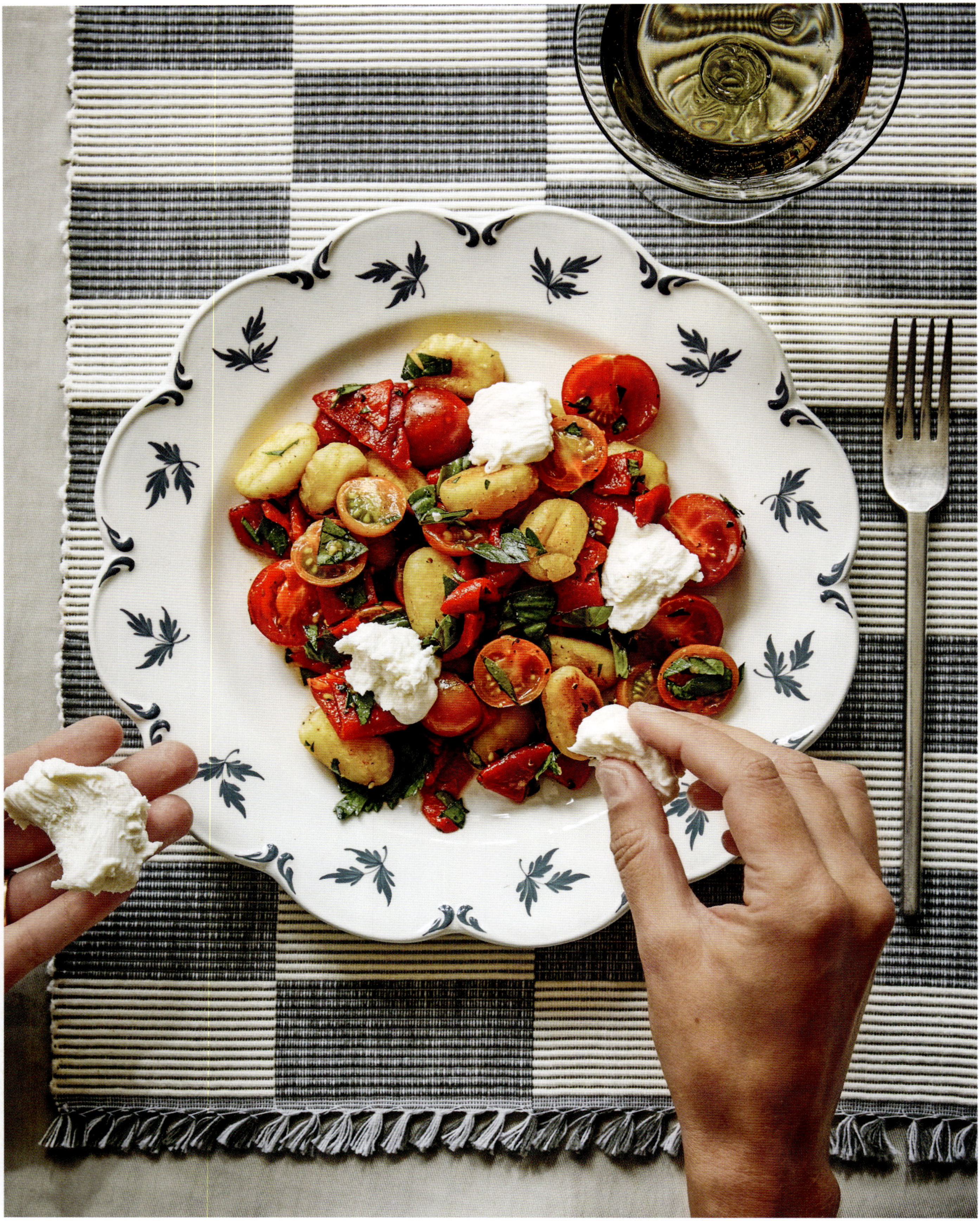

Weeknight Cooking

In order to qualify as a weeknight recipe, a recipe needs to meet these criteria:

- ❖ **TIME:** Perhaps the most important tenet of all, weeknight recipes must come together quickly. There's no hard and fast rule to say all the recipes must be complete within a certain time frame, since everyone's skill levels vary, but I've tried to cover a range of recipes. There are dishes that can be made in under 10 minutes, others that can be on the table in 30 minutes, and some that take little active time but might be in the oven for 20 minutes, giving you just enough time to unwind. What you can be sure about is none of the recipes here require you to be married to the kitchen for an afternoon to get dinner on the table.

- ❖ **EFFORT:** Tied closely to time is the amount of effort a recipe requires. Weeknight recipes shouldn't require fancy tools or an endless list of ingredients to prepare. Whenever possible, I've opted for shortcuts like slicing an onion over dicing, which may not seem groundbreaking but saves both time and effort. The goal here is to deliver recipes that you can make with little effort while offering flexibility.

- ❖ **INGREDIENTS:** Specialty ingredients have no place in weeknight cooking. The recipes here lean on pantry staples and highlight canned or jarred items that cut down on time. I've also made use of single ingredients that deliver big flavors, like chili powder, chile crisp, miso, and red curry paste. This is the time to make use of quicker-cooking proteins, like boneless, skinless chicken breast, ground turkey, or shrimp. Cooking on a weeknight also means utilizing store-bought or ready-made ingredients like puff pastry and rotisserie chicken.

- ❖ **EASE:** While this section is not entirely a collection of one-pot or one-pan recipes, weeknight meals should require as few pans and utensils as possible. Whenever applicable I've listed substitutions or swaps, or called out elements of dishes that can be made ahead or skipped entirely.

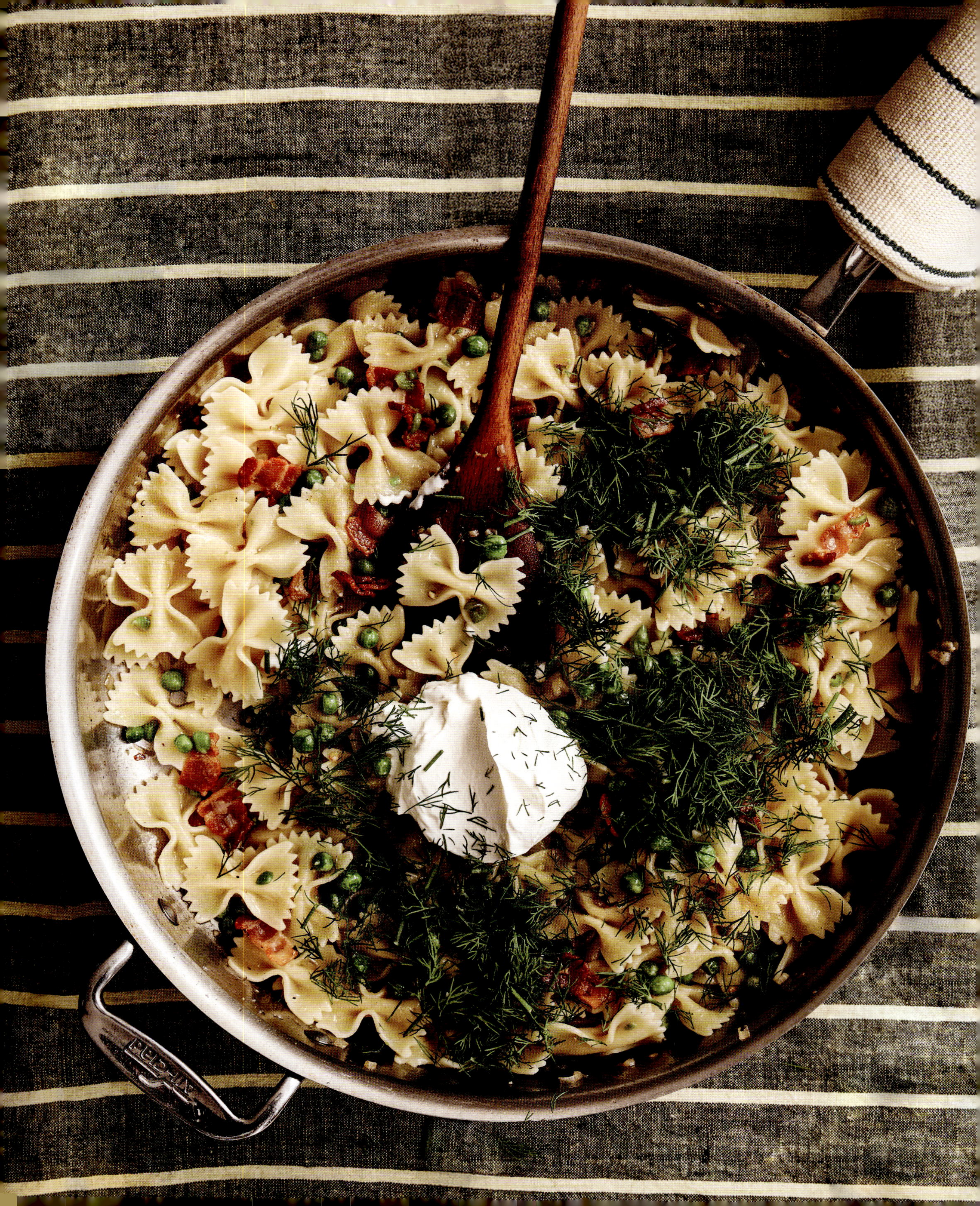

NIGHTS

PASTA

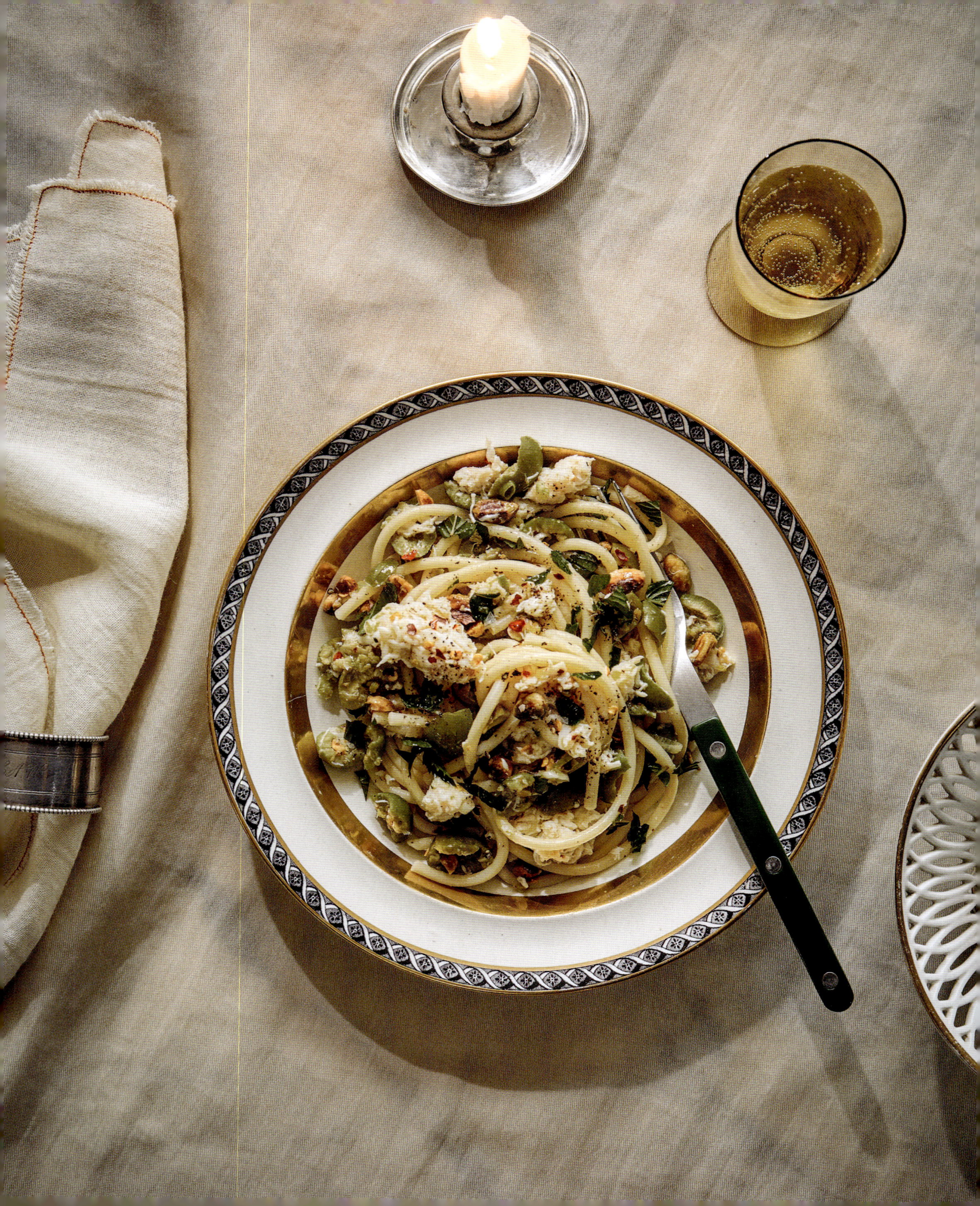

Crab Pasta with Pistachios and Olives

Hear me out—I know crab is pricey, but it doesn't take much to make this dish shine. While crab may not seem like a weeknight meal, this comes together in under fifteen minutes and couldn't be easier to assemble. There are olives for saltiness, pistachios for crunch, and herbs and lemon to keep it bright and punchy. At the same time, it's festive enough to serve for a special occasion.

NOTES: Swap in canned tuna for crab if that's more your thing. I add the mint at the end so that it doesn't brown with the heat of the pasta. Leftovers can be stored in an airtight container in the refrigerator for up to 3 days.

1. Bring a large pot of salted water to a boil over high heat. Add the pasta and cook until al dente according to the package instructions. Drain the pasta in a colander.

2. While the pasta is boiling, add the crab, olives, pistachios, scallions, lemon zest, lemon juice, olive oil, red pepper flakes, and 1 teaspoon salt to a large bowl and stir to combine.

3. Add the pasta to the bowl with the crab and toss to combine. Add the mint, toss again, and serve.

Serves 4 to 6

Kosher salt

1 (16-ounce) box long pasta of choice

1 (8-ounce) container lump crabmeat, picked through for shells

1 cup pitted Castelvetrano olives, coarsely chopped

1 cup raw shelled pistachios, coarsely chopped

4 scallions, thinly sliced

Zest and juice of 1 lemon (about 2 tablespoons juice)

1 tablespoon extra-virgin olive oil

½ teaspoon red pepper flakes

1 cup packed fresh mint leaves, coarsely chopped

Not-Your-Mom's Pasta Salad

This warm-weather dish is a constant at summer barbecues, but it's also ideal for nights when your enthusiasm for cooking is low, when you want to meal prep, or when you need a dish to pass at a potluck. No shame to Mom, but my pasta salad is a far cry from the mayo-slicked macaroni salads of our youth. I've channeled Italian antipasti spread and studded the pasta salad with tomatoes, creamy Castelvetrano olives, salami, feta, and a ton of herbs. The key to good pasta salad is to let it absorb the vinaigrette before serving, which will intensify the flavor. To do this, make sure you let the pasta fully cool to room temperature before serving. Or better yet, refrigerate it overnight.

NOTES: To make the pasta salad vegetarian, leave out the salami. Basil browns in the refrigerator, so wait until you're ready to serve to add it in. Pasta salad can be stored in an airtight container in the refrigerator for up to 3 days.

1. Bring a large pot of salted water to a boil over high heat. Add the pasta and cook until al dente according to the package instructions. Drain the pasta in a colander.

2. While the pasta is boiling, add the tomatoes, olives, salami, scallions, garlic, pepper, 1 teaspoon salt, vinegar, and olive oil to a large bowl, and stir to combine.

3. Add the pasta to the bowl and stir to combine. Let the pasta cool to room temperature and refrigerate until serving.

4. Just before serving, add the feta, parsley, and basil and stir to combine.

Serves 4 to 6

Kosher salt

1 (16-ounce) box pasta of choice

2 cups cherry tomatoes, halved

1 cup pitted Castelvetrano olives, coarsely chopped

1 (3-ounce) package salami, thinly sliced (about 1 cup; optional)

1 bunch scallions, thinly sliced

1 large garlic clove, grated

1 teaspoon freshly ground black pepper

¼ cup sherry vinegar

¼ cup extra-virgin olive oil

1½ cups crumbled feta cheese

½ bunch flat-leaf parsley, finely chopped (about 1 cup)

1 cup coarsely chopped fresh basil leaves

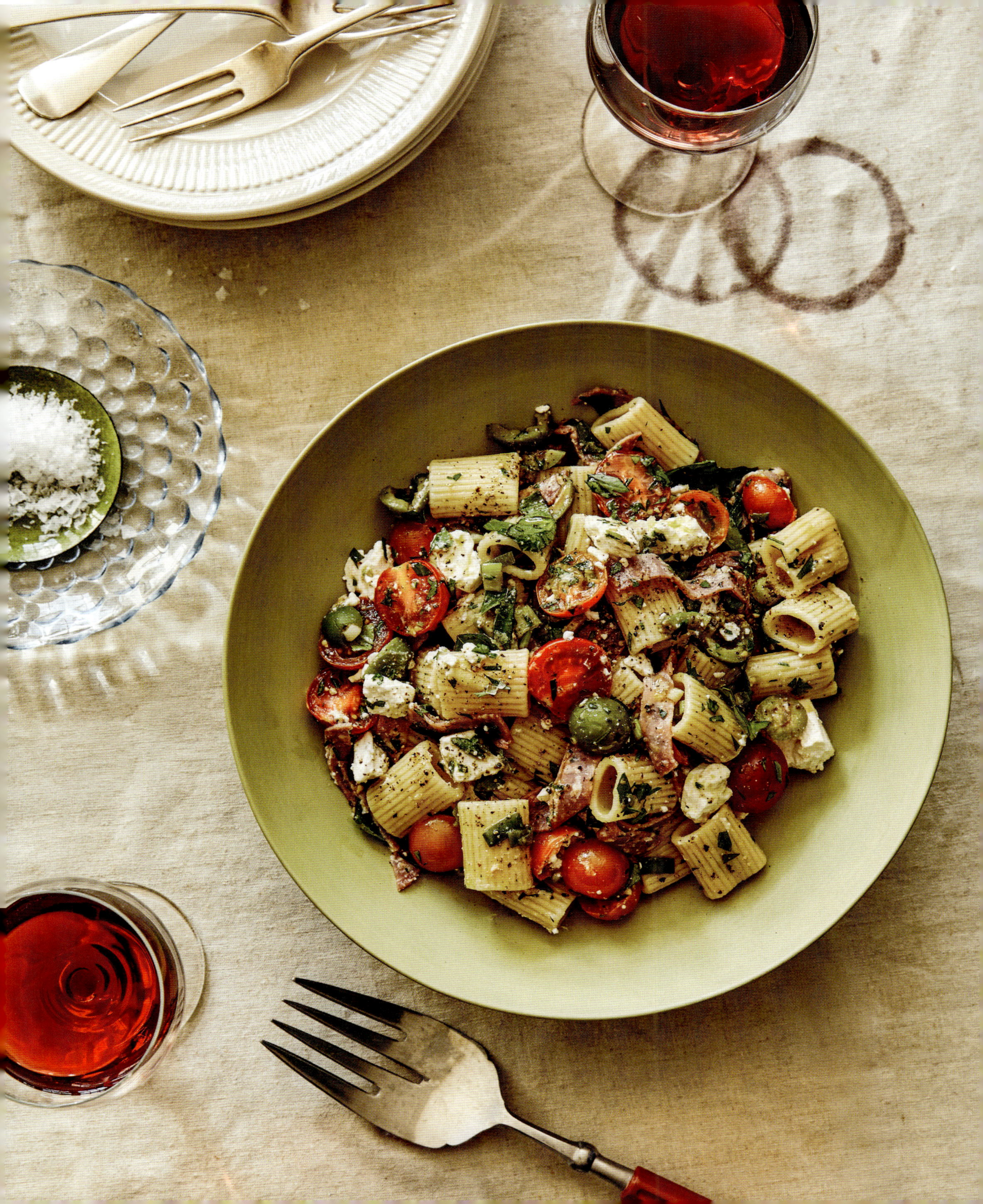

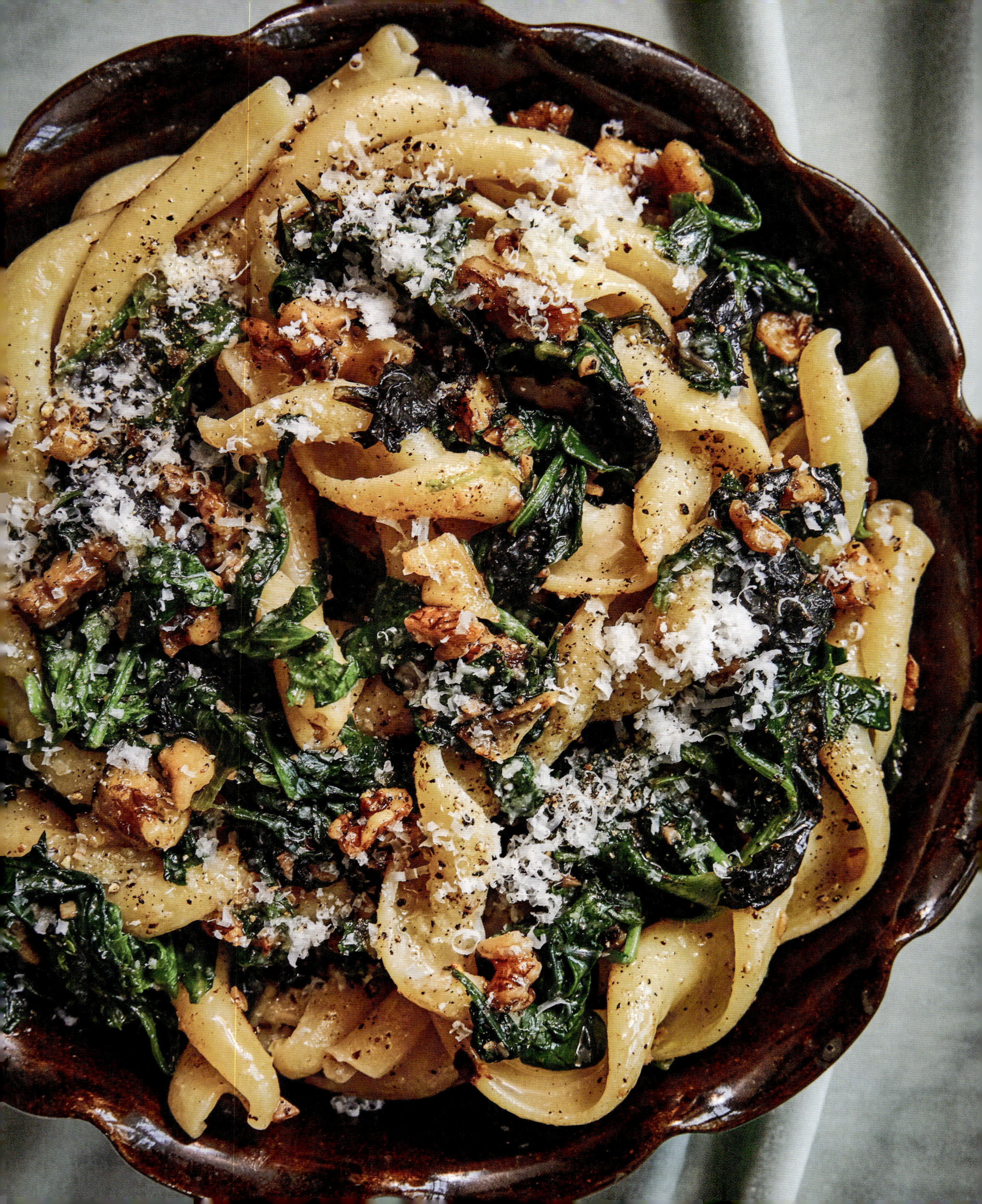

Pasta with Brown Butter Wilted Greens and Walnuts

If, like me, you often buy a box of mixed greens with big intentions, only to have them slowly wither in the back of the refrigerator, this recipe is for you. It's a pantry pasta that gets the bulk of flavor from cooking the butter until nutty and golden brown, along with a generous amount of garlic. While a 10-ounce box may seem like a lot, the greens wilt down in minutes once they touch the heat of the pan.

NOTES: I call for a box of mixed greens here, but any assortment of greens will work to sauté, like spinach, kale, mustard greens, radicchio, or arugula. The point is to use something you have on hand. You can use any type of nut you'd like in place of walnuts, such as pecans, hazelnuts, pine nuts, or pistachios. While you can also leave them out, I like the crunch they add. Leftover pasta can be stored in an airtight container in the refrigerator for up to 2 days.

Serves 4 to 6

Kosher salt

1 (16-ounce) box short pasta of choice

6 tablespoons (¾ stick) unsalted butter

¾ cup walnuts or other nut of choice, coarsely chopped

4 garlic cloves, minced

1 teaspoon freshly ground black pepper

¼ teaspoon red pepper flakes

1 (10-ounce) box mixed greens

1 cup freshly grated Parmigiano Reggiano cheese

1. Bring a large pot of salted water to a boil over high heat. Add the pasta and cook until al dente according to the package instructions. Drain the pasta in a colander.

2. Melt the butter in a large pan over medium-high heat, swirling the pan occasionally. When the butter has melted and become foamy, reduce the heat to medium-low and cook until the butter is lightly golden brown and smells nutty, 3 to 4 minutes. Add the walnuts, garlic, 1 teaspoon salt, the black pepper, and the red pepper flakes and cook, stirring, until aromatic, about 30 seconds.

3. Increase the heat to medium-high, add the mixed greens to the pan, and cook until the greens are wilted, 1 to 2 minutes. Remove the pan from the heat. Add the pasta and Parmigiano and stir to combine. Serve immediately.

Tomato Sauce with Pancetta, White Beans, and Rosemary

The only pasta my husband ever wants is rigatoni with red sauce. While I love this classic dish, I'm always trying to find ways to make it a little more interesting without much legwork. It turns out pancetta, salt-cured pork belly with a flavor similar to bacon, is the answer. I've added white beans, too, which are often found in Italian sauces but rarely make an appearance stateside. The beans deliver protein and some welcome texture. Serving the sauce with pasta makes for an easy weeknight dinner, but it'd be equally good with crusty bread.

NOTES: If you can't find pancetta, bacon will work in its place. To make it vegetarian, leave the pancetta out entirely. Sauce can be stored in an airtight container in the refrigerator for up to 5 days or frozen for up to 3 months.

Serves 4 to 6

Kosher salt

1 (16-ounce) box pasta of choice

¾ pound pancetta, cut into ¼-inch pieces

1 medium yellow onion, coarsely chopped

1 (15-ounce) can white beans, drained and rinsed

3 garlic cloves, minced

Leaves from 2 to 3 rosemary sprigs, finely chopped (about 1 tablespoon)

½ teaspoon red pepper flakes

¼ cup tomato paste

1 (28-ounce) can whole peeled tomatoes

½ teaspoon freshly ground black pepper

1 cup freshly grated Parmigiano Reggiano cheese, plus more for serving

1. Bring a large pot of salted water to a boil over high heat. Add the pasta and cook until al dente according to the package instructions. Reserve 1 cup of the pasta cooking water, then drain the pasta in a colander.

2. While the pasta is cooking, set a separate large pot or Dutch oven over medium-high heat and fry the pancetta, stirring occasionally, until it is cooked through and crispy, 10 to 12 minutes. Use a slotted spoon to transfer the pancetta to a paper towel–lined plate.

3. In the same pot, add the onion to the pancetta fat and cook, stirring occasionally, until lightly golden, 3 to 5 minutes. Add the beans, garlic, rosemary, and red pepper flakes and cook until aromatic, about 1 minute.

4. Add the tomato paste and cook, stirring until well combined, until the color turns a deep brick-red, about 2 minutes.

5. Use your hands to crush the tomatoes directly into the pot, along with their juices, and stir to combine. Add the black pepper and 1 teaspoon salt and stir to combine. Simmer until the sauce has started to thicken, about 5 minutes.

6. Add the reserved pasta water and cheese and stir to combine. Reduce the heat to medium-low and simmer until saucy and thickened, about 5 minutes. Add the pasta and cooked pancetta and stir to combine. Serve the pasta topped with more grated cheese.

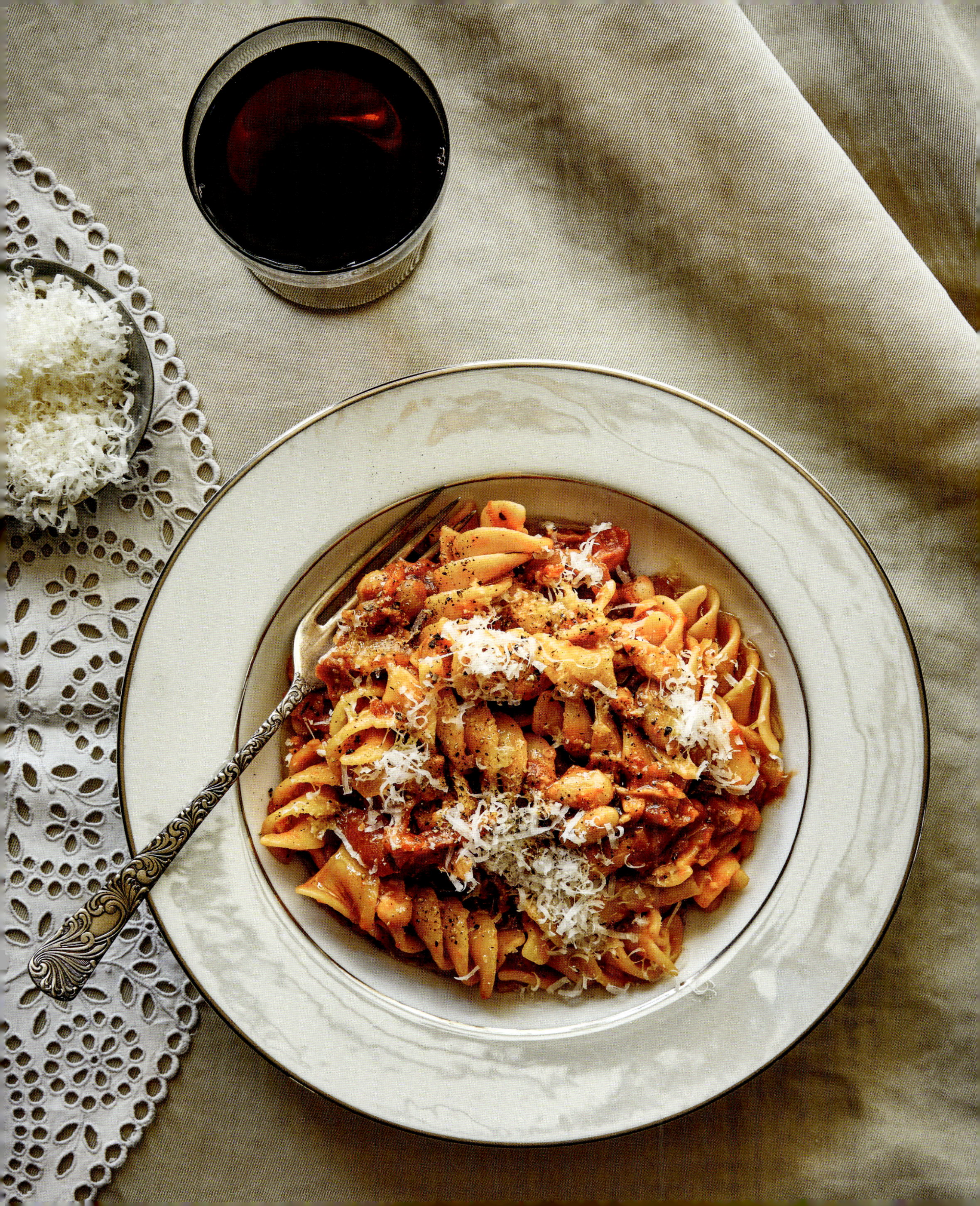

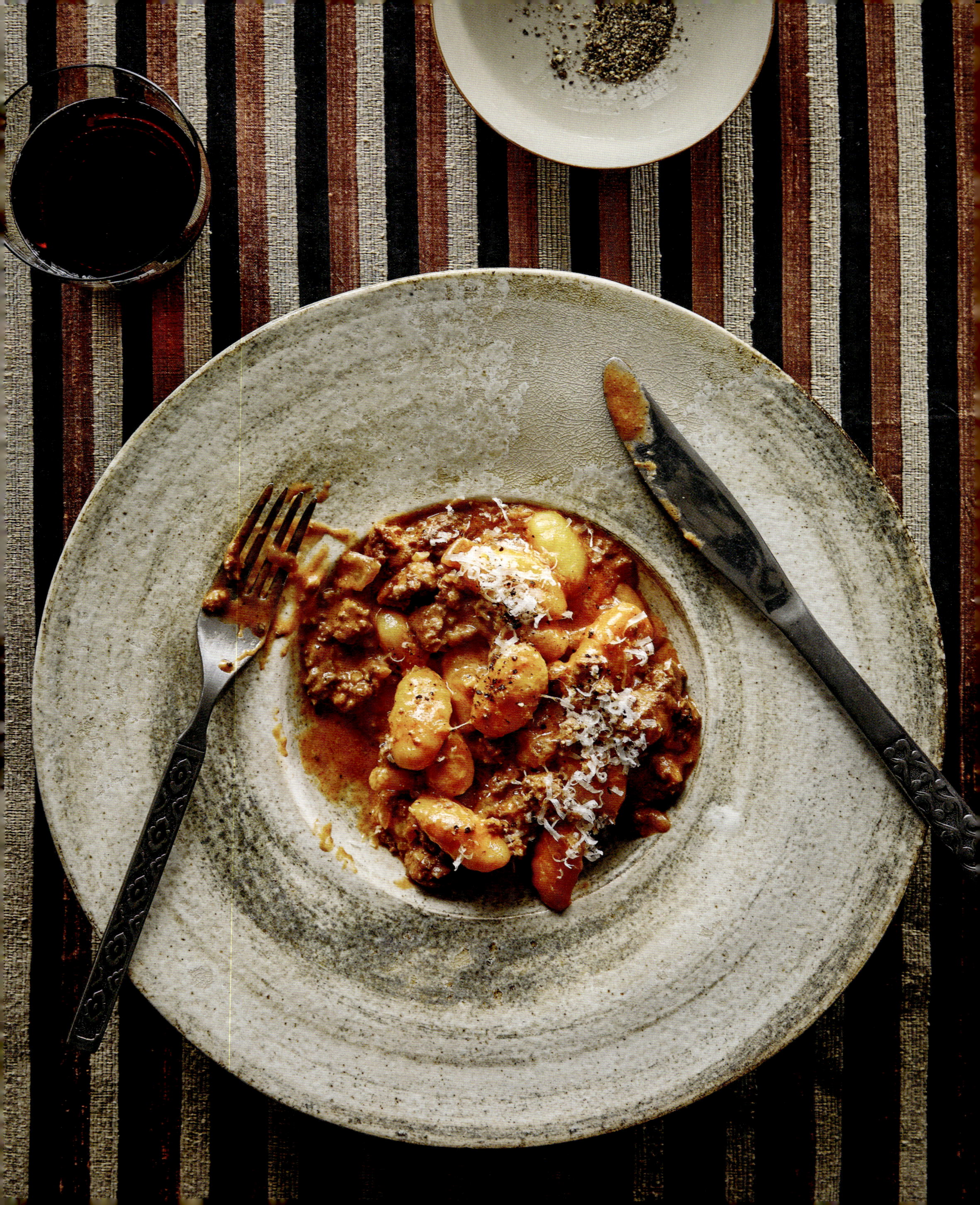

One-Pot Gnocchi Ragù

While ragù typically takes hours to simmer on the stove, this quick-cooking version can be made in under thirty minutes. By adding the gnocchi directly to the ragù, you cut down on dishes while simultaneously ensuring that the sauce clings to the ridges of the gnocchi in every bite.

NOTES: This can be made with any ground meat of your choosing, like pork, lamb, turkey, or chicken. Leftover ragù can be stored in an airtight container in the refrigerator for up to 3 days.

Serves 4

- 1 tablespoon extra-virgin olive oil
- 1 medium yellow onion, finely chopped
- 3 garlic cloves, minced
- ¼ cup tomato paste
- 1 pound ground beef
- 1½ teaspoons kosher salt
- 1 teaspoon freshly ground black pepper
- 1½ cups vegetable stock or chicken stock
- ¾ cup heavy cream
- 1 (16-ounce) package shelf-stable gnocchi
- Freshly grated Parmigiano Reggiano cheese, for serving

1. Heat the olive oil in a large high-sided saucepan over medium-high heat. When the oil begins to shimmer, add the onion and cook, stirring occasionally, until lightly golden, about 7 minutes. Add the garlic and cook until aromatic, about 1 minute. Add the tomato paste and cook until it turns brick-red, about 2 minutes.

2. Add the ground beef, salt, and pepper and cook, using a wooden spoon to break up the meat, until browned and cooked through, about 7 minutes. Add the stock and cream and stir to combine. Add the gnocchi and stir it into the ragù, making sure that each piece is submerged in the sauce. Reduce the heat to medium and cook, stirring every minute or so, until the gnocchi is tender and cooked through, about 5 minutes.

3. Serve topped with Parmigiano Reggiano.

NIGHTS | PASTA

Stovetop Mac and Cheese

No shame in using the boxed stuff, but trust me, homemade mac and cheese is so much better. Don't let the prospect of making a cheese-spiked béchamel intimidate you. With a handful of pantry staples and ten minutes of time, this cheesy sauce is begging to be mixed with your pasta of choice (although I'm partial to shells). I've opted for cheddar, for that classic mac and cheese taste and its meltiness capabilities, and Gruyère, for its nutty flavor. You can add in other cheeses you have on hand or create an entirely new combination—just make sure at least one of the cheeses melts easily, like low-moisture mozzarella, Fontina, provolone, or goat cheese.

NOTE: Mac and cheese can be stored in an airtight container in the refrigerator for up to 3 days or in the freezer for up to 3 months.

Serves 4 to 6

Kosher salt

1 (16-ounce) box short pasta of choice

2 tablespoons unsalted butter

2 tablespoons all-purpose flour

2 cups whole milk

1 tablespoon Dijon mustard

1 garlic clove, grated

1 teaspoon sweet paprika

1 teaspoon freshly ground black pepper

½ teaspoon ground turmeric

2 cups coarsely grated Gruyère cheese

2 cups coarsely grated sharp cheddar cheese

1. Bring a large pot of salted water to a boil over high heat. Add the pasta and cook until al dente according to the package instructions. Drain the pasta in a colander.

2. Melt the butter in a separate large pot over medium-high heat. Add the flour and whisk until it is golden brown and the mixture has a nutty aroma, about 2 minutes. Add the milk, mustard, garlic, paprika, pepper, turmeric, and 1 teaspoon salt and cook, whisking frequently, until the sauce thickens and coats the back of a spoon, 6 to 8 minutes.

3. Add the Gruyère and cheddar and stir until smooth. Add the pasta and stir until glossy. Serve immediately.

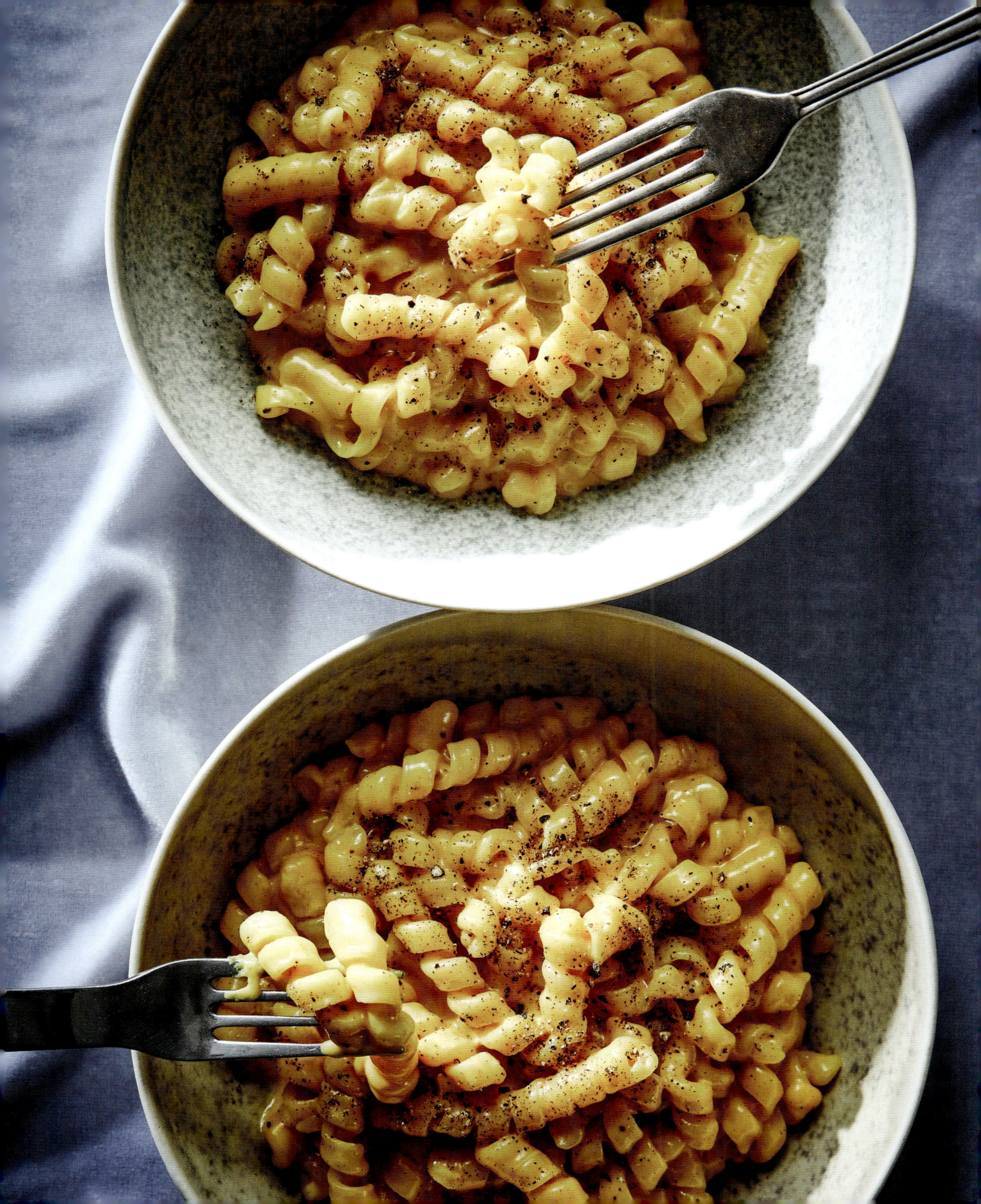

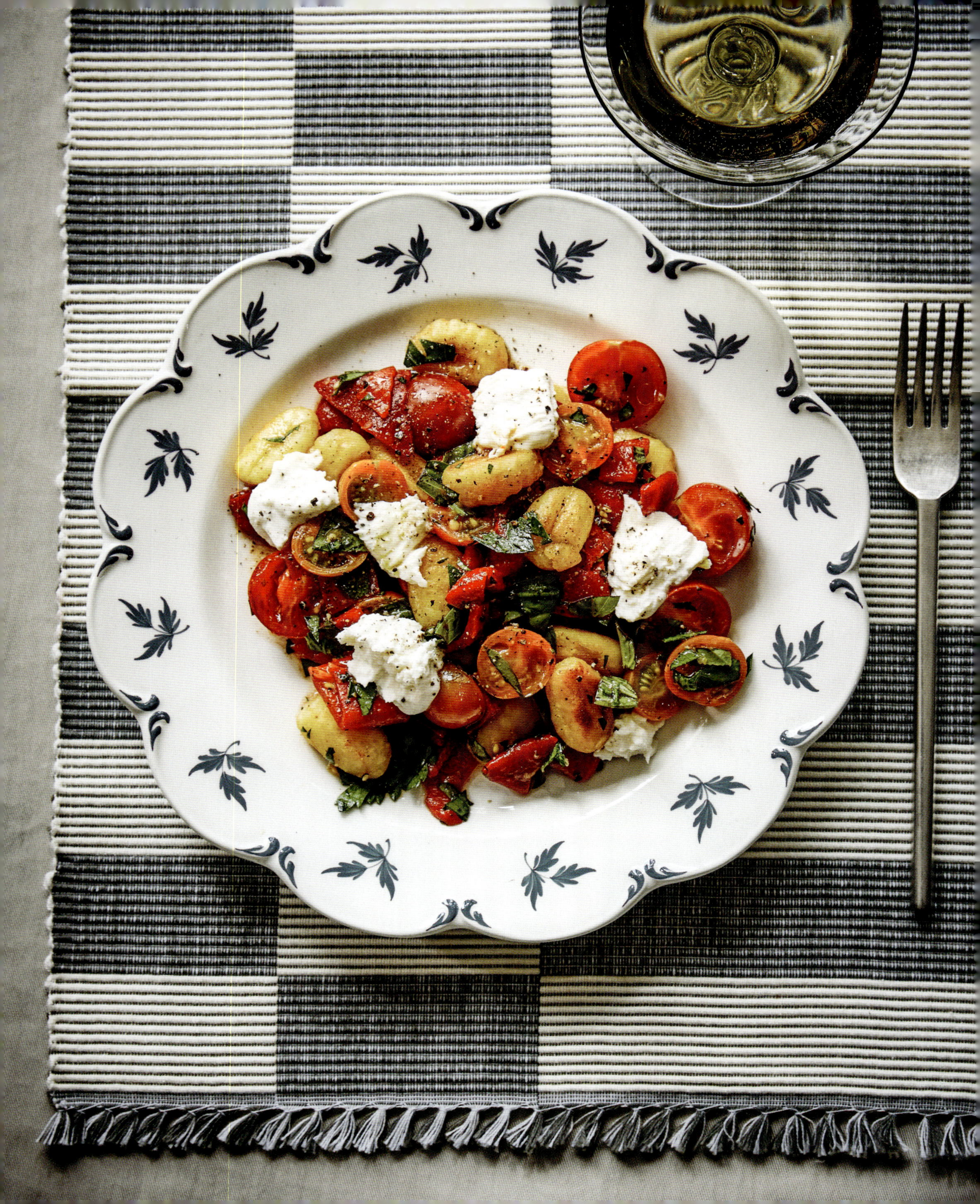

Crispy Gnocchi Caprese

While the practice of making crispy gnocchi from scratch dates back to ancient Rome, recipe developer Ali Slagle more recently popularized taking shelf-stable gnocchi and crisping it in a pan for a similar effect. This technique ensures a golden brown exterior and a pillowy, tender interior. It's slightly more involved than a traditional pasta caprese, but this dish still comes together quickly while leaning on all the classic flavors. Roasted red peppers and tomatoes are bathed in a garlicky mixture of sherry vinegar and olive oil before getting tossed with crispy gnocchi, hunks of torn mozzarella, basil, and parsley.

NOTE: I'm a leftover girl through and through, but I'm sad to say this dish doesn't hold up well the next day. If you must, reheat it in a microwave or on the stovetop until the mozzarella has melted, which transforms the dish into something more akin to a vinegary pizza.

Serves 4

- 1 (12-ounce) jar roasted red peppers, drained and coarsely chopped
- 2 cups cherry tomatoes, halved
- 3 tablespoons extra-virgin olive oil
- 2 tablespoons sherry vinegar
- 1 large garlic clove, grated
- 1 teaspoon kosher salt
- ½ teaspoon freshly ground black pepper
- 1 (16-ounce) package shelf-stable gnocchi
- 1 (8-ounce) ball mozzarella, roughly torn
- 1 cup fresh basil, coarsely chopped
- ¼ bunch flat-leaf parsley, coarsely chopped (about ½ cup)

1. Stir together the red peppers, tomatoes, 1 tablespoon of the olive oil, vinegar, garlic, salt, and black pepper in a large bowl.

2. Heat the remaining 2 tablespoons olive oil in a large pan over medium-high heat. When the oil begins to shimmer, add the gnocchi and cook, stirring occasionally, until golden brown on both sides, 7 to 8 minutes.

3. Transfer the gnocchi to the bowl with the red pepper mixture and stir to combine. Add the mozzarella, basil, and parsley and stir to combine. Serve immediately.

Udon Noodles with Peanut Sauce

Peanut sauce is the ultimate fix to your weeknight dinner woes. Made with pantry staples, it comes together in under five minutes, making it ideal to whip up on nights when you can't muster much more time in the kitchen. If you're not familiar, sambal oelek is an Indonesian chile sauce spiked with vinegar and salt that tastes like you're cooking with fresh chiles (without the fuss). I love udon noodles for their bouncy texture and bite, but you could use whatever noodles you have on hand, like rice noodles, soba, ramen, or gasp, even spaghetti in a pinch.

NOTES: If you don't have sambal oelek on hand, use another chile garlic sauce or sriracha, or simply leave it out. Peanut sauce can be stored in an airtight container in the refrigerator for up to 5 days. Before serving, let it sit at room temperature for at least 1 hour to loosen up. Once assembled, leftovers can be stored in an airtight container in the refrigerator for up to 3 days.

1. Combine the peanut butter, soy sauce, sesame oil, rice vinegar, sambal oelek, honey, garlic, ginger, lime zest, lime juice, and ¼ cup hot water in a food processor and process until smooth. Transfer the peanut sauce to a large bowl.

2. Bring a large pot of salted water to a boil over high heat. Add the udon noodles and cook according to the package instructions. Reserve 1 cup of the noodle cooking water, then drain the noodles in a colander.

3. Add the noodles to the bowl with the peanut sauce and use tongs to toss until well coated. If you want a looser sauce, add a splash of the reserved cooking water.

4. Top with the cucumbers, scallions, and peanuts and serve immediately.

Serves 4 to 6

½ cup smooth peanut butter

¼ cup low-sodium soy sauce

3 tablespoons toasted sesame oil

2 tablespoons rice vinegar

1 tablespoon sambal oelek

2 tablespoons honey

2 garlic cloves, grated

1 (1-inch) knob fresh ginger, grated

Zest and juice of 2 limes (about ¼ cup juice)

Kosher salt

4 (7-ounce) packages udon noodles

4 Persian cucumbers, thinly sliced

2 bunches scallions, thinly sliced

Roasted peanuts, coarsely chopped, for serving

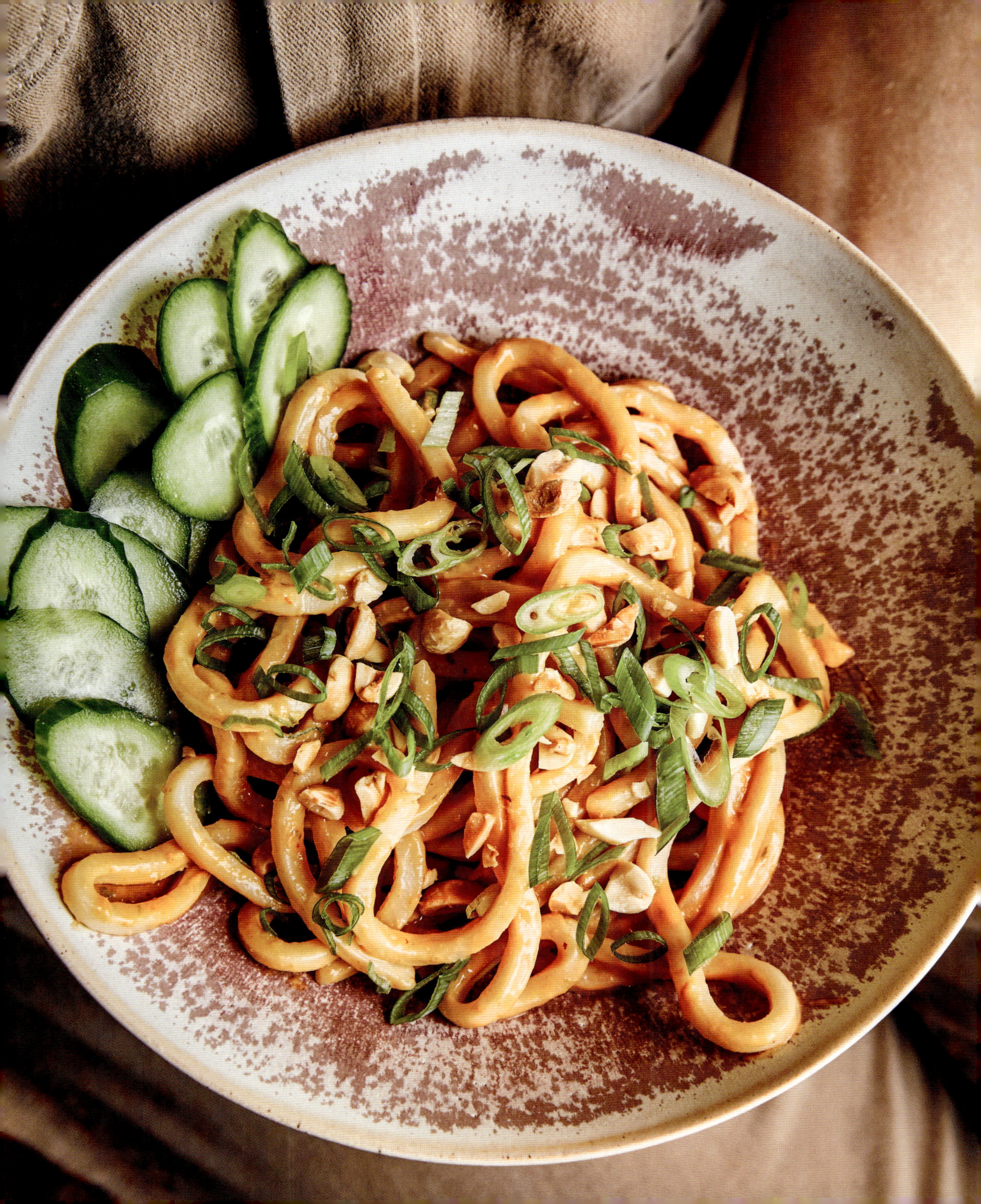

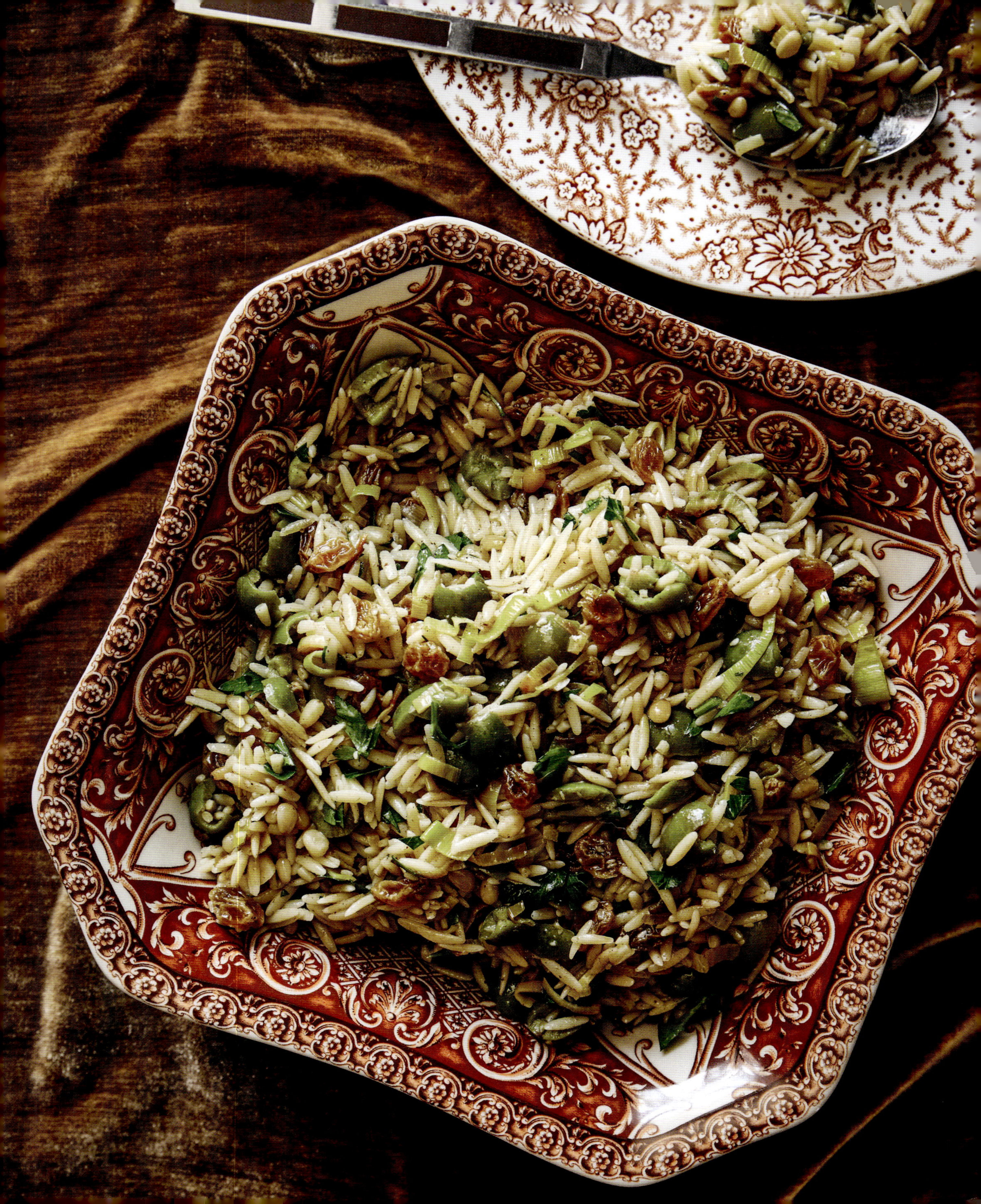

Orzo with Leeks, Olives, and Golden Raisins

Rarely does orzo get to break out of its Greek-inspired pasta salad shackles. But given the opportunity, this petite pasta can be so much more. Here, orzo gets treated more like a grain with a handful of Middle Eastern–leaning ingredients. The hot olive oil not only blooms the za'atar making it more aromatic, but also plumps up the golden raisins, almost rehydrating them to their original grape shape. While I love eating this as a main dish, it works equally well as a side.

NOTES: The joy of this recipe is that you can easily adapt it to what ingredients you have on hand. If you don't like golden raisins or olives, leave them out. If you have a different type of nut, add it in. Leftovers can be stored in an airtight container in the refrigerator for up to 4 days.

1. Bring a large pot of salted water to a boil over high heat. Add the orzo and cook until al dente according to the package instructions. Drain the orzo in a colander.

2. While the orzo is cooking, heat the olive oil in a large pan over medium-high heat. When the oil begins to shimmer, add the leeks and cook, stirring occasionally, until softened and bright green, about 5 minutes. Add the olives, raisins, pine nuts, garlic, and za'atar and cook, stirring occasionally, until deeply aromatic, about 2 minutes.

3. Transfer the orzo and the leek mixture to a large bowl. Add the parsley, lemon juice, and 2 teaspoons salt and stir to combine. Serve the orzo hot or let it cool to room temperature and store it in an airtight container to serve later, chilled or at room temp.

Serves 4 to 6

Kosher salt

1½ cups orzo

½ cup extra-virgin olive oil

3 medium leeks, white and light green parts only, well washed and thinly sliced

1 cup pitted Castelvetrano olives, roughly torn

1 cup golden raisins

½ cup pine nuts

3 garlic cloves, minced

1 tablespoon za'atar

½ bunch flat-leaf parsley, coarsely chopped (about 1 cup)

Juice of 1 lemon (about 2 tablespoons)

Pasta with Bacon, Peas, Sour Cream, and Dill

On nights when my fridge is looking sparse and the idea of spending any more time than necessary in the kitchen feels impossible, I turn to this pasta. It's creamy and comforting, and comes together in under thirty minutes. It's a safe bet that I always have a bag of frozen peas in the freezer, a pack of bacon, and some sort of dairy. While I like using sour cream for its ease, you could easily swap in heavy cream (and simmer it for a few minutes before adding the pasta), or even plain full-fat yogurt. Dill brightens the dish up, but fresh parsley or basil works, too.

NOTES: If you reach the stage after adding the garlic and the pasta isn't done, remove the pan from the heat until you're ready to add the pasta. Leftover pasta can be stored in an airtight container in the refrigerator for up to 3 days.

Serves 4 to 6

Kosher salt

1 (16-ounce) box pasta of choice

6 strips bacon, cut crosswise into ½-inch-wide pieces

1 large shallot, finely chopped

1 (10-ounce) bag frozen peas, thawed (about 2 cups)

3 garlic cloves, minced

½ teaspoon freshly ground black pepper

¼ teaspoon red pepper flakes

1 cup full-fat sour cream

½ cup coarsely chopped fresh dill

1. Bring a large pot of salted water to a boil over high heat. Add the pasta and cook until 1 minute shy of al dente according to the package instructions. Reserve ½ cup of the pasta cooking water, then drain the pasta in a colander.

2. While the pasta is cooking, heat a large skillet over medium-high heat. When the pan is warm, fry the bacon until cooked through and beginning to crisp, about 7 minutes, or until the bacon is your desired crispiness. Use a slotted spoon to remove the bacon from the pan and transfer to a paper towel–lined plate, leaving the remaining bacon fat in the pan.

3. Add the shallot to the pan and cook, stirring occasionally, until translucent, golden, and aromatic, 4 to 5 minutes. Add the peas, garlic, black pepper, red pepper flakes, and 1 teaspoon salt and cook, stirring, until the garlic is aromatic, about 1 minute.

4. Add the pasta, reserved pasta water, and sour cream to the skillet and stir to combine until the pasta is glossy, about 1 minute. Add the bacon and dill to the pasta and stir to combine.

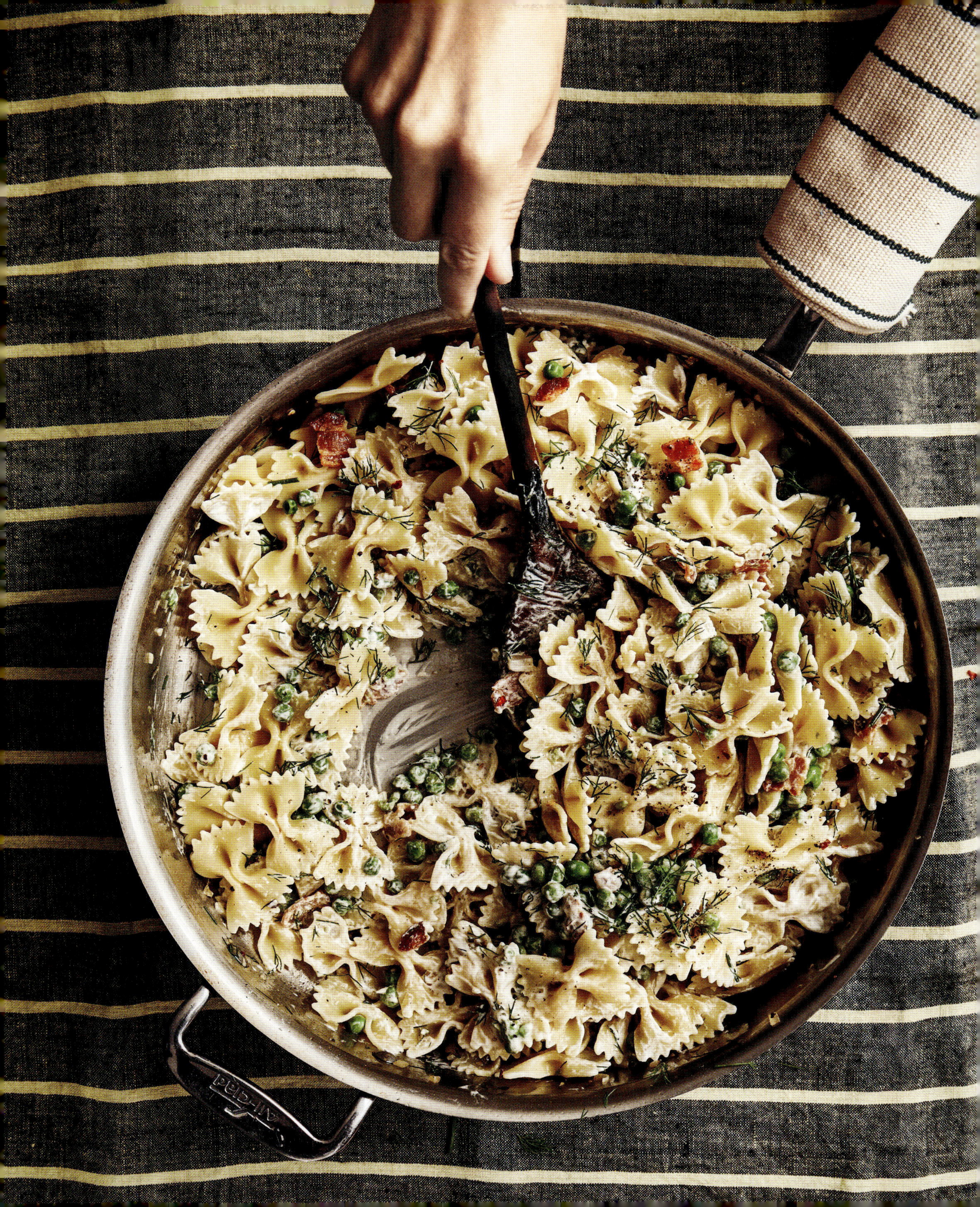

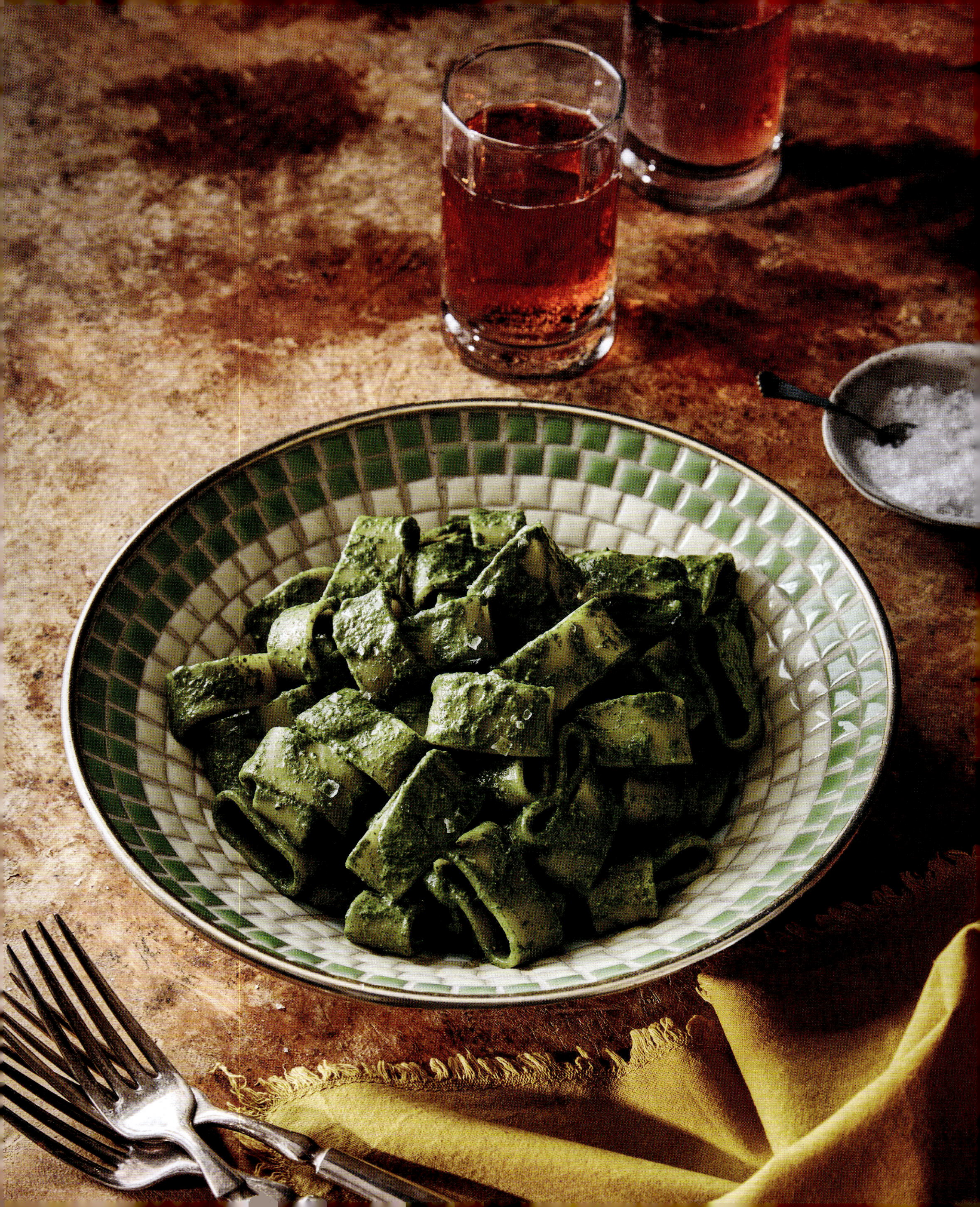

Creamy Green Pasta

This pasta is my ideal way to not-so-sneakily incorporate more greens (my eternal quest) into dinner. While the sauce is spinach-forward, the flavor is tempered with heavy cream, garlic, and cheese, making it something the whole family can get on board with. This silky sauce can be used with any type of pasta, but I favor shapes that ensure the sauce gets into every nook and cranny.

NOTES: Frozen spinach can be used in place of fresh. The sauce can be made up to 24 hours in advance and stored in an airtight container in the refrigerator until ready to use. Once assembled, leftover pasta can be stored in an airtight container for up to 3 days.

Serves 4 to 6

- 1 tablespoon extra-virgin olive oil
- 10 ounces spinach
- 4 garlic cloves, minced
- ½ cup heavy cream
- ½ cup freshly grated Parmigiano Reggiano cheese
- Kosher salt
- 1 teaspoon freshly ground black pepper
- 1 (16-ounce) box short pasta of choice, such as fusilli, rigatoni, shells, or orecchiette
- Juice of 1 lemon (about 2 tablespoons)

1. Heat the olive oil in a large pan over medium-high heat. When the oil begins to shimmer, add the spinach and garlic and cook, stirring, until the spinach is just wilted, about 1 minute.

2. Transfer the spinach mixture to a blender along with the cream, Parmigiano, 1½ teaspoons salt, and the pepper. Blend on high until smooth.

3. Bring a large pot of salted water to a boil over high heat. Add the pasta and cook until al dente according to the package instructions. Reserve 1 cup of the pasta cooking water, then drain the pasta in a colander.

4. Pour the spinach mixture into a large pan and bring to a simmer over medium-high heat.

5. Add the pasta, the reserved pasta water, and the lemon juice to the pan with the spinach mixture and stir until the noodles are coated and the sauce is glossy, about 1 minute. Serve immediately.

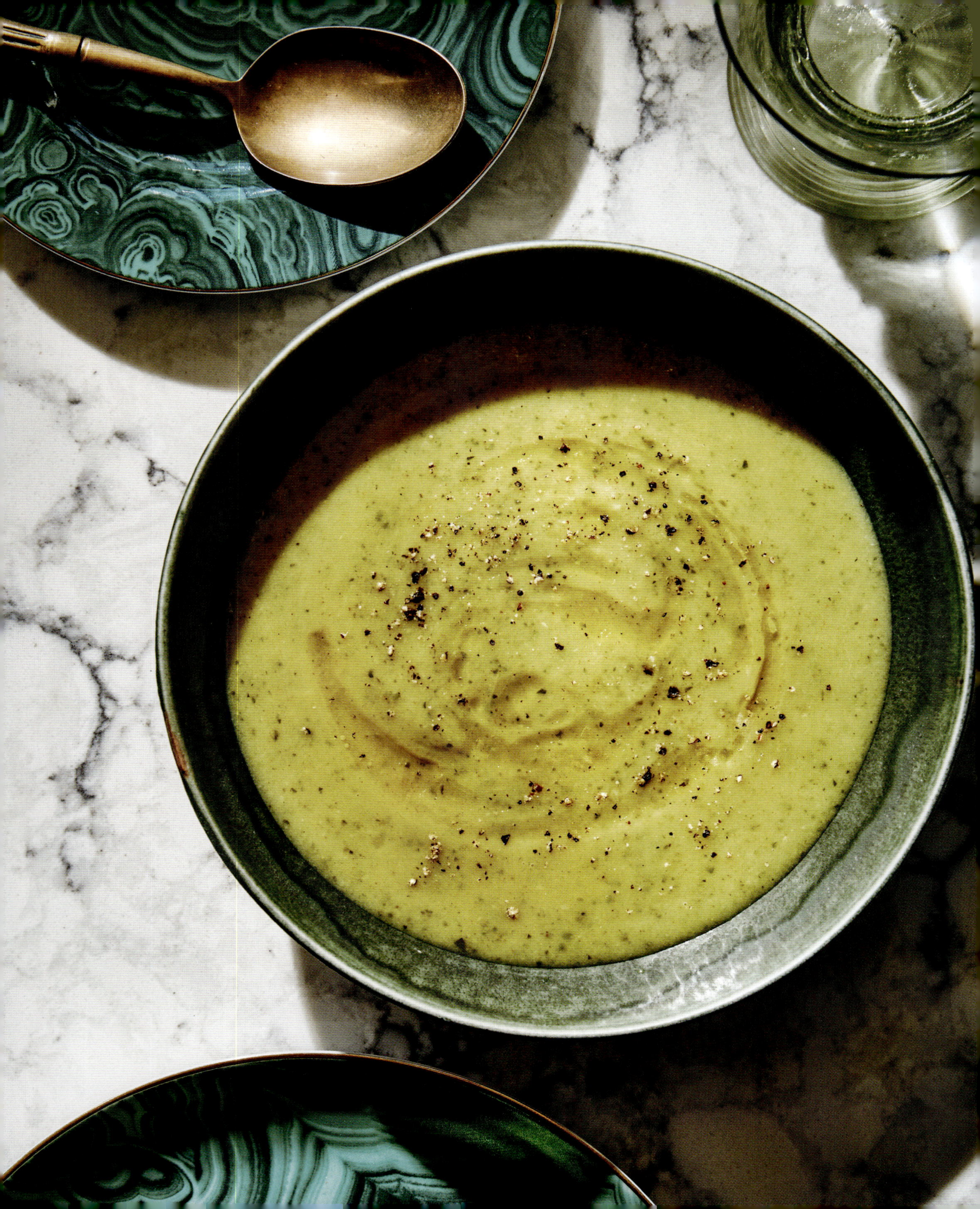

NIGHTS

SOUPS AND STEWS

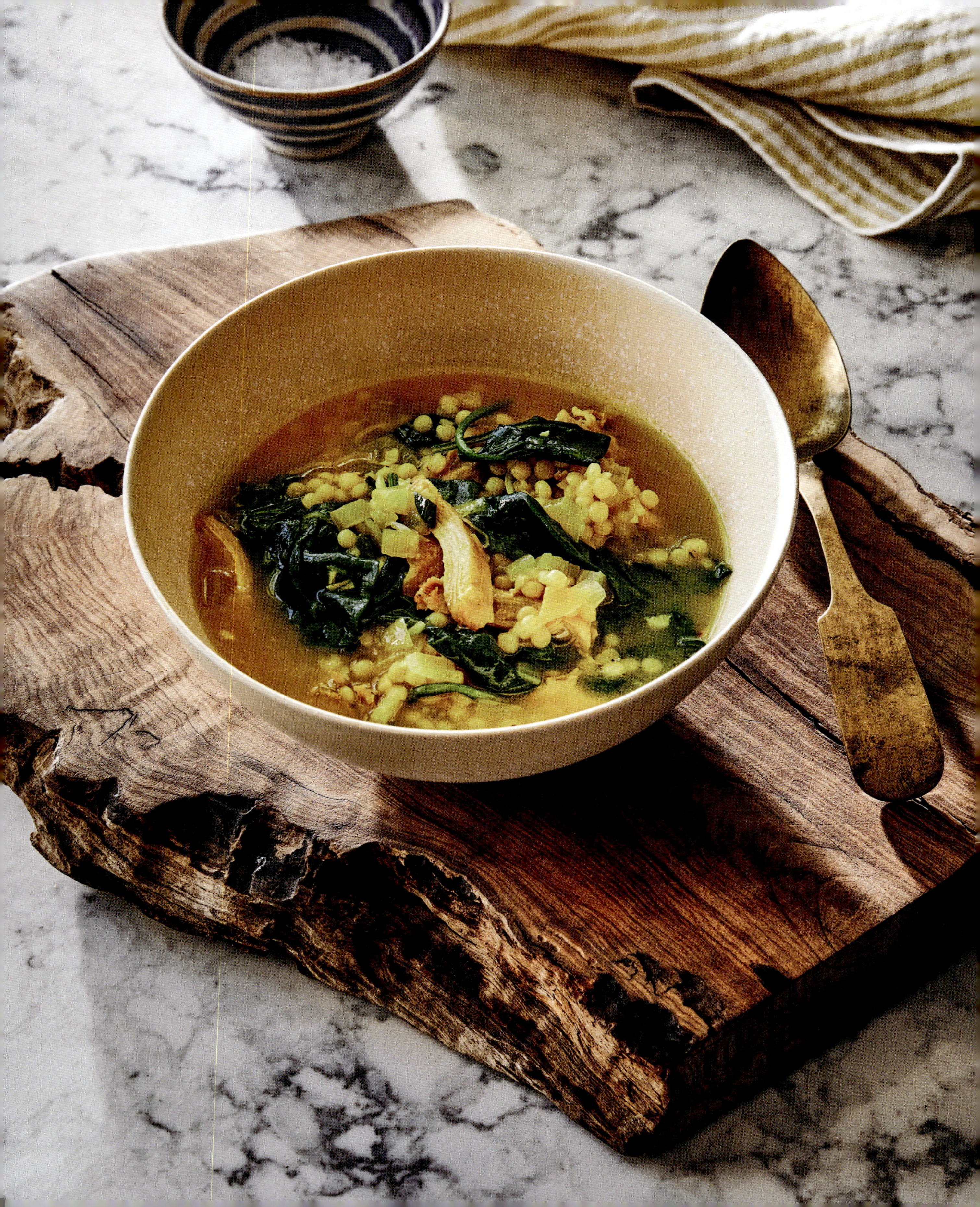

Lemon Chicken Soup for Whatever Ails You

My original plan for this soup was that it would mimic a more classic Greek-style lemon chicken soup (aka avgolemono), and then I got a cold and threw those aspirations out the window. All the home-remedy hits are here, like turmeric, garlic, ginger, and chicken stock. It's the exact soup you want to eat when you're feeling under the weather, you need a quick and comforting dish, or you want something to bring to a friend who's having a rough time.

NOTES: This is a good time to make use of leftover or rotisserie chicken if you have it on hand. If so, skip ahead to where you sauté the onions and celery. The soup can be stored in an airtight container in the refrigerator for up to 3 days. Just note that the spinach may discolor with time.

Serves 4

- 1½ pounds boneless, skinless chicken thighs
- 1½ teaspoons kosher salt
- 2 teaspoons freshly ground black pepper
- 1 tablespoon extra-virgin olive oil
- 1 medium yellow onion, finely chopped
- 3 celery stalks, finely chopped
- 3 garlic cloves, minced
- 1 (1-inch) knob fresh ginger, coarsely chopped (about 1 tablespoon)
- 1 teaspoon ground turmeric
- 8 cups chicken stock
- 1½ cups Israeli couscous
- 1 (5-ounce) box baby spinach
- Juice of 1 lemon (about 2 tablespoons)

1. Pat the chicken thighs dry with paper towels. Season both sides with 1 teaspoon of the salt and 1 teaspoon of the pepper.

2. Heat the olive oil in a large pot or Dutch oven over medium-high heat. When the oil begins to shimmer, add the chicken thighs and cook, undisturbed, until golden brown, about 8 minutes. Flip the thighs over and cook until golden, about 7 minutes more. Transfer the chicken thighs to a plate and let sit until cool enough to touch. Shred the chicken with your hands.

3. In the same pot, add the onion and celery and cook, stirring occasionally, until beginning to soften and lightly golden, about 5 minutes. Add the garlic, ginger, turmeric, and the remaining 1 teaspoon pepper and ½ teaspoon salt and cook, stirring, until aromatic, about 1 minute. Add the stock and couscous and bring to a low boil. Reduce the heat to medium-low and simmer until the couscous is cooked through, about 10 minutes.

4. Add the shredded chicken, spinach, and lemon juice, and stir to combine. Cook, stirring occasionally, until the spinach has wilted, about 1 minute. Serve immediately.

Chickpea Curry

Of all the recipes I've ever developed, this is the one I turn to the most, and for good reason. Inspired by Indian chana masala, this curry comes together using pantry staples (think canned chickpeas, canned tomatoes, and coconut milk) and is as quick to put together as it is comforting. Because it's vegan, it's an easy dish to have in your back pocket for times when you've volunteered to drop off food and are unsure of dietary restrictions or preferences. Every time I do, I'm always asked for the recipe—and you will be, too!

NOTES: This is a great moment to lean into store-bought crispy shallots. If you want to make them yourself, pour ¾ cup neutral oil into a large pan and heat it over medium heat. When the oil begins to simmer, reduce the heat to medium-low, add 6 to 8 thinly sliced shallots, and cook, stirring occasionally, until golden brown and crispy, about 30 minutes. It won't look like anything is happening to the shallots initially, but keep going—I promise they'll get crispy. Transfer the shallots to a paper towel–lined plate to drain and season with salt. Leftover chickpea curry can be stored in an airtight container in the refrigerator for up to 3 days.

Serves 4 to 6

- 1 tablespoon extra-virgin olive oil
- 1 large yellow onion, thinly sliced
- 3 large garlic cloves, minced
- 1 tablespoon curry powder
- 2 teaspoons kosher salt
- 2 teaspoons ground cumin
- 1 teaspoon ground turmeric
- 1 teaspoon ground ginger
- ½ teaspoon red pepper flakes (optional)
- 1 (28-ounce) can whole peeled tomatoes
- 2 (15-ounce) cans chickpeas, drained and rinsed
- 1 (15-ounce) can unsweetened full-fat coconut milk
- 2 cups vegetable stock
- Juice of 1 lime (about 2 tablespoons)

FOR SERVING

- Cooked rice
- Coarsely chopped fresh cilantro
- Crispy shallots

1. Heat the olive oil in a large pot or Dutch oven over medium-high heat. When the oil begins to shimmer, add the onion and cook, stirring occasionally, until softened, golden brown, and deeply aromatic, 6 to 7 minutes. Add the garlic, curry powder, salt, cumin, turmeric, ginger, and red pepper flakes (if using) and cook until deeply aromatic, about 30 seconds.

2. Use your hands to crush the tomatoes as you add them to the pot. Add the chickpeas, coconut milk, and stock, stir to combine, and bring to a low boil. Reduce the heat to medium-low and simmer for 20 minutes. Add the lime juice and stir to combine.

3. Serve the chickpea curry over rice, topped with cilantro and crispy shallots.

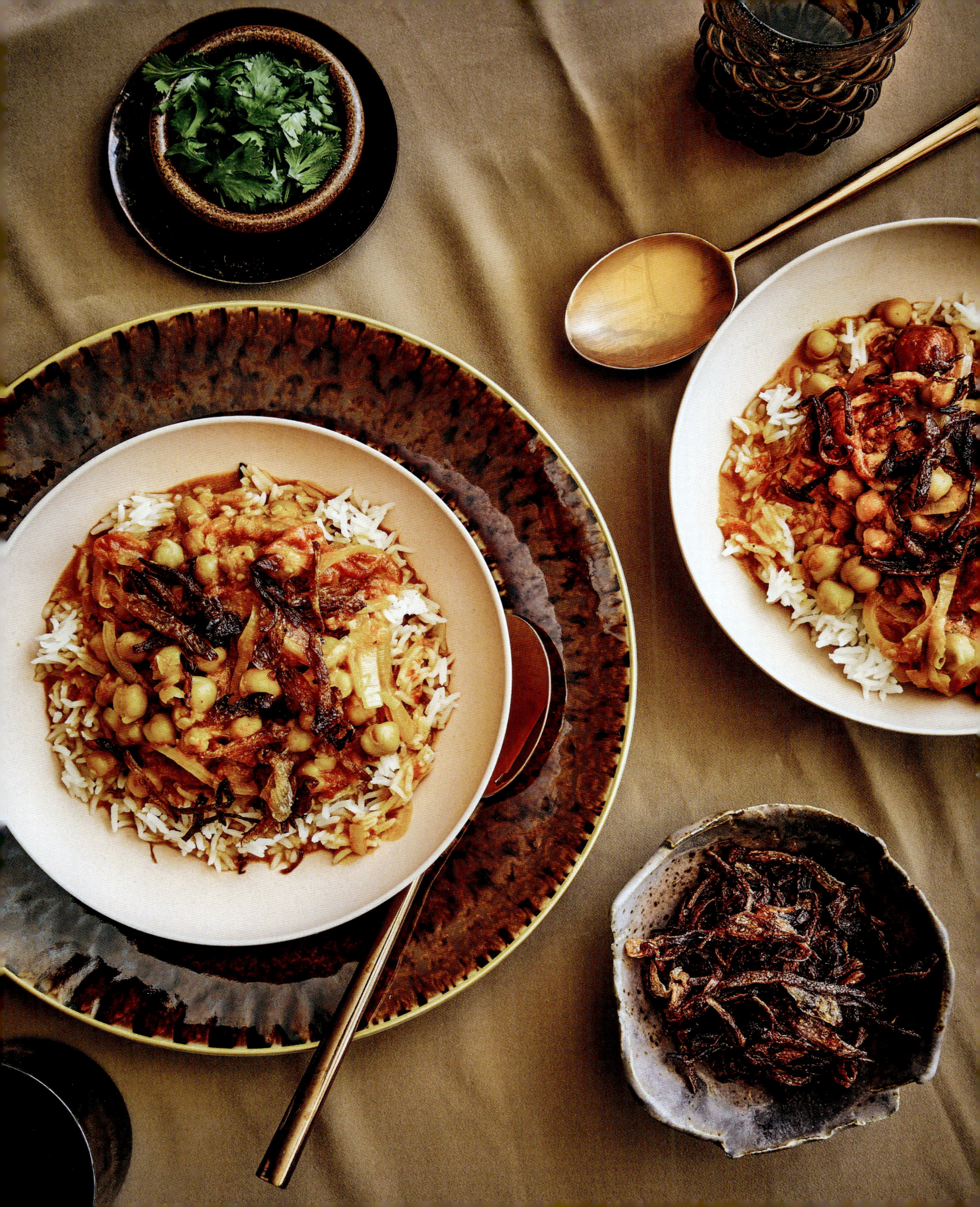

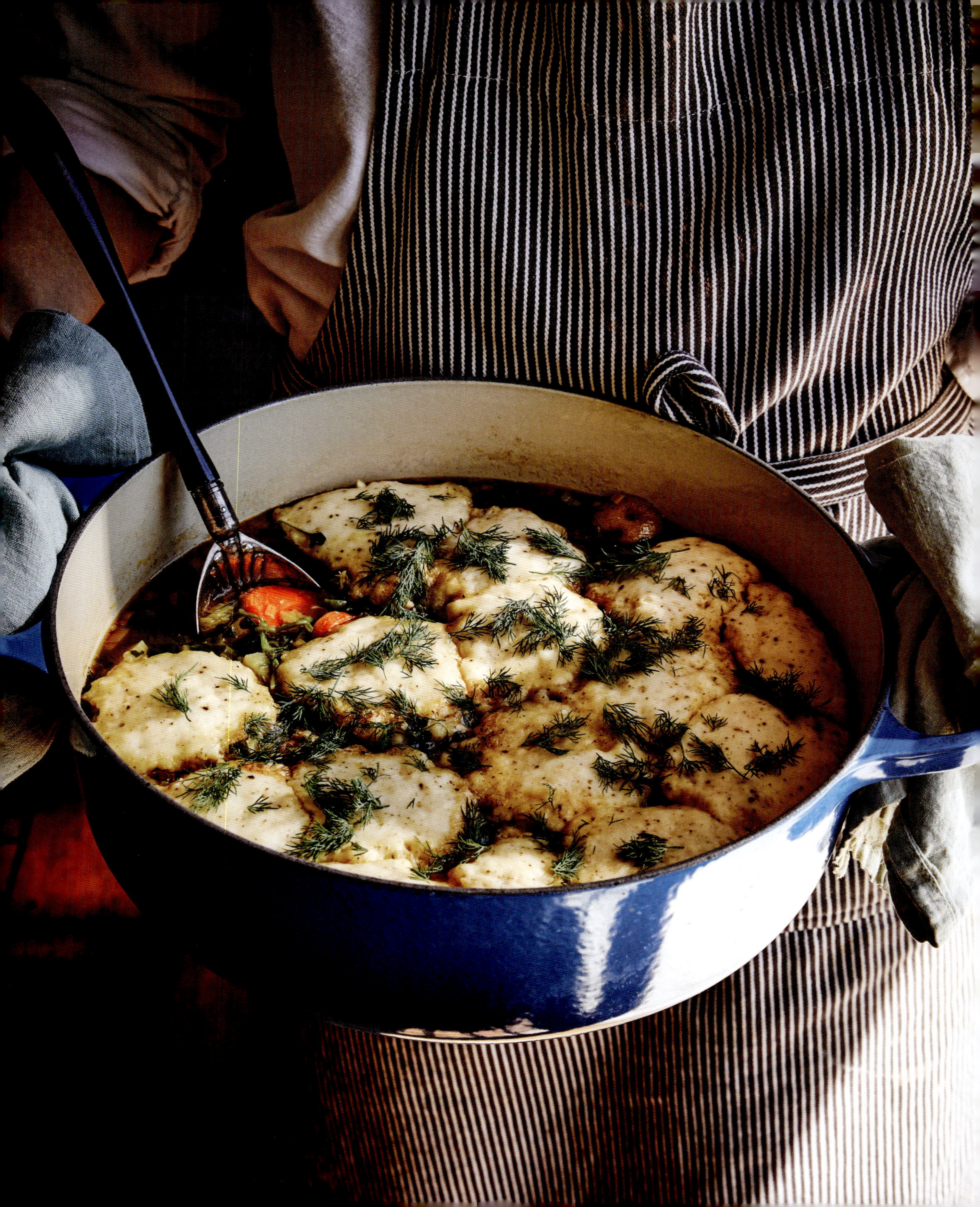

Spring Vegetable Soup with Dumplings and Dill

Topped with tender pepper-flaked dumplings and a shower of dill, this hearty soup is something I crave as soon as the temperature drops. My love for this Southern-inspired stew began over a decade ago when I was living in Los Angeles and had the flu. My friend Hannah delivered a pot of piping-hot chicken and dumplings to my doorstep as I was just starting to turn a corner. Maybe it was because it was the first real food I had in days, or maybe Hannah's cooking is just that good (both are true), but I've been a fan ever since. This vegetarian take highlights the produce that begins to emerge at the market in that crossover of winter and spring. Luckily, you can find all of it at your local grocery store.

NOTE: Leftover soup can be stored in an airtight container in the refrigerator for up to 3 days.

Serves 4 to 6

SOUP

- 1 tablespoon extra-virgin olive oil
- 2 medium leeks, white and light green parts only, well washed and thinly sliced
- 3 medium carrots, thinly sliced on an angle
- 3 medium celery stalks, thinly sliced on an angle
- 1 pound new potatoes, cut into ½-inch pieces
- 3 garlic cloves, minced
- 1 tablespoon unsalted butter
- 1 tablespoon all-purpose flour
- 6 cups vegetable stock
- 2 teaspoons kosher salt
- 1 teaspoon freshly ground black pepper

DUMPLINGS

- 1½ cups all-purpose flour
- 2 teaspoons baking powder
- 1½ teaspoons kosher salt
- 1 teaspoon freshly ground black pepper
- ½ teaspoon baking soda
- 1 cup whole milk

- 1 (4-ounce) bag watercress
- 1 (10-ounce) bag frozen peas
- ¼ cup fresh dill, coarsely chopped, for serving

1. **Make the soup:** Heat the olive oil in a large pot or Dutch oven over medium-high heat. When the oil begins to shimmer, add the leeks, carrots, and celery and cook, stirring occasionally, until they begin to soften, about 5 minutes. Add the potatoes and garlic and cook until aromatic, about 1 minute.

2. Add the butter and flour and stir until the flour is well incorporated, about 2 minutes. Add the stock, salt, and pepper and bring to a boil. Reduce the heat to medium and simmer for 5 minutes.

3. **Meanwhile, make the dumplings:** Whisk together the flour, baking powder, salt, pepper, and baking soda in a medium bowl. Add in the milk and use a spatula to mix until a shaggy dough forms.

4. Add the watercress and peas to the soup and stir to combine. Then use a tablespoon to drop the batter in clumps onto the top of the stew. Place the lid on the pot. Cook, without peeking, for 12 minutes, then check to see if the dumplings have puffed up and are cooked through. If not, cook for about 3 minutes more.

5. Top with the dill and serve immediately.

Roasted Tomato and Red Pepper Soup

Tomato soup can be so much more than just a companion to grilled cheese. This version cuts down on the active cook time by roasting canned tomatoes and a bell pepper along with aromatics to caramelize the ingredients, creating a greater depth of flavor in a short amount of time.

NOTES: To make the soup vegan, omit the heavy cream. This recipe can be easily doubled, or even tripled. Soup can be stored in an airtight container for up to 3 days or frozen for up to 3 months.

Serves 4

- 1 (28-ounce) can whole tomatoes
- 1 medium yellow onion, thinly sliced
- 1 red bell pepper, thinly sliced
- 4 garlic cloves, peeled
- ¼ cup extra-virgin olive oil
- 1½ teaspoons kosher salt
- 1½ teaspoons freshly ground black pepper, plus more for serving
- 4 cups vegetable stock or chicken stock
- 1 tablespoon balsamic vinegar
- Heavy cream, for serving

1. Preheat the oven to 425°F.
2. Place the tomatoes and their juices in a 9×13-inch baking dish and use your hands to crush them. Add the onion, bell pepper, garlic, olive oil, 1 teaspoon of the salt, and 1 teaspoon of the black pepper, and stir to combine. Transfer to the oven and roast for 20 minutes. Stir, then roast until the onion and pepper have softened, the garlic is fork-tender, and the tomatoes are jammy, about 20 minutes more.
3. Transfer the roasted tomato mixture to a large pot along with the stock, balsamic vinegar, remaining ½ teaspoon salt, and remaining ½ teaspoon black pepper. Bring to a low boil over medium-high heat, then reduce the heat to medium-low and simmer for 10 minutes.
4. Working in batches, carefully transfer the soup to a blender and pulse until smooth. (Alternatively, use a food processor or blend directly in the pot with an immersion blender.)
5. Serve the soup with a swirl of heavy cream and some more black pepper.

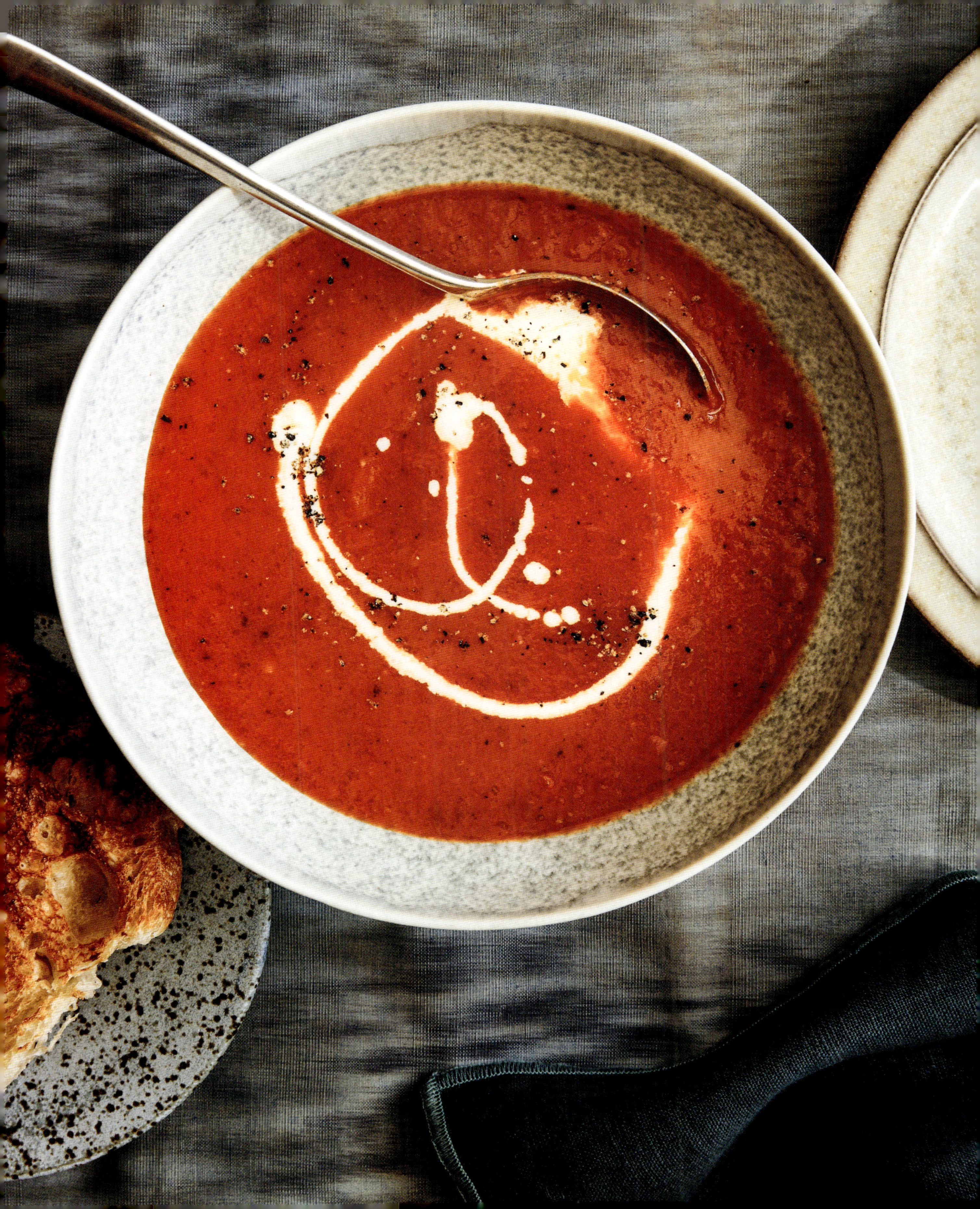

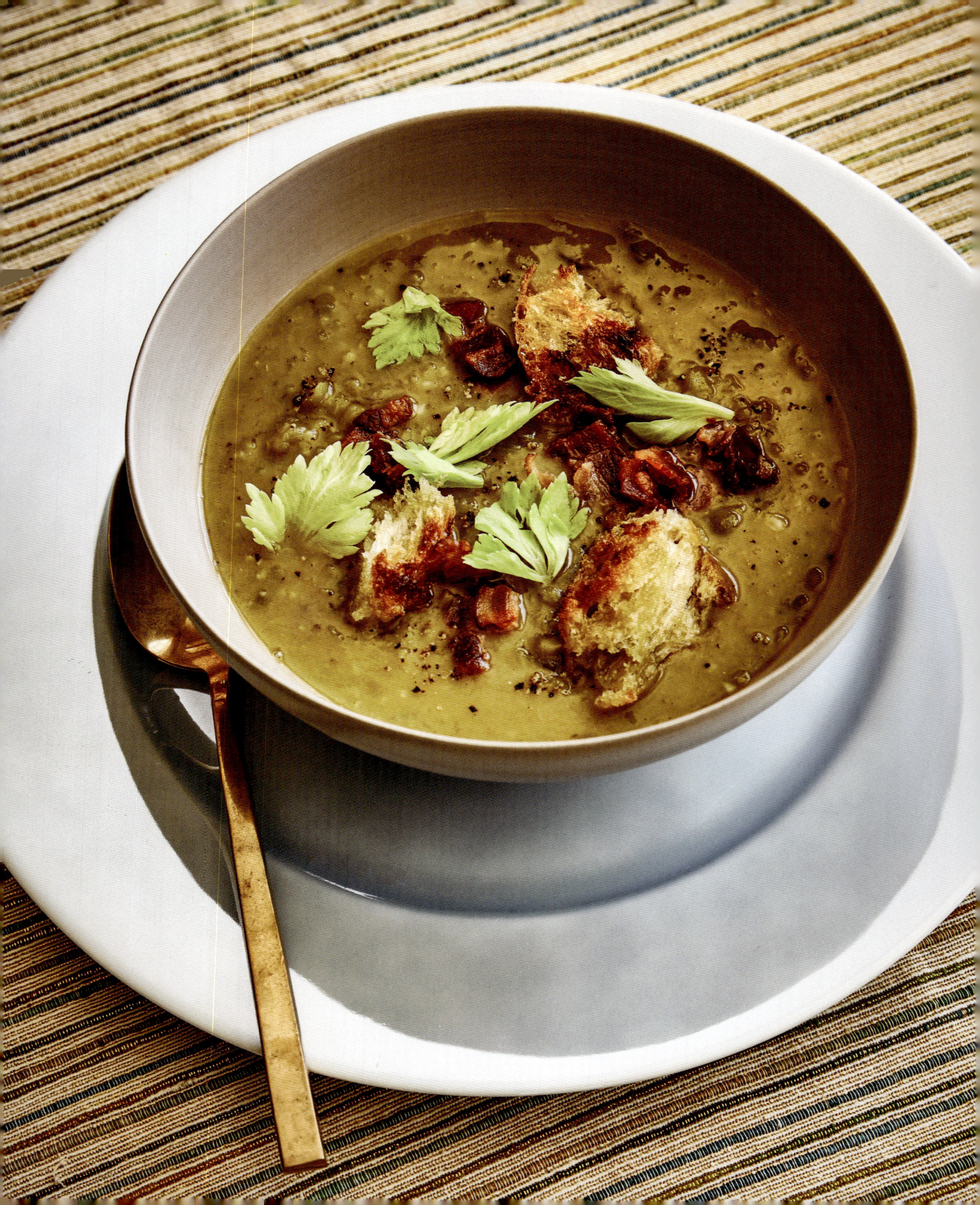

Split Pea Soup with Bacon and Croutons

I have a vivid memory of making a snarky comment in front of my professor during my first few weeks of culinary school about how boring split pea soup was. He smirked and proceeded to prove me so wrong. You see, the key to great split pea soup is coaxing the flavor out of the peas. When cooked correctly, you'll have a cozy, comforting soup that has you coming back for more. The celery here—both stalk and leaves—keeps the flavor on the bright side, which I always welcome in cold weather.

NOTES: This soup can be made vegan by omitting the bacon and cooking the onions and celery in 1 tablespoon of olive oil. It can be stored in an airtight container in the refrigerator for up to 3 days or frozen for up to 3 months.

Serves 4 to 6

- 8 strips bacon, cut into ½-inch slices
- 1 medium yellow onion, finely chopped
- 1 celery stalk, finely chopped
- 3 garlic cloves, minced
- 10 cups vegetable stock or chicken stock
- 2 cups green split peas
- 1 dried bay leaf
- 1¼ teaspoons kosher salt
- 1 teaspoon freshly ground black pepper
- 3 tablespoons extra-virgin olive oil
- 4 cups roughly torn bread, such as sourdough or ciabatta
- ½ cup celery leaves (see Notes, page 83)

1. Cook the bacon in a large pot over medium-high heat, stirring occasionally, until it is cooked through and reaches your desired crispiness level, 5 to 7 minutes. Use a slotted spoon to transfer the bacon to a paper towel–lined plate.

2. Add the onion and celery and cook, stirring frequently, until softened and golden, about 5 minutes. Add the garlic and cook, stirring, until aromatic, about 1 minute.

3. Add the stock, split peas, bay leaf, 1 teaspoon of the salt, and the pepper and bring to a boil. Reduce the heat to medium-low and simmer, stirring occasionally, until the peas are tender, 40 to 45 minutes. Discard the bay leaf.

4. While the soup is simmering, heat the olive oil in a large pan over medium-high heat. When the oil begins to shimmer, add the bread and cook, stirring occasionally, until golden brown on all sides, 4 to 5 minutes. Season with the remaining ¼ teaspoon salt.

5. Serve the soup topped with the crispy bread, bacon, and celery leaves.

Pasta e Ceci

This Roman dish toes the line between soup and stew. There are more versions than I care to count—after all, it's been around for a few thousand years—but this one leans on a handful of pantry staples. The whole thing comes together quickly as the ditalini cooks directly in the soup, cutting down on dishes and time. While not traditional, I like to toss in a handful of buttery panko to add some texture, along with a good dusting of Parm, before serving.

NOTES: If you don't have ditalini, use another small, short pasta shape like elbow macaroni, stelline, or even orzo. Pasta e ceci can be stored in an airtight container in the refrigerator for up to 3 days.

Serves 4

- 2 tablespoons extra-virgin olive oil
- 1 medium yellow onion, coarsely chopped
- 4 garlic cloves, minced
- 2 teaspoons finely chopped fresh rosemary
- ½ teaspoon red pepper flakes
- ¼ cup tomato paste
- 1 (15-ounce) can chickpeas, drained and rinsed
- 1½ teaspoons kosher salt, plus more as needed
- ½ teaspoon freshly ground black pepper
- 6 cups chicken stock or vegetable stock
- 1 cup ditalini or other small pasta of choice
- 2 tablespoons unsalted butter
- ¾ cup panko breadcrumbs
- Freshly grated Parmigiano Reggiano cheese, for serving

1. Heat the olive oil in a large pot over medium-high heat. When the oil begins to shimmer, add the onion and cook, stirring occasionally, until golden brown, 3 to 4 minutes.

2. Add the garlic, rosemary, and red pepper flakes, and stir until aromatic, about 1 minute.

3. Add the tomato paste and cook, stirring, until the tomato paste has darkened to a brick-red color, about 2 minutes.

4. Add the chickpeas, salt, and black pepper and stir until combined. Add the stock and bring to a boil. Add the ditalini and cook until al dente according to the package instructions.

5. **Meanwhile, make the crispy panko:** Melt the butter in a small pan over medium heat. Add the panko and cook, stirring continuously, until golden brown, about 2 minutes. Transfer the panko to a paper towel–lined plate and season with salt.

6. Serve the pasta e ceci sprinkled with the crispy breadcrumbs and lots of grated Parmigiano Reggiano.

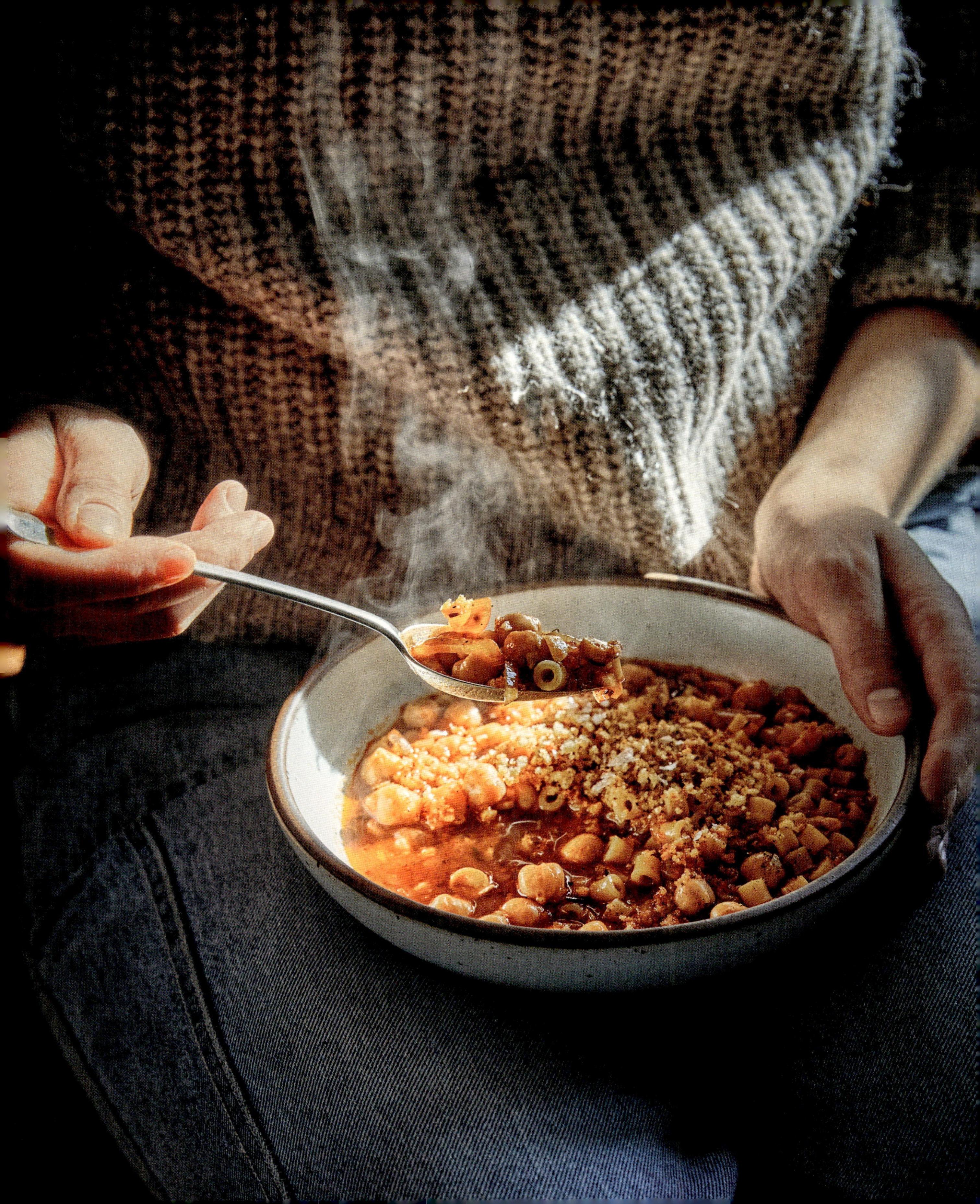

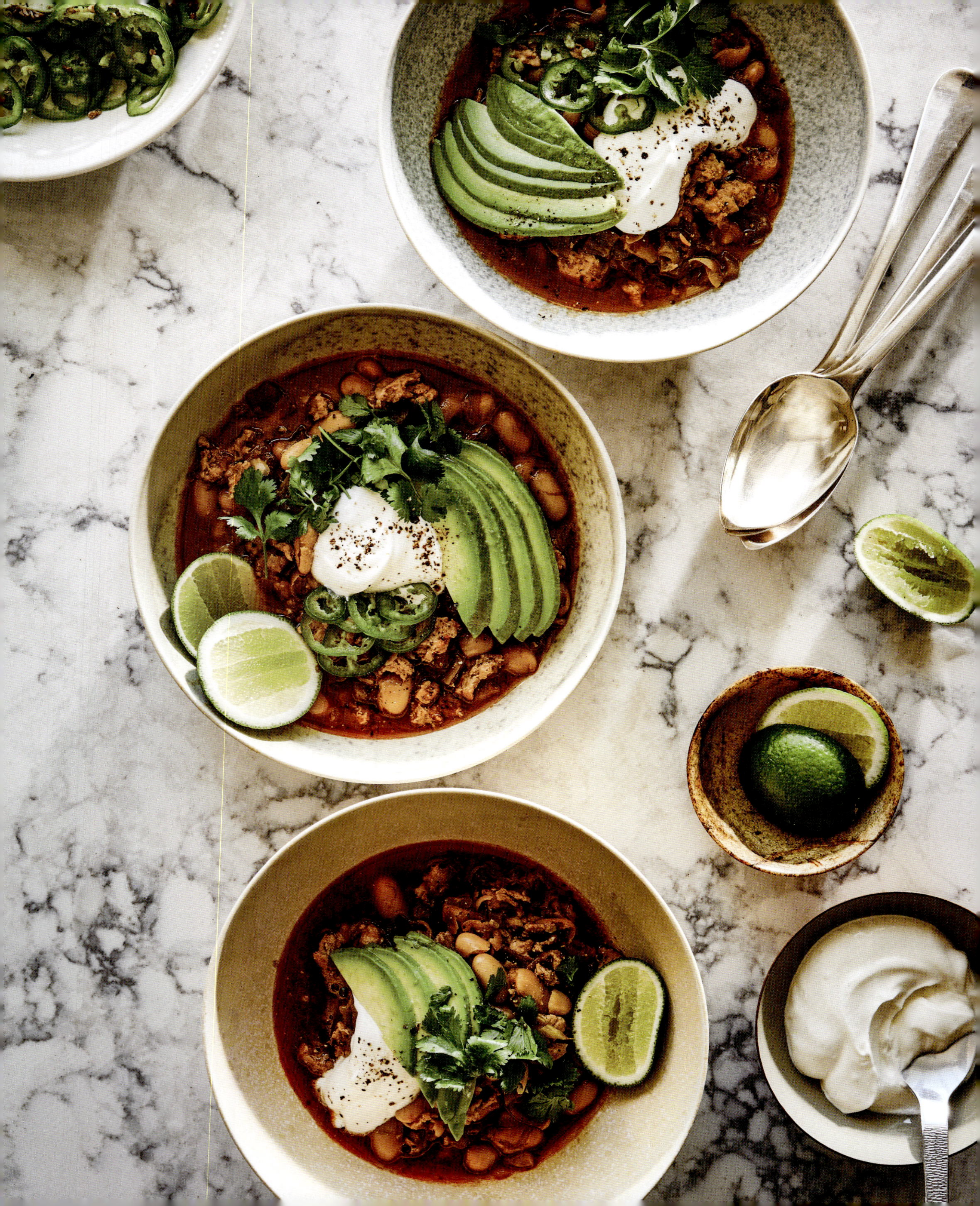

White Turkey Chili

I don't associate the words "light" and "chili," but if there were ever a time to put them together, this would be it. Typically made with pulled meat, this recipe utilizes ground turkey for faster cooking, which means dinner is in your reach in an even shorter time. Mashing half the beans makes for a thicker soup and more interesting texture than if you were to add them all in whole. While toppings are always optional, I personally think they're the best part about chili.

NOTE: Chili can be stored in an airtight container in the refrigerator for up to 3 days or frozen for up to 3 months.

1. Use a fork or potato masher to mash half the beans in a medium bowl until chunky.

2. Heat the olive oil in a large pot or Dutch oven over medium-high heat. When the oil begins to shimmer, add the onion and cook, stirring occasionally, until the onion pieces become lightly golden and begin to soften, 3 to 4 minutes. Add the turkey, salt, and black pepper and cook, using a wooden spoon to break up the meat, until browned and cooked through, about 7 minutes. Add the green chiles, garlic, cumin, paprika, oregano, and cayenne and stir until aromatic, about 1 minute.

3. Add the mashed beans and the whole beans, along with the stock, and stir to combine. Bring the chili to a low boil, then reduce the heat to medium-low and simmer until slightly thickened, about 15 minutes.

4. Serve the chili with a squeeze of lime juice and top with avocado, sour cream, jalapeños, and cilantro.

Serves 4 to 6

3 (15-ounce) cans great northern beans, drained and rinsed

1 tablespoon extra-virgin olive oil

1 medium yellow onion, finely chopped

1 pound ground turkey (preferably dark meat)

2 teaspoons kosher salt

1 teaspoon freshly ground black pepper

2 (4-ounce) cans green chiles, drained

3 garlic cloves, minced

2 teaspoons ground cumin

1 teaspoon sweet paprika

1 teaspoon dried oregano

¼ teaspoon cayenne pepper

4 cups chicken stock

FOR SERVING

Lime wedges

1 avocado, sliced

Sour cream

Fresh cilantro

Sliced jalapeños

Salmon, Potato, and Corn Chowder

A good chowder is all about balancing your cream-to-stock ratio. Too much cream, and you're sipping on something more akin to a fishy latte (not preferable). Too much stock, and you're missing the point of chowder. Loaded with potatoes, corn, and hunks of salmon, this chowder hits all the right notes. It's creamy and comforting, but still has a brightness, thanks to lime juice and jalapeño.

NOTES: You can use Yukon Gold potatoes for this recipe instead of new potatoes—just make sure to cube them into ¾-inch pieces. Salmon can be swapped for a white fish, like halibut, cod, or even bass. Leftover chowder can be stored in an airtight container in the refrigerator for up to 3 days or frozen for up to 3 months.

1. Melt the butter in a large pot or Dutch oven over medium-high heat. Add the onion and celery and cook, stirring occasionally, until the onion is translucent, about 5 minutes. Add the potatoes, garlic, salt, pepper, and paprika and cook until the garlic is aromatic, about 1 minute. Add the wine and cook until the alcohol burns off, about 2 minutes. Add the stock and corn and bring to a boil. Cook until the potatoes are fork-tender, about 10 minutes.

2. Pat the salmon dry with paper towels and season on all sides with salt. Add the salmon, cream, and jalapeños to the pot and cook until the salmon is just cooked through, about 3 minutes. Add the lime juice and scallions and stir to combine. Serve immediately.

Serves 4

3 tablespoons unsalted butter

1 medium yellow onion, finely chopped

3 celery stalks, thinly sliced

1 pound new potatoes, halved

3 garlic cloves, minced

2 teaspoons kosher salt, plus more for seasoning

1 teaspoon freshly ground black pepper

1 teaspoon sweet paprika

½ cup dry white wine, such as sauvignon blanc or pinot grigio

4 cups vegetable, fish, or chicken stock

2 cups frozen corn

1½ pounds salmon, cut into 1-inch pieces

1½ cups heavy cream

2 medium jalapeños, thinly sliced

Juice of 2 limes (about ¼ cup)

1 bunch scallions, thinly sliced

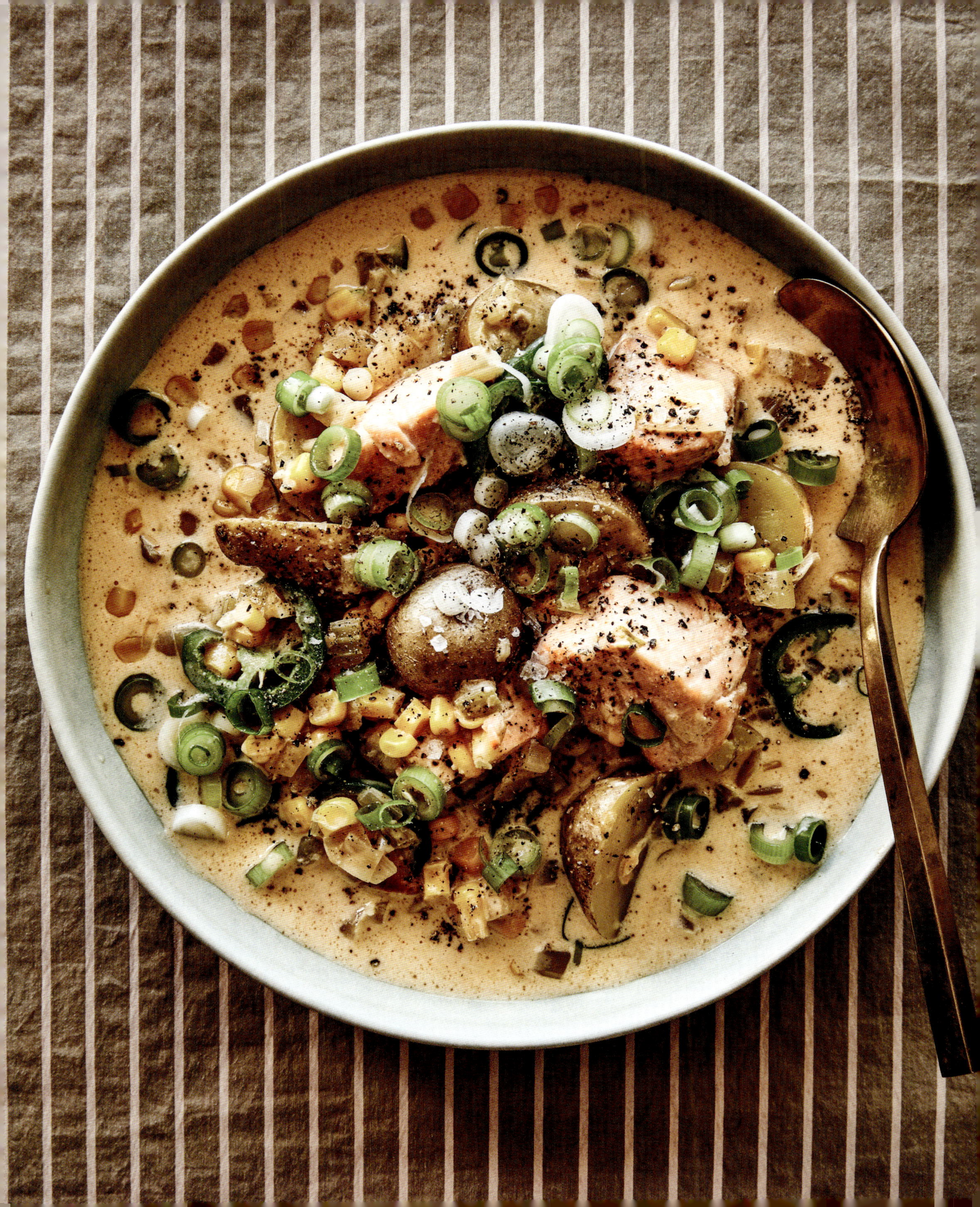

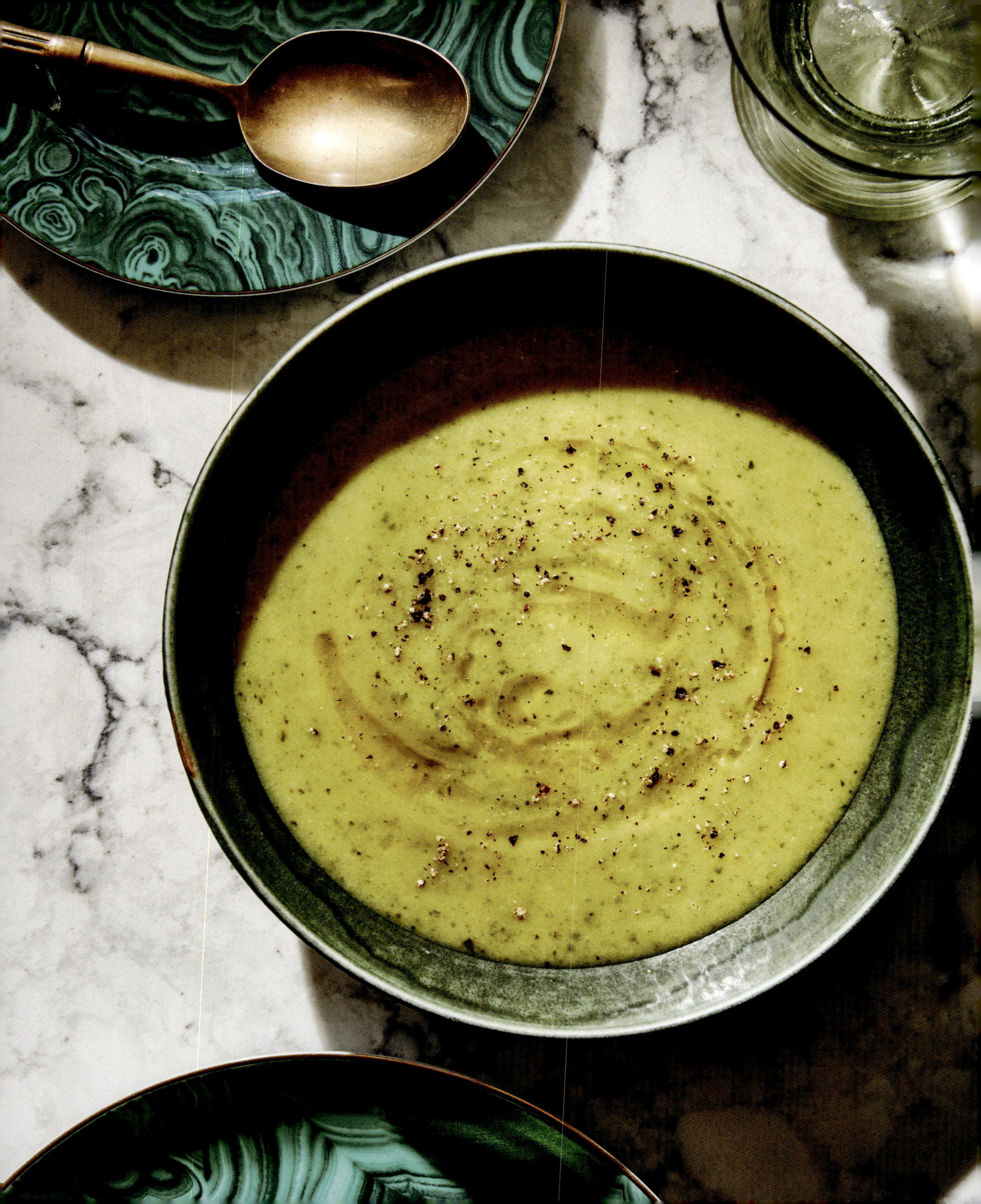

Zucchini Soup

Somewhere between late summer and early fall, zucchini takes off. If you've ever tried growing it, you know that even one plant will leave you with an overwhelming abundance, and no matter how much zucchini bread you bake, it never seems to make a dent. This soup is my personal favorite vehicle for zucchini. It's easy to make but has a complex taste, thanks to curry powder and cumin, which bring out the warmth of the vegetable. It's appropriate for when zucchini is in season, as the nights begin to cool off, but I also love freezing it so I can cling to the taste of summer once winter rolls through. Make sure not to overcook the zucchini; it should be tender but not mushy and remain bright green.

NOTES: This serves more than the other soup recipes in this chapter for the sole purpose of using up zucchini and freezing some for winter. The soup can be stored in an airtight container in the refrigerator for up to 3 days or in the freezer for up to 3 months.

Serves 6 to 8

- 2 tablespoons extra-virgin olive oil, plus more for serving
- 2 medium yellow onions, coarsely chopped
- 3½ pounds zucchini, coarsely chopped
- 4 garlic cloves, coarsely chopped
- 2 teaspoons curry powder
- 2 teaspoons kosher salt
- 1 teaspoon freshly ground black pepper
- 1 teaspoon ground cumin
- 6 cups vegetable stock

1. Heat the olive oil in a large pot or Dutch oven over medium-high heat. When the oil begins to shimmer, add the onions and cook, stirring occasionally, until softened and lightly golden, about 5 minutes.

2. Add the zucchini and cook, stirring occasionally, until the zucchini has begun to soften but the skin is still bright green, about 10 minutes.

3. Add the garlic, curry powder, salt, pepper, and cumin and cook, stirring, until aromatic, about 1 minute.

4. Add the stock and bring to a boil. Reduce the heat to medium and simmer until the zucchini is easily pierced with a knife but still green, about 10 minutes.

5. Working in batches, carefully transfer the soup to a blender and pulse until smooth. (Alternatively, use a food processor or blend directly in the pot with an immersion blender.)

6. Serve the soup with a drizzle of olive oil.

Red Coconut Curry with Tofu

Jarred red curry paste and a can of coconut milk can take you far on a weeknight. Gussied up with aromatics and lime, the curry tastes more complex than it is (the true barometer for weeknight cooking success). This is a great time to use up any leftover vegetables you have in the fridge, like broccoli, snow peas, carrots, or even sliced kale. Add them along with the tofu and simmer until cooked through.

NOTES: Peanuts are optional, but I love the crunch they add. You can also serve this with flatbread as an alternative to rice. Curry can be stored in an airtight container in the refrigerator for up to 3 days or frozen for up to 3 months.

Serves 4

- 2 (16-ounce) packages extra-firm tofu
- 1 tablespoon extra-virgin olive oil
- 1 medium yellow onion, thinly sliced
- 2 medium red bell peppers, thinly sliced
- 4 garlic cloves, minced
- 1 (1½-inch) knob fresh ginger, minced
- 3 tablespoons red curry paste
- 1 (14-ounce) can unsweetened full-fat coconut milk
- 1½ cups vegetable stock
- Zest and juice of 1 lime (about 2 tablespoons juice)
- 2 teaspoons kosher salt

FOR SERVING
Cooked white rice

½ cup salted peanuts, coarsely chopped

½ bunch cilantro, coarsely chopped (about 1 cup)

1. To remove moisture, place the tofu blocks on paper towels, top with more paper towels, and place a weight on top, such as a rimmed baking sheet topped with a cast-iron pan. Let stand for at least 10 minutes or up to 1 hour. Remove the weight and paper towels and cut the tofu into ½-inch cubes.

2. Heat the olive oil in a large pot over medium-high heat. When the oil begins to shimmer, add the onion and peppers and cook, stirring occasionally, until softened, about 7 minutes.

3. Add the garlic and ginger and cook, stirring, until aromatic, about 1 minute. Add the red curry paste and cook, stirring, for about 2 minutes. Add the coconut milk, stock, lime zest, and salt and bring to a simmer. Add the tofu and simmer until the tofu is warmed through and the curry has slightly thickened, about 10 minutes. Add the lime juice and stir to combine.

4. Serve the curry over rice, topped with peanuts and cilantro.

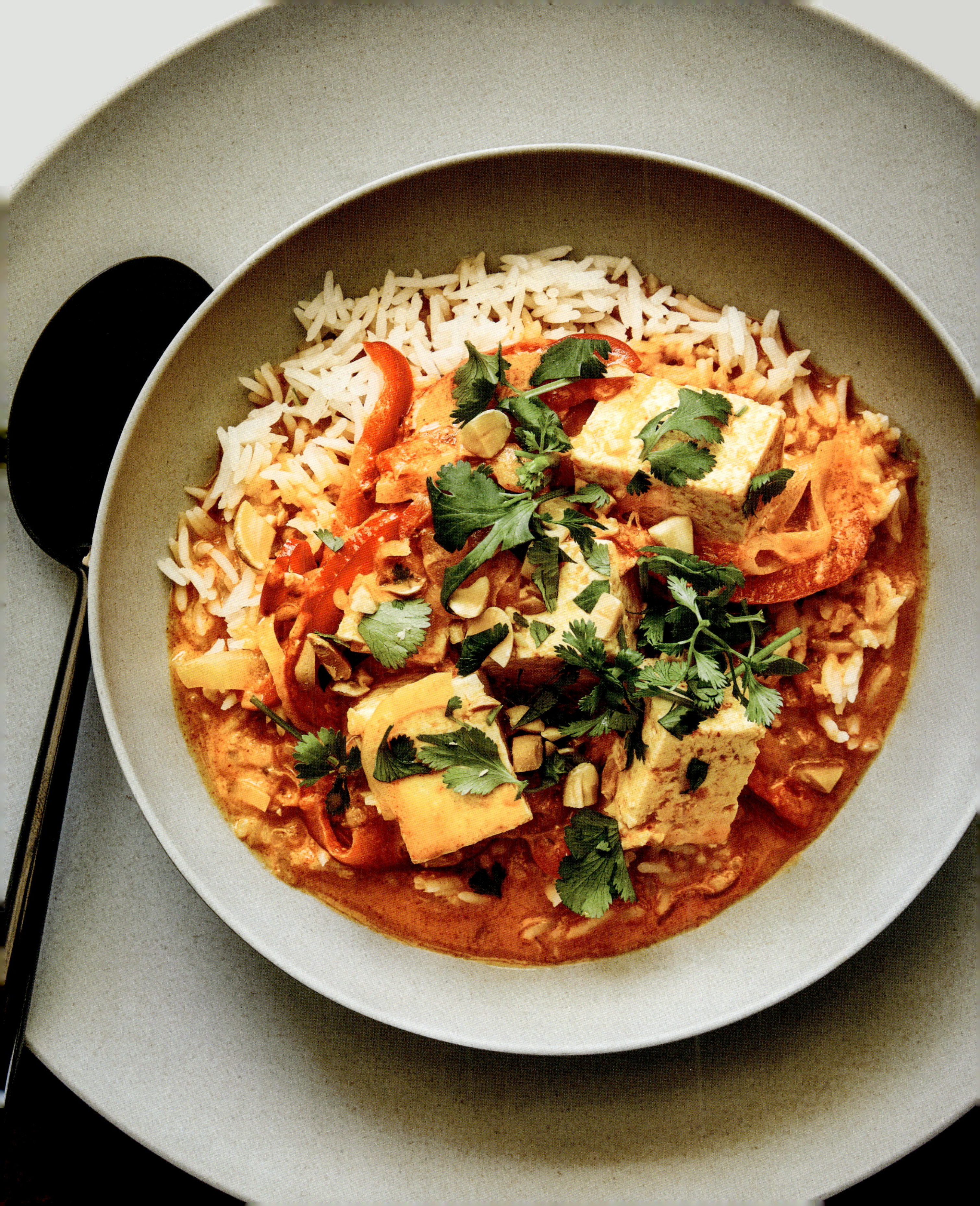

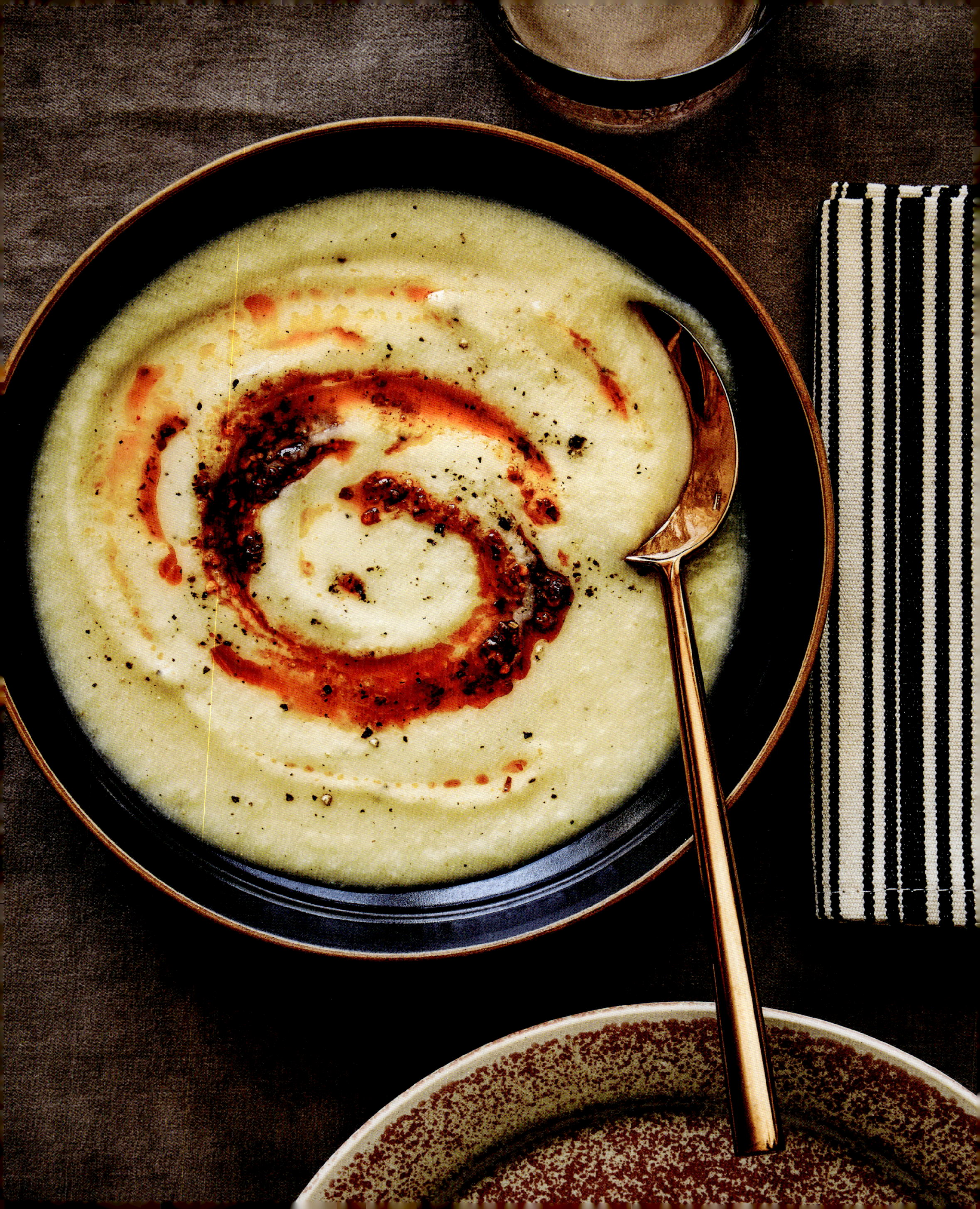

Creamy Cauliflower Soup with Chile Crisp

Cauliflower is one of those vegetables that can take on any cooking preparation or flavor combination. Here, cauliflower transforms into a cozy cold-weather soup laden with aromatics like garlic and ginger and topped with chile crisp for a bit of heat and texture. Don't be fooled by the intense creaminess: This soup happens to be vegan. I used a trick from my mom for this recipe—a dash of curry powder adds warmth and body to soup, without adding any distinctly curry flavor. This is a great time to make use of all the great store-bought chile crisp brands available these days, like Onino, Lao Gan Ma, Fly by Jing, KariKari, and Momofuku.

NOTE: The soup can be stored in an airtight container in the refrigerator for up to 3 days or in the freezer for up to 3 months.

Serves 4

- 2 tablespoons extra-virgin olive oil
- 2 large shallots, thinly sliced
- 3 garlic cloves, thinly sliced
- 1 (1-inch) knob fresh ginger, coarsely chopped (about 1 tablespoon)
- 1 large head cauliflower, separated into florets (about 10 cups)
- 4 cups vegetable stock
- 2 teaspoons kosher salt
- 1 teaspoon freshly ground black pepper
- ½ teaspoon curry powder
- Zest and juice of 1 lime (about 2 tablespoons juice)
- Chile crisp, for serving

1. Heat the olive oil in a large pot with a lid or a Dutch oven over medium-high heat. When the oil begins to shimmer, add the shallots and cook, stirring occasionally, until softened and lightly golden brown, about 4 minutes.

2. Add the garlic and ginger and cook until aromatic, about 1 minute. Add the cauliflower, stock, salt, pepper, and curry powder and bring to a boil. Place the lid on the pot, reduce the heat to medium-low, and simmer until the cauliflower is knife-tender, 15 to 20 minutes.

3. Working in batches, carefully transfer the soup to a blender and pulse until smooth. (Alternatively, blend the soup directly in the pot with an immersion blender.) Transfer the smooth soup back to the pot and add the lime zest and lime juice and stir to combine.

4. Serve the soup with a drizzle of chile crisp.

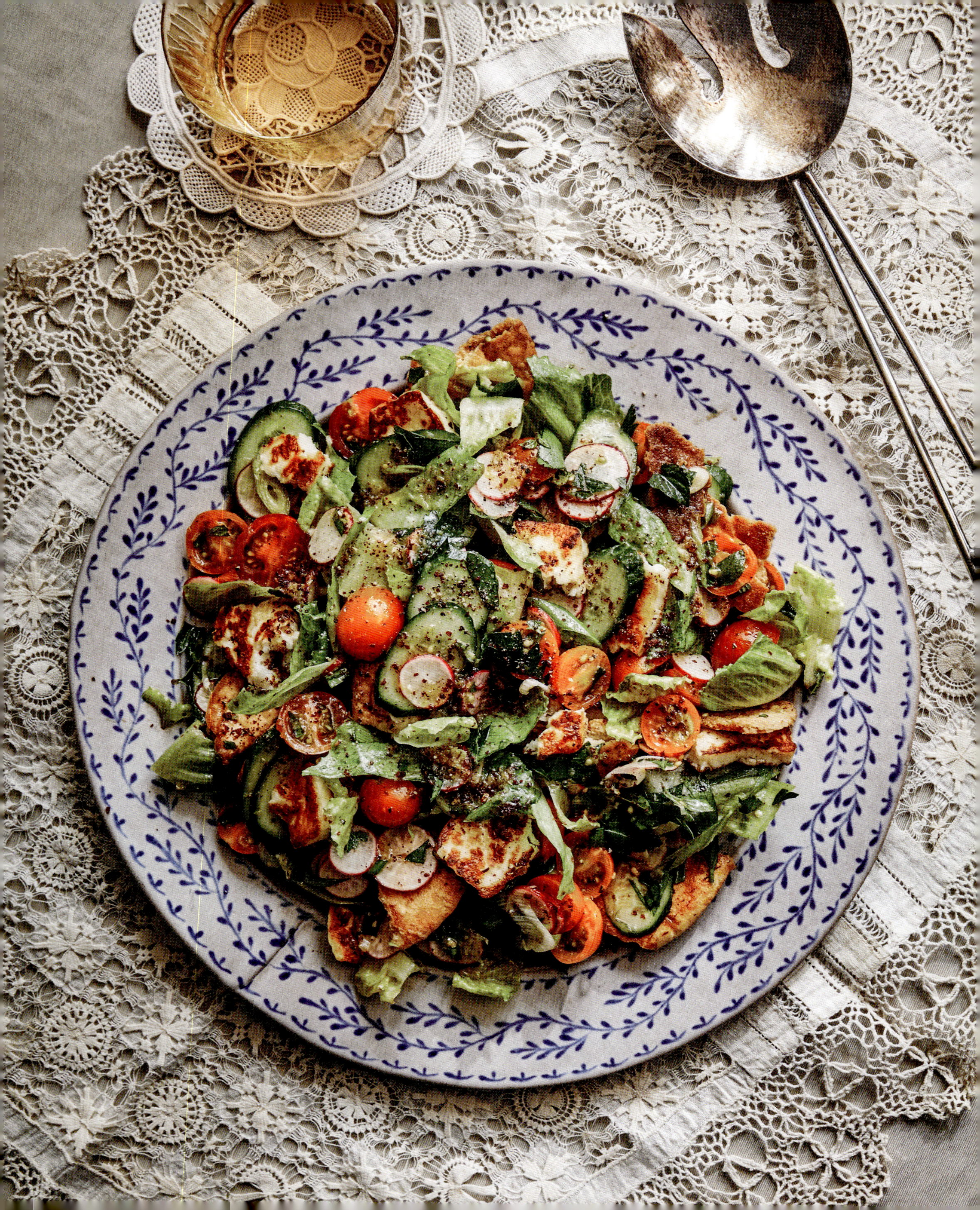

VEGETABLE MAINS, SIDES, AND SALADS

NIGHTS

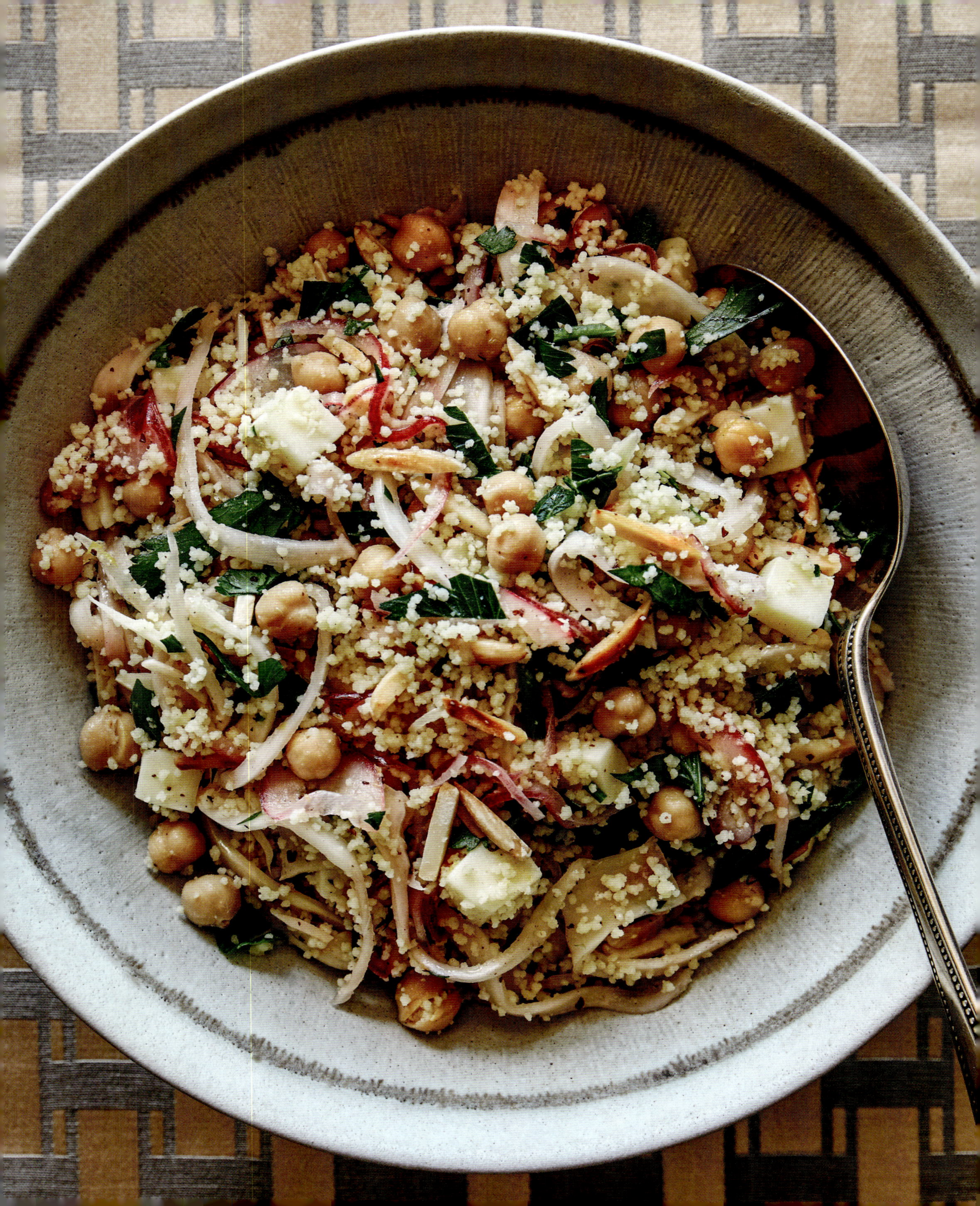

Couscous and Chickpea Salad

Made with quick-cooking couscous and canned chickpeas, this dish comes together in ten minutes. The onion and fennel macerate in the lemon juice and salt, which takes out the bite while keeping the crunch. I originally intended this recipe to use feta (which you could still use!), but during the last test, I decided to swap in Fontina on a whim. I love that the Fontina holds its shape, while softening in the couscous. This salad is satisfying enough to eat all on its own but makes a great side, too.

NOTES: You can leave the cheese out if you want to keep it vegan. If you're short on time you can skip toasting the almonds. Couscous and chickpea salad can be stored in an airtight container in the refrigerator for up to 3 days.

Serves 4

- 1 medium fennel bulb, stalks removed, bulb thinly sliced
- 1 small red onion, thinly sliced
- Zest and juice of 2 lemons (about ¼ cup juice)
- 2 tablespoons extra-virgin olive oil
- 1½ teaspoons kosher salt
- 1 teaspoon ground sumac
- 1 cup vegetable stock or chicken stock
- 1 cup couscous
- 1 cup raw slivered almonds
- 1 (15-ounce) can chickpeas, drained and rinsed
- 6 ounces Fontina cheese, cubed
- 1 bunch flat-leaf parsley, coarsely chopped (about 2 cups)

1. Combine the fennel, red onion, lemon zest, lemon juice, olive oil, salt, and sumac in a medium bowl and stir.

2. Place the stock in a medium pot over high heat. When it begins to boil, remove the pot from the heat and add the couscous, stirring to combine. Place the lid on the pot and let stand for 5 minutes.

3. Set a small pan over medium heat. When the pan is hot, add the almonds and cook, stirring, until toasted, 1 to 2 minutes.

4. Add the couscous, toasted almonds, chickpeas, Fontina, and parsley to the bowl with the fennel and stir until well combined, then serve.

Socca with Arugula Salad

Socca, or *farinata* in Italian, refers to an unleavened savory chickpea pancake that's often eaten as street food along the Mediterranean coast. There's some debate on where socca originated, with some claiming its roots come from Nice, France, and others attesting the dish comes from Genoa, Italy. It's my go-to quick dish whenever I'm craving something a little lighter, because it's affordable, comes together quickly, and is exceptionally delicious for something with so few ingredients. Made with chickpea flour, water, and olive oil (yes, it's gluten-free!), the socca batter is poured over a large, hot skillet and cooked for a few minutes until the edges get crispy and the center is tender. While traditionally it is served with a good dose of olive oil and salt, I like taking a cue from salad pizza and topping it with a simple arugula and fennel salad, although any toppings of choice would work well here.

NOTES: Although the batter can be made well in advance, socca is best served hot.

Serves 2 as a main or 4 as an appetizer

SOCCA
- 1 cup chickpea flour
- ½ teaspoon kosher salt
- ½ teaspoon freshly ground black pepper
- 3 tablespoons extra-virgin olive oil

SALAD
- 1 medium fennel bulb, stalks removed, bulb thinly sliced
- Juice of 1 lemon (about 2 tablespoons)
- 3 tablespoons extra-virgin olive oil
- ½ teaspoon kosher salt
- 3 cups loosely packed arugula
- ½ cup shaved Parmigiano Reggiano cheese

1. **Make the socca:** Combine the chickpea flour, 1 cup water, the salt, pepper, and 2 tablespoons of the olive oil in a medium bowl and whisk until smooth. Cover with a kitchen towel and let rest at room temperature for at least 30 minutes or up to 12 hours.

2. Position a rack in the upper third of the oven and set a cast-iron or stainless-steel pan in the center of the rack. Preheat the oven to 450°F.

3. When the oven has preheated, carefully remove the hot pan and switch the oven to broil. Pour the remaining 1 tablespoon olive oil into the hot pan and swirl it around the pan to coat. Pour the batter into the pan, swirling until it covers the entire bottom. Return the pan to the center of the oven rack. Broil the socca until the edges are lightly crispy and the top is golden brown and cooked through, 5 to 7 minutes, depending on the strength of your broiler.

4. **When the socca begins cooking, start the salad:** Place the fennel, lemon juice, olive oil, and salt in a medium bowl and stir to combine. Let sit at room temperature while the socca broils.

5. Let the socca cool in the pan for about 5 minutes. In the meantime, add the arugula and Parmigiano Reggiano to the bowl of fennel and toss to combine.

6. Top the socca with the arugula and fennel salad and serve immediately.

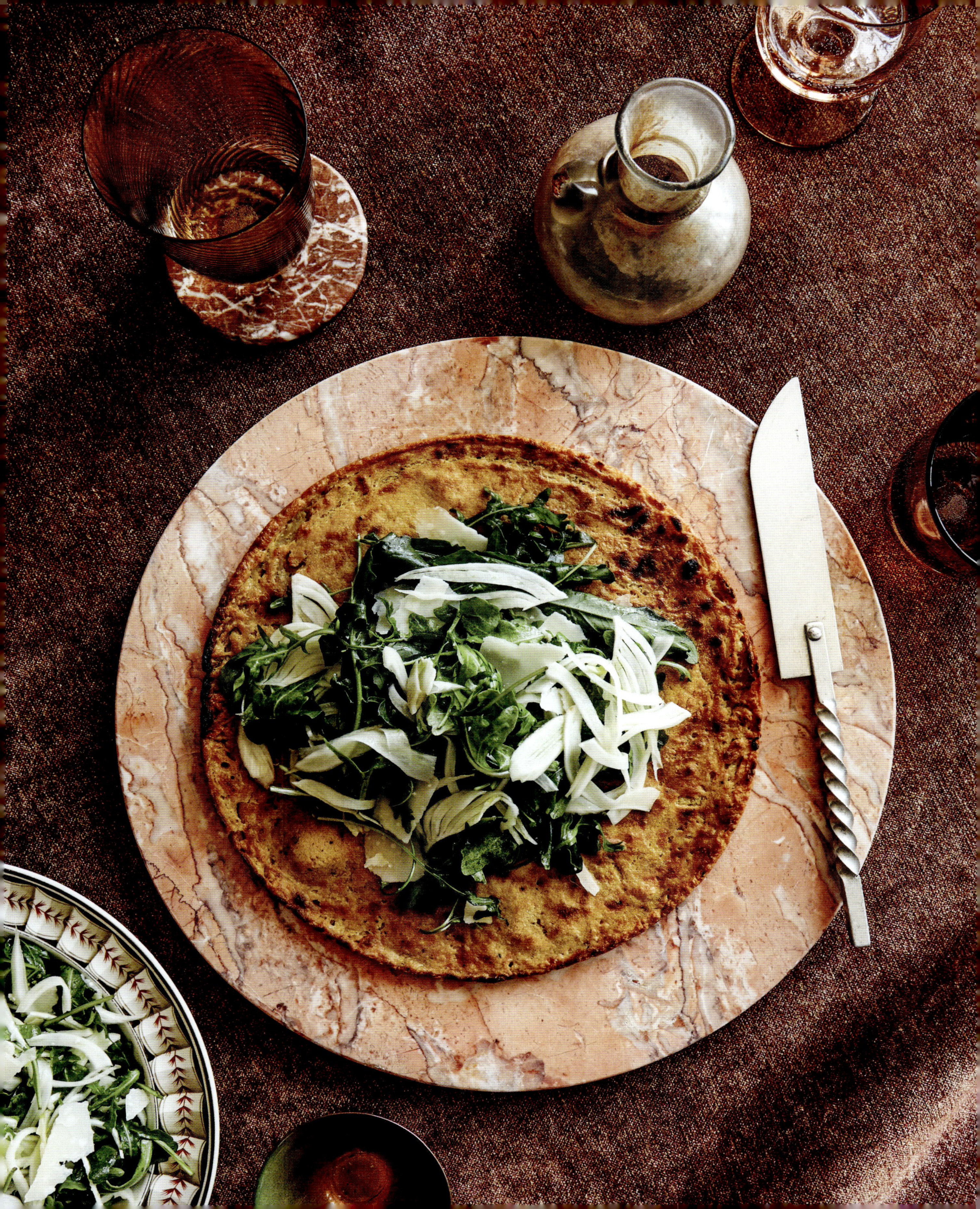

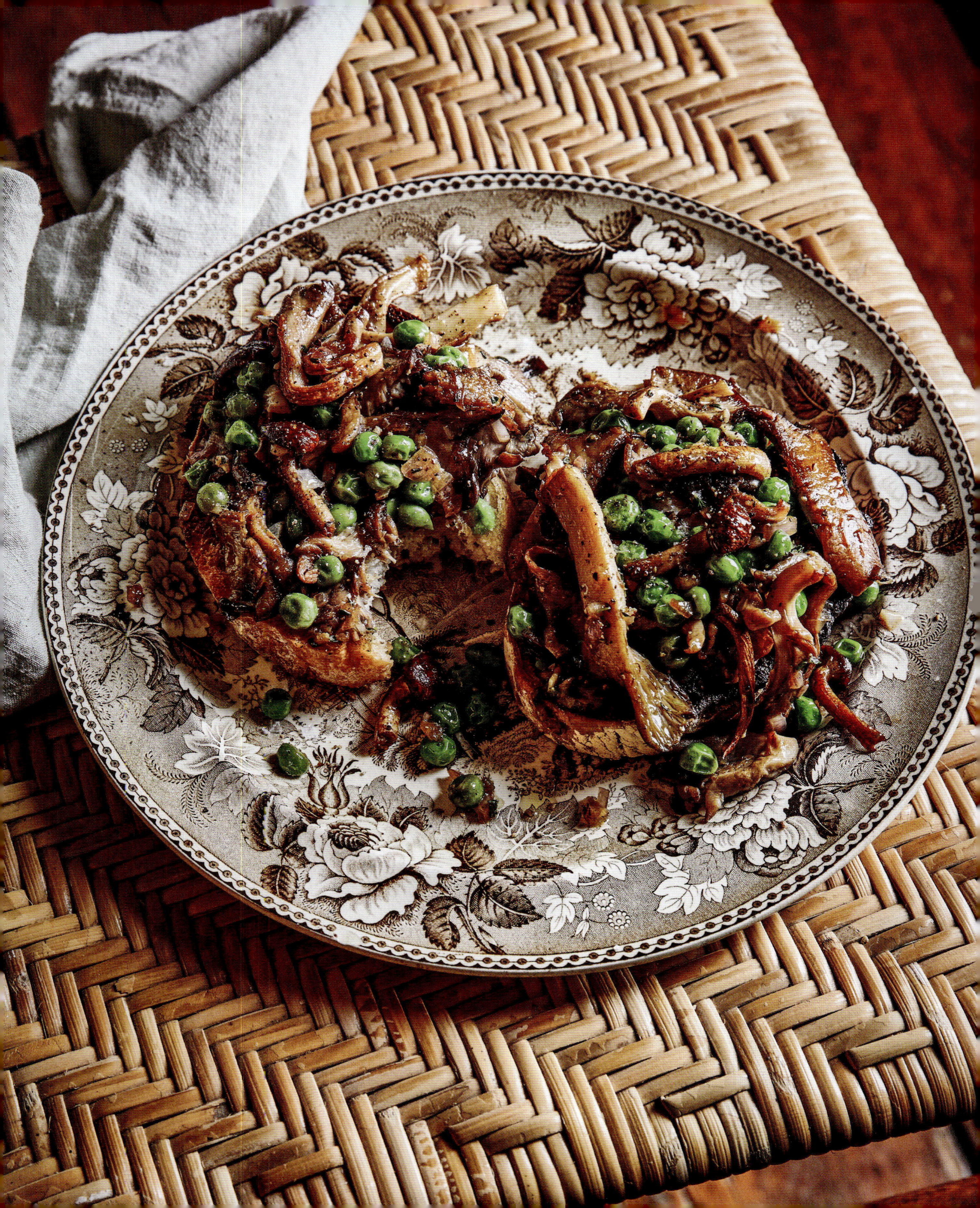

Mushroom and Pea Toast

Eating a straight-up sandwich for dinner isn't my vibe, but there's something about open-faced toast that feels different. Whenever I get my hands on a beautiful bushel of mushrooms, my go-to is serving them on toast to really highlight the flavor. This recipe is all about coaxing out umami, using soy sauce, vinegar, and butter to create a glossy sauce around the seared mushrooms. While I love this as a quick meal, you can also serve it in smaller portions for a snack.

NOTES: Leftover mushroom and peas can be stored in an airtight container in the refrigerator for up to 3 days. If using leftovers, just toast the bread when ready to serve.

1. Heat the olive oil in a large pan over medium-high heat. When the oil begins to shimmer, add the mushrooms and cook, stirring occasionally, until the mushrooms are golden brown, about 8 minutes.

2. Add the peas, shallot, garlic, thyme, salt, and pepper and cook, stirring, until the shallot begins to soften and is deeply aromatic, about 2 minutes. Add the butter, soy sauce, and vinegar and cook, stirring, until the butter has melted and the mushrooms are glossy, about 1 minute.

3. Serve the mushrooms and peas spooned over the toast.

Serves 2 to 4

- 2 tablespoons extra-virgin olive oil
- 1 pound assorted mushrooms, stemmed and thinly sliced
- 1 cup frozen peas, thawed
- 1 large shallot, finely chopped
- 2 garlic cloves, minced
- 2 teaspoons finely chopped fresh thyme
- 1 teaspoon kosher salt
- 1 teaspoon freshly ground black pepper
- 2 tablespoons unsalted butter
- 1 tablespoon soy sauce
- 1 tablespoon sherry vinegar
- 4 slices bread of choice, toasted

Roasted Broccoli and Crispy Chickpeas with Tahini Dressing

Made with grocery store staples, this protein-packed dish comes together in under thirty minutes. Broccoli and chickpeas get tossed in the same seasoning and roasted together on one sheet pan until charred and crispy. The idea came from my friend Leah, who swears by tossing the veg into a bowl with lemony tahini dressing as soon as they're out of the oven. This ensures each bite is amply coated in sauce and makes this more of a standalone meal than a side salad (although it's great for that, too).

NOTES: If you're wary of spice, cut the cayenne down to ¼ teaspoon or simply omit it. Leftover broccoli and chickpeas can be stored in an airtight container in the refrigerator for up to 3 days.

Serves 4

- 2 medium heads broccoli, cut into florets and tender stems thinly sliced (about 8 cups)
- 2 (15-ounce) cans chickpeas, drained and rinsed
- ¼ cup plus 2 tablespoons extra-virgin olive oil
- 2 teaspoons ground cumin
- 2 teaspoons kosher salt
- 1 teaspoon freshly ground black pepper
- ½ teaspoon cayenne pepper
- ¼ cup tahini
- Zest and juice of 2 lemons (about ¼ cup juice)
- 2 tablespoons hot water
- 1 small red onion, thinly sliced

1. Preheat the oven to 425°F.

2. Combine the broccoli, chickpeas, ¼ cup of the olive oil, the cumin, 1½ teaspoons of the salt, the black pepper, and cayenne in a large bowl and toss until well coated. Transfer the mixture to a rimmed baking pan in an even layer. If the sheet pan is too crowded, use two baking sheets. Roast until the broccoli is charred and tender and the chickpeas are crispy, about 25 minutes.

3. While the broccoli and chickpeas are roasting, combine the tahini, lemon zest, lemon juice, hot water, remaining 2 tablespoons olive oil, and remaining ½ teaspoon salt to the bottom of the same bowl that you tossed the broccoli in and whisk until smooth.

4. Add the roasted broccoli, chickpeas, and red onion to the bowl with the tahini dressing and toss until well combined. Serve immediately.

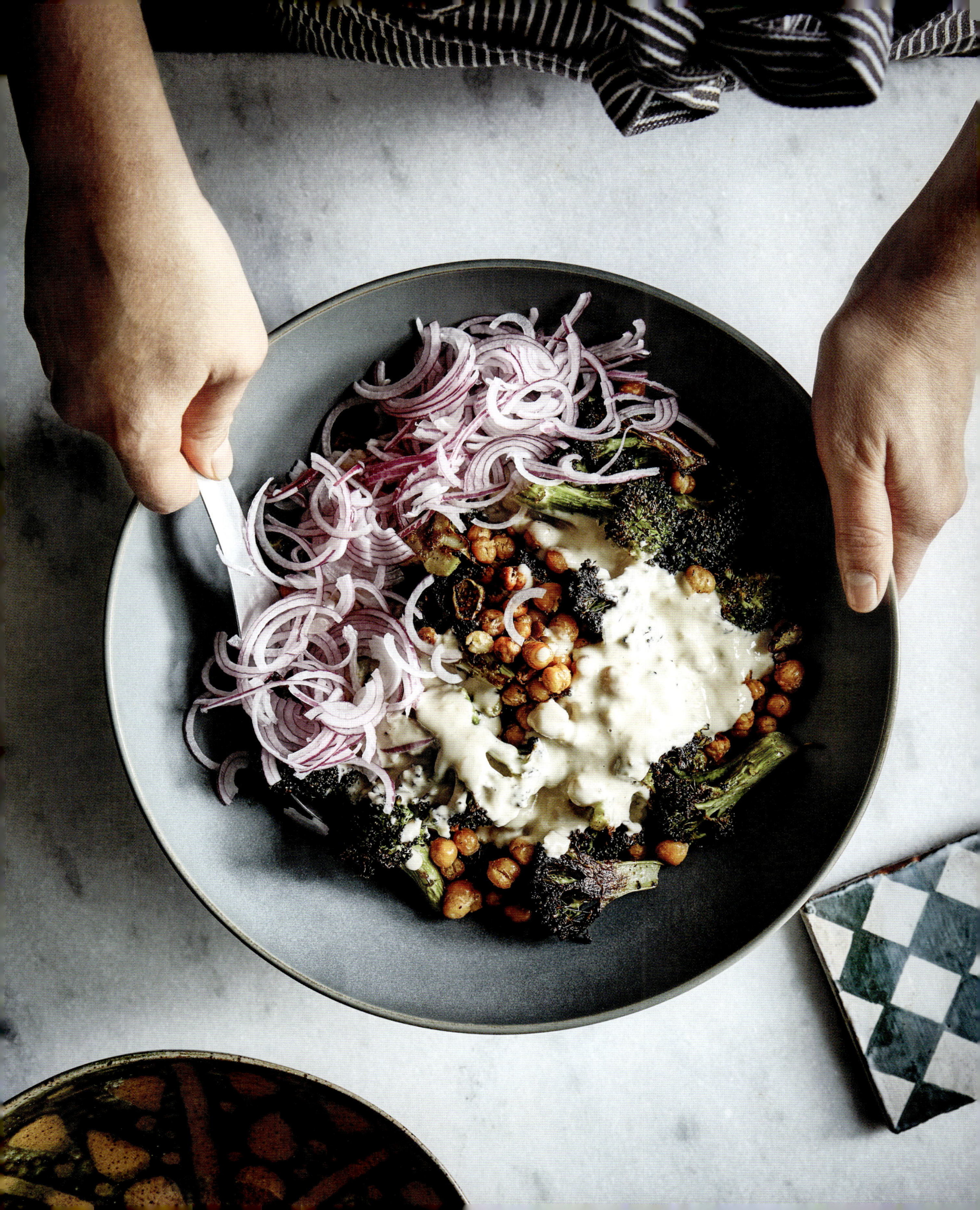

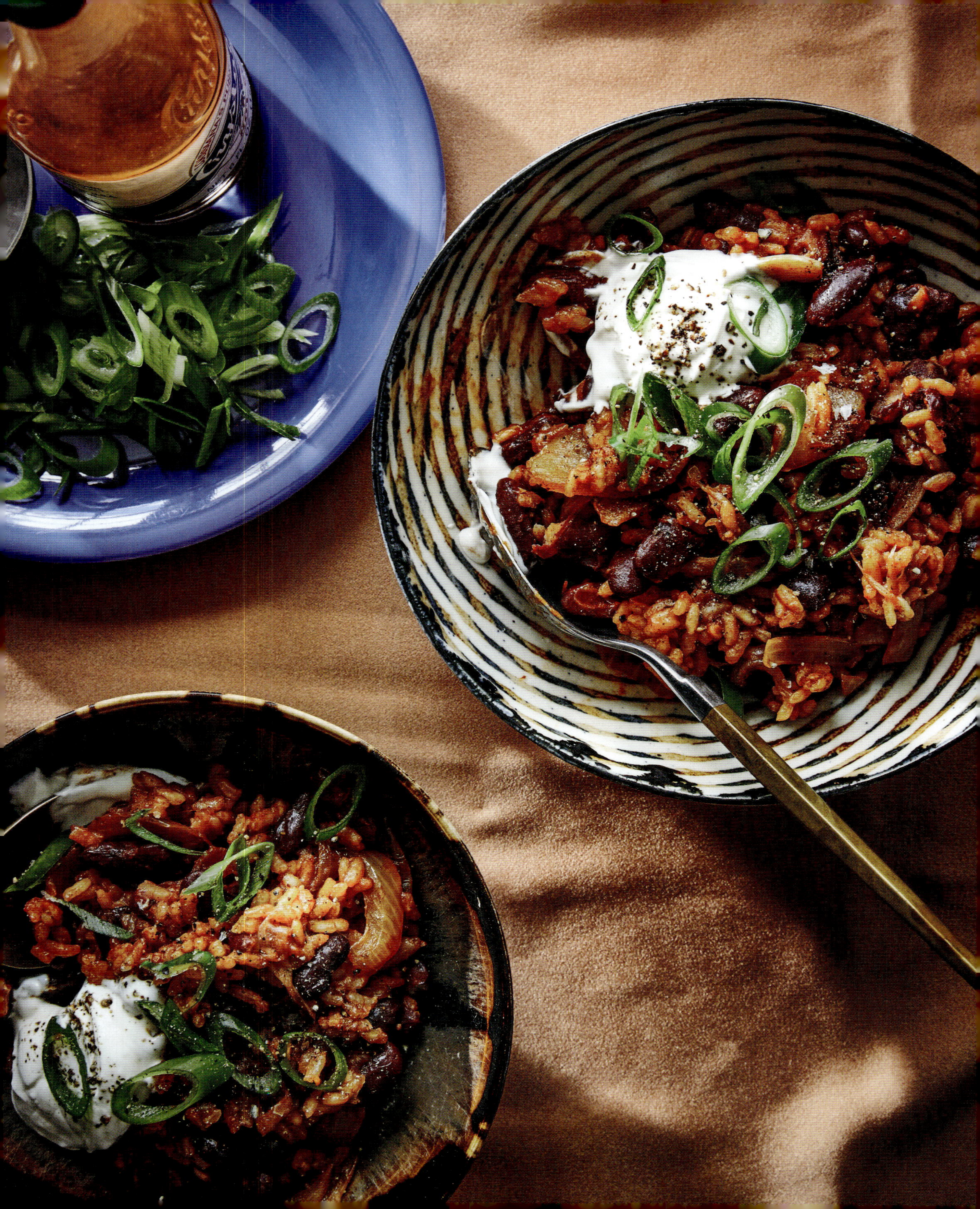

One-Pot Rice and Beans

Red beans and rice pilaf were on our weekly rotation growing up. I've carried on that tradition, but combined the dishes into one pot. It's filling, affordable, and most importantly, delicious. I've leaned on two flavor heavy hitters to do most of the legwork here: chili powder and Louisiana-style hot sauce, which is frankly more about adding acidity than heat and helps cut down on the cook time without sacrificing flavor.

NOTES: If you don't have Louisiana-style hot sauce, you can swap in white wine vinegar. Similarly, if you're trying to steer clear of alcohol, add ½ cup more stock in its place. Leftover rice and beans can be stored in an airtight container in the refrigerator for up to 3 days.

Serves 4

- 1 tablespoon extra-virgin olive oil
- 2 medium yellow onions, thinly sliced
- 4 garlic cloves, thinly sliced
- ½ cup tomato paste
- 1 tablespoon chili powder
- ½ cup dry white wine, such as sauvignon blanc or pinot grigio
- 2 (15-ounce) cans red kidney beans, drained and rinsed
- 2 cups vegetable stock or chicken stock
- 1½ cups short-grain white rice
- 2 teaspoons kosher salt
- 1 teaspoon freshly ground black pepper
- 1 tablespoon Louisiana-style hot sauce, such as Crystal
- Sour cream, for serving
- Thinly sliced scallions, for serving

1. Heat the olive oil in a medium pot over medium-high heat. When the oil begins to shimmer, add the yellow onions and cook, stirring occasionally, until they begin to soften and become lightly golden brown, about 7 minutes. Add the garlic and cook until aromatic, about 1 minute.

2. Add the tomato paste and chili powder and cook until it turns a brick-red color and is deeply aromatic, about 2 minutes.

3. Add the wine and scrape up any brown bits on the bottom of the pan, cooking until the alcohol burns off, about 2 minutes. Add the beans, stock, rice, salt, and pepper, and stir to combine. Bring the mixture to a boil, then place the lid on the pot and simmer until the rice is cooked through, 20 to 25 minutes, depending on which brand of rice you use. Let stand with the lid on for at least 5 minutes.

4. Stir in the hot sauce and serve immediately with sour cream and scallions on the side.

Summer Squash Casserole with Buttery Ritz Crackers

I didn't eat many casseroles growing up, but I've come to appreciate them in adulthood for their ease and convenience. This one is particularly good. This recipe is a riff on a dish my mother-in-law makes every year when summer squash abounds. The concept is simple enough—squash and onions are cooked down until lightly caramelized, then folded into a cheesy batter before getting topped with buttery, crumbled Ritz crackers. In the original recipe, the squash gets cooked down until it's nearly falling apart, but I like my squash with a bit of bite, so the cooking time is reduced here.

NOTES: If you have an excess of zucchini, you could swap out the summer squash and use them in this recipe—or even use a mix of both. The crispy crackers on top are crucial for the texture, but if you don't have Ritz you could also use saltines or even oyster crackers. Leftover squash casserole can be stored in an airtight container in the refrigerator for up to 3 days.

Serves 6 to 8

- 4 tablespoons (½ stick) unsalted butter, melted, plus more for greasing
- 1 tablespoon extra-virgin olive oil
- 2 medium yellow onions, thinly sliced
- 3 pounds summer squash, thinly sliced
- 3 garlic cloves, minced
- 2 teaspoons kosher salt
- 1 teaspoon freshly ground black pepper
- 1 teaspoon sweet paprika
- ½ teaspoon red pepper flakes
- 1 (8-ounce) package full-fat cream cheese, at room temperature
- 1 cup shredded cheddar cheese
- 2 large eggs, beaten
- 7 ounces Ritz crackers (about 2 sleeves), crushed

1. Position a rack in the upper third of the oven. Preheat the oven to 375°F. Grease a 9×13-inch baking dish with butter.

2. Heat the olive oil in a large pot over medium-high heat. When the oil begins to shimmer, add the onions and cook, stirring occasionally, until lightly golden, 5 to 6 minutes.

3. Add the squash and cook, stirring occasionally, until it has softened but still holds its shape, about 10 minutes. Add the garlic, salt, black pepper, paprika, and red pepper flakes and cook, stirring, until aromatic, about 1 minute. Drain the squash mixture in a fine-mesh sieve to release any excess liquid.

4. Combine the cream cheese, cheddar, and eggs in a large bowl and stir until well combined. Add the squash mixture and stir until just combined. Transfer the mixture to the greased baking dish.

5. Combine the crackers and melted butter in a medium bowl and stir to combine. Top the squash casserole with the buttery crackers. Place the dish in the center of the oven rack and bake until the crackers are golden brown, about 20 minutes.

6. Serve immediately.

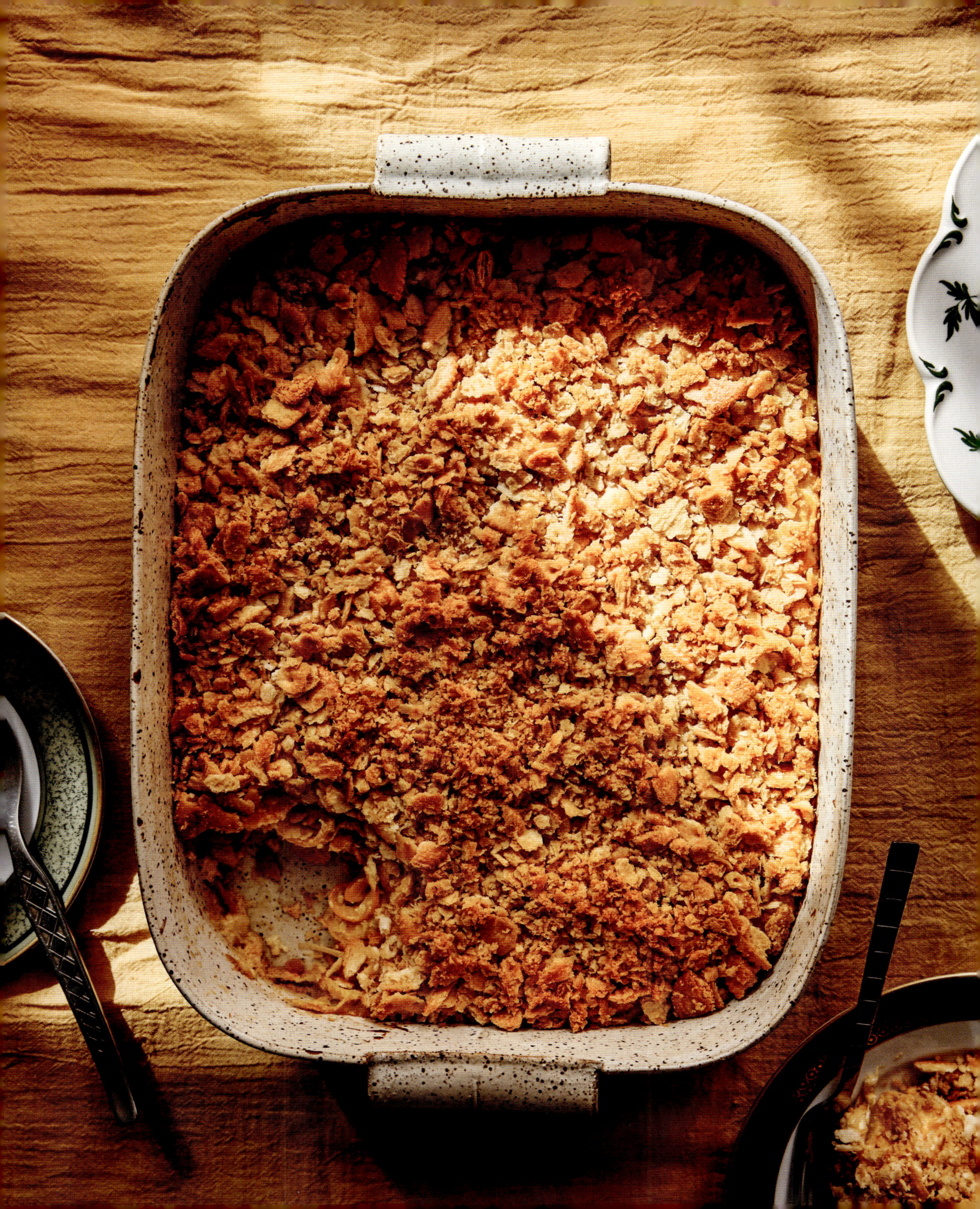

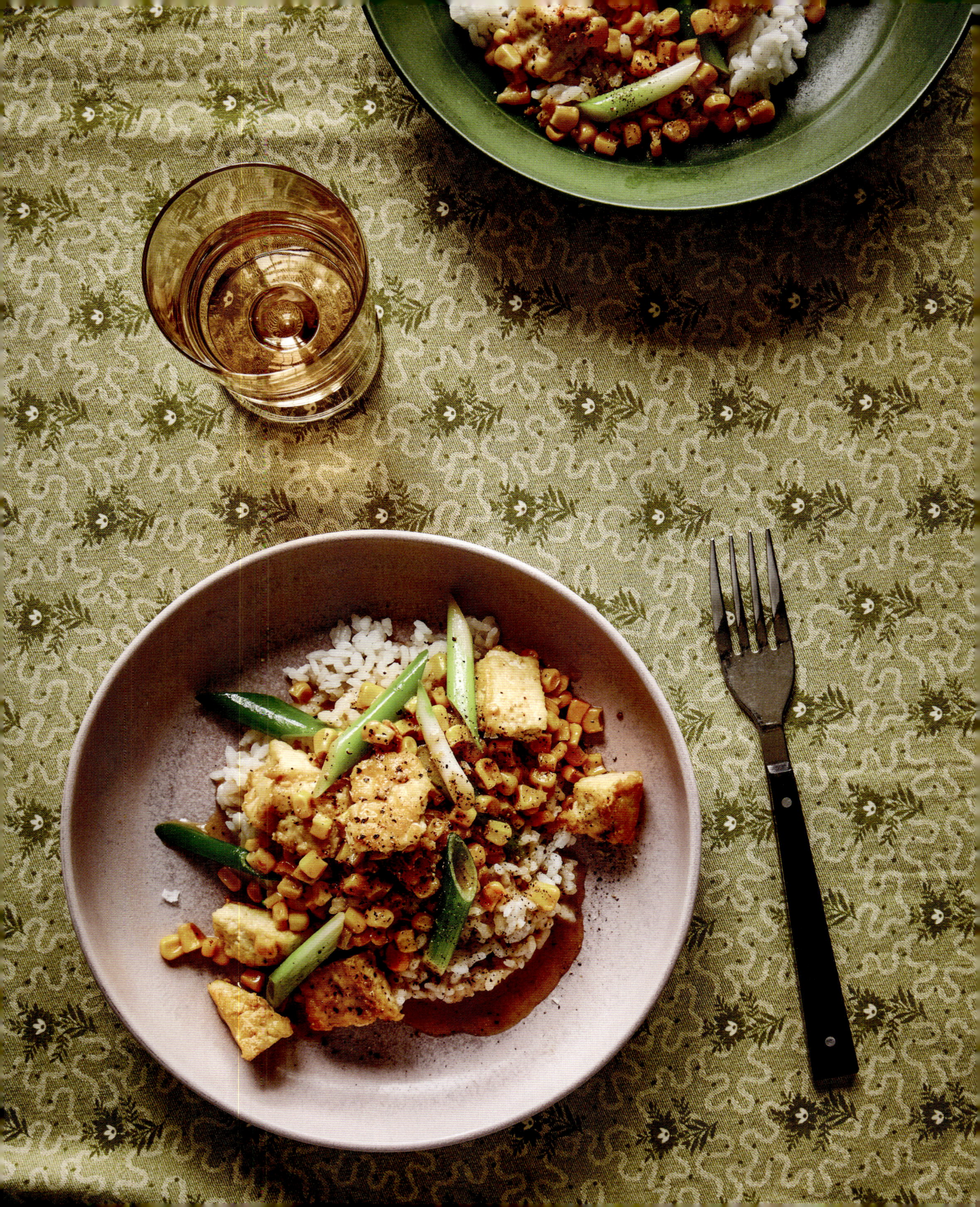

Tofu in Miso Butter Sauce with Corn

Put miso paste and butter together, and I'm on board. While tofu is the protein here, the real star of the show is the sauce. Frozen corn makes this a year-round dinner contender, although you could of course use fresh if it's in season. The key here is to thin out the miso paste and butter with boiling water until glossy enough to coat each craggy piece of seared tofu. Miso and soy sauce are inherently salty, so make sure to taste the final dish before adding more.

NOTES: Extra-firm tofu is crucial to the success of this recipe. Softer types won't be able to stand up to the pan and will crumble instead of becoming golden brown. To quickly thaw corn, microwave it or run it under hot water, and be sure to drain it through a sieve before adding to the tofu. Leftovers can be stored in an airtight container in the refrigerator for up to 2 days.

Serves 4

- 1 (16-ounce) package extra-firm tofu
- 2 tablespoons extra-virgin olive oil
- 1 (12-ounce) package frozen corn, thawed and drained
- 1 cup boiling water
- 4 tablespoons (½ stick) unsalted butter
- 2 tablespoons white miso paste
- 1 tablespoon soy sauce
- 1 teaspoon freshly ground black pepper
- ½ teaspoon kosher salt
- 2 bunches scallions, white and light green parts only, sliced into 1-inch pieces on an angle
- Cooked white rice, for serving

1. To remove moisture, place the tofu blocks on paper towels, top with more paper towels, and place a weight on top, such as a rimmed baking sheet topped with a cast-iron pan. Let stand for at least 10 minutes or up to 1 hour. Remove the weight and paper towels and use your hands to tear the tofu into bite-size pieces.

2. Heat the olive oil in a large pan over medium-high heat. When the oil begins to shimmer, add the tofu and cook, stirring every few minutes, until golden brown on all sides, 8 to 10 minutes. Transfer it to a paper towel–lined plate.

3. In the same pan, cook the corn, stirring occasionally, until lightly browned, about 3 minutes. Add the boiling water, butter, miso paste, soy sauce, pepper, and salt and stir until the mixture has slightly thickened and is smooth, about 3 minutes. Add the scallions and stir to combine, cooking for 1 minute. Add the tofu back in and stir until well coated. Serve the tofu immediately, spooned over white rice.

Kale Salad with Roasted Grapes

My cooking career began in the age of kale salads, and while they are no longer in the spotlight, they'll always be worth making in my book. The highlight of this one is the roasted grapes. While I'm not a huge raw grape fan (I know, I know), once roasted, they become less tart while having a more concentrated grape flavor. The dressing was inspired by my friend Rebekah, who makes a salad dressing that subtly incorporates tahini. The tahini makes it creamy without imparting an overpowering sesame flavor.

NOTE: Leftover kale salad can be kept in an airtight container in the refrigerator for up to 1 day.

Serves 4

- 1 medium red onion, thinly sliced
- 1 teaspoon kosher salt
- 2 cups seedless red grapes
- 2 tablespoons plus 2 teaspoons extra-virgin olive oil
- ¼ teaspoon red pepper flakes
- 1 cup whole raw walnuts, coarsely chopped
- Juice of 2 lemons (about ¼ cup)
- 3 tablespoons tahini
- 1 teaspoon Dijon mustard
- 1 teaspoon maple syrup
- 1 large bunch lacinato kale, stems removed, leaves stacked and thinly sliced
- ½ head medium radicchio, leaves roughly torn

1. Preheat the oven to 400°F.

2. Add the red onion to a large bowl and sprinkle with ½ teaspoon of the salt. Let sit while you prepare the rest of the salad.

3. Combine the grapes, 2 teaspoons of the olive oil, and the red pepper flakes in a 9-inch square baking dish and toss until coated. Bake for 15 minutes. Add the walnuts to the dish and stir to combine. Bake until the walnuts are toasted and the grapes look shriveled and charred in some places, about 5 minutes more.

4. Combine the lemon juice, tahini, mustard, maple syrup, remaining 2 tablespoons olive oil, and remaining ½ teaspoon salt in a glass measuring cup or small bowl and whisk well.

5. Add the kale and radicchio to the bowl with the red onion and drizzle with the dressing. Use your hands to massage the kale mixture until it has reduced by half and appears wilted, about 1 minute. Add the roasted grape and walnut mixture to the bowl and toss to combine. The kale salad can be made up to 30 minutes before serving.

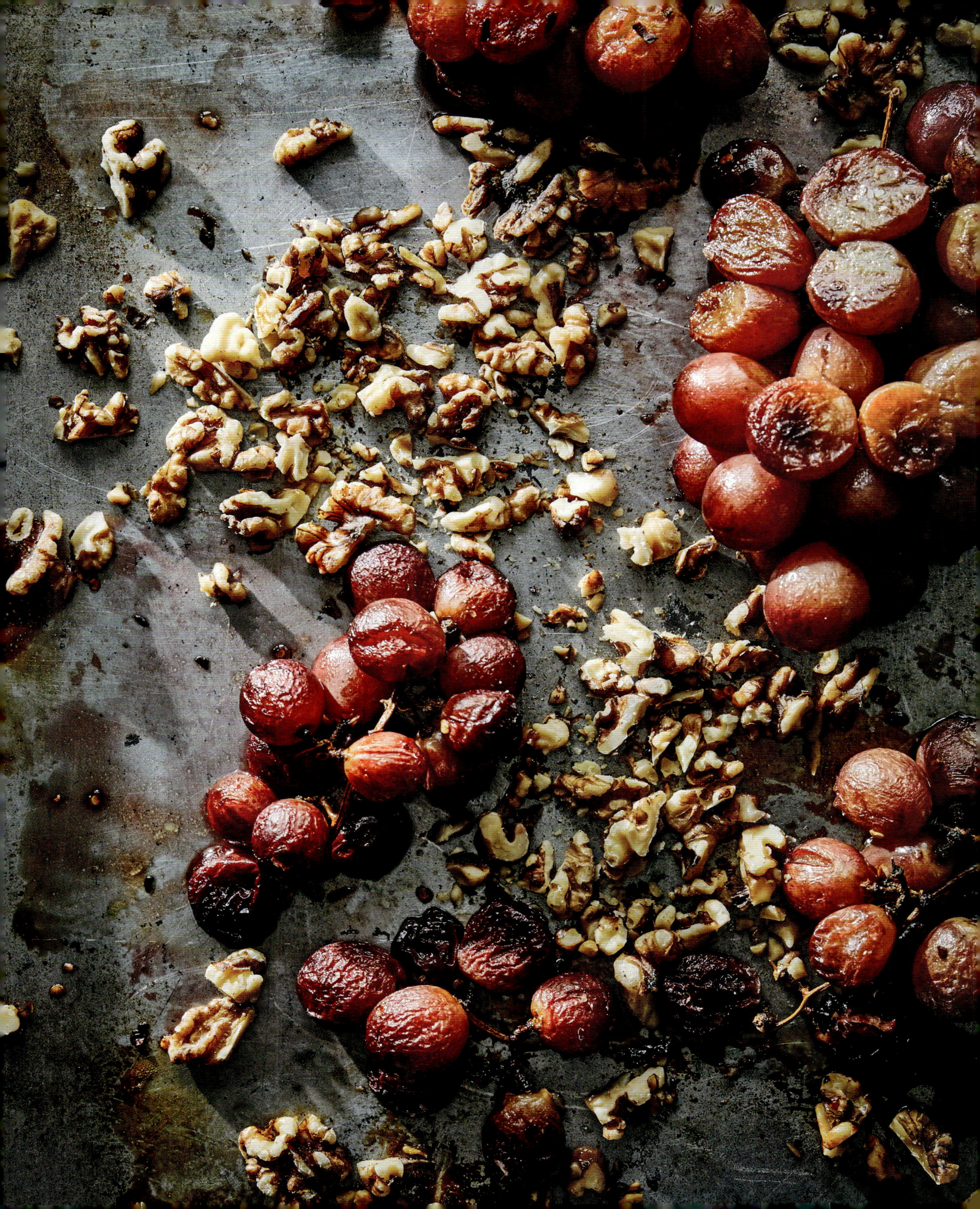

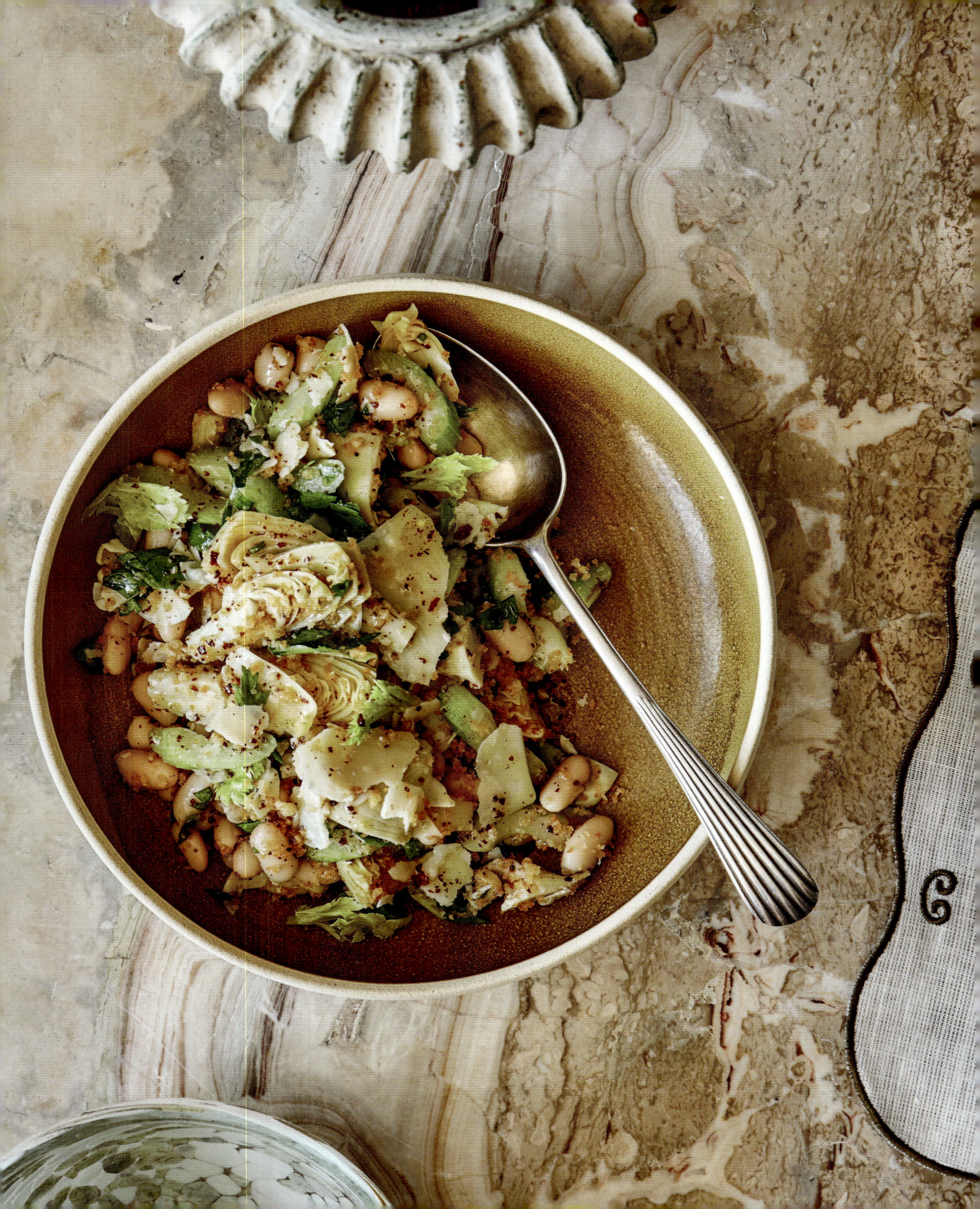

Marinated White Beans and Artichokes

I've been on a canned artichoke kick for a while now, and use them in as many preparations as possible. Here, artichokes are mixed with white beans in a zesty marinade before getting showered with crispy panko breadcrumbs and shaved Parm. It's crunchy, creamy, and bright all in one. While this dish feels particularly fitting for warm weather, it works year-round. I love it as a meal, but it also plays nicely as a side with grilled steak, chicken, or salmon.

NOTES: Celery leaves are typically found on the inner stalks of a bunch of celery. If you've never used them before, they add a great subtle celery flavor to any dish. If your bunch of celery is missing the leaves, simply leave them out. If you don't have canned white beans, chickpeas or kidney beans will work, too. Store any leftovers in an airtight container in the refrigerator for up to 3 days. Store leftover panko separately and add it just before serving.

Serves 4

- 5 tablespoons extra-virgin olive oil
- 1 cup panko breadcrumbs
- 1¼ teaspoons kosher salt
- 2 tablespoons red wine vinegar
- 1 teaspoon ground sumac
- ½ teaspoon red pepper flakes
- 1 (15-ounce) can white beans, drained and rinsed
- 2 (15-ounce) cans artichoke hearts, drained
- 4 medium celery ribs, thinly sliced
- ½ bunch flat-leaf parsley, coarsely chopped (about 1 cup)
- ¾ cup shaved Parmigiano Reggiano cheese
- ½ cup celery leaves, coarsely chopped

1. Heat 1 tablespoon of the olive oil in a medium pan over medium heat. When the oil begins to shimmer, add the panko and cook, stirring, until golden brown, 3 to 5 minutes. Transfer the panko to a paper towel–lined plate and season with ¼ teaspoon of the salt.

2. Add the remaining ¼ cup olive oil, vinegar, remaining 1 teaspoon salt, the sumac, and the red pepper flakes to a medium bowl and whisk to combine.

3. Add the white beans, artichoke hearts, celery, parsley, Parmigiano Reggiano, and celery leaves, and stir to combine. Just before serving, mix in the crispy panko.

Everything Bagel Tomato Panzanella

Come summertime, there's no shortage of panzanellas parading through my kitchen. For me, the real highlight of produce season is when tomatoes start showing up. While there's nothing better than eating them straight from the vine, a panzanella is a great way to use copious amounts of tomatoes without doing too much to them. This version is like a deconstructed bagel, minus the smoked salmon. To really lean into the bagel of it all, I've utilized everything bagel spice in the dressing, which does the heavy lifting in terms of adding a more complex flavor. Drizzled over tomatoes, shaved fennel, red onion, and crispy, craggy pieces of fried bread, this panzanella is everything I want in a summer salad.

NOTES: To make your own everything bagel seasoning, combine 1 tablespoon poppy seeds, 1 tablespoon toasted sesame seeds, 1 tablespoon dried garlic, 1 tablespoon dried onion, and 2 teaspoons coarse salt. I've opted for cherry tomatoes since they're bite-size, but you can chop up any in-season tomatoes. The dressing can be made up to 3 days in advance and stored in an airtight container in the refrigerator. The tomatoes, fennel, and red onion can be sliced and salted and left to rest, covered, at room temperature for up to 8 hours. Just be sure to drain any excess liquid that may have pooled in the bottom of the bowl. Once assembled, the salad is best eaten immediately.

Serves 4

- ½ cup full-fat sour cream
- Zest and juice of 2 lemons (about ¼ cup juice)
- 2 tablespoons everything bagel spice blend, plus more for serving
- 1½ teaspoons kosher salt, plus more to taste
- 2 cups cherry tomatoes, halved
- 1 large fennel bulb, stalks removed, bulb thinly sliced
- 1 small red onion, thinly sliced
- 2 tablespoons extra-virgin olive oil
- 3 cups roughly torn sourdough bread
- ½ cup coarsely chopped fresh dill

1. Combine the sour cream, lemon zest, lemon juice, everything bagel spice blend, and ½ teaspoon of the salt in a glass measuring cup and whisk until smooth.

2. Combine the tomatoes, fennel, red onion, and remaining 1 teaspoon salt in a medium bowl and stir. Let sit for at least 5 minutes at room temperature.

3. Heat the olive oil in a large pan over medium heat. When the oil begins to shimmer, add the bread and cook, stirring occasionally, until golden brown on all sides, 5 to 6 minutes. Transfer the bread to a serving platter and season with salt.

4. Add the tomatoes, fennel, red onion, and dill to the serving platter and toss to combine. Drizzle the dressing on the panzanella and sprinkle more everything bagel blend on top. Serve immediately.

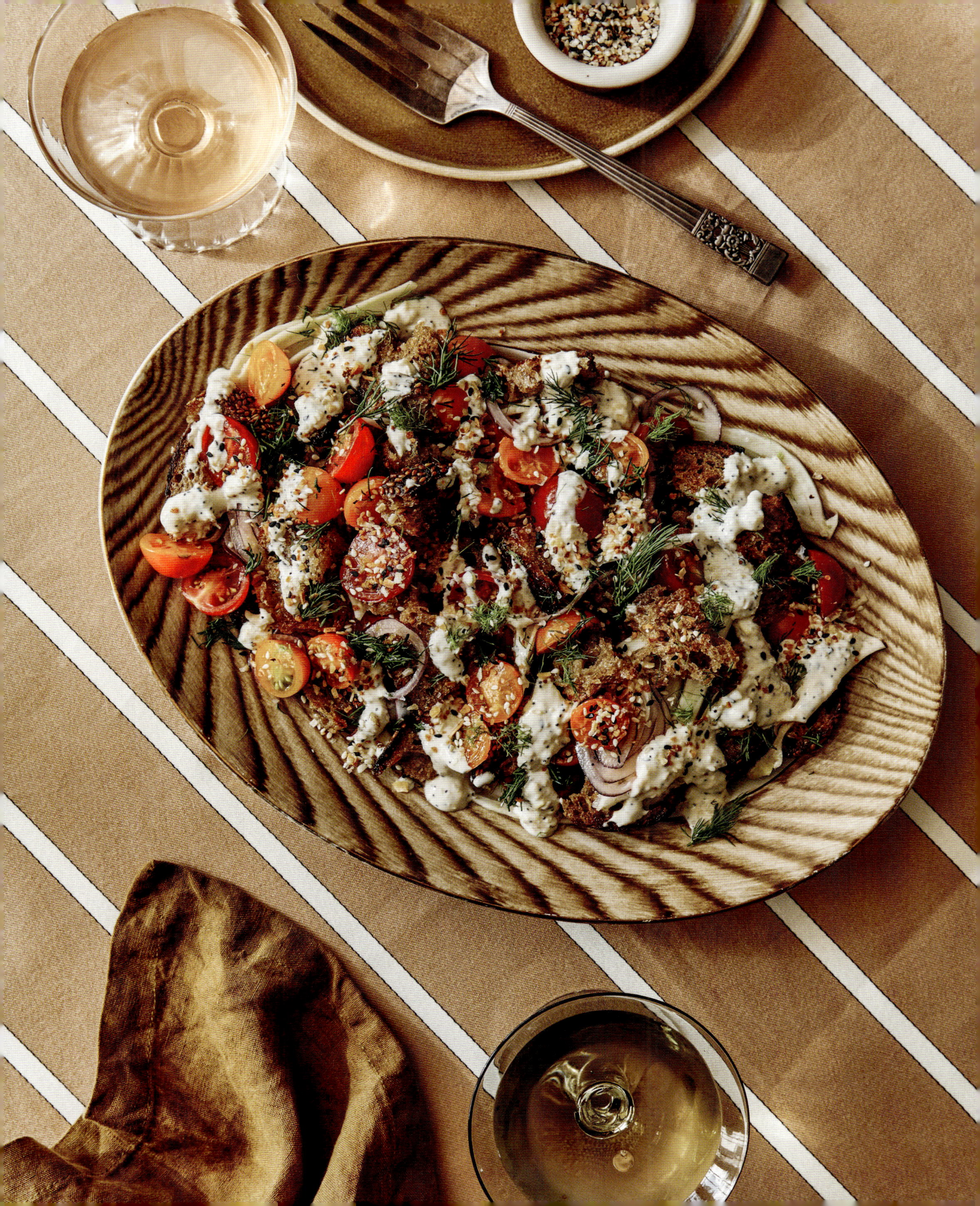

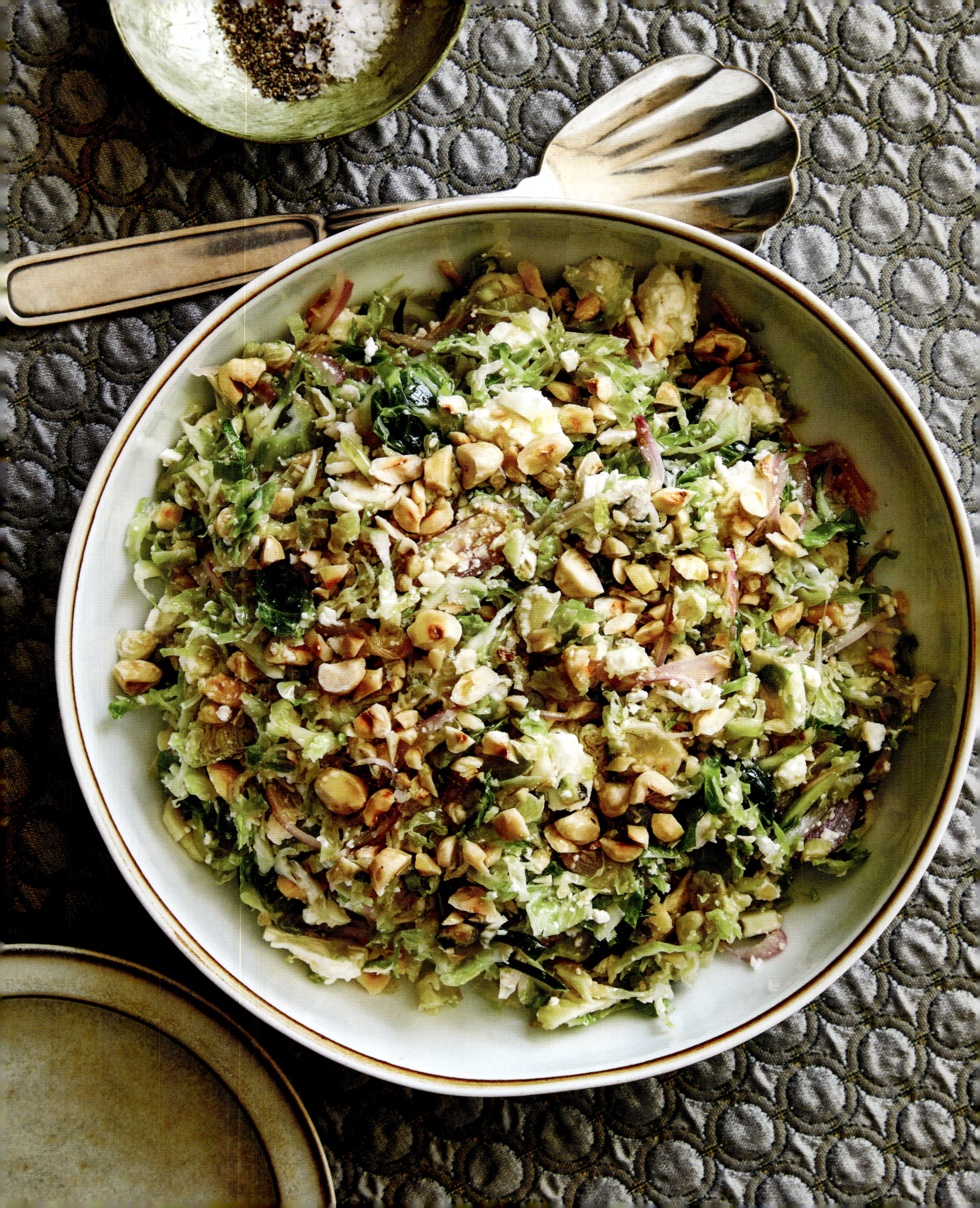

Brussels Sprout Salad with Hazelnuts and Feta

If you're a salad-for-dinner person, this is a great option when Brussels sprouts are in season, although you could also serve it as a side with your favorite protein. My chef friend Antonio and I made a more involved version of this salad for a Thanksgiving we hosted together based on a dish he was serving at his restaurant. After that, it became part of my weekly rotation. This iteration is friendly for home cooks, cutting down on time while keeping the essence of the salad. While this may seem like a lot of vinegar, the sprouts soak it right up. Don't skip massaging the Brussels sprouts, which coaxes out the tenderness (and makes them easier to digest).

NOTES: This is a good time to lean on preshredded Brussels sprouts, which you can sometimes find in the produce section of your grocery store. Since the Brussels sprouts below are trimmed, opt for a 12-ounce bag of shredded sprouts. While this dish can be eaten right away, it's also sturdy enough to be made ahead of time. You can store it in an airtight container in the refrigerator for up to 3 days.

1. Combine the vinegar, shallot, garlic, and salt in a large bowl and stir well. Let sit at room temperature for 5 minutes. Add the olive oil and whisk to combine.

2. Add the Brussels sprouts and use your hands to massage until they have shrunk by half, about 1 minute. Add the hazelnuts and feta and toss until well combined.

Serves 4

- ¼ cup red wine vinegar
- 1 medium shallot, thinly sliced
- 1 garlic clove, grated
- 1 teaspoon kosher salt
- 3 tablespoons extra-virgin olive oil
- 1 pound Brussels sprouts, trimmed and thinly sliced
- ½ cup hazelnuts, finely chopped
- 6 ounces crumbled feta cheese

Cheesy Potato and Pinto Bean Tacos

There's a hole-in-the-wall restaurant in Boyle Heights in Los Angeles that has the best bean-and-cheese burritos that I've ever had. Now that I live three thousand miles away, I've tried to re-create the joy of these burritos in taco form with a few tweaks. To make them a little more substantial for a weeknight dinner, I've added potatoes. The beans and potatoes are treated like ground beef: heavily spiced with chili powder, cumin, and paprika, along with aromatics.

NOTES: The potatoes can be boiled, drained, and stored in the refrigerator for up to 3 days. The cooked potato-bean mixture can be stored in an airtight container in the refrigerator for up to 3 days.

1. Place the potatoes in a medium pot, add cold water to cover, and generously season with salt. Bring to a boil over high heat and cook until the potatoes are easily pierced with a knife, about 10 minutes. Drain the potatoes in a colander.

2. Heat 2 tablespoons of the olive oil in a large pan over medium-high heat. When the oil begins to shimmer, add the potatoes and use a measuring cup to smash them down until flattened. Cook, stirring occasionally, until golden brown in places, 10 to 12 minutes. Transfer the potatoes to a bowl.

3. Pour the remaining 1 tablespoon olive oil into the same pan and add the onion and beans. Cook, stirring occasionally, until the onion has softened, about 5 minutes. Add the potatoes back to the pan along with the garlic, salt, pepper, chili powder, cumin, and paprika, and stir to combine. Cook until aromatic, about 1 minute.

4. Add the cheese and stir until fully melted throughout, about 1 minute.

5. Use the cheesy potato and beans to fill the tortillas and serve the tacos immediately with lime wedges, hot sauce, and pickled red onions on the side.

Serves 4

1 pound Yukon Gold potatoes, cut into 1-inch cubes

Kosher salt

3 tablespoons extra-virgin olive oil

1 medium yellow onion, thinly sliced

1 (15-ounce) can pinto beans, drained and rinsed

3 garlic cloves, minced

2 teaspoons kosher salt

1 teaspoon freshly ground black pepper

1 teaspoon chili powder

1 teaspoon ground cumin

1 teaspoon sweet paprika

1 (8-ounce) bag shredded Mexican-style cheese blend

FOR SERVING

Tortillas of choice

Lime wedges

Hot sauce

Pickled red onions

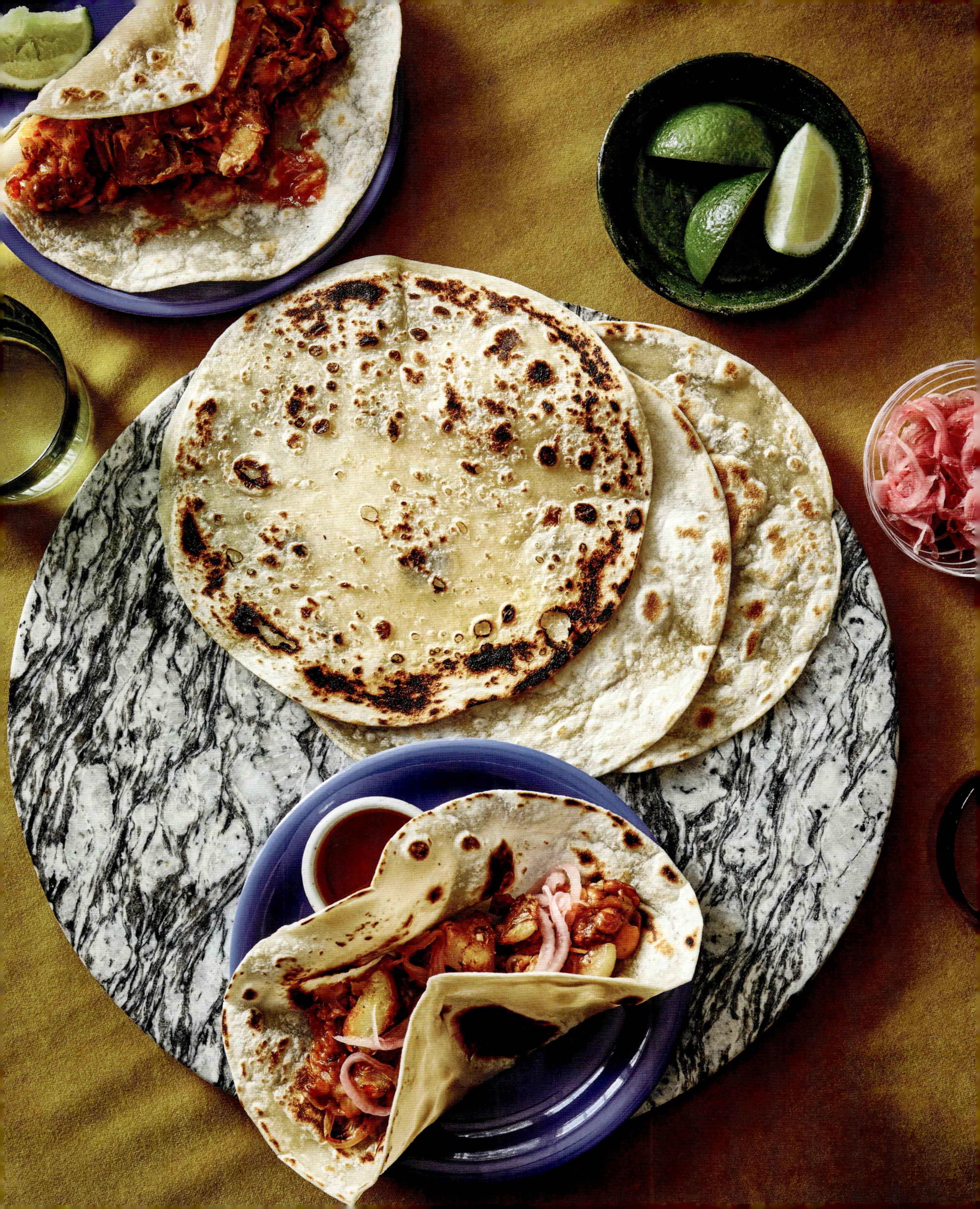

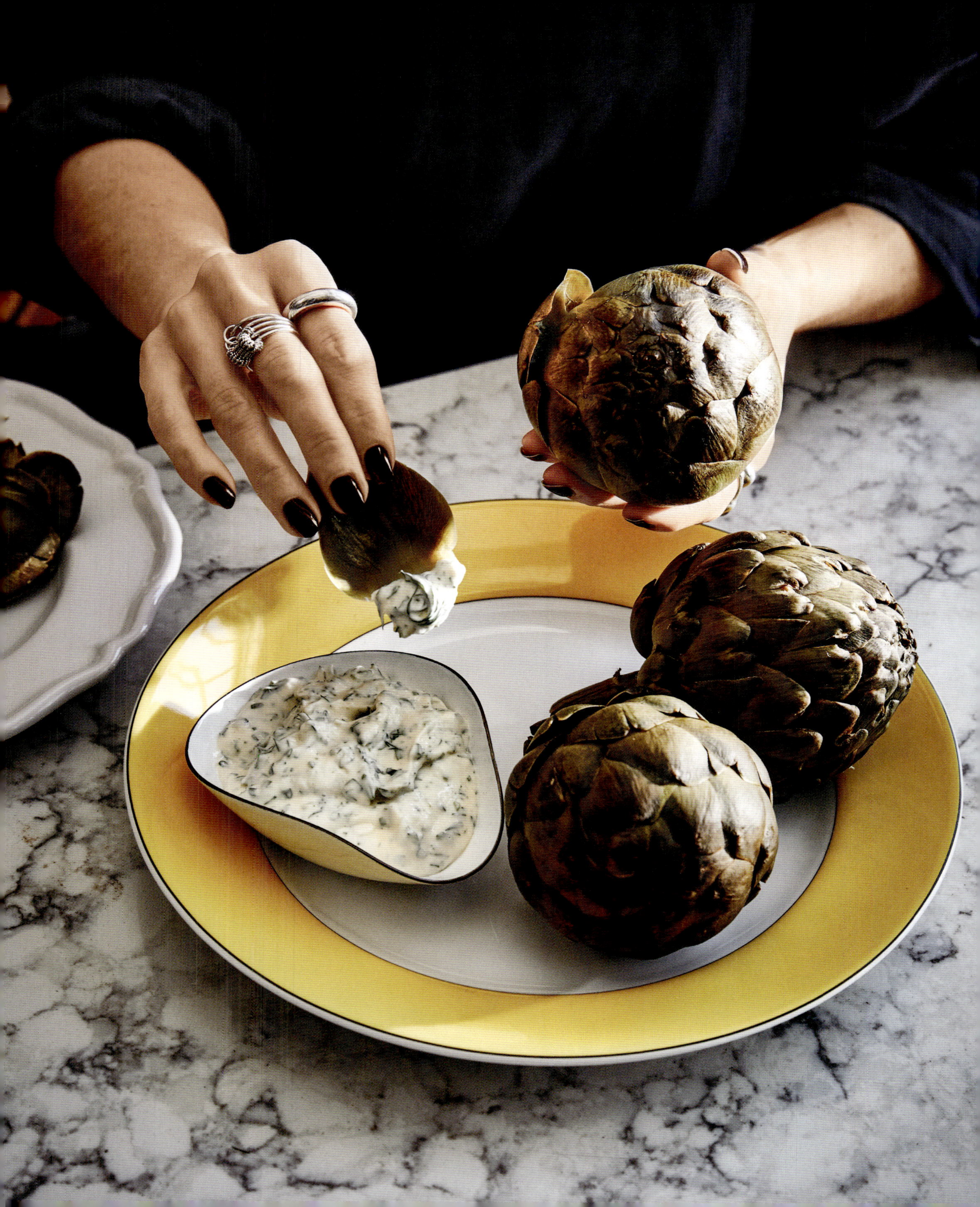

Artichokes with Herb Aioli

I've had so many friends tell me they've never dared make artichokes. I get it—while I love grilled artichoke, there's rarely a time when I want to spend two hours painstakingly trimming the end of each spiky leaf. Instead, I skip the whole prepping ordeal and go for the tried-and-true method I grew up with: boiling. By boiling the artichokes until tender, the leaves make the optimal vehicle for sauce, and the whole preparation requires about five minutes of prep time. Here I've paired them with a cheater aioli, filled with herbs and spiked with vinegar, which complements the earthy flavor of artichokes. I say "cheater" because I use store-bought mayonnaise, but you could make your own should the desire strike. Serve with a side salad and crusty bread for a lighter dinner, or as an appetizer when you're looking to impress.

NOTES: The artichokes can be boiled up to 3 days in advance of serving. The aioli can be made up to 3 days in advance and stored in an airtight container in the refrigerator. This recipe can easily be doubled (or tripled!); just make sure to use a big enough pot that the artichokes stay submerged in the water.

Serves 4

- 4 artichokes, stem ends trimmed
- Juice of 1 lemon (about 2 tablespoons)
- 3 large garlic cloves: 2 smashed, 1 grated
- 2 teaspoons kosher salt
- 1 teaspoon whole black peppercorns
- 1 dried bay leaf
- 1½ cups mayonnaise
- ½ bunch flat-leaf parsley, finely chopped (about 1 cup)
- ½ cup loosely packed fresh dill, finely chopped
- 1 tablespoon champagne vinegar

1. Combine the artichokes, lemon juice, 2 smashed garlic cloves, salt, pepper, and bay leaf in a large pot and fill with cold water. Set the pot over medium-high heat and bring to a boil. Boil the artichokes until a knife is easily inserted into the stem, 45 to 55 minutes, depending on the size of the artichoke. Drain the artichokes in a colander.

2. While the artichokes are boiling, combine the mayonnaise, 1 grated garlic clove, parsley, dill, and vinegar in a small bowl and stir well.

3. Serve the artichokes with the herb aioli.

Tofu with Scallion Garlic Ginger Oil

In the last few years, I've become a tofu convert. Seared, fried, or baked, tofu can take on so many different flavor profiles. Here, the tofu is prepared simply so that it can act as a vessel for the oil, which is somewhere between doctored-up chile crisp and a classic Chinese sizzling scallion oil. It's the type of thing you'll want to spoon over noodles, fish, jammy eggs—everything, really.

NOTES: The tofu can be stored in an airtight container in the refrigerator for up to 3 days, but note that it will lose its crispiness. The oil can be stored in an airtight container in the refrigerator for up to 5 days, although I doubt it will last that long.

Serves 4

TOFU

2 (16-ounce) packages extra-firm tofu

2 tablespoons extra-virgin olive oil

2 tablespoons soy sauce

2 tablespoons cornstarch

1 tablespoon toasted sesame oil

SCALLION GARLIC GINGER OIL

½ cup neutral oil

2 bunches scallions, thinly sliced

1 (1½-inch) knob fresh ginger, minced

4 garlic cloves, minced

1 tablespoon chile crisp

3 tablespoons soy sauce

1 tablespoon rice vinegar

1 tablespoon toasted sesame oil

1 teaspoon sugar

Cooked white rice, for serving

---

1. **Make the tofu:** To remove moisture, place the tofu blocks on paper towels, top with more paper towels, and place a weight on top, such as a rimmed baking sheet topped with a cast-iron pan. Let the tofu drain for at least 30 minutes or up to 8 hours. Remove the weight and paper towels. Set the tofu on its side and slice it into thirds horizontally. Slice the each piece into 6 rectangles.

2. Preheat the oven to 400°F. Line a rimmed baking sheet with parchment paper.

3. Combine the olive oil, soy sauce, cornstarch, and sesame oil in a medium bowl and whisk until smooth. Add the tofu and toss to coat.

4. Transfer the tofu to the prepared baking sheet in an even layer. Bake until golden and slightly crispy, about 30 minutes.

5. **Make the scallion garlic ginger oil:** Heat the neutral oil in a small pot over medium-high heat. When the oil begins to shimmer, add the scallions, ginger, garlic, and chile crisp and cook until sizzling and bright green, about 3 minutes. Remove the pot from the heat and add the soy sauce, rice vinegar, sesame oil, and sugar and whisk to combine.

6. Serve the tofu over the rice with a generous drizzle of the scallion garlic ginger oil.

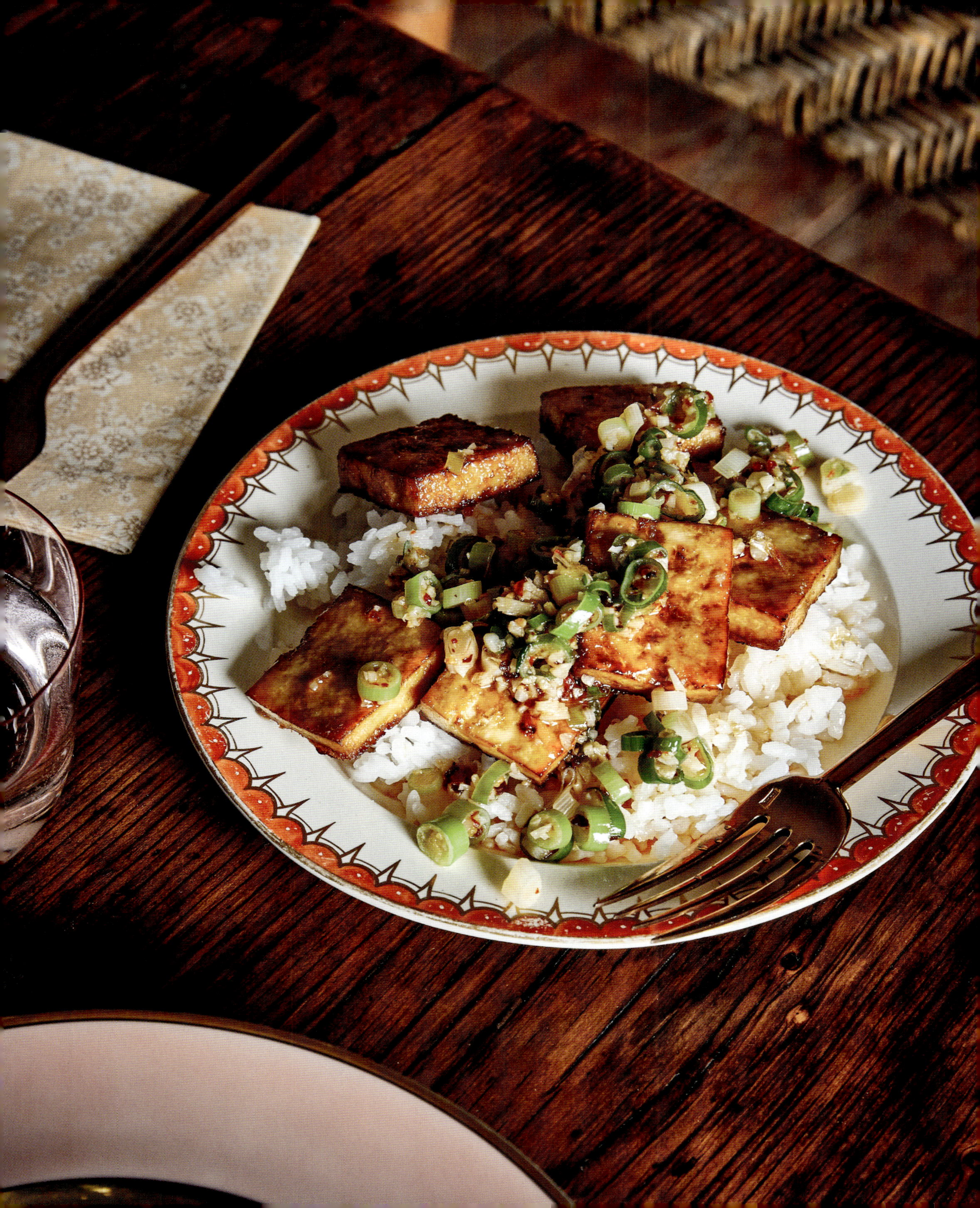

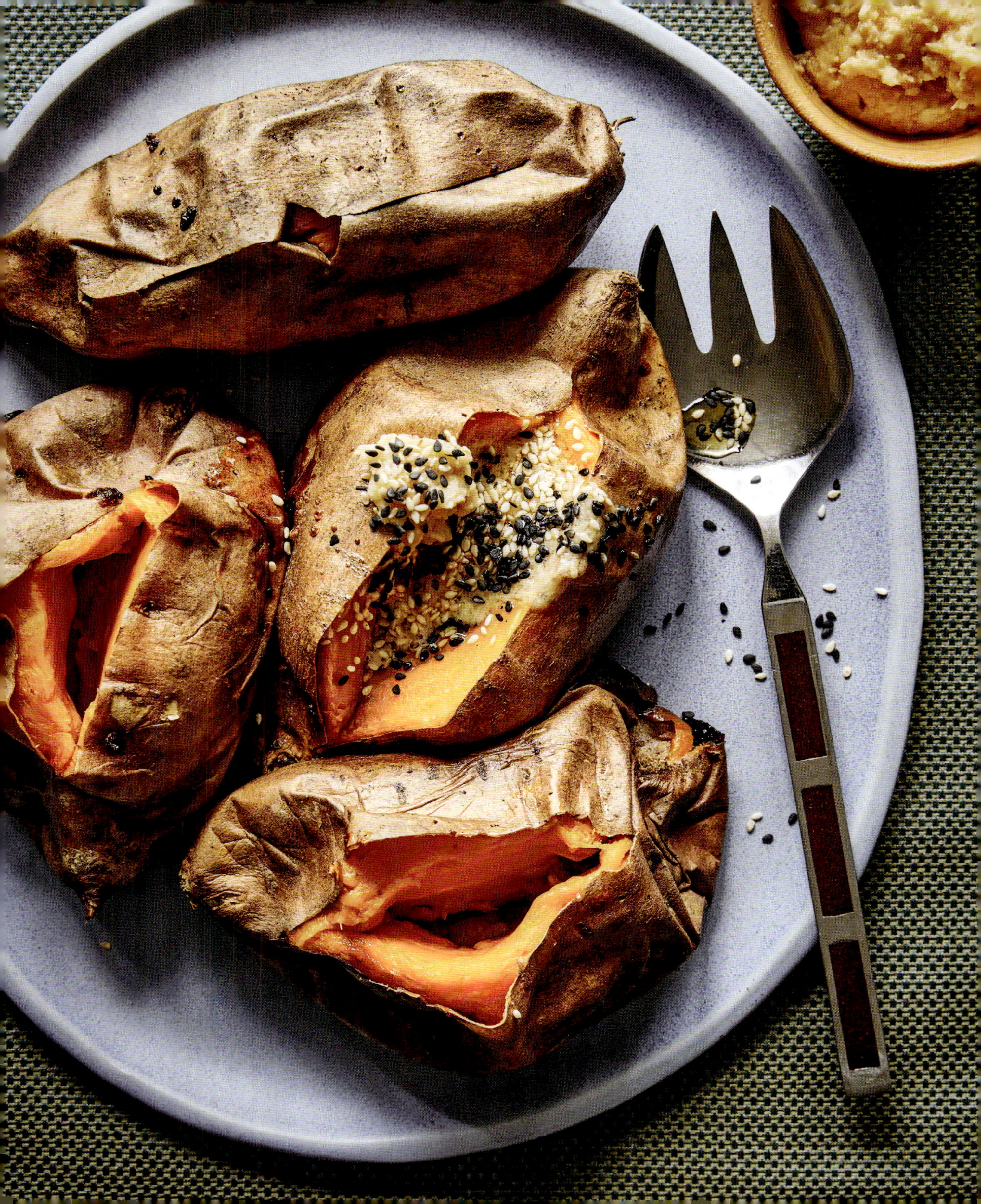

Sweet Potatoes with Miso Sesame Butter

Something that takes an hour in the oven doesn't scream weeknight friendly, but this side dish is so simple that I think it still fits the bill. The compound butter comes together quickly but packs a ton of flavor, thanks to miso paste and sesame oil. While showering the potatoes in sesame seeds is optional, I like the texture they add.

NOTE: The roasted sweet potatoes and miso sesame butter can be stored in separate airtight containers in the refrigerator for up to 5 days.

Serves 4

- 4 medium sweet potatoes
- 1 tablespoon extra-virgin olive oil
- 4 tablespoons (½ stick) unsalted butter, at room temperature
- 2 tablespoons white miso paste
- 1 teaspoon toasted sesame oil
- 1 tablespoon sesame seeds (optional)

1. Preheat the oven to 400°F.
2. Place the sweet potatoes on a rimmed baking sheet and rub with olive oil. Use the tines of a fork to prick holes all over the potatoes. This will help steam release as they cook.
3. Bake the potatoes until easily pierced with a knife, about 1 hour.
4. Meanwhile, combine the butter, miso, and sesame oil in a small bowl and stir well.
5. Split the potatoes down the center, add a dollop of miso sesame butter, and top with sesame seeds, if desired. Serve immediately.

Roasted Broccolini and Banana Peppers over Ricotta

This is decidedly a side dish, but I think it pairs well with any protein you might want to make on a weeknight, like crispy chicken thighs, seared salmon, or sautéed shrimp. While broccolini and hazelnuts are nothing new, I've added in pickled banana peppers, which contribute acidity and heat. Serve it over a bed of ricotta for that ideal balance of creamy, crunchy, tart, and salty in every bite.

NOTE: The broccolini and banana peppers can be stored in an airtight container in the refrigerator for up to 3 days.

Serves 4

- 3 bunches broccolini, ends trimmed
- ¾ cup drained jarred pickled banana pepper slices
- 2 tablespoons extra-virgin olive oil
- 1 teaspoon kosher salt
- ¼ cup hazelnuts, coarsely chopped
- 3 garlic cloves, thinly sliced
- 1 (8-ounce) container full-fat ricotta
- Zest of 1 lemon

1. Preheat the oven to 425°F.

2. Place the broccolini and banana peppers on a rimmed baking sheet, drizzle with olive oil, and season with salt. Use your hands to toss until well coated, then transfer to the oven. Roast for 20 minutes. Sprinkle the hazelnuts and garlic over the broccolini and use a spatula to toss to combine. Roast until the broccolini is charred and the hazelnuts are toasted, about 5 minutes.

3. Add the ricotta and lemon zest to a small bowl and stir to combine.

4. Spread the ricotta on a serving platter and top with the broccolini mixture. Serve immediately.

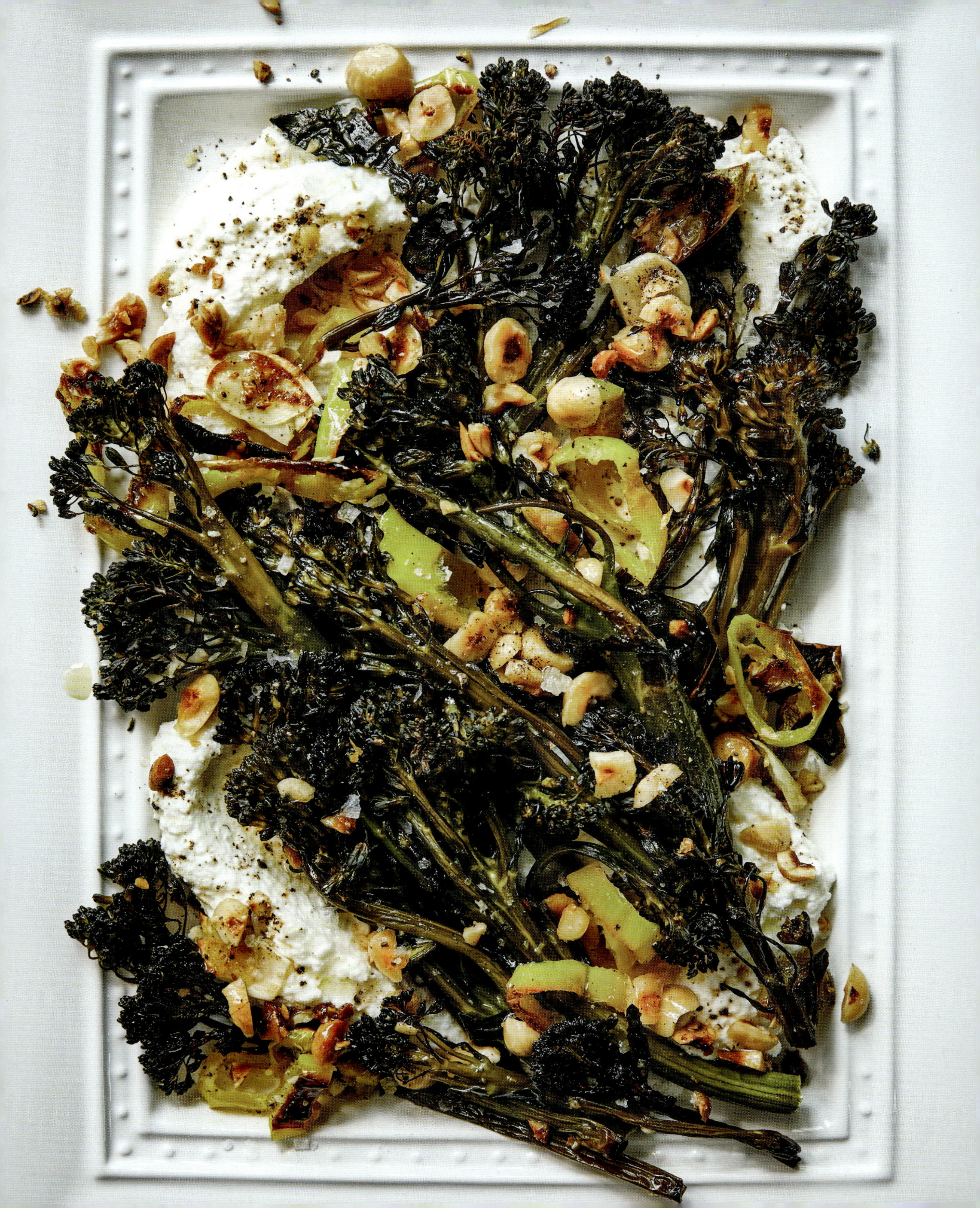

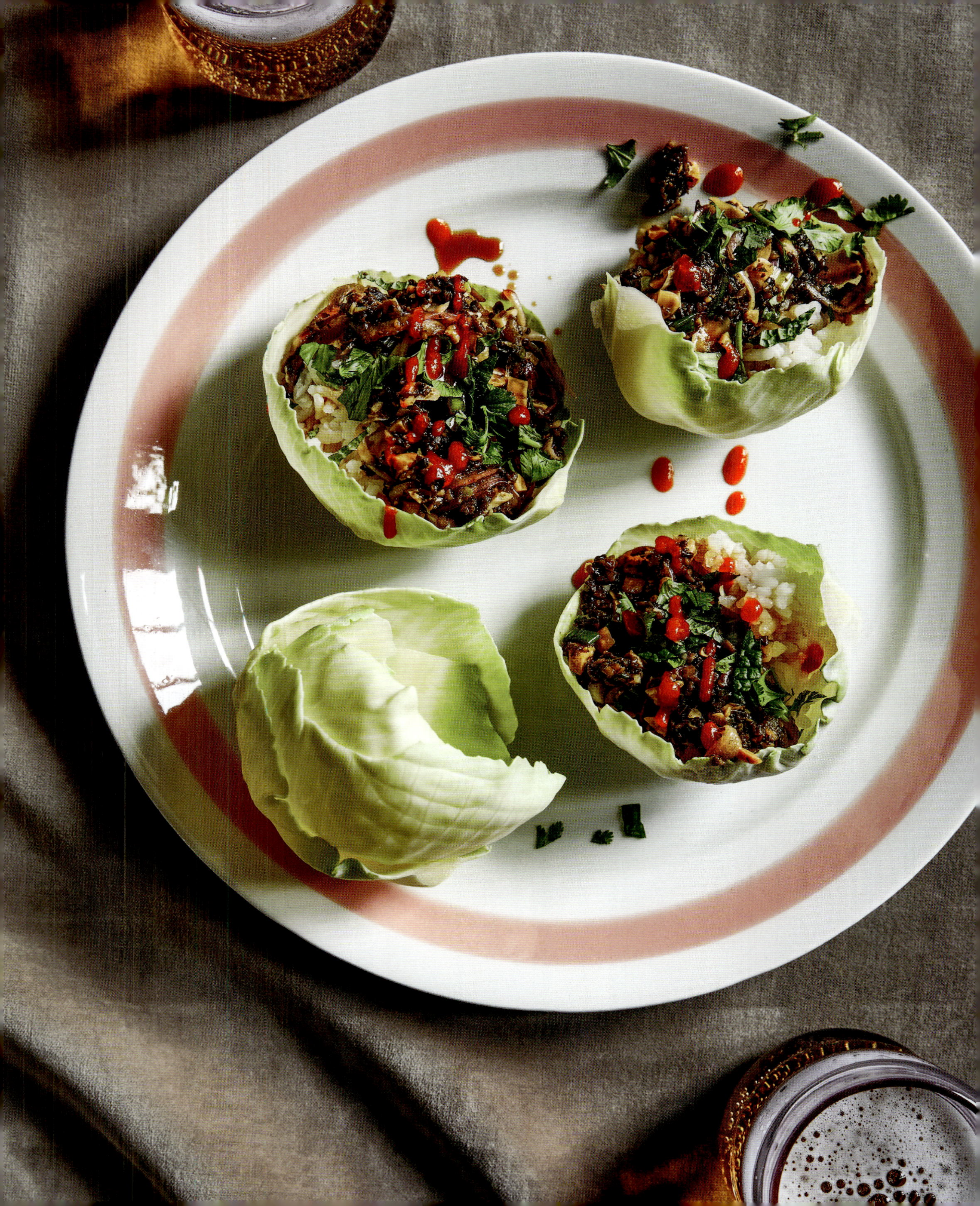

Mushroom Larb

Larb, which originated in Laos but is also eaten in the Isan region of Thailand, is traditionally made up of minced meat combined with aromatics and bright herbs. In an effort to eat a bit more veg-forward, I've swapped meat for mushrooms, and while this isn't entirely vegetarian, due to the fish sauce, it can easily be made with a vegan alternative. Authentic recipes for larb typically call for adding powdered rice, which imparts a great texture, but the reality is that step isn't weeknight friendly. In another effort to make this meal particularly low-lift, I've left out chiles and relied on sriracha to bring some heat to the dish.

NOTE: The larb can be stored in an airtight container in the refrigerator for up to 3 days.

1. Pulse the mushrooms in a food processor until coarsely chopped. (Alternatively, coarsely chop them by hand.)

2. Combine the red onion, scallions, lime zest, lime juice, peanuts, and 1 teaspoon of the salt in a medium bowl and stir.

3. Heat the olive oil in a large pan over medium-high heat. When the oil begins to shimmer, add the mushrooms and cook, stirring occasionally, until softened and golden brown in places, 10 to 12 minutes.

4. Add the garlic, soy sauce, fish sauce, sriracha, brown sugar, and remaining 1 teaspoon salt to the pan and cook until the liquid has been absorbed and the mixture is deeply aromatic, about 1 minute.

5. Transfer the mushroom mixture to the bowl with the red onion and scallions and stir to combine. Add the cilantro and mint, stir once more, and serve immediately with cabbage leaves, rice, and sriracha.

Serves 4

1½ pounds assorted mushrooms, such as cremini, shiitake, button, or oyster

1 medium red onion, thinly sliced

1 bunch scallions, thinly sliced

Zest and juice of 2 limes (about ¼ cup juice)

½ cup unsalted peanuts, coarsely chopped

2 teaspoons kosher salt

2 tablespoons extra-virgin olive oil

3 garlic cloves, minced

2 tablespoons soy sauce

2 tablespoons fish sauce

1 tablespoon sriracha, plus more for serving

2 teaspoons light brown sugar

Leaves and tender stems from ½ bunch cilantro, coarsely chopped (about 1 cup)

1 cup coarsely chopped fresh mint leaves

Green or napa cabbage leaves, for serving

Cooked white rice, for serving

Chopped Chicory Salad

A chopped salad is the ultimate pantry-staples salad to me, as the add-ins are mostly canned or jarred. To winterize this version, I've swapped romaine and tomatoes for an assortment of chicories and fennel. The real joy of this salad is that any assortment of chicories will do—just try to combine more than one variety to cut down on the bitterness of the greens. I've snuck salami into the ingredient list, which falls in line with traditional chopped salads. To make it vegetarian, simply leave it out.

NOTES: Red wine vinegar is classic in a chopped salad, but you can use sherry vinegar, champagne vinegar, or white wine vinegar in its place. If you don't have canned chickpeas, try white beans. The dressing can be stored in an airtight container in the refrigerator for up to 5 days. Once assembled, the salad is best eaten immediately.

1. **Make the salad:** Combine the onion, fennel, chicories, chickpeas, salami (if using), peppers, olives, and Parmigiano Reggiano in a large bowl and toss together.

2. **Make the dressing:** Whisk together the red wine vinegar, garlic, oregano, and salt in a small bowl. While whisking, gradually pour in the olive oil until emulsified.

3. Pour the vinaigrette over the salad and serve immediately.

Serves 4

SALAD

¼ medium red onion, thinly sliced

1 small fennel bulb, stalks removed, bulb thinly sliced

6 cups assortment torn chicories, such as endive, radicchio, Treviso, frisée, and escarole

1 (15-ounce) can chickpeas, drained and rinsed

1 cup thinly sliced salami (optional)

⅓ cup Peppadew peppers

1 cup pitted Castelvetrano olives

½ cup shaved Parmigiano Reggiano cheese

DRESSING

¼ cup red wine vinegar

1 large garlic clove, grated

1 teaspoon dried oregano

½ teaspoon kosher salt

½ cup extra-virgin olive oil

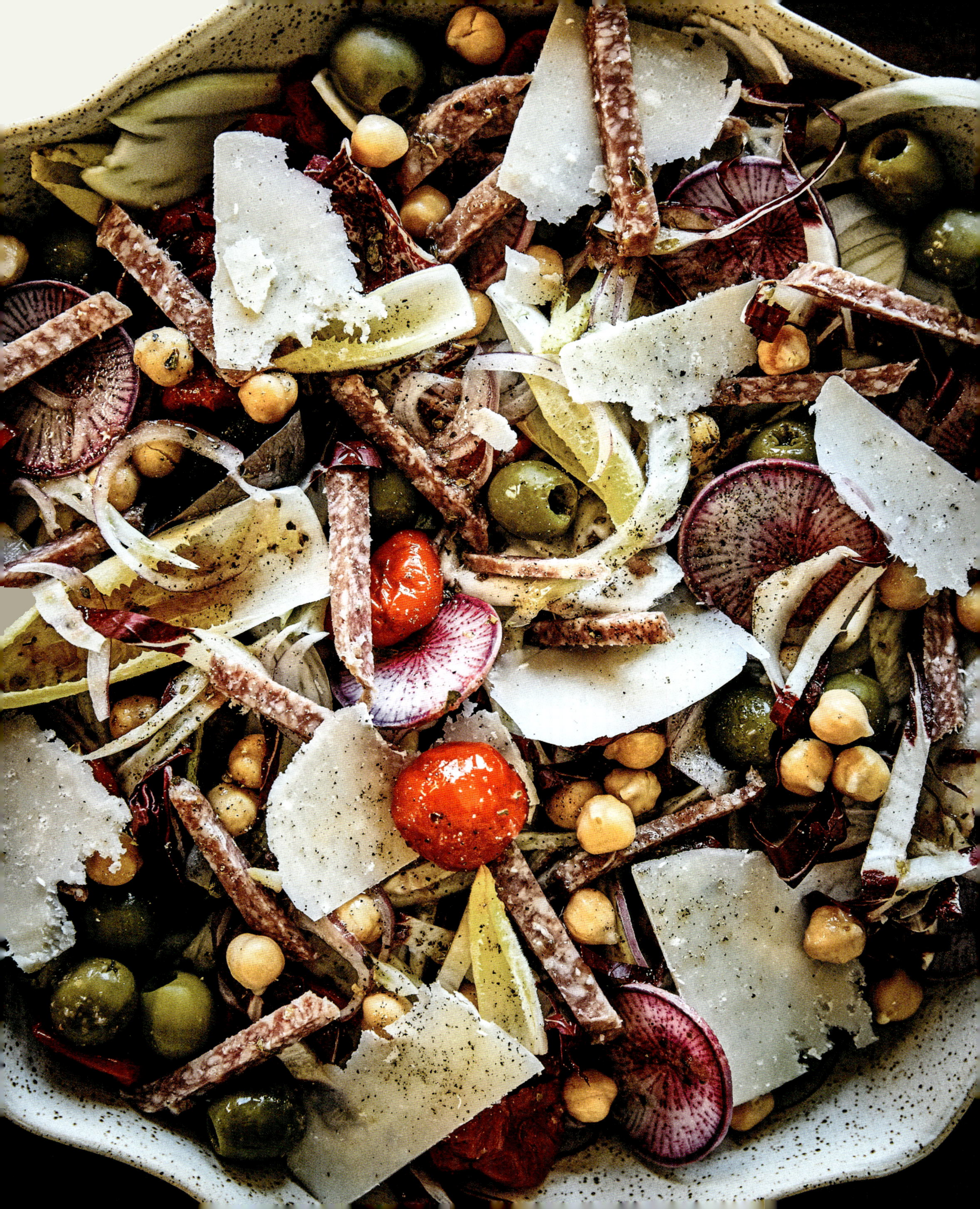

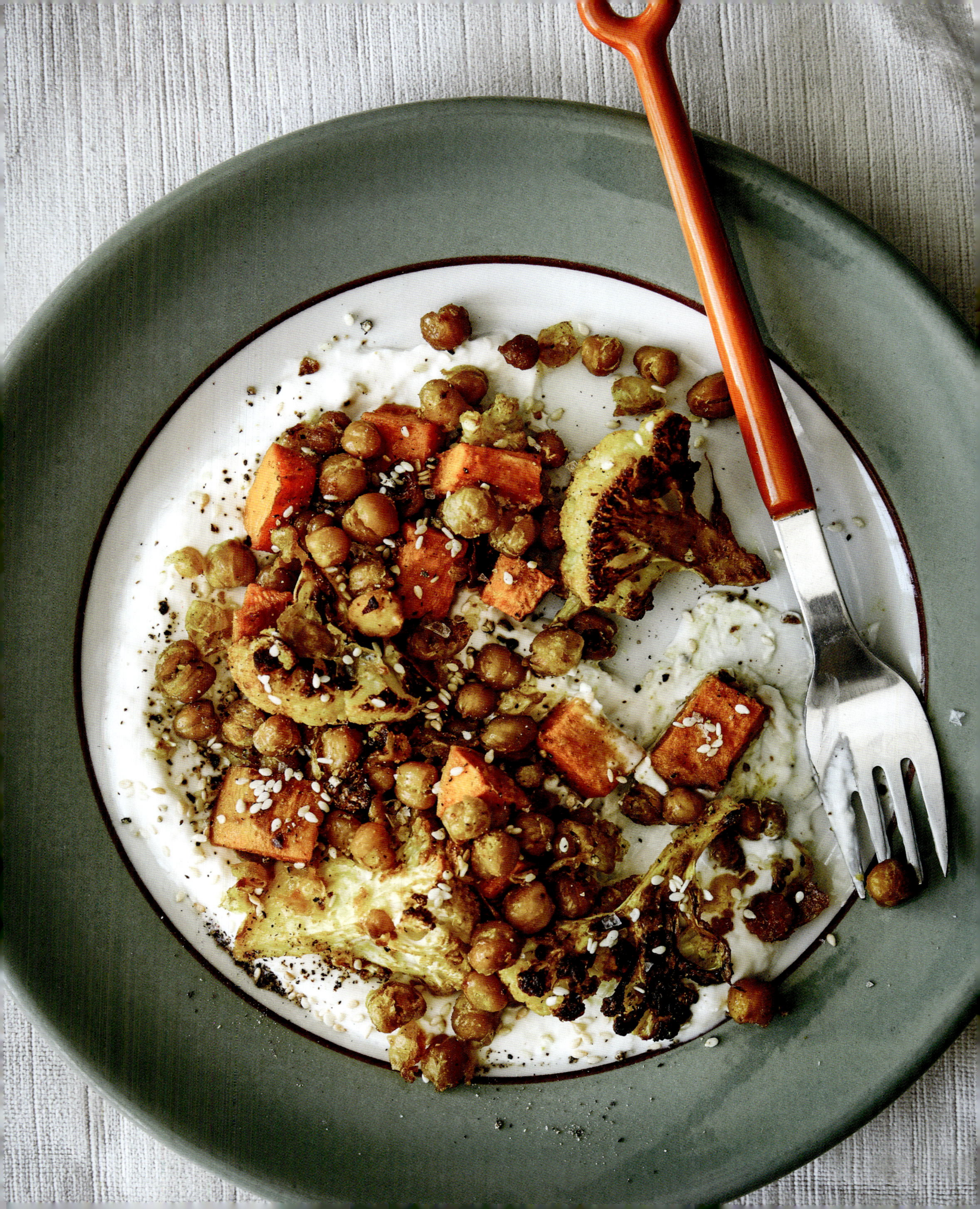

Roasted Cauliflower, Chickpeas, and Sweet Potatoes with Spiced Yogurt

I'm so sorry to ask you to break out two baking sheets on a weeknight, but hear me out. Overcrowding the pan results in soggy vegetables. For this recipe (and always) we're looking for a ton of crispy, crunchy texture to pair with the creaminess of the yogurt.

NOTE: Leftover roasted vegetables and spiced yogurt can be stored separately in airtight containers in the refrigerator for up to 3 days.

1. Preheat the oven to 425°F.

2. **Make the roasted vegetables:** Whisk together the olive oil, salt, cumin, coriander, turmeric, and pepper flakes in a large bowl. Add the sweet potatoes, cauliflower, and chickpeas and stir until well coated.

3. Divide the mixture between two rimmed baking sheets, spreading it in an even layer. Bake until the vegetables are tender and golden brown and the chickpeas are crispy, 35 to 40 minutes. Season with sesame seeds.

4. **Meanwhile, make the spiced yogurt:** Combine the yogurt, lemon zest, lemon juice, garlic, and salt in a medium bowl and stir until smooth.

5. Serve the vegetables over the spiced yogurt and season with flaky salt.

Serves 4

ROASTED VEGETABLES

⅓ cup extra-virgin olive oil

2 teaspoons kosher salt

1½ teaspoons ground cumin

1 teaspoon ground coriander

1 teaspoon ground turmeric

½ teaspoon red pepper flakes

2 medium sweet potatoes, peeled and cut into ½-inch cubes (about 2 cups)

1 small head cauliflower, separated into florets (about 5 cups)

2 (15-ounce) cans chickpeas, drained and rinsed

2 tablespoons sesame seeds

SPICED YOGURT

1 cup plain full-fat Greek yogurt

Zest and juice of 1 lemon (about 2 tablespoons juice)

2 garlic cloves, grated

½ teaspoon kosher salt

Flaky salt, for serving

Cheesy Potato Tart

I always have a pack of puff pastry in the freezer, a stash of potatoes in the cupboard, and some type of hard cheese in the refrigerator. Putting this trio of staples together creates this cheesy potato tart, which admittedly looks much more impressive than it is to execute. Potatoes and cheese are a classic combination, but the addition of puff pastry with its shatteringly flaky crust brings this into entrée territory. I love serving this with the Big Green Seedy Salad on page 108, but any green vegetable will do.

NOTES: If you don't have Gruyère, try cheddar, Monterey Jack, Fontina, or Comté. Dufour is my go-to store-bought puff pastry brand, but Pepperidge Farm or other brands will also work. This is a good time to use a mandoline if you have one, so you get perfect, thin slices of potato. Potato tart can be stored in an airtight container in the refrigerator for 24 hours, although it's best eaten fresh out of the oven.

Serves 2 to 4

- 1 large egg, beaten
- ½ pound new potatoes, cut into ⅛-inch slices
- 1 tablespoon extra-virgin olive oil
- 1 tablespoon fresh rosemary
- 2 garlic cloves, grated
- ½ teaspoon kosher salt
- ½ teaspoon freshly ground black pepper
- 1 sheet puff pastry, chilled
- 7 ounces coarsely grated Gruyère cheese (about 2 cups)
- 1 tablespoon sesame seeds

1. Preheat the oven to 400°F. Line a rimmed baking sheet with parchment paper.

2. Combine the egg with 1 tablespoon water in a small bowl and whisk well.

3. Combine the potatoes, olive oil, rosemary, garlic, salt, and pepper in a medium bowl and stir until coated.

4. On a clean work surface, roll the puff pastry sheet into a 12×14-inch rectangle. Carefully transfer the puff pastry to the prepared baking sheet. With a knife, score the pastry with just enough pressure to see the line without cutting through it, making a 1-inch-wide border around the rectangle.

5. Brush the pastry with the egg wash. Sprinkle the cheese on the rectangle in an even layer, leaving the border clear. Spread the potatoes in an even layer over the cheese.

6. Sprinkle the sesame seeds on the border around the potatoes. It's okay if some sesame seeds are on the edge of the potatoes.

7. Bake until the crust is golden brown, the potatoes are tender and golden, and the cheese has melted, about 25 minutes. Serve immediately.

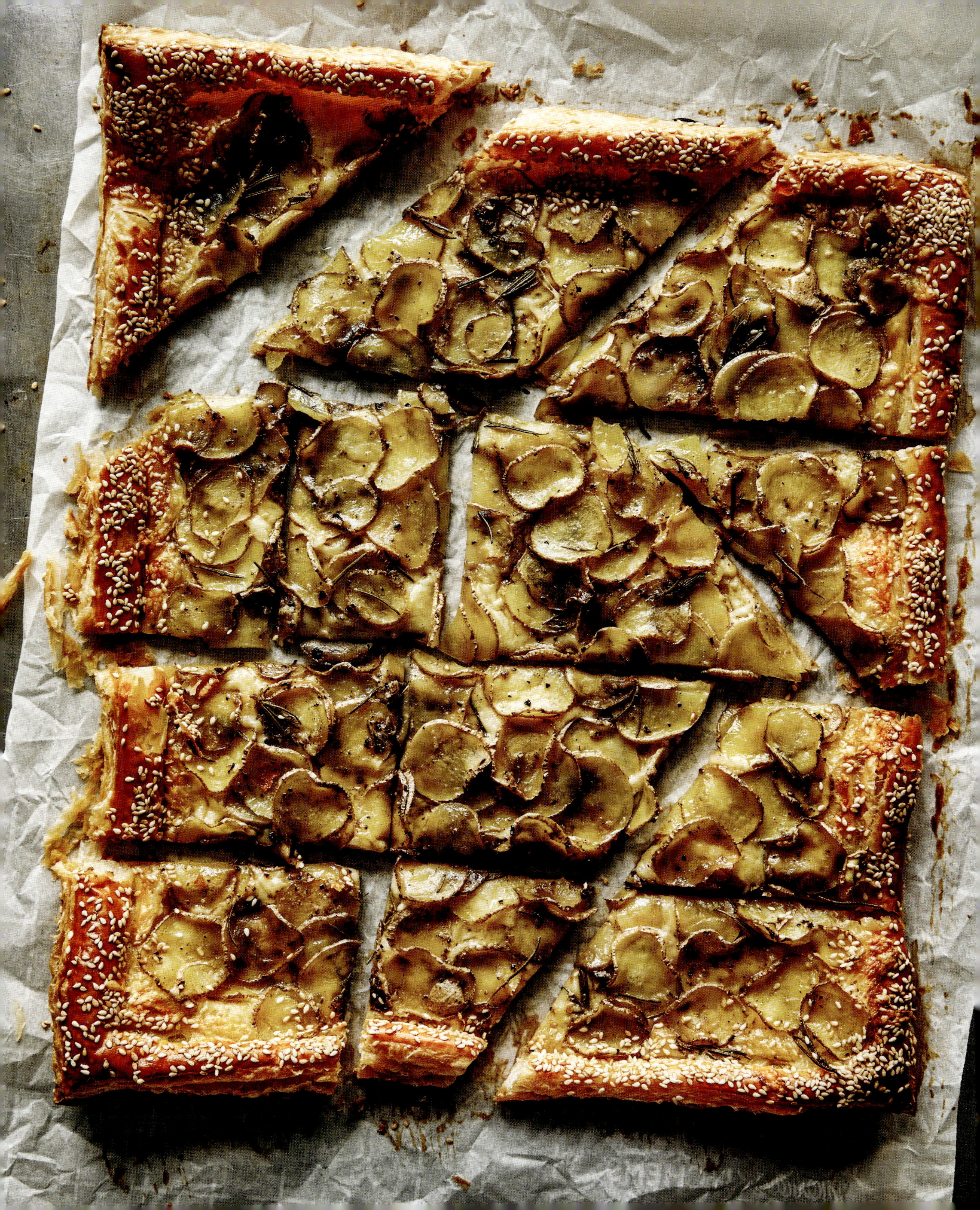

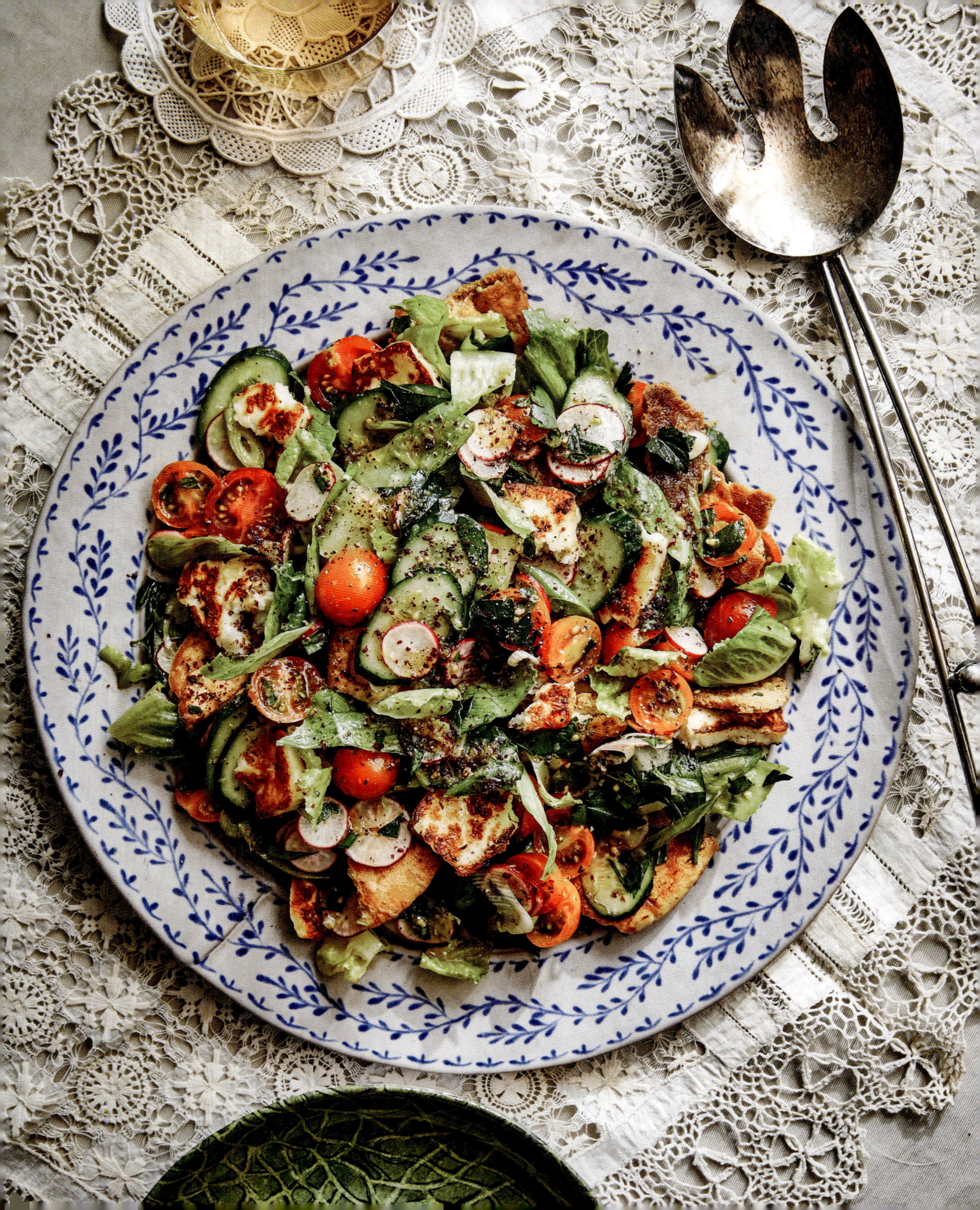

Halloumi Fattoush

Found all over the Middle East (and beyond!), there are so many iterations of this popular Lebanese salad. While tomatoes, cucumbers, and fried bread are the constants, I like gussying up my version with a showering of herbs, radishes, and a garlicky sumac-spiked dressing. To make this salad more substantial, there's enough seared Halloumi for every bite.

NOTES: If you can't find Halloumi, crumbled feta can be swapped in; just leave out the frying part. The dressing can be made up to 3 days in advance and stored in an airtight container at room temperature. Make sure to give it a good whisk before serving. Leftover salad can be stored in an airtight container in the refrigerator for up to 24 hours.

1. Preheat the oven to 350°F.

2. Place the pitas on a rimmed baking sheet. Drizzle with 2 tablespoons of the olive oil and season with ½ teaspoon of the salt. Bake until the pita is golden brown and crispy, 10 to 12 minutes. Let cool to room temperature.

3. Whisk together the lemon zest, lemon juice, garlic, pomegranate molasses (if using), sumac, pepper, and remaining ½ teaspoon salt in a glass measuring cup or small bowl to combine. While whisking, slowly drizzle in the remaining ¼ cup olive oil and whisk until smooth.

4. Heat a large nonstick pan over medium-high heat. When the pan is hot, add the Halloumi and cook, undisturbed, until golden brown on the bottom, 1 to 2 minutes. Flip and cook until the other side is golden brown, 1 to 2 minutes. Let cool slightly, then tear the Halloumi into bite-size pieces.

5. Combine the crispy pita, fried Halloumi, romaine, cucumbers, radishes, tomatoes, parsley, mint, and scallions in a large bowl and drizzle with the dressing. Use your hands to toss the salad and serve immediately.

Serves 4

- 2 pitas, roughly torn into 1-inch pieces
- 6 tablespoons extra-virgin olive oil
- 1 teaspoon kosher salt
- Zest and juice of 1 lemon (about 2 tablespoons juice)
- 2 garlic cloves, grated
- 1 teaspoon pomegranate molasses (optional)
- 1 teaspoon ground sumac
- ½ teaspoon freshly ground black pepper
- 2 (8-ounce) packages Halloumi cheese, cut into ¼-inch-thick slices and blotted dry with a paper towel
- 2 heads baby romaine, sliced into ½-inch pieces
- 3 Persian cucumbers, thinly sliced
- 2 medium watermelon radishes, or 4 red radishes, thinly sliced
- 2 cups cherry tomatoes, halved
- ¼ bunch flat-leaf parsley, coarsely chopped (about ½ cup)
- ½ cup coarsely chopped fresh mint leaves
- 1 bunch scallions, thinly sliced

Big Green Seedy Salad

I'm a firm believer that dinner is better when served with a big green salad. While a simple vinaigrette and greens usually does the trick for me, I love adding a shower of toasted seeds and radishes for some crunch and color. Serve this as a side salad or make it a main by adding your protein of choice, like grilled chicken, seared shrimp, or flaked salmon.

NOTES: You can use any greens you want for this salad, although I think the texture of the buttery lettuce works particularly well with the crunch of the seeds. Dressing and toasted seeds can be made up to 3 days in advance and stored in airtight containers at room temperature. Once assembled, the salad is best eaten immediately.

1. Set a large pan over medium heat. When the pan is hot, add the seeds and cook, stirring occasionally, until toasted, about 1 minute 30 seconds. Transfer the mixture to a bowl and season with ½ teaspoon of the salt.

2. Combine the vinegar, maple syrup, and remaining ½ teaspoon salt in a salad bowl and whisk to combine. While whisking, drizzle in the olive oil and whisk until emulsified. (Alternatively, this can be made in a jar and saved for later.) Add the butter lettuce, radish, and seed mixture and toss until well coated. Serve immediately.

Serves 4

¼ cup pumpkin seeds

¼ cup sunflower seeds

¼ cup sesame seeds

1 teaspoon kosher salt

3 tablespoons champagne vinegar

1 tablespoon maple syrup

¼ cup extra-virgin olive oil

2 medium heads butter lettuce, leaves roughly torn

1 watermelon radish, or 4 red radishes, thinly sliced

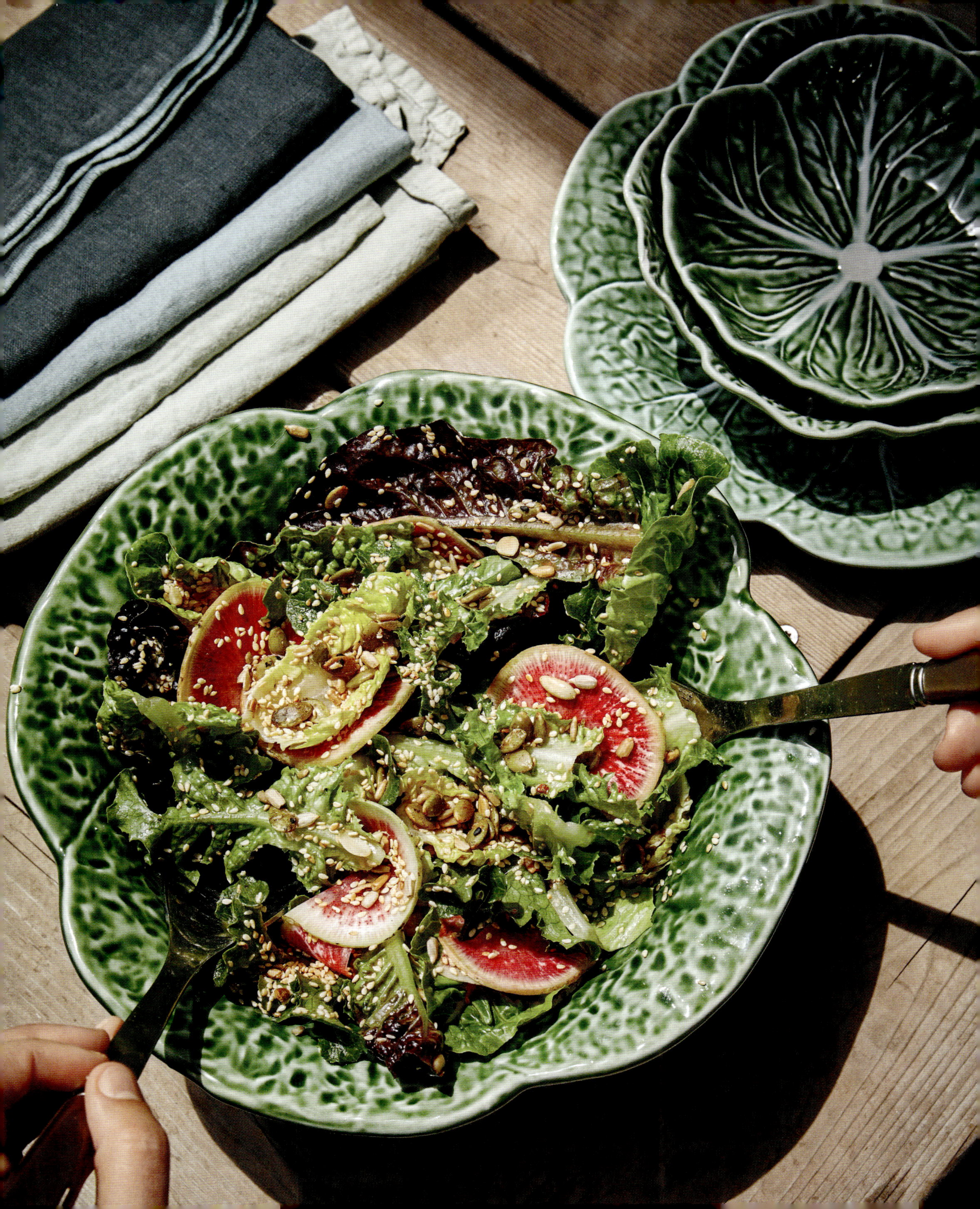

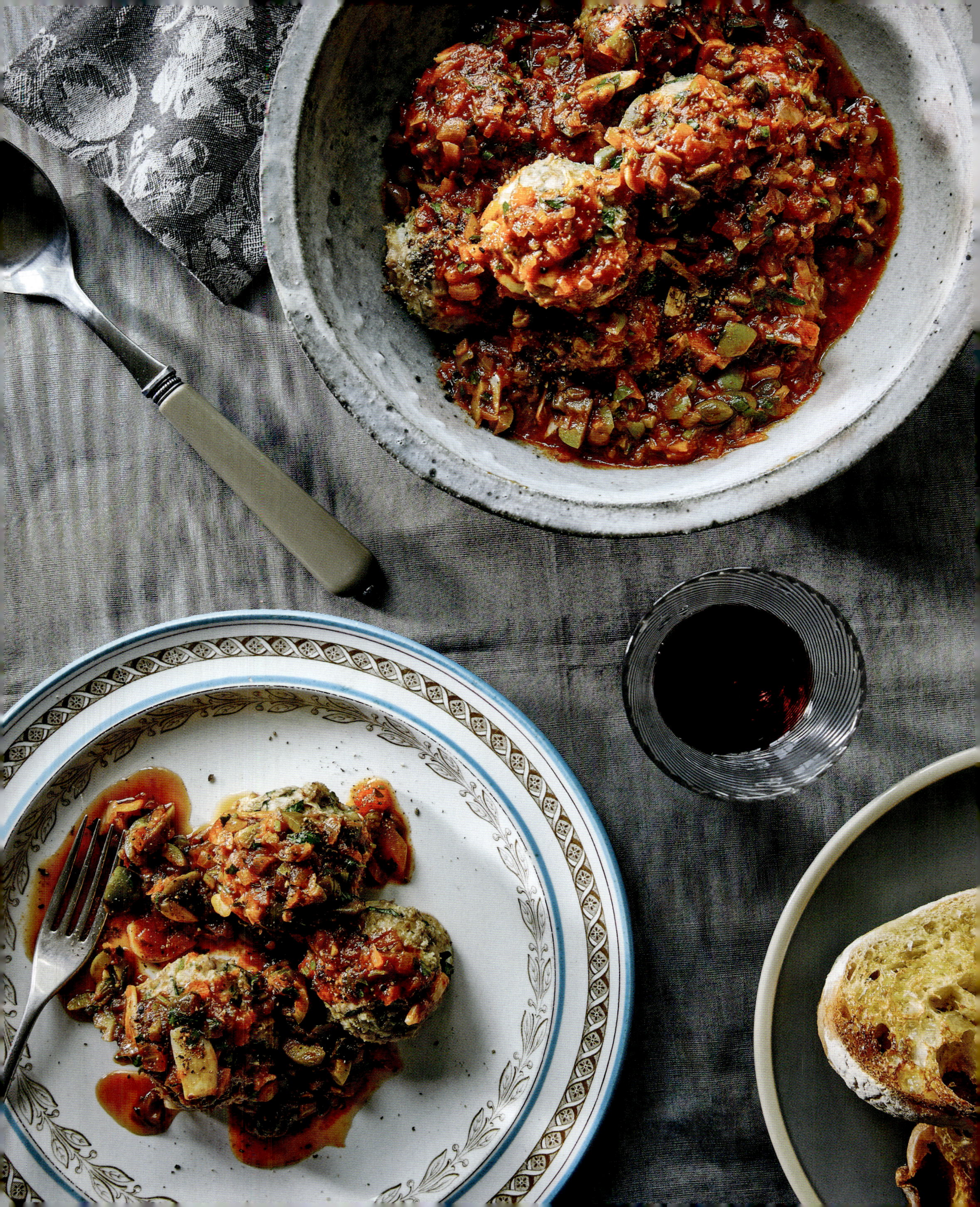

MEAT

NIGHTS

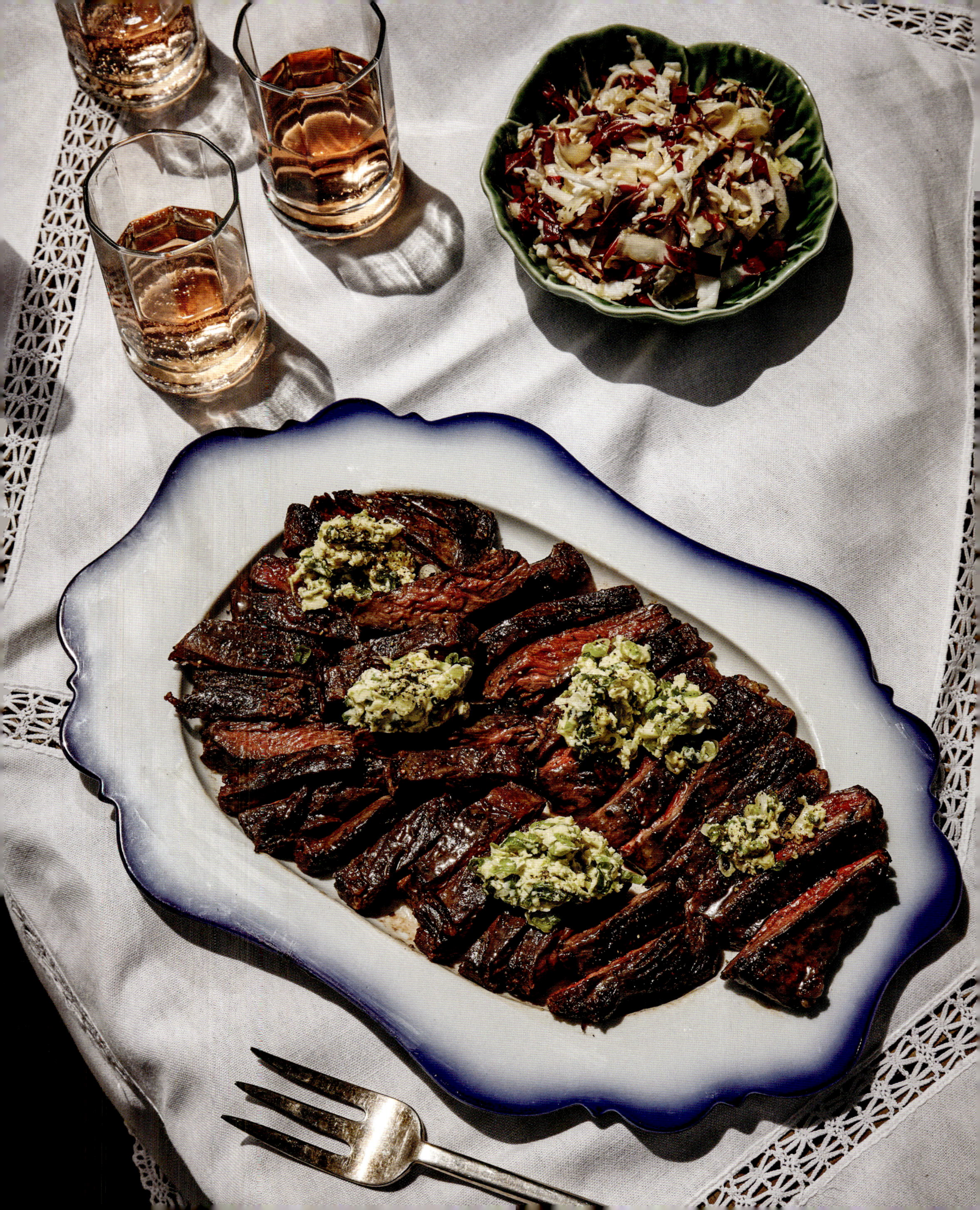

Skirt Steak with Scallion Butter and Slaw

If you're craving beef on a weeknight, there's no better option than skirt steak. This thin cut cooks even more quickly than ground beef, ensuring you can have dinner on the table in under ten (yes, ten!) minutes. The key to perfect skirt steak is to cook it quickly in a piping-hot pan, which ensures a good crust and pink center. While you could of course serve the steak as is, a simple zesty compound butter—this one flavored with scallions—adds a ton of flavor without much work. If chopping three vegetables to make the slaw on a weeknight feels overwhelming, any green vegetable will round this out.

NOTES: Compound butter simply refers to butter that gets incorporated with other ingredients. Feel free to experiment with your own versions, adding spices or herbs to create your ideal flavor combination. Leftover compound butter can be stored in an airtight container in the refrigerator for up to 1 week. Leftover steak and slaw can be stored in airtight containers in the refrigerator for up to 3 days.

1. **Make the scallion butter:** Combine the butter, scallions, lime zest, lime juice, and salt in a small bowl and use a spoon to mix well.

2. **Make the slaw:** Whisk the lime zest, lime juice, olive oil, mustard, sriracha, salt, and sugar together in a measuring cup or small bowl. Place the cabbage, Treviso, and fennel in a large bowl, drizzle with the lime vinaigrette, and toss to combine.

3. **Make the steak:** Blot the steak dry with paper towels. Generously season both sides with salt and pepper.

4. Heat the grapeseed oil in a large stainless-steel or cast-iron pan over high heat. When the oil begins to shimmer and the pan is very hot and almost smoking, add the steak and cook, without moving it, until browned, 2 to 3 minutes. Flip the steak over and cook it, without moving, until browned, 2 to 3 minutes more. Transfer the steak to a cutting board and let rest for 5 minutes.

5. Slice the steak and serve it with dollops of the scallion butter and the slaw alongside.

Serves 4

SCALLION BUTTER

4 tablespoons (½ stick) unsalted butter, at room temperature

1 bunch scallions, white and light green parts only, finely chopped (about ½ cup)

Zest of 1 lime

Juice of ½ lime (about 2 teaspoons)

½ teaspoon kosher salt

SLAW

Zest and juice of 2 limes (about ¼ cup juice)

2 tablespoons extra-virgin olive oil

2 teaspoons Dijon mustard

1 teaspoon sriracha

1 teaspoon kosher salt

1 teaspoon sugar

1 medium head napa cabbage, thinly sliced

1 head Treviso, or ½ head small radicchio, thinly sliced

1 medium fennel bulb, stalks removed, bulb thinly sliced

STEAK

2 pounds skirt steak, cut into portions that will fit the pan

Kosher salt, to taste

Freshly ground black pepper, to taste

1 teaspoon grapeseed oil

Chicken Thighs in Creamy Paprika Sauce

This recipe takes a cue from chicken paprikash, the Hungarian one-pot stew traditionally made with bone-in chicken parts and a generous amount of paprika. Here I've opted for boneless, skinless chicken thighs for faster cooking. This dish is really all about the sauce—find something to serve with it to sop it up with, like crusty bread, rice, pasta, or even boiled potatoes.

NOTES: You can make this recipe with chicken breasts or tenders, but keep in mind the cook time will need to be adjusted. Use a digital thermometer to ensure the temperature reaches 165°F. Leftover chicken and sauce can be stored in an airtight container in the refrigerator for up to 3 days.

Serves 4

- 2 pounds boneless, skinless chicken thighs
- 2½ teaspoons kosher salt
- 2 teaspoons freshly ground black pepper
- 1 tablespoon extra-virgin olive oil
- 1 medium yellow onion, coarsely chopped
- ¼ cup tomato paste
- 3 garlic cloves, minced
- 1 tablespoon all-purpose flour
- 1 tablespoon sweet paprika
- ½ cup dry white wine, such as sauvignon blanc or pinot grigio
- 1 cup heavy cream
- 1 cup chicken stock
- Juice of 1 lemon (about 2 tablespoons)

1. Pat the chicken thighs dry with paper towels. Season both sides of the thighs with 1½ teaspoons of salt and 1 teaspoon of pepper.

2. Heat the olive oil in a Dutch oven or large high-sided pan over medium-high heat. When the oil begins to shimmer, add the chicken thighs and cook, undisturbed, until golden brown, 8 to 10 minutes. Flip the chicken and cook until golden brown on the second side with an internal temperature of at least 165°F, about 8 minutes. (You might need to work in batches, depending on the size of your pan.) Transfer the chicken to a plate.

3. Reduce the heat under the pan to medium, add the onion, and cook, stirring occasionally, until softened and frizzled on the edges, about 2 minutes. Add the tomato paste and garlic and cook, stirring, until the tomato paste turns a dark red color, about 2 minutes. Add the flour and paprika and cook, stirring, for 1 minute. Add the white wine and cook, scraping up any brown bits on the bottom of the pan, until the alcohol burns off, about 1 minute.

4. Add the heavy cream, stock, remaining 1 teaspoon salt, and remaining 1 teaspoon pepper; stir to combine. Bring to a simmer and cook, stirring occasionally, until slightly thickened, about 3 minutes. Turn the heat off and add the lemon juice, stirring to combine. Add the chicken back to the pan and serve immediately.

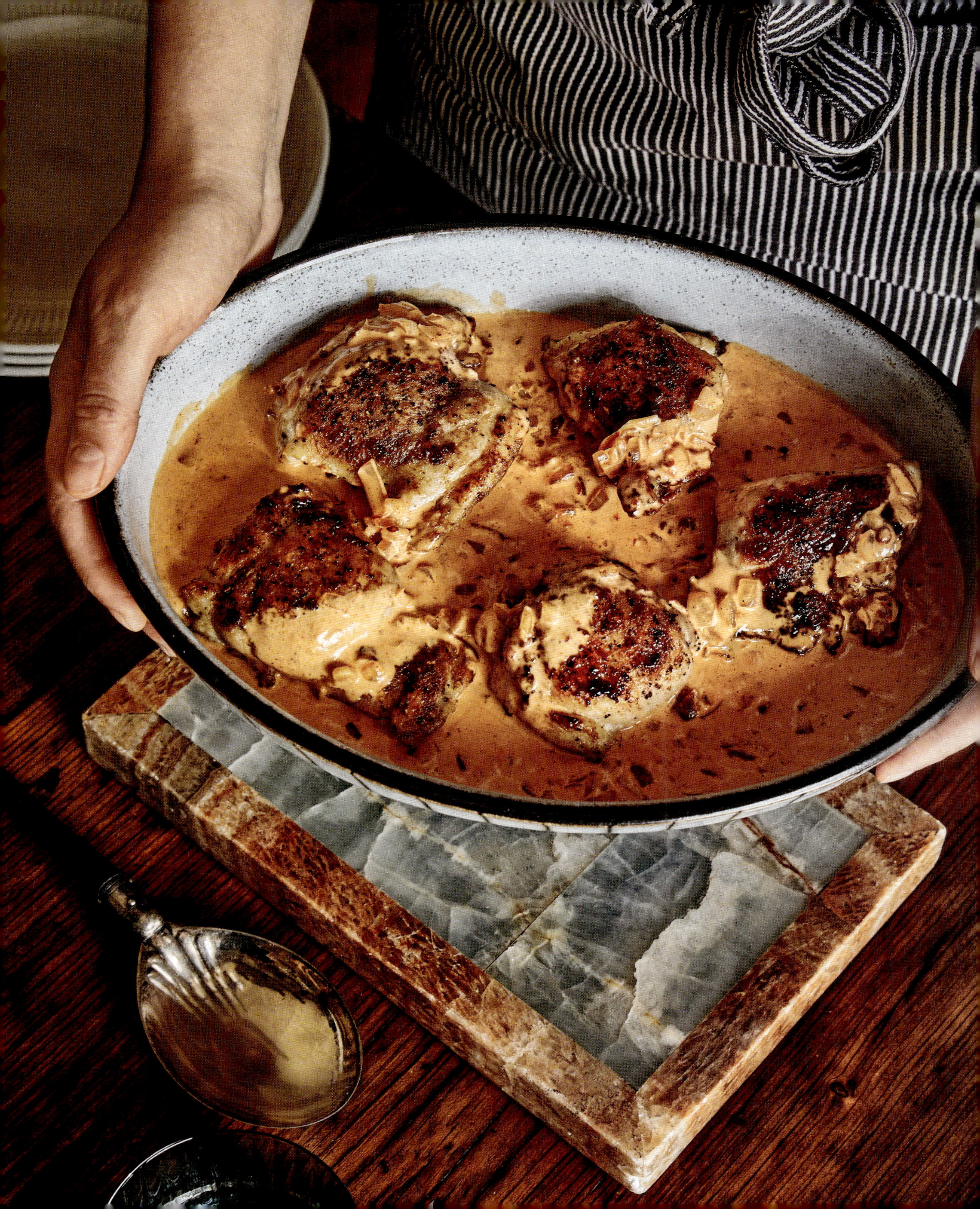

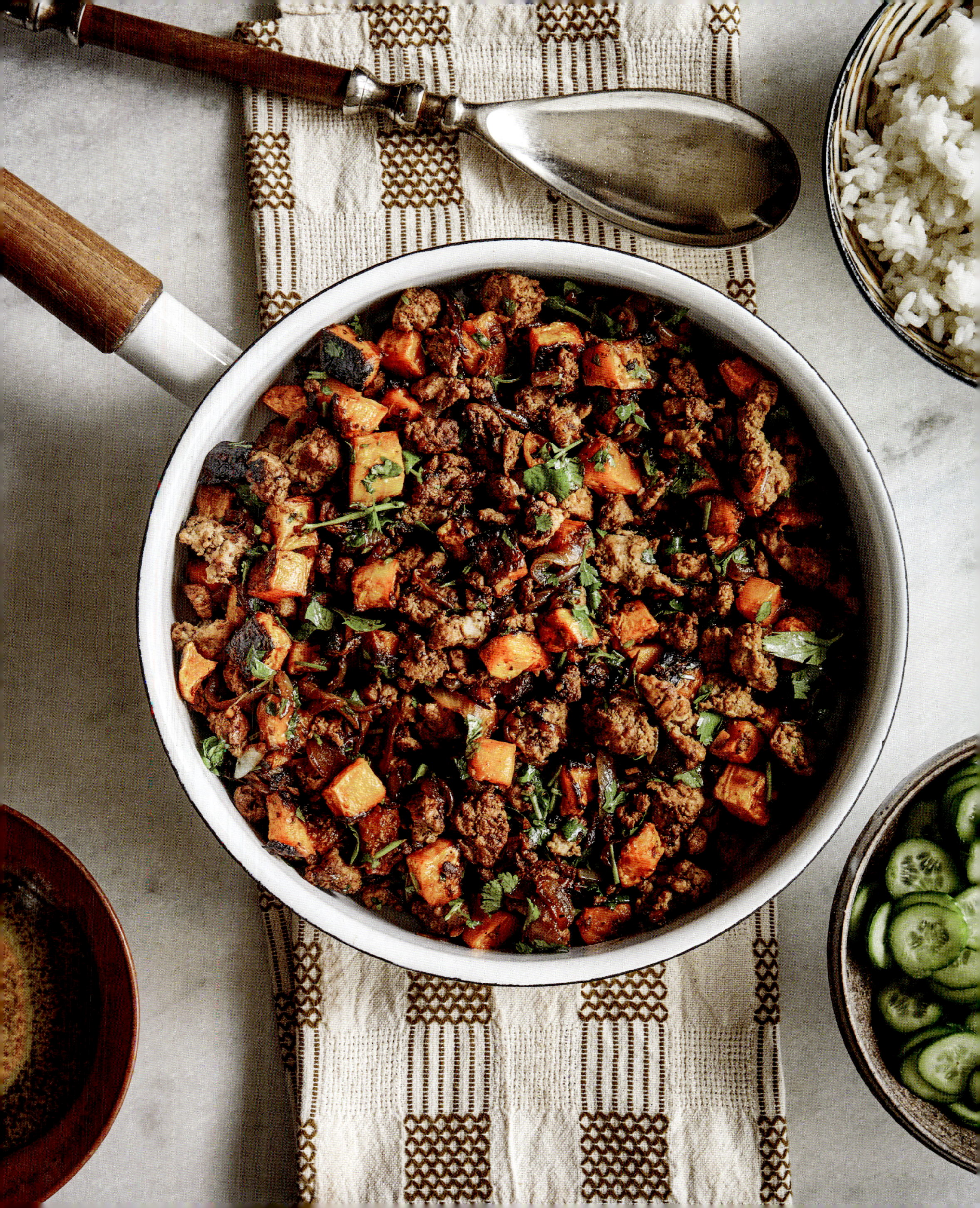

Turkey and Butternut Squash Bowl

Left to my own devices, I'd be eating bowl-centric dishes for most meals (see the Savory Breakfast Bowl on page 194). Here, ground turkey takes on my favorite flavor profile, thanks to Asian pantry staples like soy sauce, sesame oil, garlic, and ginger. While the turkey browns, the butternut squash roasts in the oven until tender. Stir it together and serve with a side of barely pickled cucumbers for a meal that's all in one.

NOTES: If you don't want to cut up your own squash, this is a good time to lean on the precut options that can be found in the produce section of your grocery store. The dish can be stored in an airtight container in the refrigerator for up to 3 days.

Serves 4

- 1 (2-pound) butternut squash, peeled, seeded, and cut into ½-inch cubes
- 3 tablespoons extra-virgin olive oil
- 2½ teaspoons kosher salt
- 6 Persian cucumbers, thinly sliced
- 3 tablespoons rice vinegar
- 1 medium yellow onion, thinly sliced
- 1 pound ground turkey (preferably dark meat)
- 3 garlic cloves, minced
- 1 (1-inch) knob fresh ginger, minced
- ½ cup dry white wine, such as sauvignon blanc or pinot grigio
- 2 tablespoons soy sauce
- 1 tablespoon toasted sesame oil
- Leaves and tender stems from 1 bunch cilantro, coarsely chopped (about 2 cups)
- Cooked grain of choice, such as rice, farro, or quinoa, for serving

1. Preheat the oven to 425°F.
2. Place the squash on a rimmed baking sheet, drizzle with 1 tablespoon of olive oil, and sprinkle on ½ teaspoon of salt. Roast until the squash is tender and browned, about 40 minutes, stirring halfway through.
3. While the squash is cooking, combine the cucumbers, 2 tablespoons of rice vinegar, and 1 teaspoon of salt in a bowl and toss well. Let sit at room temperature, stirring occasionally, until ready to serve.
4. While the squash is roasting, make the turkey. Heat the remaining 2 tablespoons olive oil in a large pan over medium-high heat. When the oil begins to shimmer, add the onion and cook, stirring occasionally, until the onion begins to turn lightly golden and soften, about 5 minutes. Add the ground turkey and use a wooden spoon to break it up, cooking until browned and cooked through, 8 to 10 minutes. Add the garlic, ginger, and remaining 1 teaspoon salt and cook until aromatic, about 1 minute.
5. Add the wine and cook, scraping up any brown bits on the bottom of the pan, until the alcohol burns off, about 2 minutes. Add the roasted squash, soy sauce, remaining 1 tablespoon rice vinegar, sesame oil, and the cilantro to the pan and stir to combine.
6. Serve the turkey over your cooked grain with the cucumbers on the side.

Rotisserie Chicken Salad with Snap Peas and Dilly Ranch

Rotisserie chicken is one of the easiest weeknight dinner hacks in the book (not my book, the book of life). There are endless possibilities of how to use up a rotisserie chicken: a meat and three; taco night; in enchiladas, soups and stews, or even pasta. My preference is to shred the chicken and pair it with crunchy romaine, radishes, and snap peas, and drench it in a dilly ranch dressing. To make it vegetarian, leave out the chicken and swap in your beans of choice.

NOTES: I call for a rotisserie chicken, since that's relatively easy to procure, but you could also use any type of leftover shredded chicken you might have on hand. Alternatively, make your own rotisserie-style chicken using the recipe on page 226. Ranch dressing can be made up to 3 days in advance and stored in an airtight container in the refrigerator. Once assembled, the salad is best eaten immediately.

1. **Make the ranch dressing:** Whisk together the mayonnaise, cream, lemon zest, lemon juice, salt, pepper, hot sauce, and dill in a small bowl.

2. **Make the salad:** Bring a small pot of salted water to a boil over high heat. Add the snap peas and cook until bright green and crisp-tender, about 1½ minutes. Drain the peas in a fine-mesh sieve and run cold water over them for 30 seconds.

3. Assemble the romaine, chicken, snap peas, and radishes in a bowl or on a serving plate. Drizzle the dressing over the salad and top with pepper and more dill to serve.

Serves 4

RANCH DRESSING

5 tablespoons mayonnaise

¼ cup heavy cream or whole milk

Zest and juice of 1 lemon (about 2 tablespoons juice)

½ teaspoon kosher salt

½ teaspoon freshly ground black pepper, plus more for serving

1 teaspoon hot sauce of choice

½ cup fresh dill, finely chopped, plus more for serving

SALAD

Kosher salt

2 cups snap peas, sliced on an angle

2 heads romaine hearts, sliced into 1-inch pieces (about 6 cups)

Meat from 1 rotisserie chicken, shredded (about 3 cups)

1 large watermelon radish, or 4 red radishes, thinly sliced

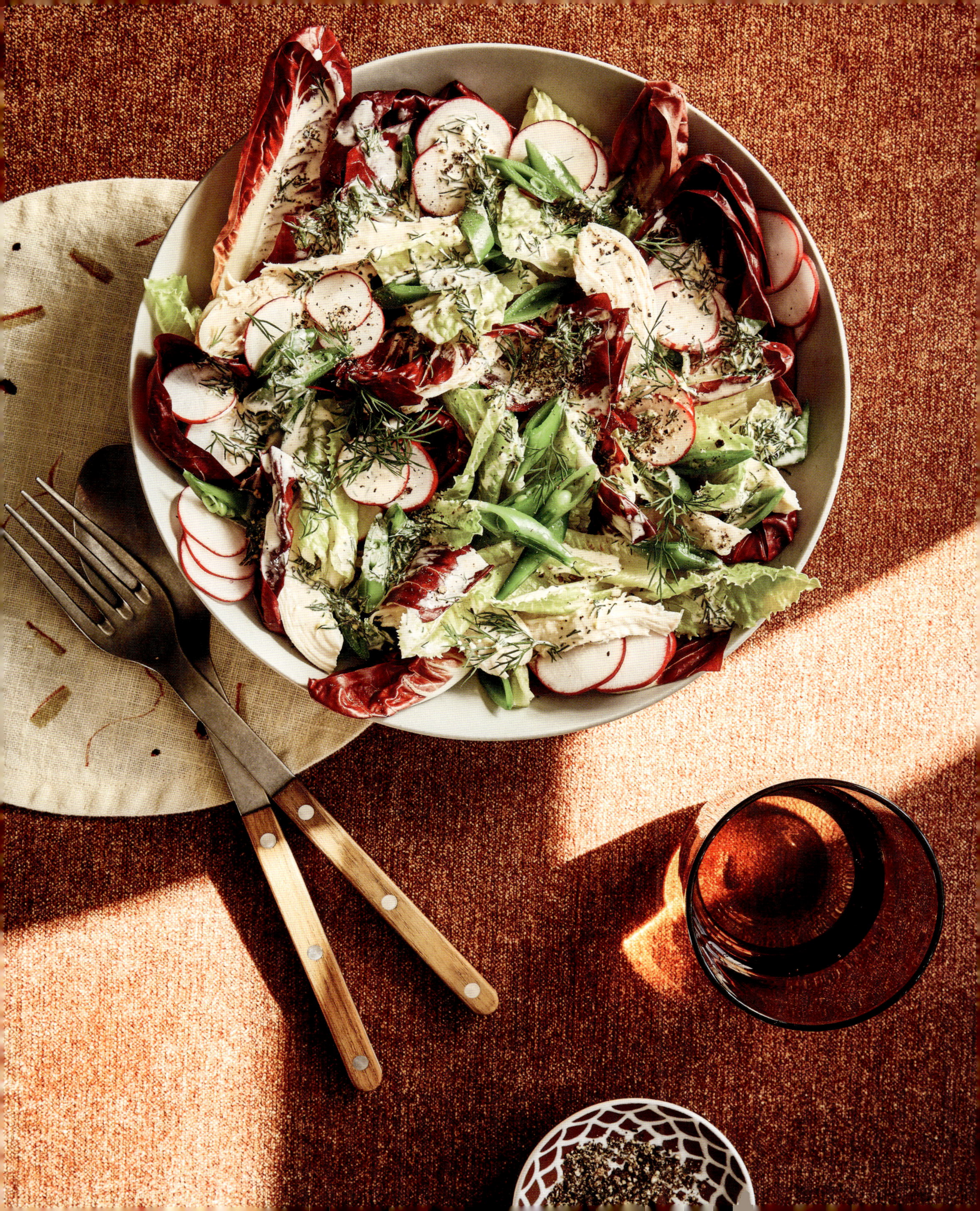

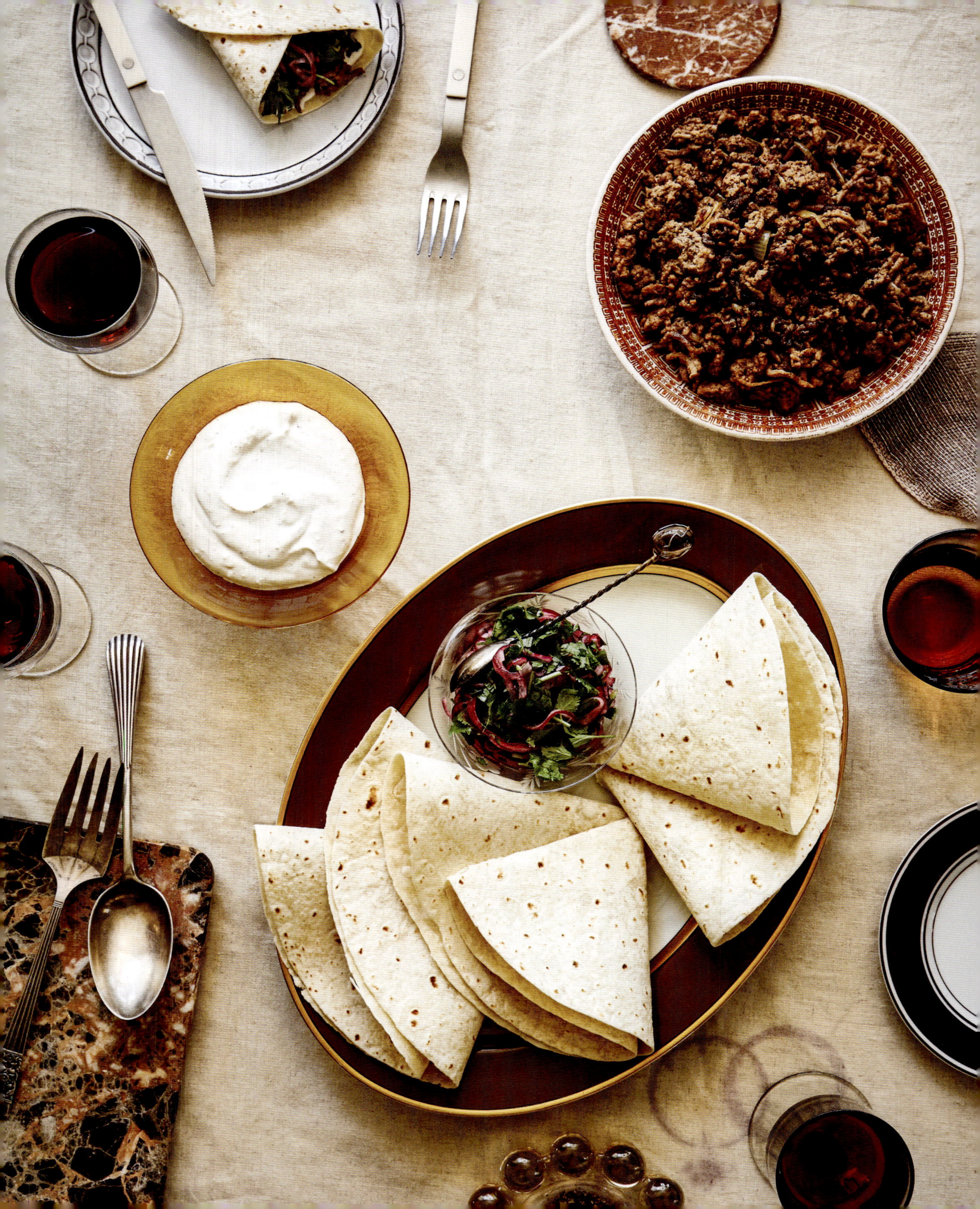

Spiced Lamb Flatbreads

I love a meal where everyone can assemble their own plates exactly to their liking, and spiced lamb flatbreads are at the top of that list, combining crunchy, herby, creamy, and savory components. While the length of this ingredient list might seem too long for a weeknight, bear with me. Both the herb salad and feta sauce can be simply stirred together in their respective bowls, and the only cooking involved is for the lamb, which takes under ten minutes. As Ina says, store-bought flatbread is fine, and even encouraged here.

NOTES: This recipe can be made with other types of ground meat, like beef, chicken, or turkey. Store each of the elements in a separate airtight container in the refrigerator for up to 3 days.

Serves 4

HERB SALAD

1 small red onion, thinly sliced

Juice of 1 lemon (about 2 tablespoons)

½ teaspoon kosher salt

1 bunch cilantro, coarsely chopped (about 2 cups)

1 cup coarsely chopped fresh mint leaves

FETA SAUCE

¾ cup full-fat sour cream

¾ cup crumbled feta cheese

Juice of 1 lemon (about 2 tablespoons)

½ teaspoon kosher salt

½ teaspoon freshly ground pepper

SPICED LAMB

1 tablespoon extra-virgin olive oil

1 large yellow onion, thinly sliced

2 teaspoons kosher salt

2 teaspoons ground cumin

1 teaspoon freshly ground black pepper

1 teaspoon ground coriander

1 teaspoon sweet paprika

2 pounds ground lamb

4 flatbread or pitas, warmed, for serving

1. **Make the herb salad:** Stir together the red onion, lemon juice, and salt in a small bowl. Let sit at room temperature for 5 minutes. Add the cilantro and mint and stir to combine.

2. **Make the feta sauce:** Combine the sour cream, feta, lemon juice, salt, and pepper in a food processor and process until smooth, about 30 seconds. (Alternatively, mix the ingredients by hand in a small bowl for a chunkier sauce.)

3. **Make the spiced lamb:** Heat the olive oil in a large pan over medium-high heat. When the oil begins to shimmer, add the onion and cook, stirring occasionally, until aromatic and golden, about 3 minutes. Add the salt, cumin, pepper, coriander, and paprika and cook, stirring, until deeply aromatic, about 30 seconds. Add the lamb and cook, using a wooden spoon to break up the meat and stirring occasionally, until browned and cooked through, 8 to 10 minutes.

4. For each serving, spread some feta sauce over a flatbread or on the inside of a pita. Add a generous scoop of the lamb and top with herb salad. Serve immediately.

Sheet-Pan Sausage with Corn, Peach, and Cucumber Salad

This summery sheet-pan dinner celebrates the bounty of the season and couldn't be simpler to put together. I've always been into salads that combine raw and roasted elements—they result in a great texture (and flavor) contrast. Here, roasted peaches and corn get stirred into a simple cucumber salad spiked with lime juice and scallions. Chorizo plays nicely with the salad, thanks to its spice, but you could use any other type of sausage you favor, even plant-based versions.

NOTES: Since the peaches get roasted, you can use unripe ones in this preparation. After roasting they'll be soft and slightly caramelized. Store leftover sausage and corn salad in the refrigerator for up to 3 days.

1. Position a rack in the upper third of the oven. Preheat the oven to 425°F.

2. Place the corn and peaches on a rimmed baking sheet and drizzle with 1 tablespoon of the olive oil. Use your hands to coat all the ingredients with the oil. Place the sausage on the baking sheet. Bake in the center of the oven rack until the peaches have softened and the sausage is cooked through, about 25 minutes.

3. Meanwhile, combine the cucumbers, scallions, lime zest, lime juice, salt, and remaining 2 tablespoons olive oil in a medium bowl and stir.

4. Add the cooked peaches and cilantro to the bowl with the cucumbers. Place the corn on a cutting board and remove the kernels, then transfer them to the bowl with the cucumbers and stir to combine.

5. Serve the sausage warm alongside the salad.

Serves 4

4 ears corn, shucked

4 yellow peaches, diced

3 tablespoons extra-virgin olive oil

2 pounds chorizo sausage

4 Persian cucumbers, thinly sliced

1 bunch scallions, white and light green parts only, thinly sliced

Zest and juice of 2 limes (about ¼ cup juice)

1 teaspoon kosher salt

½ bunch cilantro, coarsely chopped (about 1 cup)

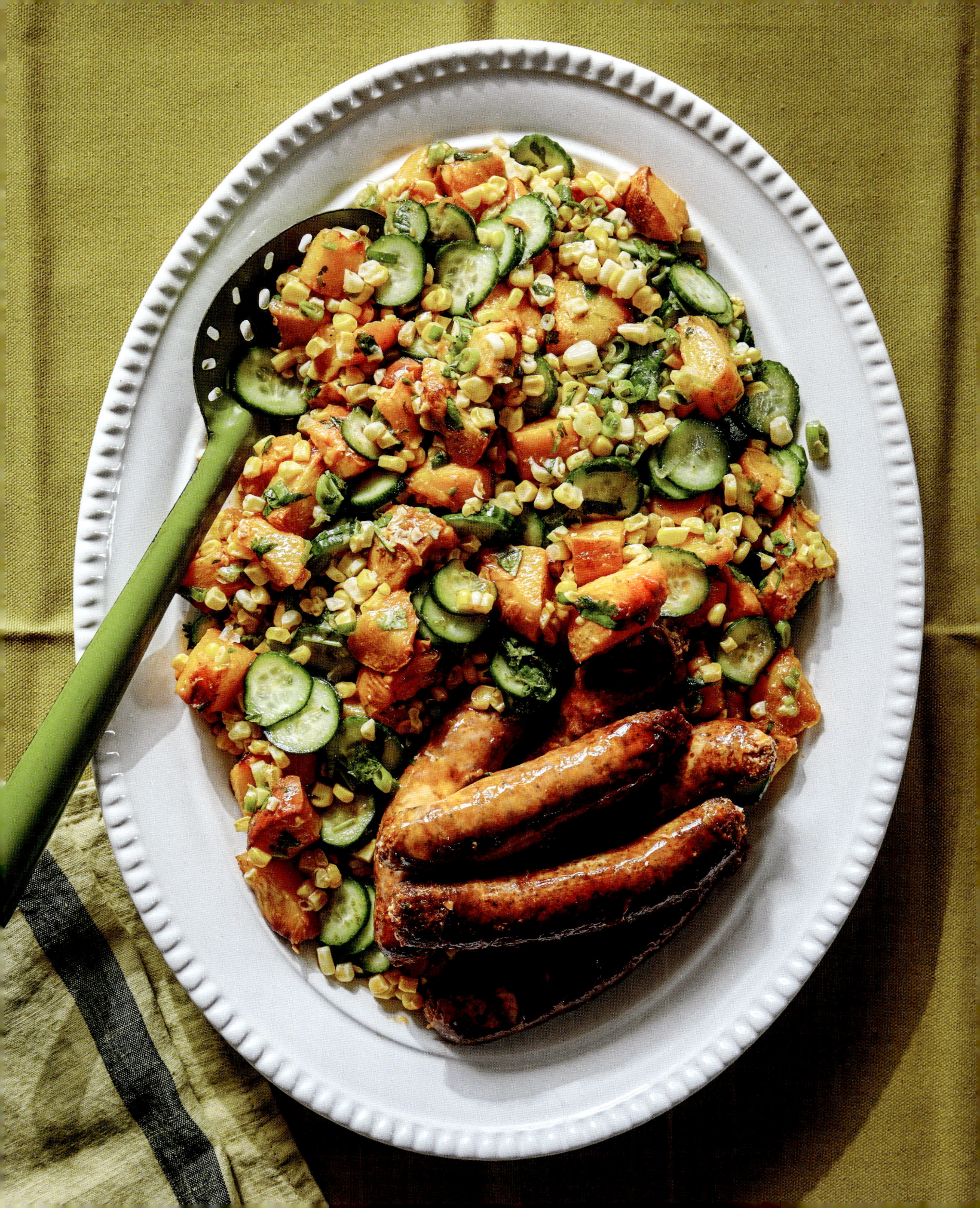

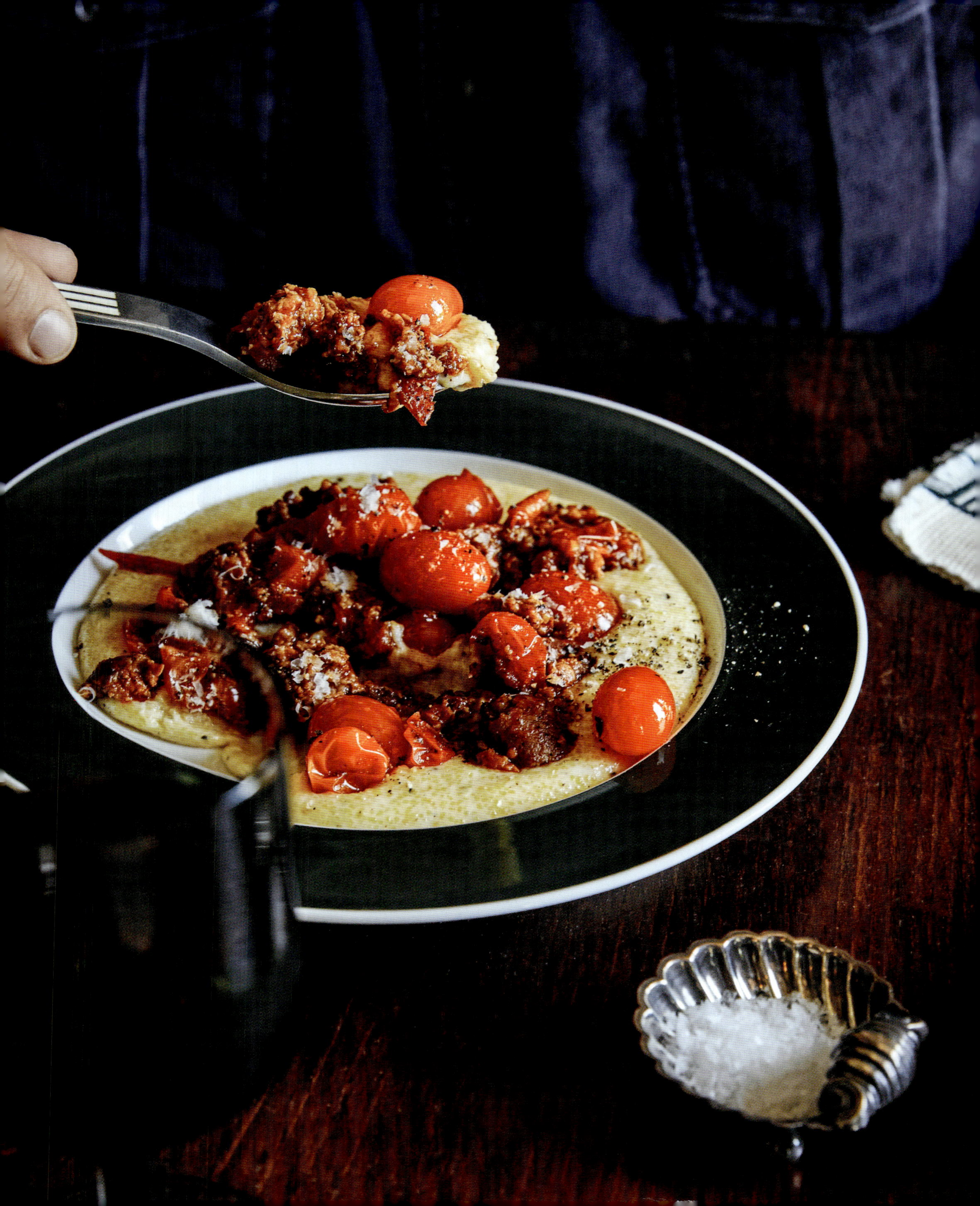

Polenta with Saucy Sausage and Tomatoes

I love a dish that does double duty by being easy to execute while also feeling special enough to serve friends. Cheesy polenta is topped with a simple sauce made of sausage, charred tomatoes, tomato paste, and wine, which results in an umami bomb of flavor that tastes more complex than it is. Polenta gets a bad rap for being a labor-intensive dish, but I'm here to tell you that you can make it in under ten minutes. You can also serve this sauce over pasta, or even with crusty bread.

NOTES: This sauce can be made up to 3 days ahead and stored in an airtight container in the refrigerator; heat it up when you're ready to eat. Polenta is best eaten immediately; however, leftovers can be stored in an airtight container in the refrigerator for up to 3 days.

1 **Make the sauce:** Set a large pan over medium-high heat. When the pan is warm, add the sausage and cook, using a wooden spoon to break up the meat, until browned and cooked through, 8 to 10 minutes. Use a slotted spoon to transfer the sausage to a paper towel–lined plate to drain.

2 Add the tomatoes and olive oil to the pan and cook, stirring occasionally, until blistered, about 5 minutes. Add the tomato paste and salt and stir to combine. Cook until the tomato paste is bright red, about 2 minutes. Add the wine and cook until alcohol burns off, about 2 minutes. Return the sausage to the pan and stir to combine. Remove the pan from the heat.

3 **Make the polenta:** Combine the stock, milk, and salt in a medium pot and bring to a boil over high heat. Reduce the heat to low and add the polenta. Cook, whisking continuously, until the mixture has thickened, 5 to 7 minutes. Add the Parmigiano Reggiano and pepper and whisk until fully combined, about 1 minute.

4 Serve the polenta topped with the sauce.

Serves 4

SAUCE

2 pounds hot Italian sausage, casings removed

4 cups cherry tomatoes

1 tablespoon extra-virgin olive oil

¼ cup tomato paste

1 teaspoon kosher salt

½ cup dry white wine, such as sauvignon blanc or pinot grigio

POLENTA

2 cups vegetable stock or chicken stock

2 cups whole milk

1 teaspoon kosher salt

1 cup polenta

1½ cups freshly grated Parmigiano Reggiano cheese

1½ teaspoons freshly ground black pepper

Couscous with Merguez, Broccoli, and Halloumi

Couscous is one of those ingredients I repeatedly turn to on busy weeknights. Combined with sheet-pan cooking, you can have this dish on the table in under thirty minutes. While you can gussy up couscous with any combination of ingredients (see the couscous salad with chickpeas and shaved fennel on page 67), I particularly love bulking it up with sausage to make a well-rounded meal. The key to sheet-pan cooking is combining ingredients that all cook at the same time. Here, merguez, broccoli, and Halloumi do just that.

NOTES: You can swap pistachios for other nuts you have on hand, like pine nuts or hazelnuts, or simply leave them out. Leftovers can be stored in an airtight container in the refrigerator for up to 3 days.

Serves 4

1 medium head broccoli, cut into florets (about 5 cups)

1 (8-ounce) package Halloumi, cut into ½-inch cubes

4 tablespoons extra-virgin olive oil

1½ teaspoons kosher salt

1 pound merguez sausage, casing removed

1¼ cups vegetable stock or chicken stock

1¼ cups couscous

Zest and juice of 2 lemons (about ¼ cup juice)

1 garlic clove, grated

1 cup shelled raw unsalted pistachios, coarsely chopped

1. Preheat the oven to 425°F.

2. Add the broccoli and Halloumi to a rimmed sheet pan and drizzle with 2 tablespoons of the olive oil and ½ teaspoon of the salt. Using your hands, toss to combine and spread in an even layer. Add the merguez in clumps around the pan. Bake until the merguez is cooked through, the Halloumi is melted, and the broccoli is roasted and knife-tender, about 25 minutes.

3. **Meanwhile, make the couscous:** Pour the stock into a medium pot and set it over high heat. When the stock begins to boil, remove the pot from the heat and add the couscous, stirring to combine. Place the lid on the pot and let sit for 5 minutes.

4. Whisk together the remaining 2 tablespoons olive oil, the lemon zest, lemon juice, garlic, and remaining 1 teaspoon salt in a medium bowl. Add the couscous and pistachios and stir until well combined. Add the broccoli, sausage, and Halloumi and stir to combine. Serve immediately.

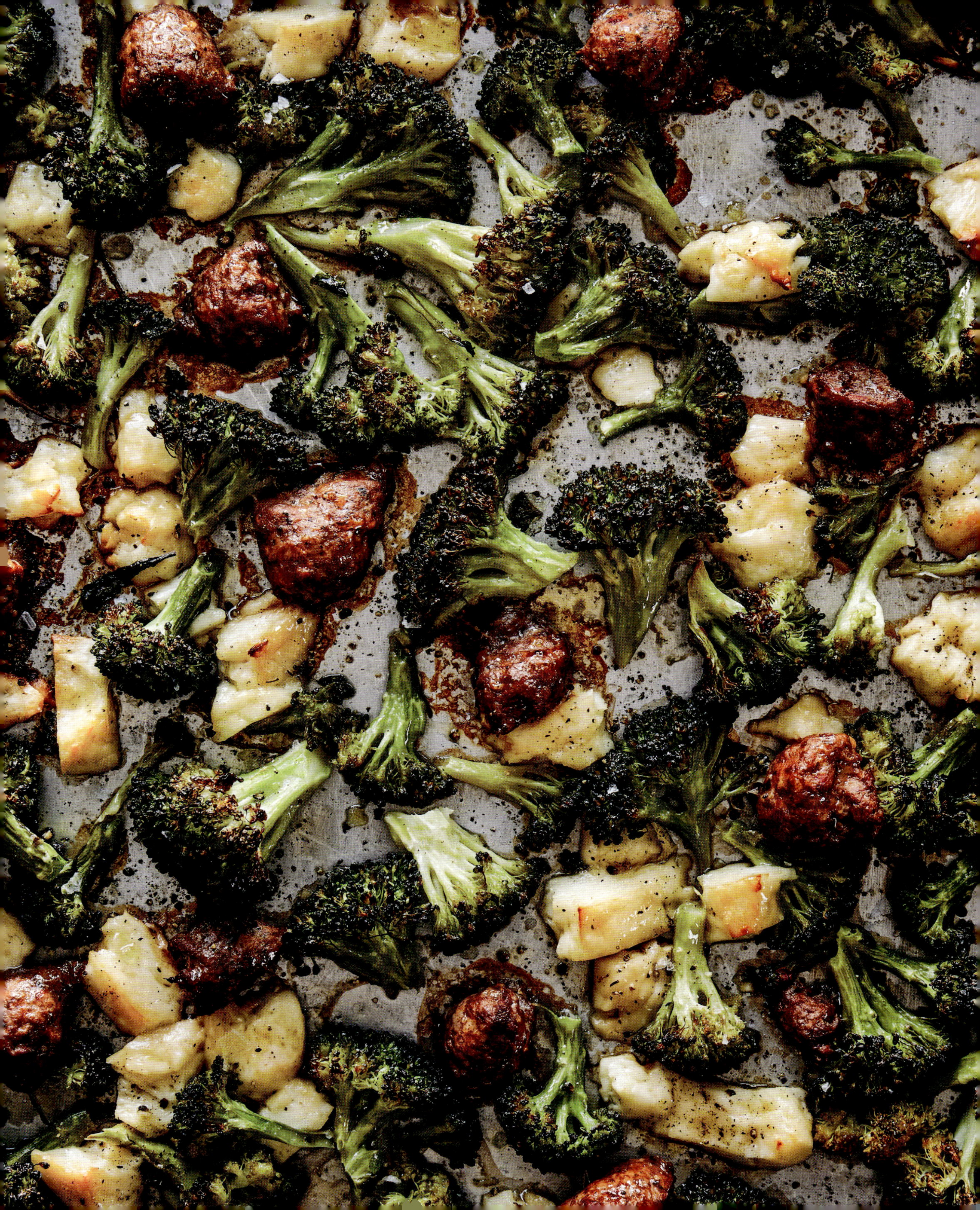

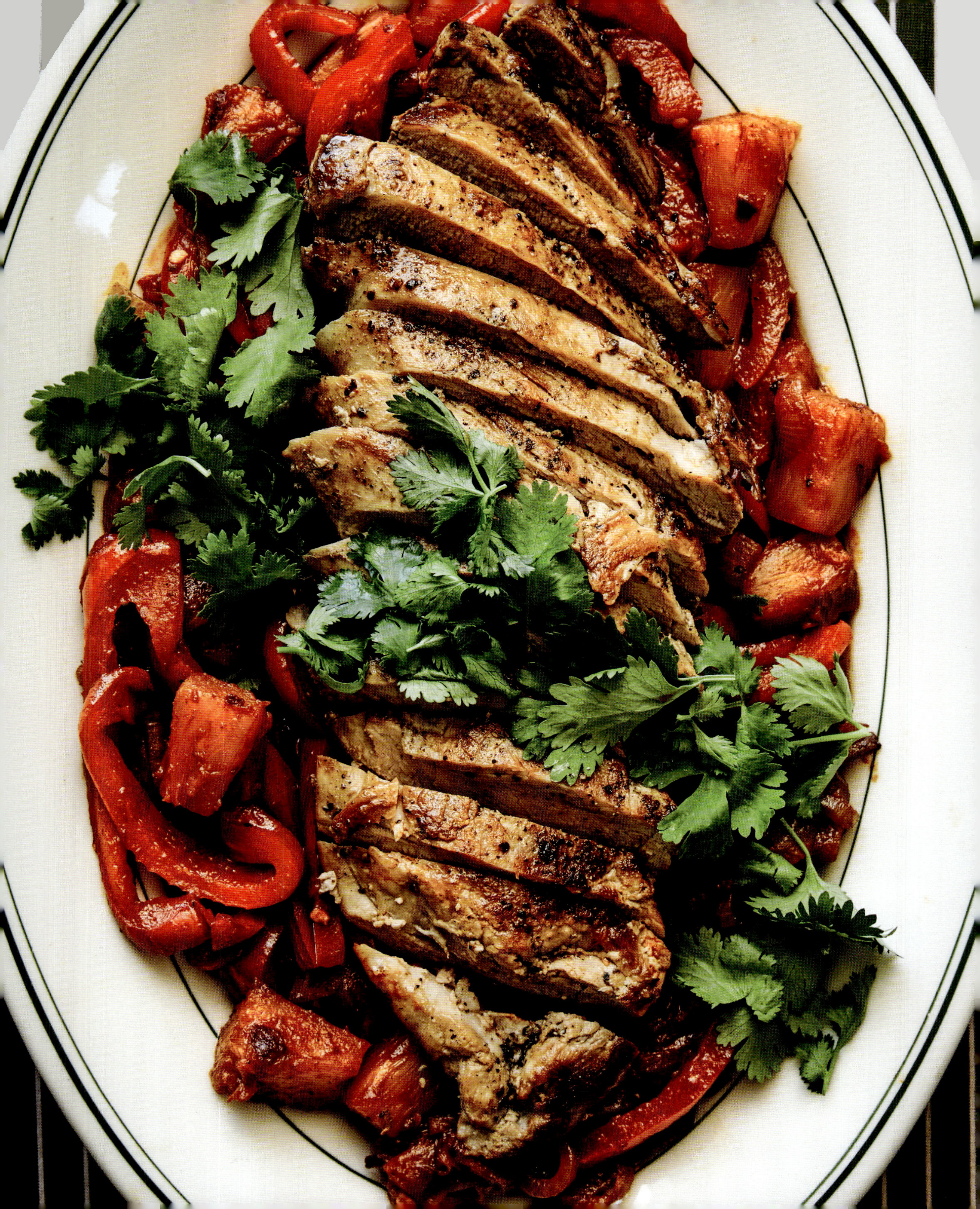

Pork Tenderloin with Pineapple and Peppers

Pork tenderloin, not to be confused with pork loin, is one of those cuts that's sneakily apt for a weeknight. After it has been browned on all sides, the pork tenderloin finishes cooking in the oven, leaving you the perfect amount of time to make a side, clean up, have a drink, or all three. Pork and pineapple are a classic combination in Hawaiian cooking, and thus this dish feels almost tropical to me. However, since canned pineapple and bell peppers are stocked year-round, this dish is evergreen for all seasons, not just summer. The sauce is an umami bomb of flavors, thanks to tomato paste and soy sauce, which pair well with the pork. I like serving it with cooked rice to sop up all the sauciness.

NOTES: This dish can be easily doubled for a crowd. If you're abstaining from alcohol, you can swap the wine for chicken or vegetable stock. Leftovers can be stored in an airtight container in the refrigerator for up to 3 days.

Serves 4

- 1 (1½-pound) boneless pork tenderloin
- 1½ teaspoons kosher salt
- 1 teaspoon freshly ground black pepper
- 1 tablespoon grapeseed oil
- 2 red bell peppers, thinly sliced
- 1 (16-ounce) can pineapple chunks, drained
- 1 medium yellow onion, thinly sliced
- ¼ cup tomato paste
- 1 tablespoon light brown sugar
- 1½ teaspoons sweet paprika
- 1 teaspoon red pepper flakes
- 1 cup dry white wine, such as sauvignon blanc or pinot grigio
- 2 tablespoons soy sauce
- ½ bunch cilantro, coarsely chopped (about 1 cup)

1. Preheat the oven to 425°F.
2. Pat the pork tenderloin dry on all sides with paper towels. Season with salt and black pepper.
3. Heat the grapeseed oil in a cast-iron or stainless-steel pan over medium-high heat. When the oil begins to shimmer, add the tenderloin and sear on all sides until browned, 2 to 3 minutes per side. Remove the tenderloin from the pan and set aside on a plate.
4. Combine the bell peppers, pineapple, and onion in the pan and cook, stirring occasionally, until softened, about 8 minutes.
5. Add the tomato paste, brown sugar, paprika, and red pepper flakes and stir until well combined and the tomato paste turns brick-red, about 1 minute.
6. Add the wine and soy sauce and cook until the alcohol has burned off, about 2 minutes.
7. Place the tenderloin on top of the peppers and transfer the pan to the oven until the internal temperature of the tenderloin reaches 135°F, 15 to 18 minutes.
8. Transfer the pork tenderloin to a cutting board to rest for 5 minutes before slicing. Serve the pork tenderloin with the pepper mixture, topped with cilantro.

Grilled Chicken Sandwiches

Grilled chicken always reminds me of summertime barbecues, but one dreary February night, my friends Rose and James invited me to dinner and served up a platter of chicken sandwiches that was a winter revelation. The sandwiches were simple—a squishy bun slathered in mayo with a stack of bread-and-butter pickles and a perfectly grilled chicken thigh—and I couldn't get enough. Of course, the chicken can be cooked over the grill, but a cast-iron pan will do as well.

To make this truly weeknight friendly, marinate the chicken ahead of time so when it comes to cooking, you've got only ten minutes in the kitchen. The chicken needs at least thirty minutes to bathe in the marinade, and then another thirty minutes to rest at room temperature, so plan accordingly. Lesson learned: There's no need to relegate grilled chicken to warmer weather.

NOTES: Pickle juice may seem like an unlikely ingredient, but it acts as a meat tenderizer, resulting in extra-juicy chicken thighs. Not only that, but it also adds a hit of tang to the marinade. Leftover chicken thighs can be stored in an airtight container in the refrigerator for up to 3 days.

Serves 4 to 6

- ½ cup soy sauce
- 3 tablespoons plus 2 teaspoons grapeseed oil
- 3 tablespoons honey
- 3 tablespoons bread-and-butter pickle juice from the jar
- 2 teaspoons hot sauce of choice
- 3 large garlic cloves, grated
- 1½ teaspoons kosher salt
- 1 teaspoon freshly ground black pepper
- 2 pounds boneless, skinless chicken thighs
- Mayonnaise, for serving
- 4 to 6 burger buns, toasted
- Bread-and-butter pickles, for serving

1. Whisk the soy sauce, 3 tablespoons of the grapeseed oil, the honey, pickle juice, hot sauce, garlic, salt, and pepper together in a medium bowl. Add the chicken thighs, making sure each of them is covered by the marinade. Cover with plastic wrap and transfer to the refrigerator to marinate for at least 30 minutes or up to 24 hours. Before cooking, let the chicken sit at room temperature for 30 minutes.

2. Heat the remaining 2 teaspoons oil in a large cast-iron or stainless-steel pan over medium-high heat. When the oil is shimmering, drain the excess marinade from the chicken and then add the thighs to the pan and cook until golden brown and charred, 5 to 6 minutes. Flip the chicken over and cook until cooked through and golden brown and a digital thermometer registers 165°F, about 5 minutes. (Alternatively, grill the chicken.)

3. Spread mayonnaise on the cut side of each bun. Assemble the sandwiches, layering on the chicken and pickles, and serve immediately.

NIGHTS AND WEEKENDS

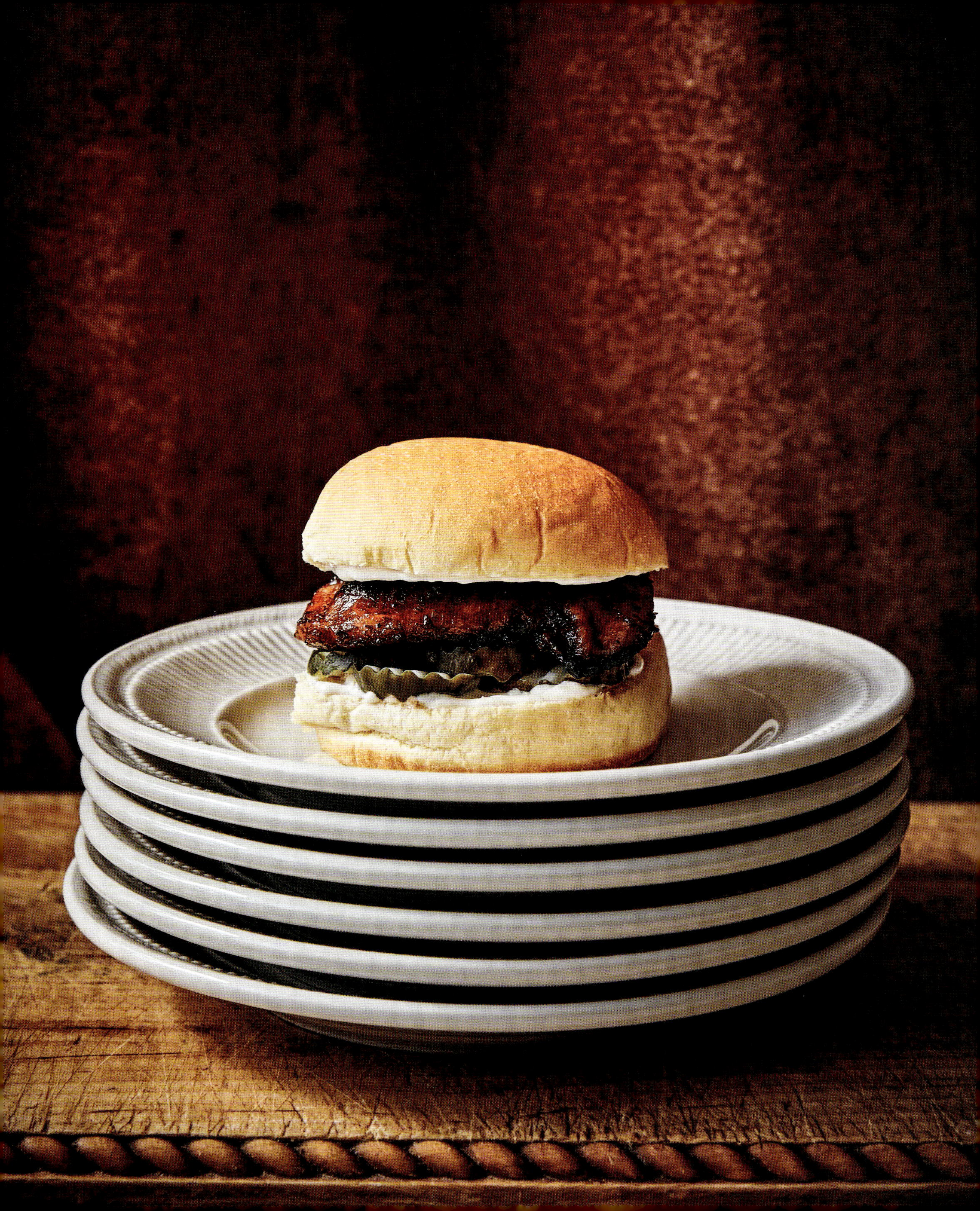

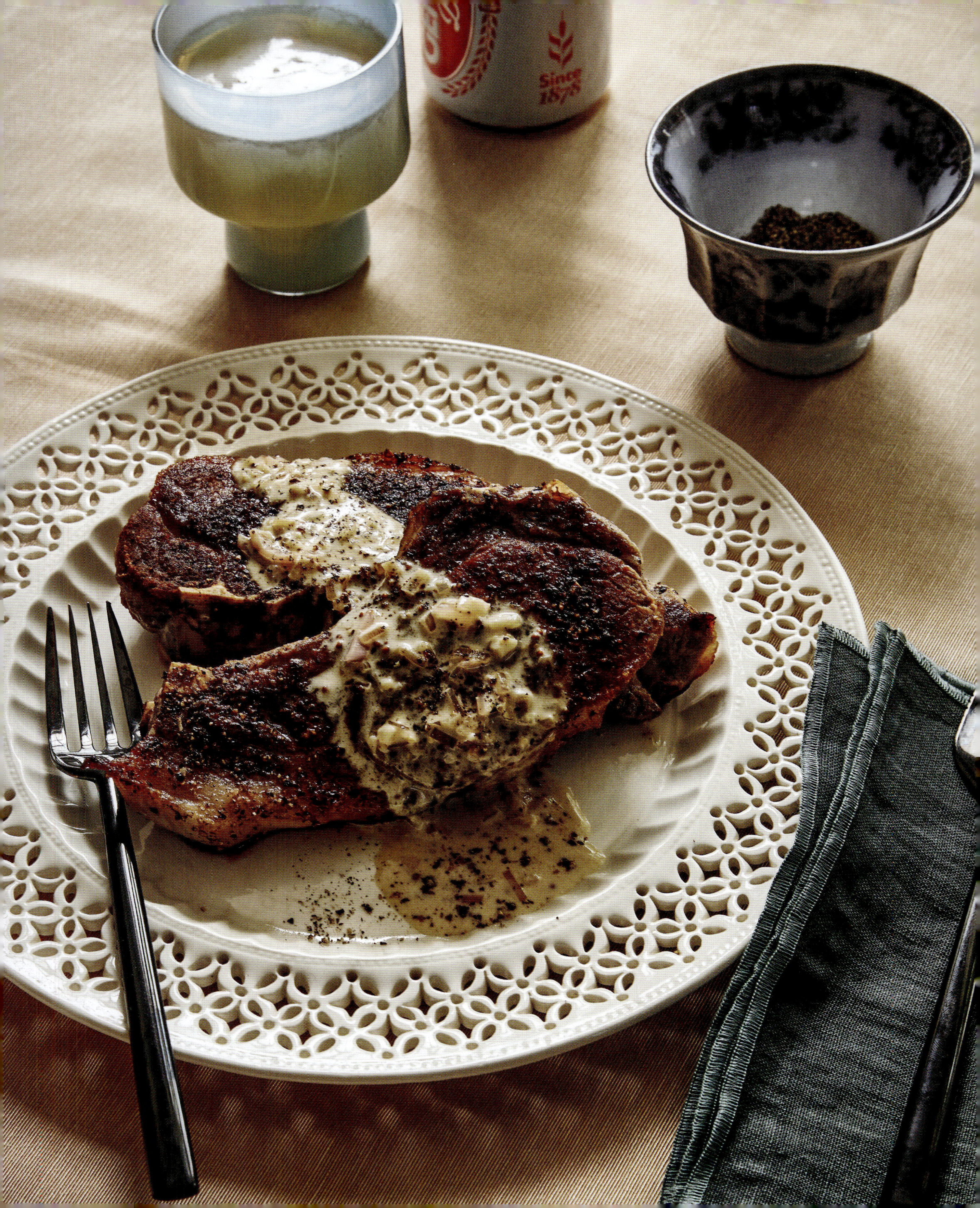

Pork Chops au Poivre

Au poivre might be one of the most beloved of the French sauces, or at least it's mine. I've swapped out steak, with which au poivre is typically served, for pork chops and draped them in this creamy black peppercorn pan sauce. Seriously, I've been known to eat it by the spoonful on more than one occasion. This recipe captures all the same flavors of traditional au poivre but omits flambéing (adding alcohol to a pan until it catches fire), which is decidedly not weeknight friendly or for the faint of heart. Instead, I finish the sauce with sherry vinegar, which helps balance it with some acidity, no flame required.

NOTES: You can of course serve this with steak. See the recipe on page 210 for instructions on cooking rib eye. Leftover pork chops au poivre can be stored in an airtight container in the refrigerator for up to 3 days.

Serves 4

- 4 (1-inch-thick) bone-in pork chops (about 2 pounds total)
- 2 tablespoons plus 1 teaspoon freshly ground black pepper
- 2½ teaspoons kosher salt
- 2 teaspoons grapeseed oil
- 2 tablespoons unsalted butter
- 1 large shallot, finely chopped
- 4 garlic cloves, minced
- ¾ cup heavy cream
- 1 tablespoon whole-grain mustard
- 1 tablespoon sherry vinegar

1. Preheat the oven to 350°F.

2. Pat the pork chops dry on both sides with paper towels. Season with 2 tablespoons of the pepper and 2 teaspoons of the salt.

3. Heat the grapeseed oil in a large stainless-steel or cast-iron pan over high heat. When the pan is very hot and the oil begins to shimmer, add the pork chops and cook, undisturbed, until golden brown, about 3 minutes. Flip the pork chops over and cook until golden brown, about 2 minutes. Turn the pork chops so that the fat cap is touching the pan and cook, undisturbed, until golden brown, about 1 minute. Set the pork chops flat in the pan and transfer it to the oven. Cook until the internal temperature reaches 140°F, about 8 minutes. Transfer the pork chops to a cutting board to rest while you make the pan sauce.

4. Set the pan over medium heat. Add the butter, shallot, and garlic to the pan and cook, stirring, until the butter has melted, about 1 minute. Add the cream, mustard, and remaining 1 teaspoon pepper and stir to combine. Cook until slightly thickened, about 1 minute. Add the vinegar and remaining ½ teaspoon salt and stir to combine, about 30 seconds. Remove the pan from the heat.

5. Serve the pork chops with the sauce poured over the top.

Turkey Meatballs with Puttanesca Sauce

Made with turkey, these meatballs are still juicy and tender but have a slightly lighter texture than those made with beef. My preferred method of cooking meatballs is always to bake them to cut down on cleaning and free up your hands—which in this case can then be used to make a quick puttanesca-style sauce.

NOTES: You can swap in ground beef, pork, or chicken for the turkey. If not making pasta, use 2 cups boiling water in place of the pasta water. Meatballs and sauce can be stored in an airtight container in the refrigerator for up to 3 days.

Serves 4 to 6

Kosher salt

1 (16-ounce) box long pasta of choice

1 pound ground turkey (preferably dark meat)

2 medium yellow onions, finely chopped

½ cup panko breadcrumbs

½ cup freshly grated Parmigiano Reggiano cheese

1 large egg, beaten

½ bunch flat-leaf parsley, finely chopped (about 1 cup)

1 teaspoon freshly ground black pepper

1 tablespoon extra-virgin olive oil

½ cup pitted Castelvetrano olives, coarsely chopped

2 tablespoons capers, drained and rinsed

4 garlic cloves, thinly sliced

1 teaspoon dried oregano

½ teaspoon red pepper flakes

½ cup tomato paste

1 tablespoon sherry vinegar

1. Preheat the oven to 400°F.

2. Bring a large pot of salted water to a boil over high heat. Add the pasta and cook until al dente according to the package instructions. Reserve 2 cups of the pasta cooking water, then drain the pasta in a colander.

3. Combine the ground turkey, half the onions, the panko, Parmigiano Reggiano, egg, half the parsley, 1 teaspoon salt, and ½ teaspoon of the black pepper in a medium bowl and use your hands to combine; do not overmix.

4. Form the mixture into 1½-inch balls and place them on a rimmed baking sheet 2 inches apart. Bake until cooked through, 18 to 20 minutes, or until an instant-read thermometer reaches 165°F.

5. Meanwhile, heat the olive oil in a large pan over medium-high heat. When the oil begins to shimmer, add the remaining chopped onions and cook, stirring occasionally, until lightly golden brown, about 4 minutes. Add the olives, capers, garlic, oregano, red pepper flakes, and ½ teaspoon salt and cook until aromatic, about 1 minute. Add the tomato paste and cook, stirring until combined, until the tomato paste turns a brick-red color, about 2 minutes.

6. Add the reserved pasta water and cook, scraping up any brown bits on the bottom of the pan, until the sauce is slightly thickened and deeply aromatic, about 5 minutes. Remove the pan from the heat, add the remaining parsley and the sherry vinegar, and stir to combine.

7. Add the drained pasta to the sauce and toss to combine until the pasta is well coated and glossy. Add the meatballs to the pan and serve immediately.

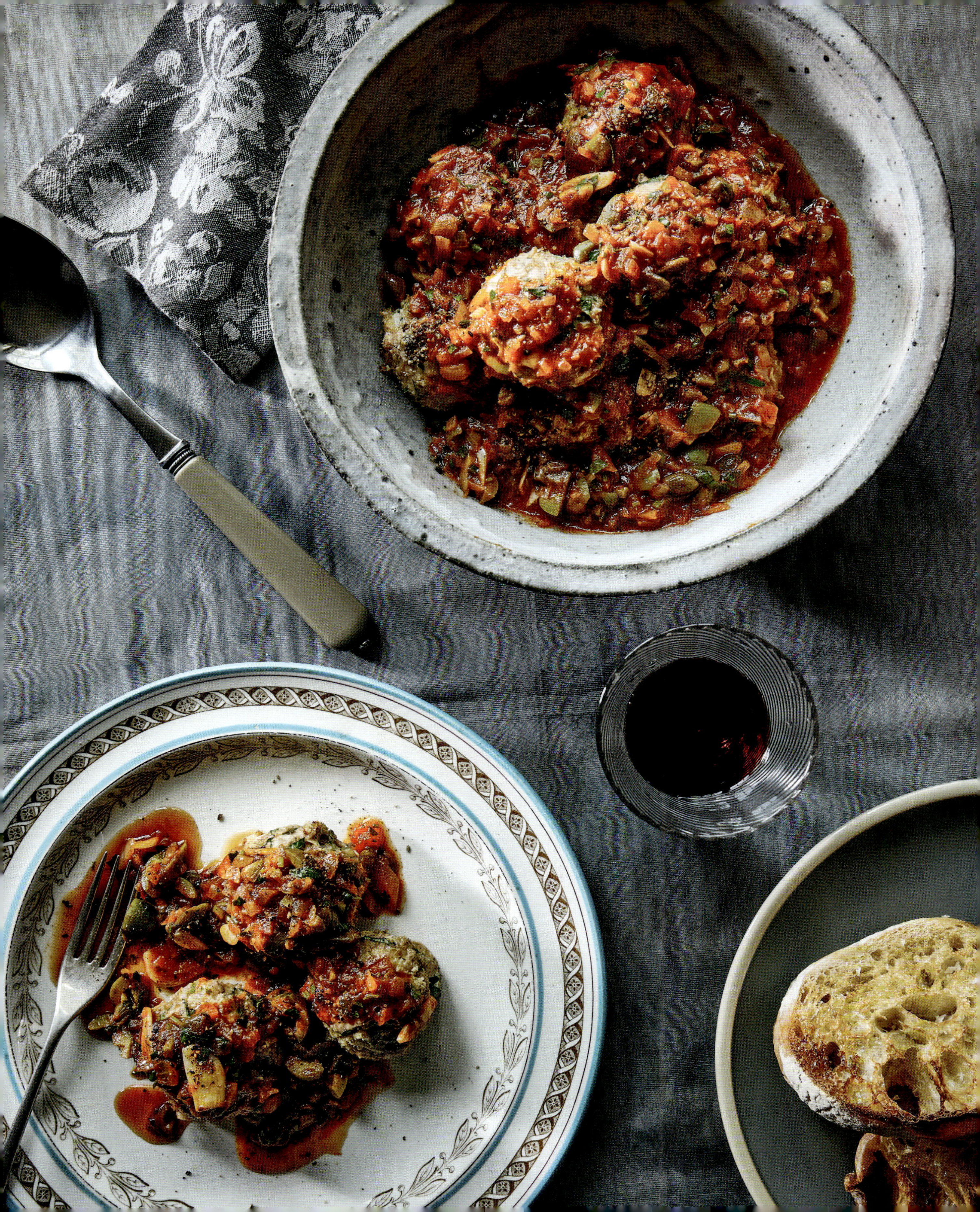

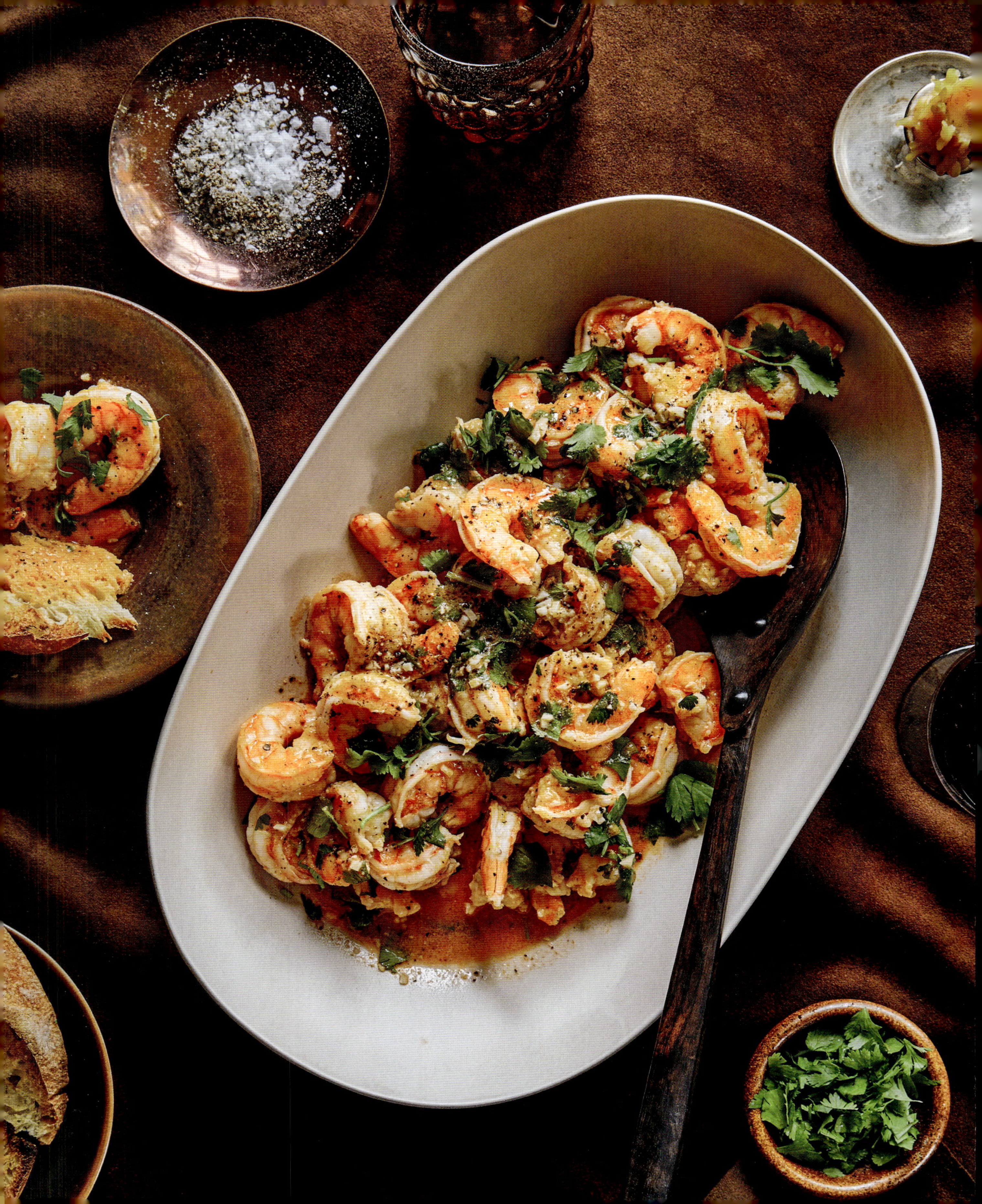

FISH

NIGHTS

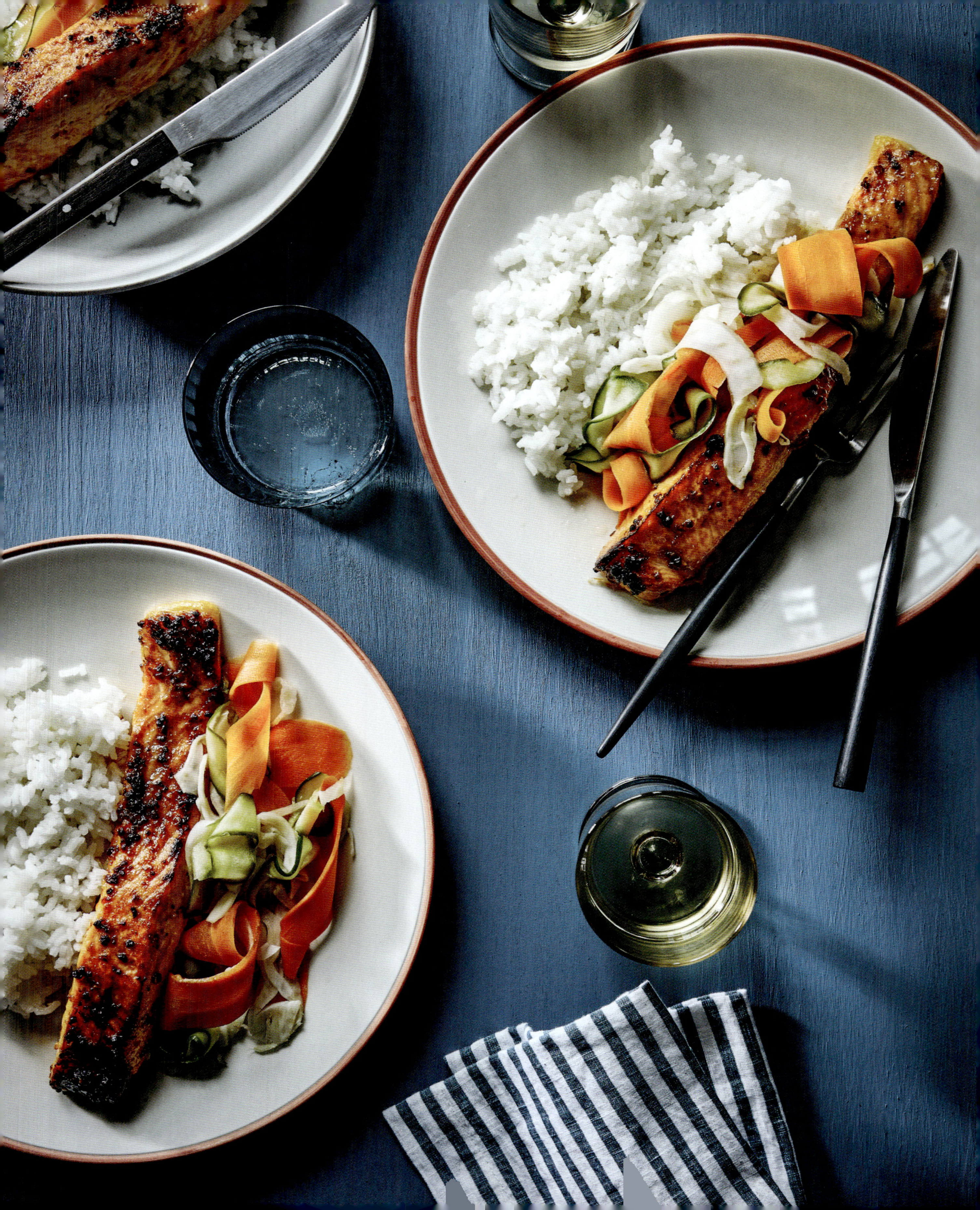

Chile Crisp Salmon with Quick Pickle Salad

If you're not keeping a jar of chile crisp in the pantry to drizzle over, well, just about everything, we need to talk. This popular condiment by way of China combines the heat of hot sauce with some necessary crunch. Chile crisp does the heavy lifting in terms of flavor here. When mixed with mayonnaise and brown sugar to make a glaze, it caramelizes under the broiler and creates a browned crust while the fish stays tender and flaky. While you could serve the salmon with any sides, I love how it pairs with this punchy salad of shaved quick-pickled vegetables. The acidity balances the richness of the fish while adding some crunch.

NOTES: Use a vegetable peeler to get just the right thin cucumber and carrot slices. The quick pickles can be stored in an airtight container in the refrigerator for up to 5 days. The salmon can be stored in an airtight container in the refrigerator for up to 3 days.

Serves 4

QUICK PICKLES

1 cup rice vinegar

2 tablespoons sugar

1 tablespoon kosher salt

2 garlic cloves, peeled

3 Persian cucumbers, thinly sliced lengthwise

2 medium carrots, thinly sliced lengthwise

1 medium fennel bulb, stalks removed, bulb thinly sliced

SALMON

2 tablespoons mayonnaise

1 tablespoon chile crisp

2 teaspoons light brown sugar

4 (6-ounce) center-cut, skin-on salmon fillets

Cooked white rice, for serving

1. **Make the quick pickles:** Combine the vinegar, sugar, salt, and garlic with 1 cup water in a medium pan and heat over medium-high heat, stirring, until the sugar is dissolved and the mixture begins to boil. Remove the pan from the heat and add the cucumbers, carrots, and fennel. Let sit at room temperature for at least 20 minutes or up to 2 hours.

2. **Make the salmon:** Preheat the broiler to high. Line a rimmed baking sheet with aluminum foil.

3. Combine the mayonnaise, chile crisp, and brown sugar in a small bowl and stir well. Pat the salmon dry on both sides with paper towels. Divide the mayonnaise mixture into fourths and place a dollop on each piece of salmon. Use your hands to coat the salmon on both sides with the mayonnaise mixture and transfer it to the prepared baking sheet, skin-side down.

4. Broil the salmon until the interior is pink and it is easily flaked with a fork, 5 to 8 minutes, depending on the thickness of the salmon. (For salmon that's ½ inch thick, you can assume it'll take between 5 and 6 minutes. For thicker cuts, add more time.)

5. Serve the salmon with the rice and pickled vegetables.

Cod in Green Sauce

Cod is a gateway fish for those who might be nervous to make fish at home, thanks to its inherently forgiving nature. It's light and flaky with a mellow, sweet flavor and will still be delicious even slightly overcooked. You can bake it, sear it in a pan, grill it on skewers, or poach it in sauce like I do here. This punchy sauce goes heavy on the greens and lime and is good enough to eat all on its own. The coconut milk at the base of the sauce adds creaminess rather than overpowering coconut flavor. I call for one and a half pounds of cod, since that feeds four, but you could up the quantity to two or even three pounds of fish, depending on how many you're serving. I spoon extra sauce over rice to eat alongside it.

NOTES: Green sauce can be made up to 1 day in advance and kept in an airtight container in the refrigerator. Cooked cod can be stored in an airtight container in the refrigerator for up to 3 days.

Serves 4

1½ pounds cod fillets

Kosher salt

1 (15-ounce) can unsweetened full-fat coconut milk

2 cups spinach, coarsely chopped

Leaves and tender stems from ½ bunch cilantro, coarsely chopped (about 1 cup)

½ cup fresh mint leaves

¼ cup extra-virgin olive oil

Zest and juice of 2 limes (about ¼ cup juice)

3 garlic cloves, coarsely chopped

1 medium jalapeño, coarsely chopped

Cooked white rice, for serving

1. Pat the cod dry with paper towels and season with salt.

2. Combine the coconut milk, spinach, cilantro, mint, olive oil, lime zest, lime juice, garlic, jalapeño, and 1½ teaspoons salt in a blender and blend on high until bright green and smooth, about 30 seconds.

3. Transfer the green sauce to a large pan and bring to a simmer over medium heat.

4. Carefully place the cod in the simmering sauce and cover the pan. Cook until the cod is just cooked through and easily flakes with a fork, about 10 minutes.

5. Serve the cod and green sauce over the rice.

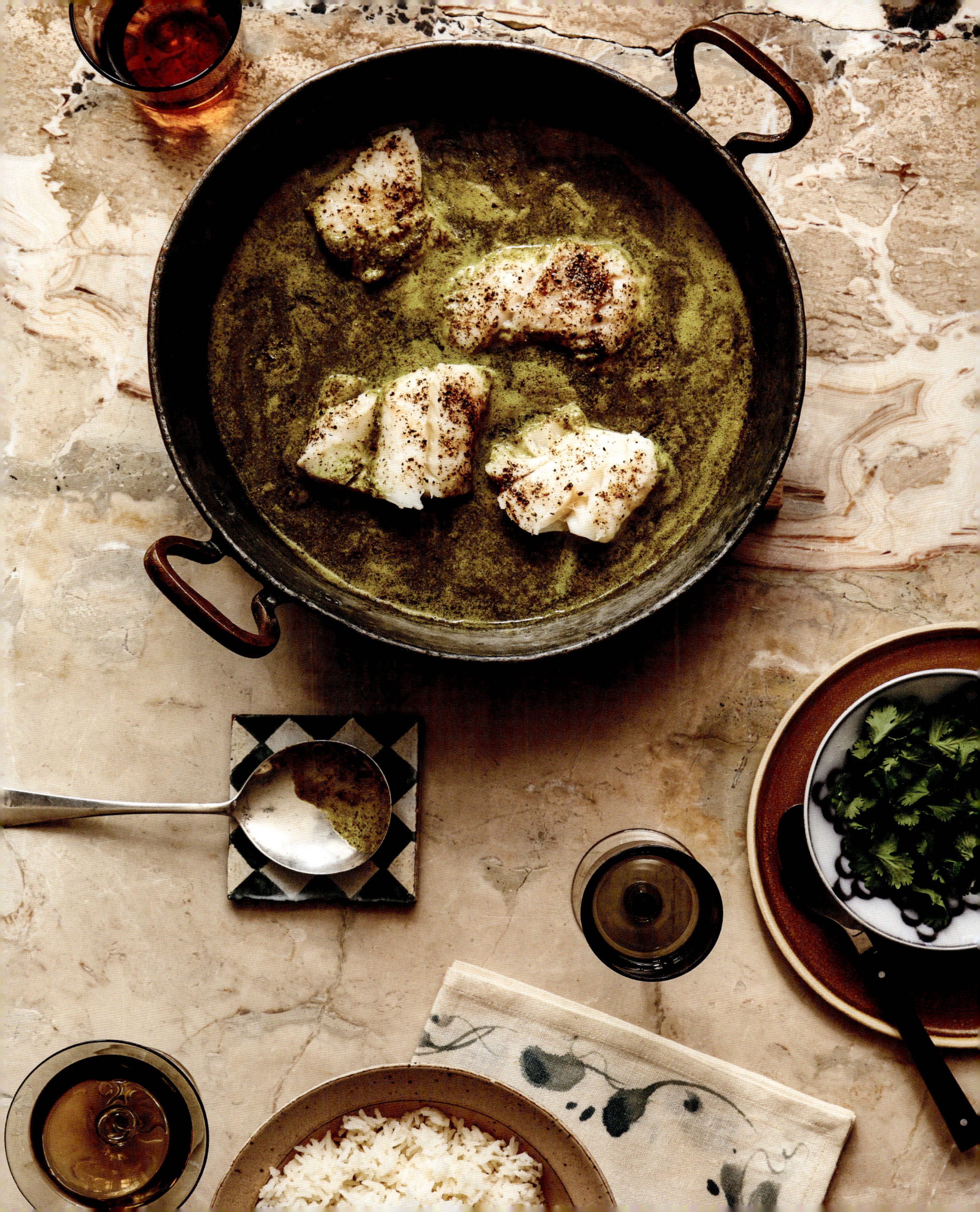

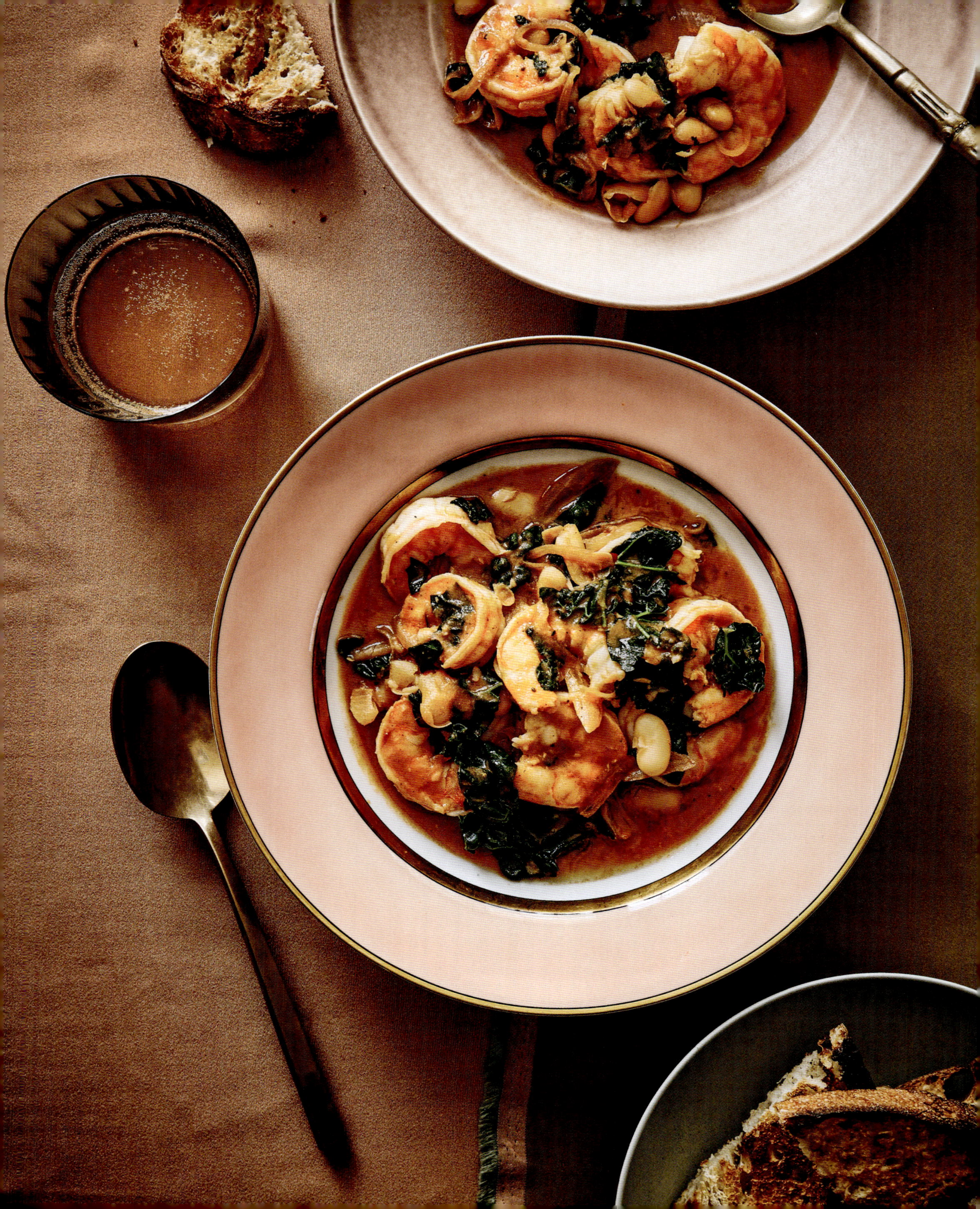

Saucy Shrimp with Beans and Greens

Packed with protein and greens, this is the type of meal I often turn to on a weeknight. Better yet, it's made in one pan. Once the sauce is finished, the shrimp are added and gently poached, ensuring they don't get overcooked. Be sure to serve this dish with something like rice, a crusty baguette, or pasta to sop up the saucy bits.

NOTES: You can use any type of canned bean you have on hand in place of great northern beans, like cannellini, pinto, or kidney. Leftover shrimp and beans can be stored in an airtight container in the refrigerator for up to 3 days.

Serves 4

- 1½ pounds shrimp, peeled and deveined
- 1½ teaspoons kosher salt
- 2 tablespoons extra-virgin olive oil
- 2 large shallots, thinly sliced
- 2 garlic cloves, minced
- 2 tablespoons tomato paste
- 2 (15-ounce) cans great northern beans, drained and rinsed
- 1 teaspoon freshly ground black pepper
- ½ teaspoon red pepper flakes
- ¼ cup dry white wine, such as sauvignon blanc or pinot grigio
- 1½ cups vegetable stock or chicken stock
- 2 tablespoons unsalted butter
- 1 bunch greens, such as kale, Swiss chard, spinach, or watercress, coarsely chopped (about 4 cups)
- Juice of 1 lemon (about 2 tablespoons)

1. Pat the shrimp dry with paper towels. Season with ½ teaspoon of the salt.

2. Heat the olive oil in a large pan over medium-high heat. When the oil begins to shimmer, add the shallots and cook, stirring occasionally, until lightly golden, about 2 minutes. Add the garlic and cook, stirring, until aromatic, about 1 minute. Add the tomato paste and cook until the color becomes a deep red, stirring until well combined, about 2 minutes.

3. Add the beans, the remaining 1 teaspoon salt, the black pepper, and the red pepper flakes and cook, stirring, until the beans are warmed through, about 2 minutes. Add the wine and cook, scraping up any brown bits on the bottom of the pan, until the alcohol burns off, about 2 minutes.

4. Add the stock, shrimp, and butter and cook, stirring occasionally, until the shrimp turns bright pink and opaque, about 2 minutes.

5. Add the greens and cook until just wilted, about 1 minute. Remove the pan from the heat and stir in the lemon juice. Serve immediately.

Potato Salad with Pesto, Smoked Fish, and Asparagus

This is a far cry from the potato salads that you might find at a summer barbecue, although I won't stop you from bringing it to your next potluck. Here, baby potatoes are mixed with pesto and studded with flakes of smoked fish and bright green spears of asparagus, channeling the best of spring flavors. While potato salad is often thought of as a side dish, this version is filling enough to be a meal all on its own.

NOTES: To cut down on time, store-bought pesto is fine. Alternatively, you can use this pesto recipe to mix with pasta. Leftover potato salad can be stored in an airtight container in the refrigerator for up to 3 days.

1. **Make the pesto:** Combine the Parmigiano Reggiano, pine nuts, garlic, and ½ teaspoon salt in a food processor and process until finely chopped, about 30 seconds. Add the basil and process until smooth. With the motor running, add the olive oil in a steady stream and process until combined.

2. Place the potatoes in a large pot, add cold water to cover, and generously season the water with salt. Bring to a boil over high heat and cook until the potatoes are easily pierced with a knife, 10 to 12 minutes. Add the asparagus to the pot with the potatoes and boil until the asparagus is bright green and tender, about 3 minutes. Drain the potatoes and asparagus in a colander and transfer to a serving bowl. Add the pesto and smoked fish and stir to combine.

Serves 4

- 1 cup freshly grated Parmigiano Reggiano cheese
- ½ cup pine nuts
- 2 large garlic cloves, coarsely chopped
- Kosher salt
- 2 cups loosely packed fresh basil leaves
- ½ cup extra-virgin olive oil
- 1 pound new, baby, or fingerling potatoes
- 1 bunch asparagus, ends trimmed, stalks cut into 1-inch pieces on an angle
- 6 ounces smoked fish of choice, such as trout, whitefish, mackerel, or haddock, flaked

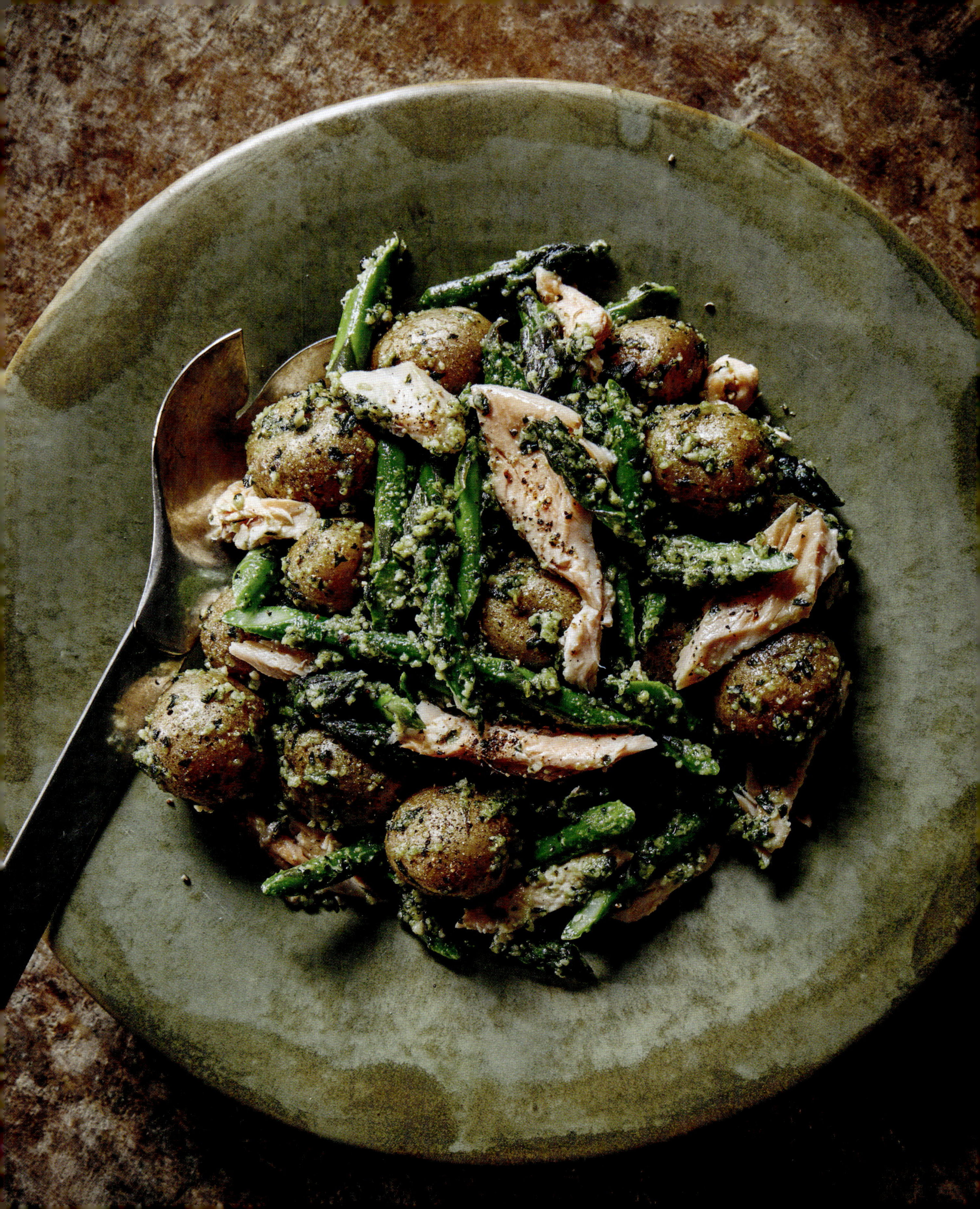

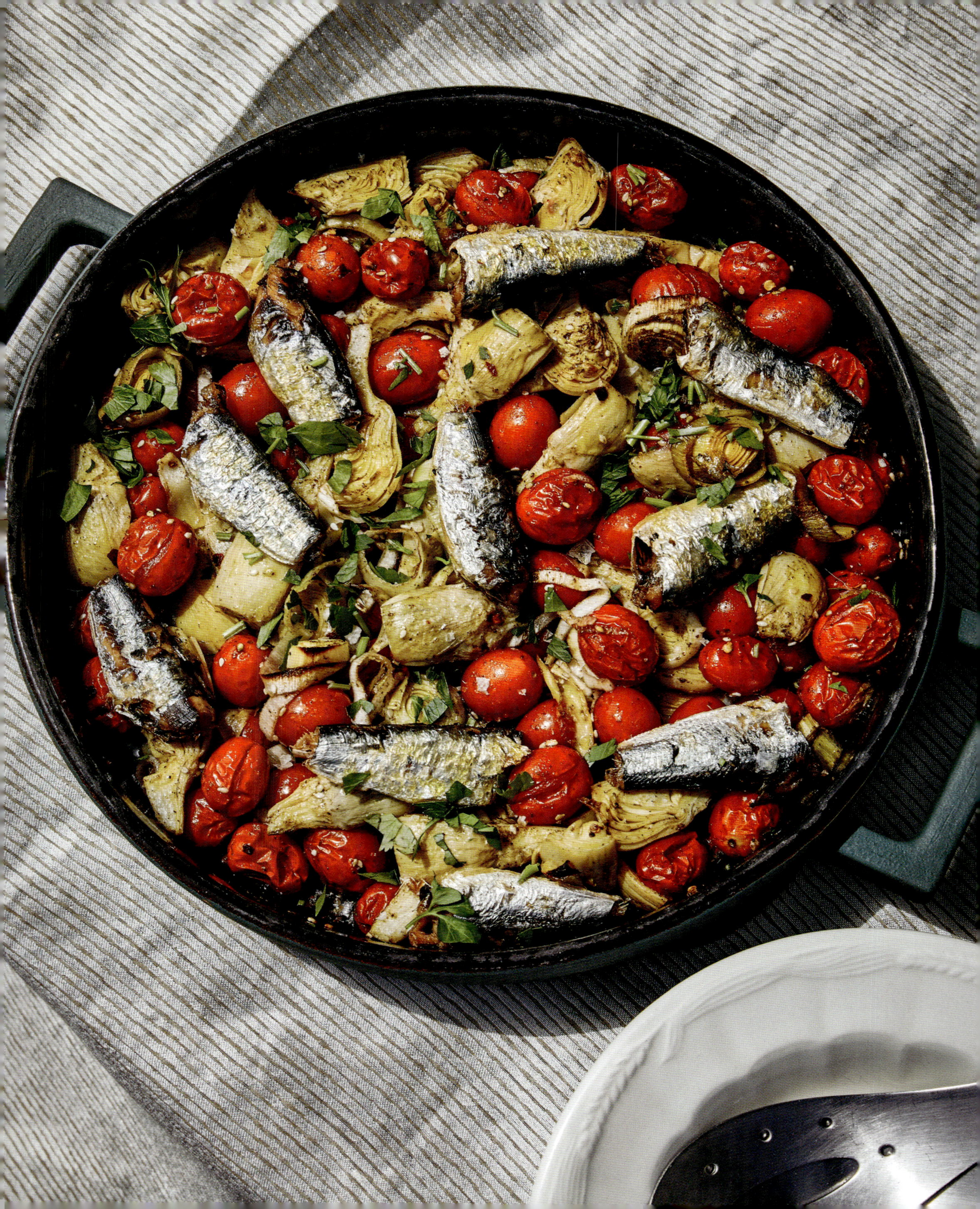

Roasted Tomatoes, Artichokes, and Leeks with Sardines

There's been a real push over the last few years to choose more sustainable seafood options. The most accessible fish on the list is always sardines. And while I love tinned sardines on toast or twirled into pasta, I wanted to come up with a way to make them part of a bigger meal. Here, tomatoes, canned artichokes, leeks, and, of course, sardines are seasoned with za'atar and roasted until the tomatoes have burst and the veg is tender. While sardines can be intense, roasting mellows the flavor.

NOTE: Leftovers can be stored in an airtight container in the refrigerator for up to 3 days.

Serves 4

4 cups cherry tomatoes

2 (14-ounce) cans artichokes, drained

2 medium leeks, white and light green parts only, well washed and thinly sliced

2 tablespoons extra-virgin olive oil

1 tablespoon za'atar

1 teaspoon kosher salt

¼ teaspoon red pepper flakes

2 (4.4-ounce) tins sardines packed in oil

2 teaspoons sherry vinegar

½ bunch flat-leaf parsley, coarsely chopped (about 1 cup)

1. Preheat the oven to 425°F.

2. Place the tomatoes, artichokes, and fennel on a rimmed baking sheet. Drizzle with olive oil and season with za'atar, salt, and red pepper flakes and toss with your hands to combine, spreading the mixture in an even layer.

3. Place the sardines on top of the vegetables and roast until the tomatoes are softened and the artichokes and fennel have charred in some places, 20 to 25 minutes. Drizzle with the vinegar and sprinkle with the parsley, then carefully stir to combine, making sure to keep the sardines intact.

4. Serve immediately.

Shrimp Salad with Horseradish Aioli Dressing

This springy salad is all about the shrimp. Poaching shrimp is my favorite back-pocket weeknight move. You can utilize it for shrimp cocktail, of course, a shrimp boil (see page 229), or here, topped over Little Gem lettuce and smothered in a horseradish-spiked aioli. Note that because this dressing is meant to be poured over, it's a little looser than a classic aioli.

NOTES: The horseradish aioli can be made up to 2 days ahead and kept in an airtight container in the refrigerator. The shrimp can be poached up to 3 days in advance and kept in an airtight container in the refrigerator. The peas are best served fresh.

1. **Make the horseradish aioli:** Whisk together the egg yolks, mustard, garlic, salt, and pepper in a medium bowl to combine. Add a few drops of olive oil and whisk to combine. Drop by drop, add the olive oil, whisking until the mixture begins to emulsify and thicken. When the mixture has thickened, slowly whisk in the rest of the olive oil, then the grapeseed oil. Add the lemon juice and horseradish and whisk to combine. Taste and adjust the seasoning.

2. **Make the salad:** Combine the lemon juice, salt, and white wine in a large pot, fill it with cold water, and bring to a boil over high heat. Add the asparagus and blanch for 2 minutes. Turn off the heat, add the shrimp and peas, and let stand until the shrimp turn pink and opaque, about 3 minutes. Drain in a colander.

3. Arrange the lettuce on a platter and top with the shrimp, asparagus, and peas. Drizzle the salad with the horseradish aioli, sprinkle with pepper, and serve immediately.

Serves 4

HORSERADISH AIOLI

2 large egg yolks

1 teaspoon Dijon mustard

1 garlic clove, grated

½ teaspoon kosher salt, plus more as needed

⅛ teaspoon freshly ground black pepper, plus more as needed

¼ cup extra-virgin olive oil

¼ cup grapeseed oil

Juice of 1 lemon (about 2 tablespoons)

2 tablespoons prepared horseradish

SHRIMP SALAD

Juice of 1 lemon (about 2 tablespoons)

2 teaspoons kosher salt

1 cup dry white wine, such as sauvignon blanc or pinot grigio

1 bunch asparagus, halved crosswise, ends trimmed

1 pound shrimp, peeled and deveined (see Notes, page 152)

1 (10-ounce) bag frozen peas, thawed

3 Little Gem lettuces, or 2 heads baby romaine, leaves separated

Freshly ground black pepper, for serving

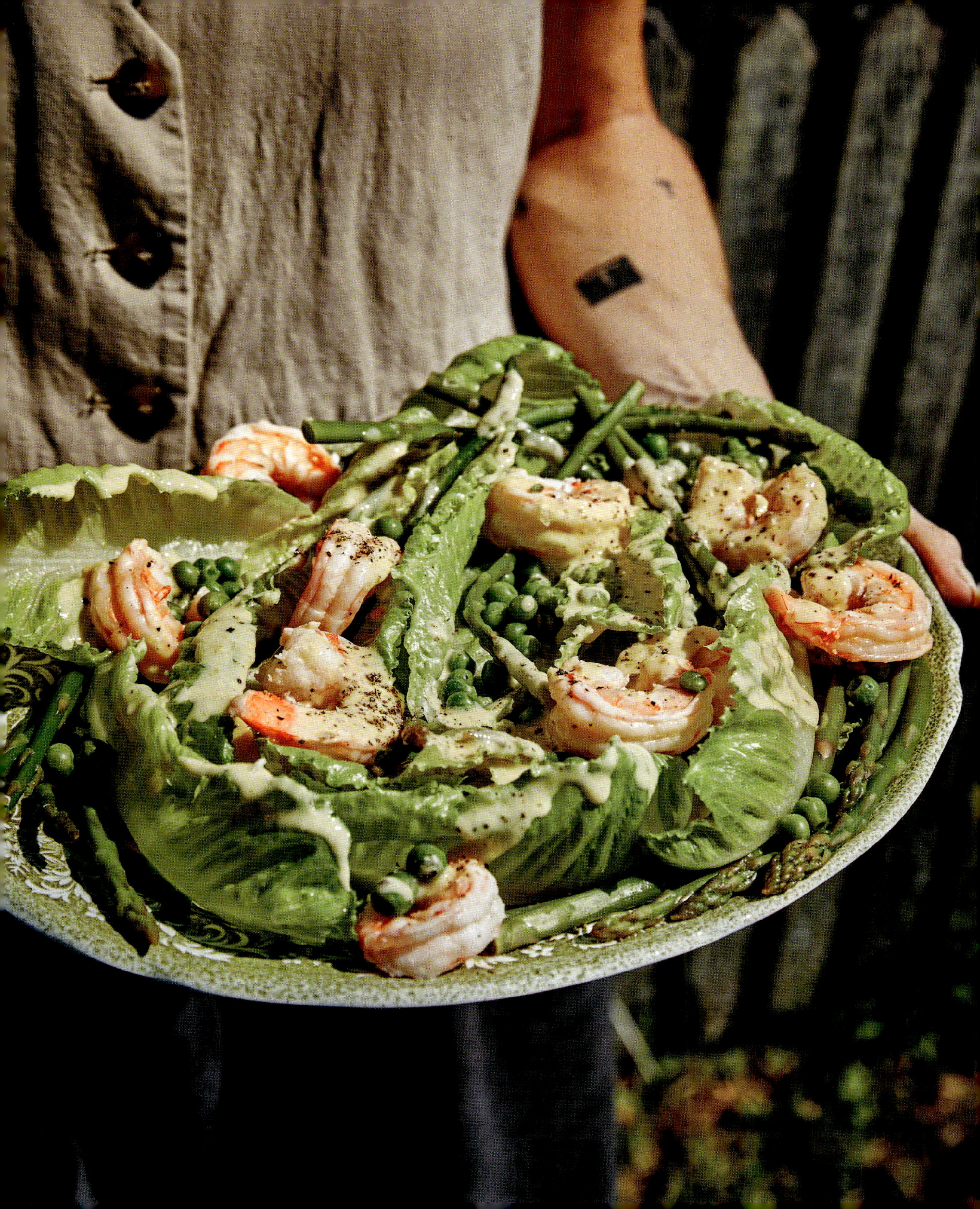

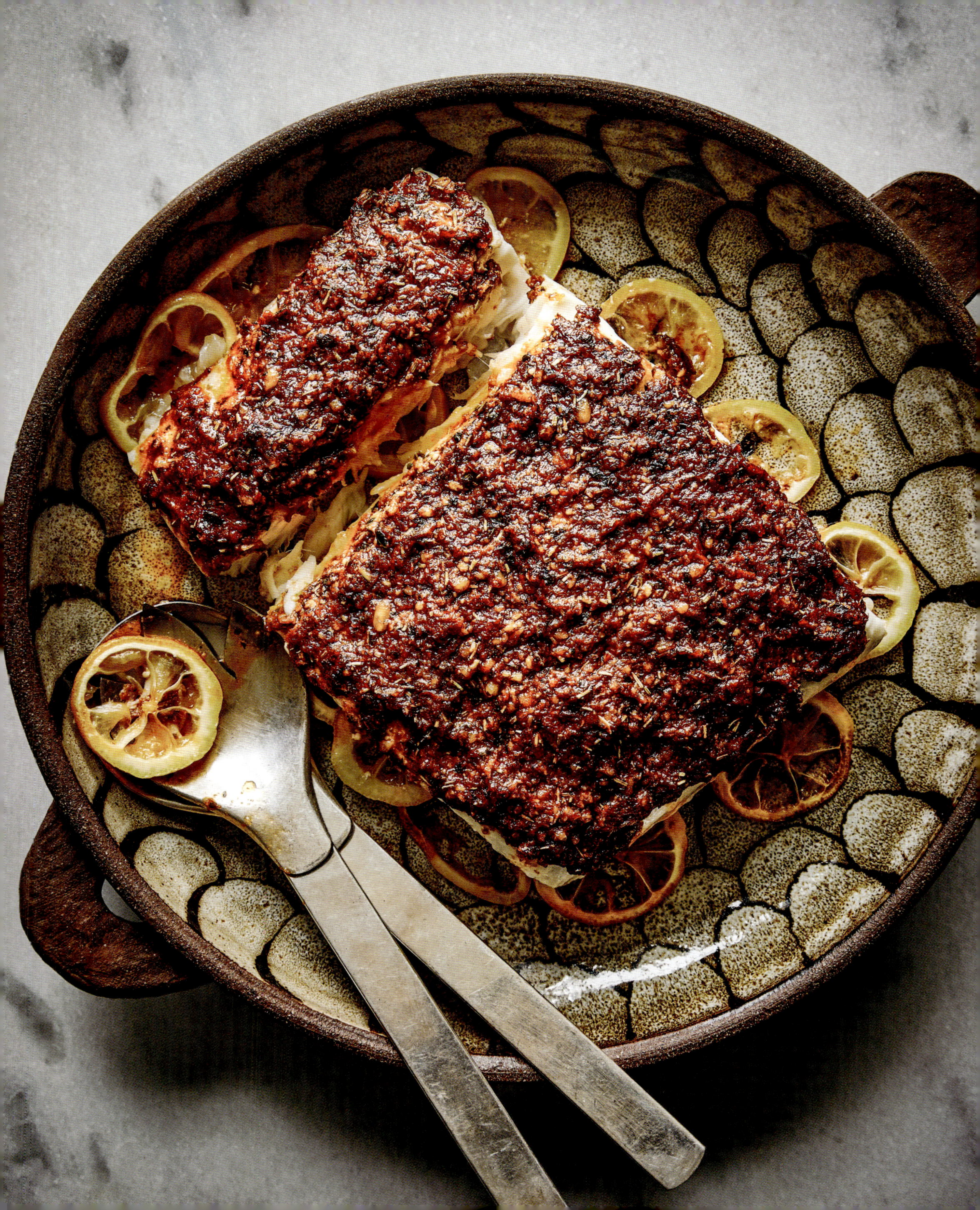

Baked Halibut with Pesto Rosso

This is a public service announcement to bring sun-dried tomatoes back into your life. Pesto rosso is a Sicilian-style pesto that uses these intensely concentrated umami-packed tomatoes in place of basil. While it differs flavor-wise from the herby green version we all know and love, pesto rosso can be used similarly—twirled into pasta, on sandwiches, or like this, draped over fish. A mild white fish like halibut (cod or grouper would work, too) acts as a blank canvas to absorb the flavors of this dynamic sauce that gets spiked with rosemary, balsamic vinegar, and pepper flakes.

NOTES: Reserve the olive oil from the jar of sun-dried tomatoes and use it as part of the olive oil that gets drizzled into the pesto (most likely you'll need to supplement it with olive oil from your pantry). This is a great way to add extra flavor while cutting down on food waste. Pesto rosso can be made up to 1 week in advance and stored in an airtight container in the refrigerator. Leftover cooked halibut can be stored in an airtight container in the refrigerator for up to 3 days.

1. Preheat the oven to 400°F.
2. **Make the pesto rosso:** Combine the sun-dried tomatoes, basil, pine nuts, Parmigiano Reggiano, garlic, rosemary, balsamic vinegar, salt, pepper, and red pepper flakes in a food processor and pulse until finely chopped. Scrape down the sides of the processor bowl with a spatula. With the motor running, add the olive oil in a steady stream and process until smooth.
3. **Make the halibut:** Spread the lemons on a rimmed baking sheet in an even layer. Pat the halibut dry with paper towels and season with salt. Transfer the halibut to the baking sheet on top of the lemons. Spread the pesto over the fillets in an even layer.
4. Bake until the halibut is cooked through and easily flakes, 13 to 15 minutes. Serve immediately.

Serves 4

PESTO ROSSO

1 cup sun-dried tomatoes packed in olive oil

½ cup loosely packed fresh basil leaves

¼ cup pine nuts

¼ cup freshly grated Parmigiano Reggiano cheese

3 garlic cloves, coarsely chopped

1 tablespoon dried rosemary

2 teaspoons balsamic vinegar

½ teaspoon kosher salt

½ teaspoon freshly ground black pepper

½ teaspoon red pepper flakes

½ cup extra-virgin olive oil

HALIBUT

2 lemons, thinly sliced and seeded

1 (2-pound) halibut fillet

1 teaspoon kosher salt

Hot Butter Garlic Shrimp

I'm an equal-opportunity shrimp lover, but my absolute favorite preparations involve copious amounts of butter and garlic. Here there's both, along with hot sauce and lime juice for a kick. Think of it like an elevated Buffalo sauce. The shrimp cooks quickly, so it's imperative you have everything prepped and ready to go before you start cooking. What you serve with this shrimp is up to you—rice, crusty bread, or even pasta are all great options.

NOTES: To cut down on prep time, buy shrimp that has already been peeled and deveined. You can find this in the frozen seafood section of your grocery store. Leftover shrimp and sauce can be stored in an airtight container in the refrigerator for up to 3 days.

Serves 4

- 2 pounds shrimp, peeled and deveined
- 1 tablespoon extra-virgin olive oil
- 1½ teaspoons kosher salt
- 1 teaspoon freshly ground black pepper
- 3 tablespoons unsalted butter
- 3 garlic cloves, minced
- 2 tablespoon hot sauce, sauce of choice
- Juice of 2 limes (about ¼ cup)
- ½ bunch cilantro, coarsely chopped (about 1 cup)

1. Pat the shrimp dry with paper towels. Heat the olive oil in a large pan over medium-high heat. When the oil begins to shimmer, add the shrimp and season with salt and pepper. Cook, without stirring, until one side of the shrimp turns pink, about 1 minute.

2. Flip the shrimp over and cook, without stirring, for 1 minute. Add the butter, garlic, and hot sauce and stir until the butter has melted and the shrimp is fully coated, about 1 minute.

3. Remove the pan from the heat, add the lime juice and cilantro, and stir to combine. Serve immediately.

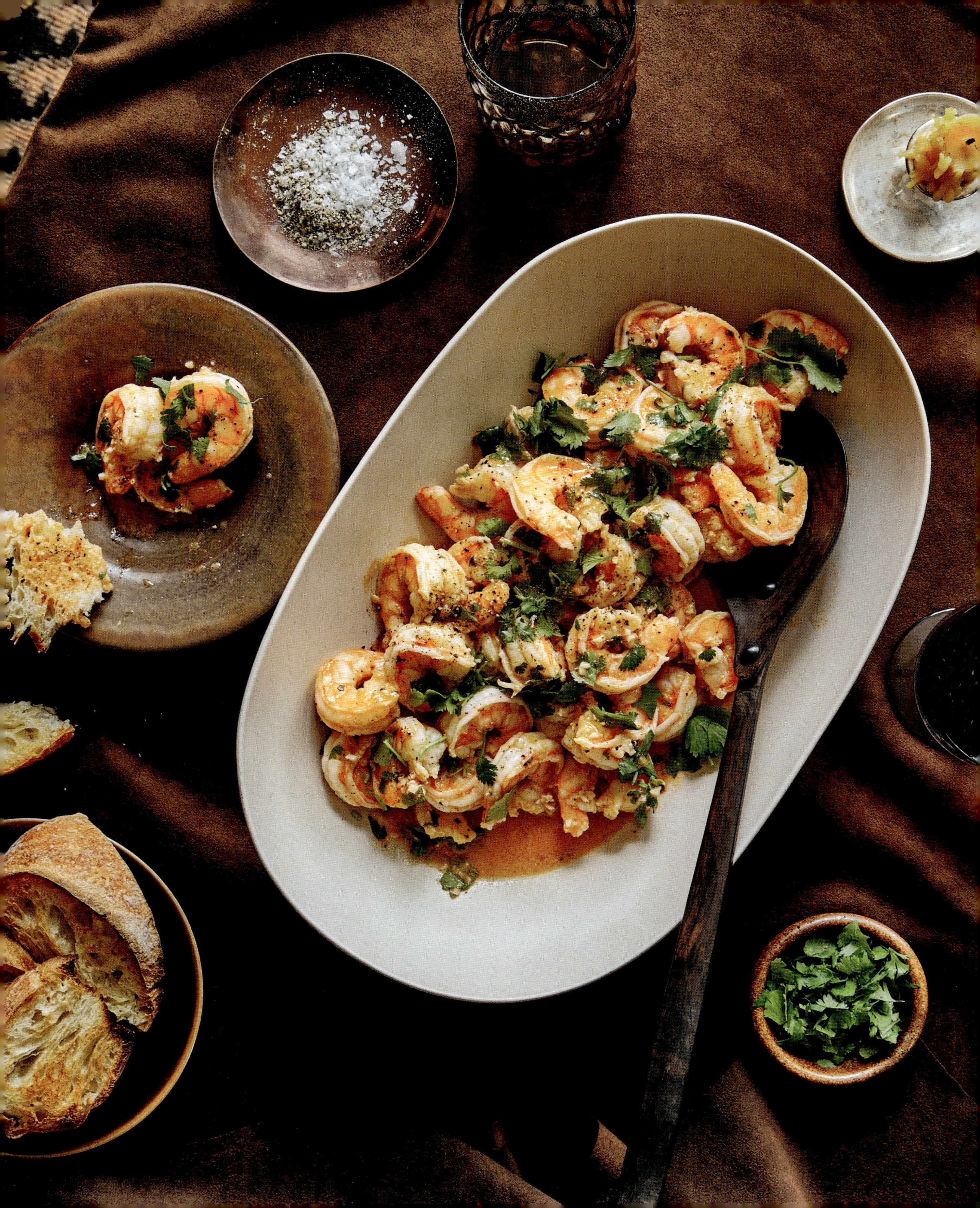

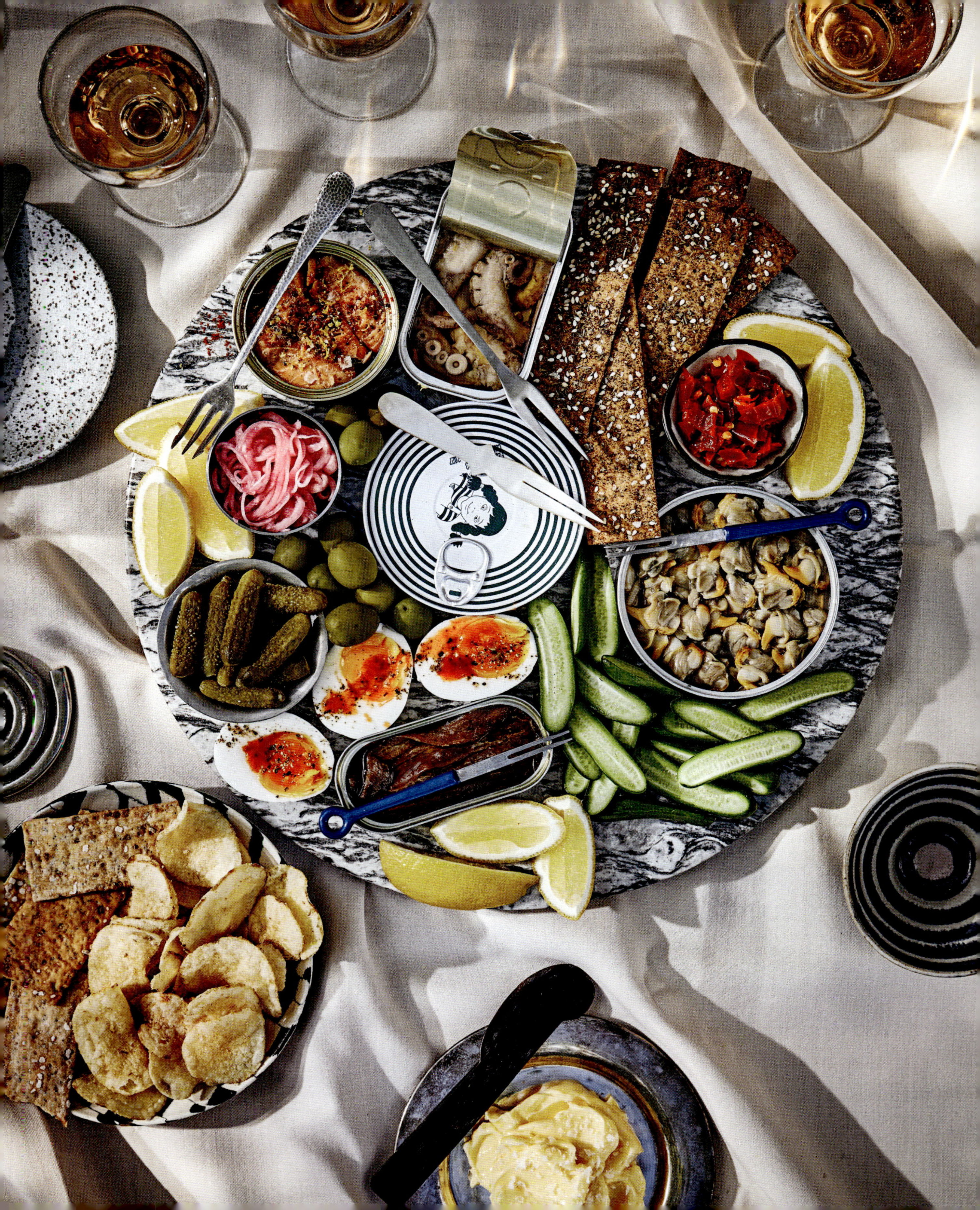

Conserva Plate

Whenever I see my friend Rebekah, I can be sure that one of our meals will be a spread of conservas, aka tinned fish. For two people who develop recipes for a living, it's always a welcome reprieve from the endless cycle of cooking and dishes to turn to a path of least resistance. I've adopted this meal on my laziest days when all I can muster is opening a jar or can. There's no real recipe, as it's essentially putting the fish on a plate with a few accoutrements. The most important thing to remember when assembling a conserva plate is that it should be *easy*. Here's how Rebekah and I do it.

- To start, figure 1 to 2 tins of fish per person. I think an assortment is always best, and there's a world of possibilities, depending on your preference—sardines, mussels, tuna, anchovies, cockles, mackerel, lobster, salmon, trout, squid, clams . . .

- Next, consider what you'll serve alongside the fish. Remember, weeknight dinners mean leaning into what's already stocked in your pantry, so any type of crackers, baguette, or sliced bread will do. A smear of room-temperature butter sprinkled with flaky sea salt is always a good idea, too. I like to include a few punchy, vinegar elements to help cut the fat of the fish, like pickled red onions and cornichons. Along that line, sliced lemon and hot sauce are musts, or even something like salsa macha or chile crisp, to add acid and heat.

- If you're looking to buff out your conserva spread, you probably have other elements on hand to gussy it up—kind of like you would a cheese spread. Mustard, olives, roasted peppers, canned artichokes, and pepperoncini are all fun sides. Sliced radishes, cucumbers, and even a side salad can make the spread feel a little more well-rounded without much heavy lifting. And of course, a side of jammy eggs is always welcome (see page 167).

WEEK

ENDS

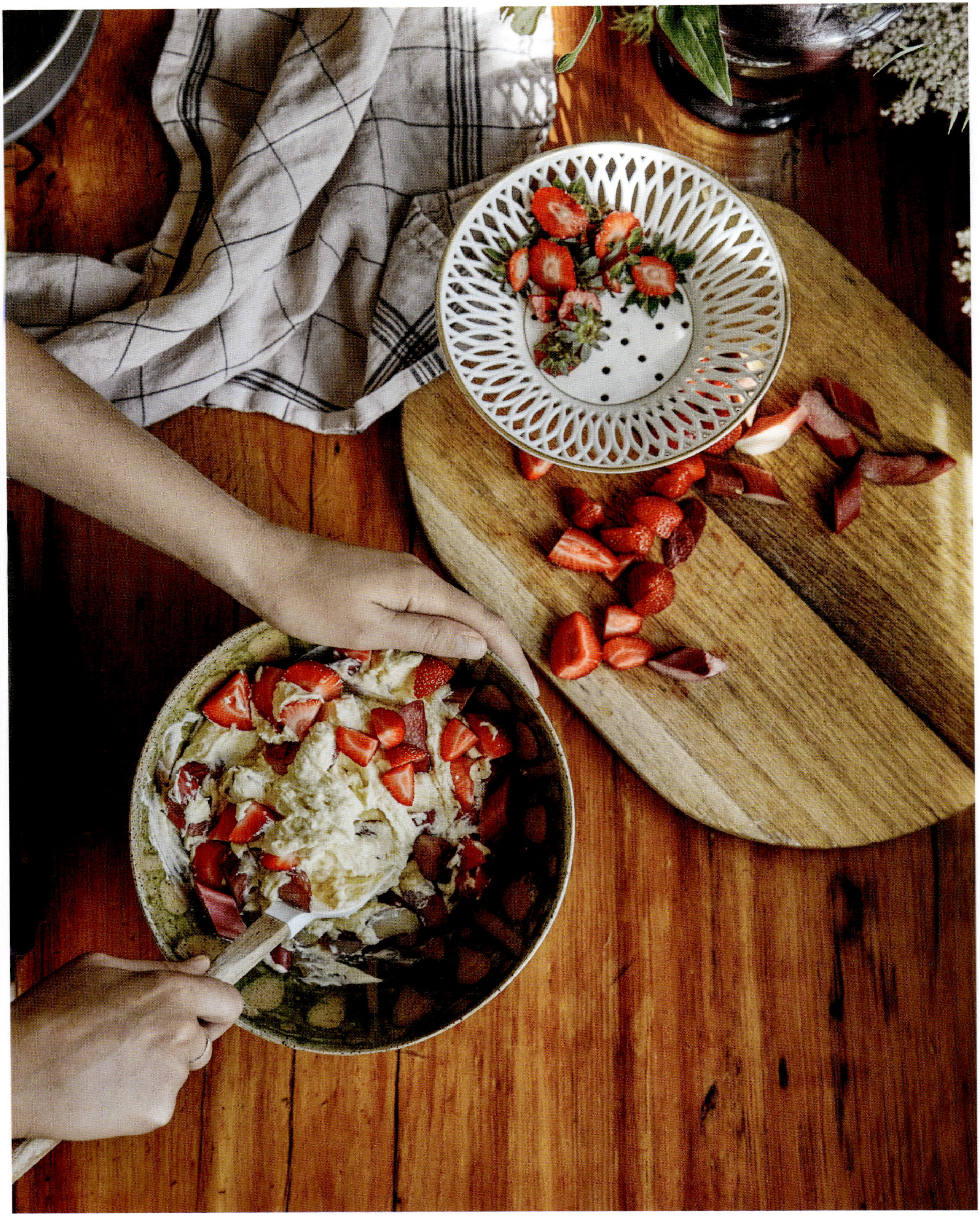

Cooking on a Weekend

The real differentiator between a meal you might make on a weeknight versus a weekend is time. Let me be clear. There's absolutely nothing stopping you from shallow-frying breaded tofu on a Tuesday or making a two-tiered Pavlova after work just because. But I want to make the boundaries of time clear between the two sets of recipes. If weeknight cooking is all about utility, cooking on the weekend is about leaning in to really enjoy the process of what you're making.

There's nothing better to me than sitting around a table, sharing a meal with the people I love. And while I've been known to host dinners throughout the week, weekends are when I'm mostly likely to pull out all the stops. They're where I have the space to put time and effort into what I'm making. Nothing delights me quite like spending Saturday morning rolling, rising, and glazing sticky buns, or taking an afternoon to dock and crimp an apple pie towering high with a brown butter crumble. Hosting means putting together a snack spread that could suffice as a meal on its own. It's having a bar set up and ready with my friends' favorite drinks, or at least everything they need to serve themselves.

The weekend recipes encompass more than dinner. The chapters in this section are meant to carry you through all the meals that you might make in a weekend, from brunch, snacks, and dinner to, of course, dessert. While the dishes here aren't hard, they take a bit more time and effort, whether that's tending to the stove to ensure each piece of lamb shoulder is braised until deeply browned, for example, or taking a few steps to create a perfectly roasted whole cauliflower.

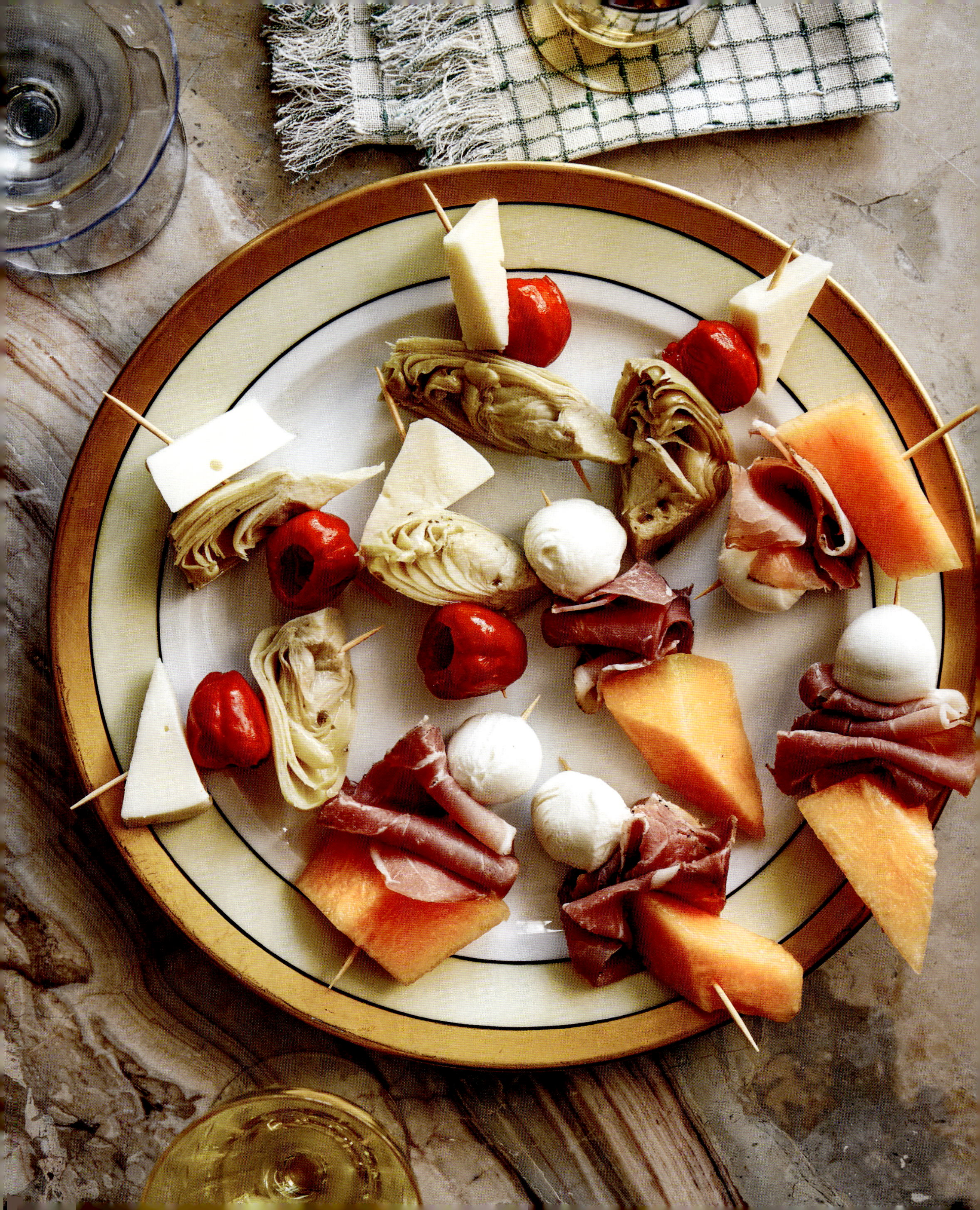

WEEKENDS

SNACKS

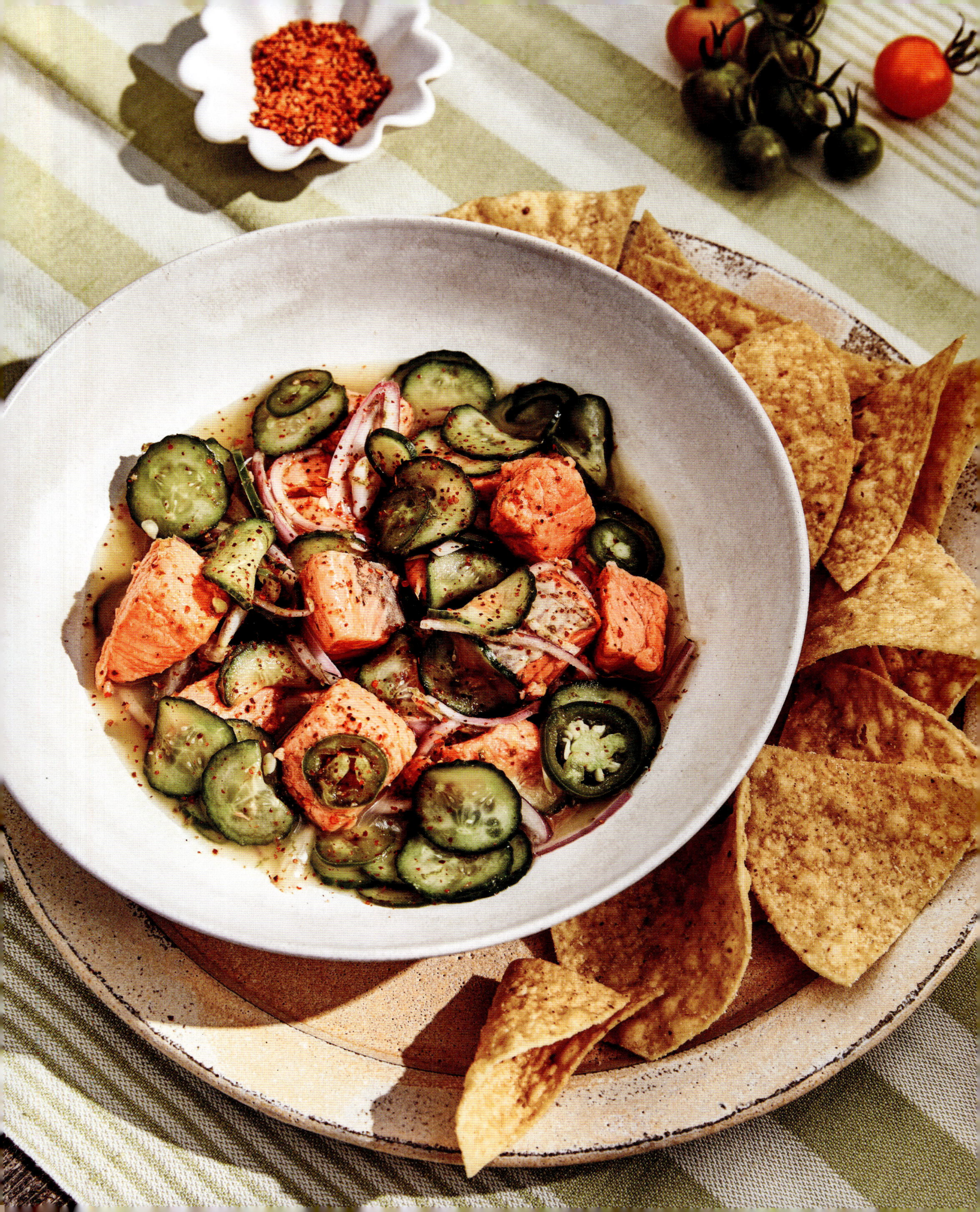

Salmon Ceviche with Cucumber and Tajín

I love ceviche for its ease—everything can be prepped ahead of time and thrown together right before your guests show up—and of course, it's also delicious. Yes, ceviche uses raw fish, and no, you shouldn't be afraid to make it. Okay, there are a couple of caveats. It's important to use the freshest fish possible. The acid from the lime juice "cooks" the fish, so don't let it marinate for too long or the fish will become tough and rubbery. This version hits all my favorite flavor notes: crunchy, spicy, and zesty.

NOTES: If you don't have salmon, you could make this with shrimp, scallops, red snapper, sea bass, grouper, or another firm-fleshed fish. While the ceviche is best eaten immediately, you can store leftovers in an airtight container in the refrigerator for up to 24 hours. Just keep in mind that the texture of the fish will change.

1. Combine the salmon, cucumbers, lime zest, lime juice, shallot, jalapeño, salt, and Tajín in a medium bowl and mix well. Make sure the fish is submerged in lime juice. If not, add more lime juice. Cover the bowl with plastic wrap and transfer to the refrigerator until the fish is opaque and just "cooked" through, 40 to 45 minutes.

2. Transfer the ceviche to a serving bowl and sprinkle with Tajín. Serve immediately, with tortilla chips.

Serves a crowd

1½ pounds salmon, skin removed, cut into ½-inch cubes

4 Persian cucumbers, thinly sliced

Zest of 2 limes

Juice of 6 limes (about 6 tablespoons), plus more if needed

1 large shallot, thinly sliced

1 jalapeño, thinly sliced

1½ teaspoons kosher salt

1 teaspoon Tajín, plus more for serving

Tortilla chips, for serving

Caramelized Shallot Dip

You'd be hard-pressed to show up at a millennial dinner party in the last five years and not be served caramelized onion dip. It's a hit for a reason: Caramelizing brings out the natural sweetness of alliums, and combining them with sour cream creates an addictive dip. I've swapped onions for shallots (my allium of choice), which offer a mellower flavor than onions.

NOTES: Caramelized shallots can be made up to 3 days in advance and stored in an airtight container in the refrigerator. If you don't have shallots, onions will of course work in their place. The sherry vinegar is crucial for the depth of flavor here: You can use red wine vinegar or champagne vinegar instead—or, in a pinch, even lemon juice.

1. Heat the olive oil in a large pan over medium-low heat. When the oil begins to shimmer, add the shallots and cook, stirring often, until deeply golden brown and aromatic, about 15 minutes. Add the salt and vinegar and cook, stirring, until the vinegar has been absorbed, about 1 minute. Remove the pan from the heat and let cool to room temperature.

2. Transfer the caramelized shallots to a medium bowl, add the sour cream, mayonnaise, and pepper, and stir to combine.

Serves a crowd

- 2 tablespoons extra-virgin olive oil
- 4 large shallots, thinly sliced (about 2 cups)
- 1 teaspoon kosher salt
- 1 tablespoon sherry vinegar
- 1 cup full-fat sour cream
- ¼ cup mayonnaise
- 1 teaspoon freshly ground black pepper
- Chips, for serving

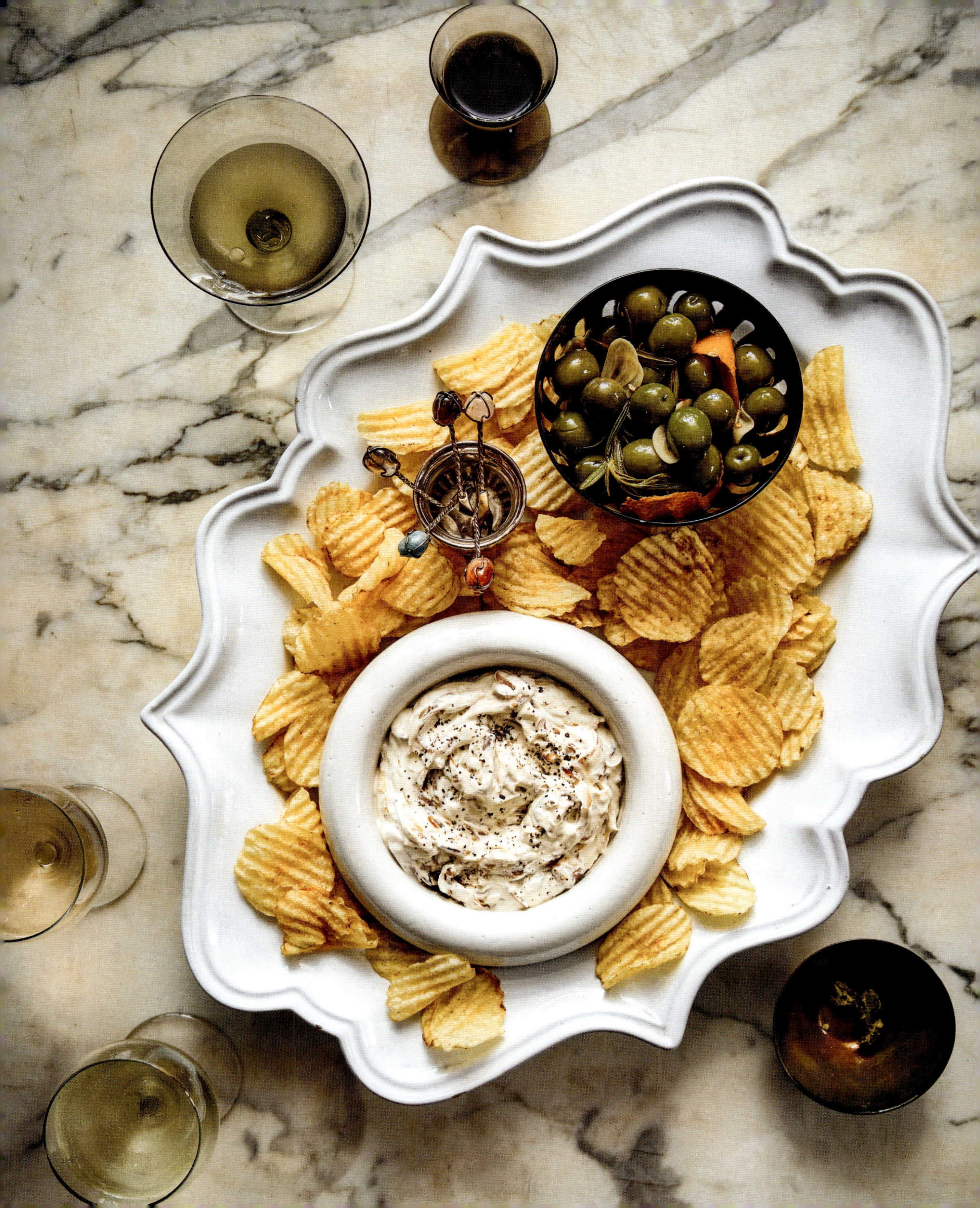

Marinated Olives in Citrus and Spices

If friends are coming over and you're in a time crunch, marinated olives are the perfect snack. They offer a wow factor with comically little effort. I always keep a jar (or three) of olives on hand for this exact reason. While I love the combination of herbs and spices listed here, you can use it as inspiration to make your own with whatever you have on hand. Lemons, thyme, peppercorns, balsamic vinegar, and bay leaves are all great options.

NOTE: Olives can be made up to 1 week in advance and kept in an airtight container in the refrigerator.

Serves 4 to 6

- ½ cup extra-virgin olive oil
- Strips of rind from 1 small orange
- 2 rosemary sprigs
- 2 garlic cloves, thinly sliced
- 1 tablespoon sherry vinegar
- ½ teaspoon red pepper flakes
- ¼ teaspoon fennel seeds
- 2 cups mixed olives

1. Combine the olive oil, orange rind, rosemary, garlic, vinegar, red pepper flakes, and fennel seeds in a small pot. Cook over medium-low heat until the garlic sizzles and smells deeply aromatic, about 3 minutes.

2. Place the olives in a jar or resealable glass container and pour the olive oil mixture over the top. Let cool to room temperature, then cover and refrigerate for at least 1 hour (preferably 24 hours) or up to 1 week.

3. Remove the olives from the refrigerator and let them sit at room temperature for 1 hour before serving.

Jammy Eggs with Mayo and Chile Oil

If you're looking for an easy, affordable, make-ahead appetizer, this is it. This preparation is so simple that a recipe is almost unnecessary—all you do is steam eggs, then add a swipe of mayonnaise, a drizzle of chile oil, and a sprinkle of flaky sea salt. Steaming eggs has become my go-to method, ensuring an easier-to-peel egg that delivers perfectly jammy eggs every time. While you could cook them longer, getting the eggs jammy is ideal for this recipe. They're not so soft that the mayonnaise slips off, but not hard enough that you might as well make deviled eggs.

NOTES: Eggs can be boiled up to 3 days in advance and kept whole. When ready to serve, simply peel, halve, and proceed with the toppings. Rather than using fresh eggs, opt for slightly older eggs—they are easier to peel. Peeling them in a bowl of water also helps the shells come off more easily.

Serves 4 to 6

6 large eggs
Mayonnaise, for serving
Chile oil, for serving
Flaky salt, for serving

1. Fill a large pot with 1 inch of water and place a steamer basket in the pot, making sure the water doesn't touch the bottom of the basket. Bring the water to a boil over high heat. Carefully add the eggs to the steamer basket, cover the pot, and cook for 9 minutes, then transfer to a bowl of cold water. Let the eggs cool in the water for at least 5 minutes or up to 1 hour.

2. Peel and halve the eggs. Add a smear of mayonnaise over the egg yolks, then drizzle them with chile oil and sprinkle with flaky salt. Serve immediately.

Jammy Eggs with Mayo and Chile Oil, page 167

Soy-Blistered Shishitos

Shishitos have become so popular over the last few years that you can almost always find them year-round in your local grocery store—seriously, my town of 3,000 people has them—so they're an ideal snack to have in your back pocket. The key to making shishitos well is to blister the hell out of them in a hot pan until they're charred all over. I like adding some soy sauce at the end for a bit more depth of flavor.

NOTES: This recipe is easily doubled, or even tripled. Shishitos are best served hot, but leftovers can be stored in an airtight container in the refrigerator for up to 2 days, if needed.

1 Heat the olive oil in a large pan over high heat. When the oil begins to shimmer and the pan is on the cusp of smoking, add the shishito peppers. Cook, stirring occasionally, until blistered on all sides, about 5 minutes. Remove the pan from the heat, add the soy sauce, and stir until combined.

2 Top the shishitos with flaky salt and serve immediately.

Serves 4

1 tablespoon extra-virgin olive oil

1 (8-ounce) bag shishito peppers

1 tablespoon soy sauce

Flaky salt, for serving

Hot Cheesy Crab Dip

A friend introduced me to hot crab dip years ago, and it's become a snack staple in my house. While I typically favor keeping seafood and cheese separate, this is an exception. It's crucial to go heavy on the cheese in this preparation. This Maryland staple mixes a quartet of dairy with lump crabmeat and a generous dose of Old Bay seasoning and hot sauce to pack a punch. I've added more acid and alliums than most recipes call for to cut the richness of the dish (and encourage you to go back for more).

NOTES: The crab dip mixture can be prepared up to 2 days in advance and kept in an airtight container in the refrigerator. When ready to serve, preheat the oven and continue as the recipe states. This recipe can be easily doubled; just make sure to use a bigger vessel than the recipe calls for.

Serves 4 to 6

- 4 ounces full-fat cream cheese, at room temperature
- 1 cup shredded cheddar cheese
- ¼ cup mayonnaise
- ¼ cup full-fat sour cream
- 1 bunch scallions, thinly sliced
- Juice of 1 lemon (about 2 tablespoons)
- 1½ teaspoons Old Bay seasoning
- 1 teaspoon Worcestershire sauce
- 1 teaspoon hot sauce of your choice
- 1 (8-ounce) container lump crabmeat, drained and picked through for shells
- Crackers, for serving

1. Position a rack in the upper third of the oven. Preheat the oven to 400°F.

2. Combine the cream cheese, ½ cup of the cheddar, the mayonnaise, sour cream, scallions, lemon juice, Old Bay, Worcestershire, and hot sauce in a medium bowl and stir well.

3. Add the crabmeat and use a spatula to fold until just combined. Transfer the mixture to an 8-inch cast-iron skillet or a similar-size oven-safe vessel and top with the remaining ½ cup cheddar. Bake in the center of the oven rack until golden brown and bubbling, about 15 minutes.

4. Serve immediately, with crackers.

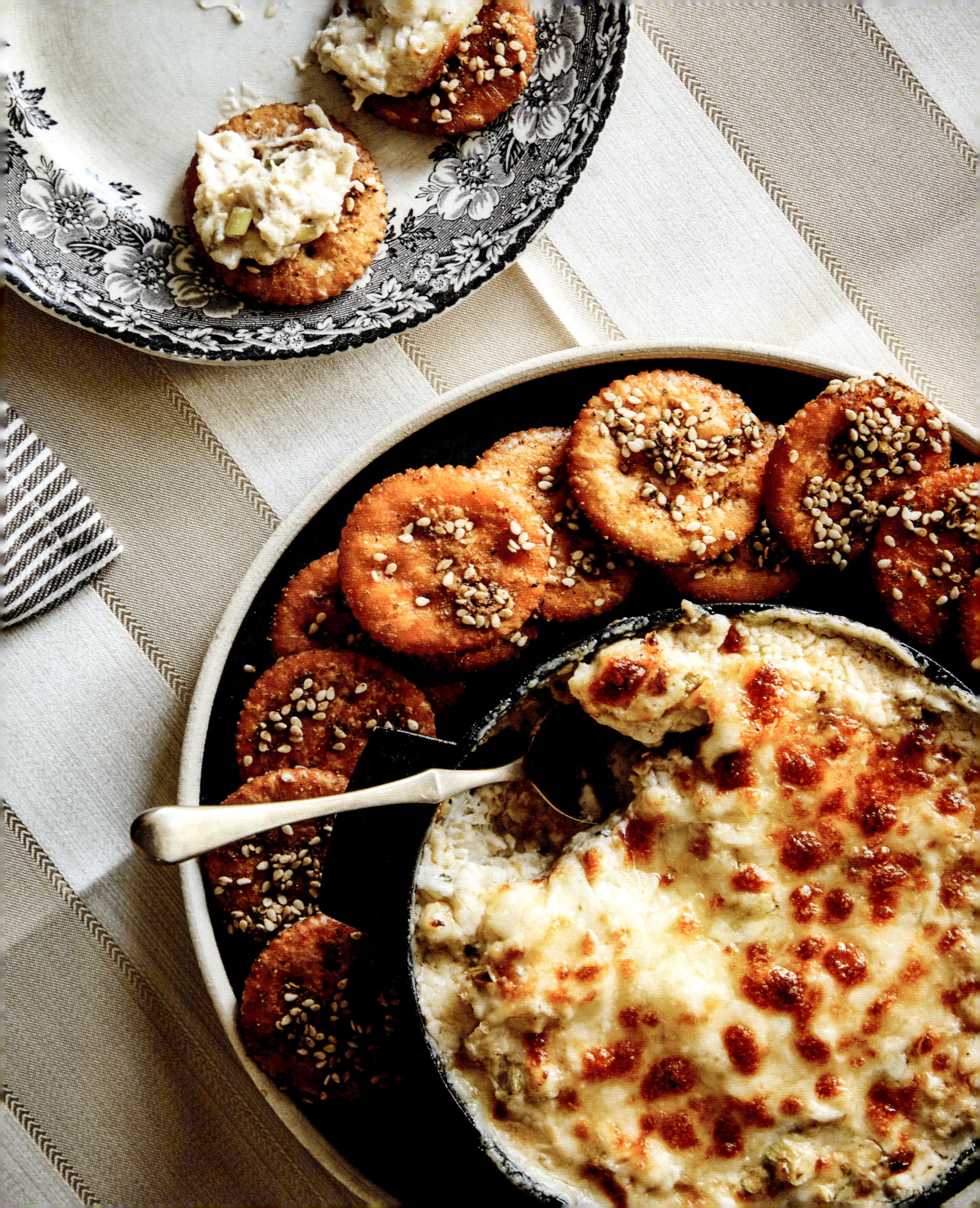

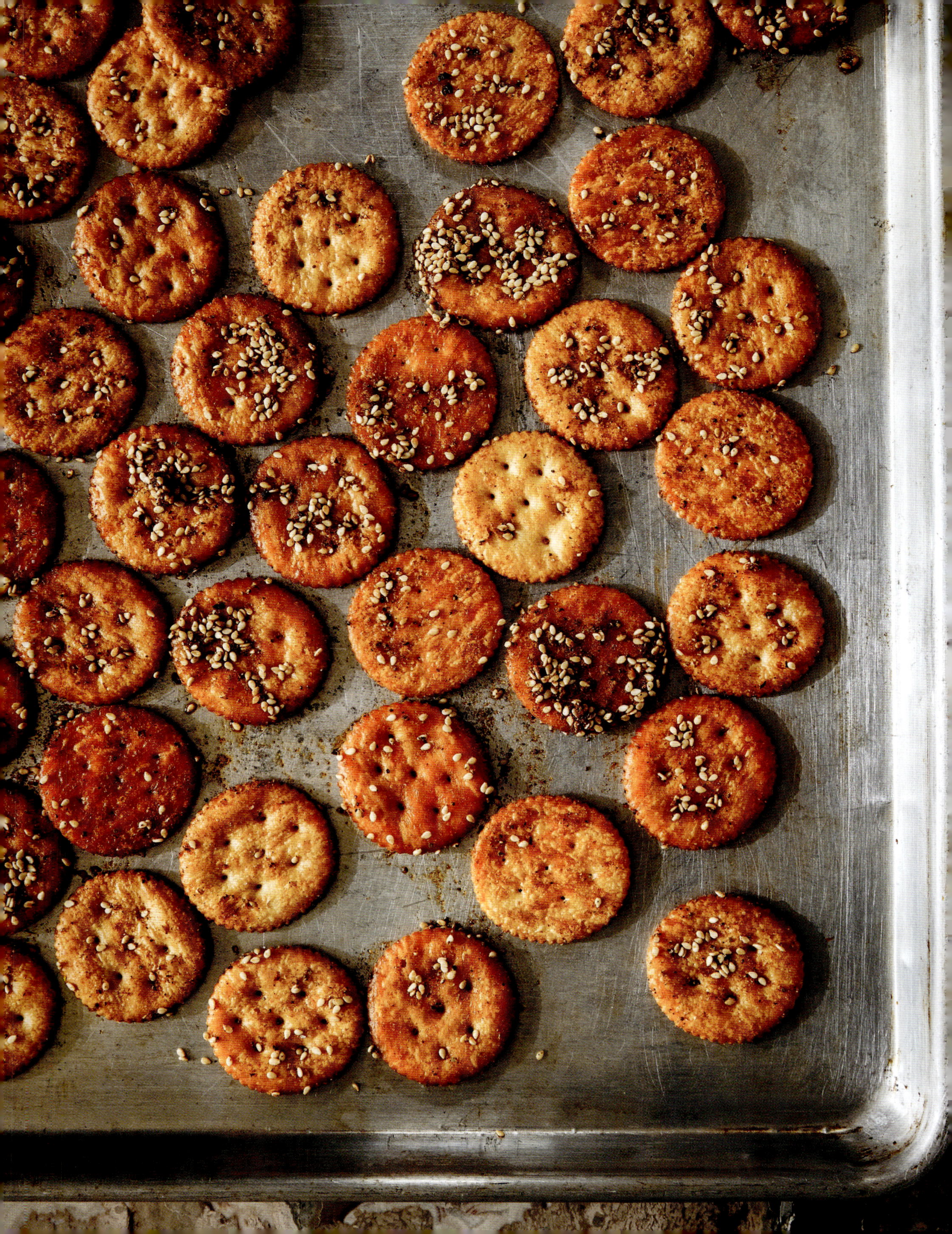

Fire Crackers

Sure, you could serve regular ol' crackers alongside dips, but why not make them the star of the show? Classically, fire crackers, sometimes called Alabama fire crackers, are plain saltines soaked in a mixture of oil and spices and then baked. The trick is to let them sit long enough in the oil mixture to become fully saturated. Once baked, the texture is reminiscent of a tortilla chip hot out of the fryer. I love the combination of sesame seeds and Old Bay, but you could totally experiment with flavors like ranch powder, Italian seasoning, Chinese five-spice, or even furikake.

NOTES: Most often fire crackers are made with saltines, but I love the flavor and texture of Ritz crackers. You could also use oyster crackers or even water crackers, as long as you make sure the amount used is 10 ounces. Crackers can be stored in an airtight container at room temperature for up to 1 week.

Serves a crowd

- ¾ cup extra-virgin olive oil
- ¼ cup sesame seeds
- ¼ cup Old Bay seasoning
- 2 teaspoons hot sauce of choice
- 2 teaspoons freshly ground black pepper
- 1 teaspoon kosher salt
- 10 ounces Ritz crackers (3 sleeves)

1. Combine the olive oil, sesame seeds, Old Bay, and hot sauce in a glass measuring cup and whisk well. Pour the oil mixture into a resealable plastic bag and add the crackers.

2. Let the crackers sit in the oil mixture for at least 2 hours, or up to 24, occasionally shaking the bag to coat the crackers.

3. Preheat the oven 300°F.

4. Place the crackers in a single layer on a rimmed baking sheet (use two pans if the crackers are crowded) and bake until golden brown and crisp, about 10 minutes. Let the crackers cool to room temperature before serving.

Everything Bagel Spice Cheese Ball

The first recipe I developed at my first job straight out of culinary school was for a cheese ball. At the time, this assignment felt like a tall order. I remember being wildly stressed about making sure the recipe was perfect. Not only did I want to impress my boss (an impossible feat), but I wanted to pay homage to the cheese ball's retro history. It turned out my stress was totally unnecessary, as the joy of a cheese ball is that it's really the perfect appetizer to make use of whatever bits of cheese you might have in the refrigerator that you need to use up. In this version, the cheese ball is rolled in everything bagel seasoning and studded with scallions. It's as delicious as an appetizer as it is smeared on a bagel. Use this recipe as a guide, but feel free to swap in whatever cheeses you have on hand as desired.

NOTES: To make your own everything bagel seasoning, refer to the recipe for Everything Bagel Tomato Panzanella on page 84. If you have any leftover cheese ball, store it in an airtight container in the refrigerator for up to 1 week.

Serves a crowd

- ½ cup everything bagel seasoning
- 1 (8-ounce) package full-fat cream cheese, at room temperature
- 1 (4-ounce) package chèvre goat cheese, at room temperature
- 2 cups shredded cheddar cheese
- 2 bunches scallions, thinly sliced
- 1 teaspoon Worcestershire sauce
- 1 teaspoon hot sauce of choice
- ½ teaspoon freshly ground black pepper
- Assorted crackers and crudités, for serving

1. Place the everything bagel seasoning in a small bowl.
2. Combine the cream cheese, goat cheese, cheddar, scallions, Worcestershire, hot sauce, and pepper in a medium bowl and use a spatula to mix well.
3. Use your hands to shape the cheese mixture into a ball. Carefully transfer the cheese ball to the bowl with the everything bagel seasoning and toss until covered in the seasoning.
4. Serve the cheese ball with assorted crackers and crudités.

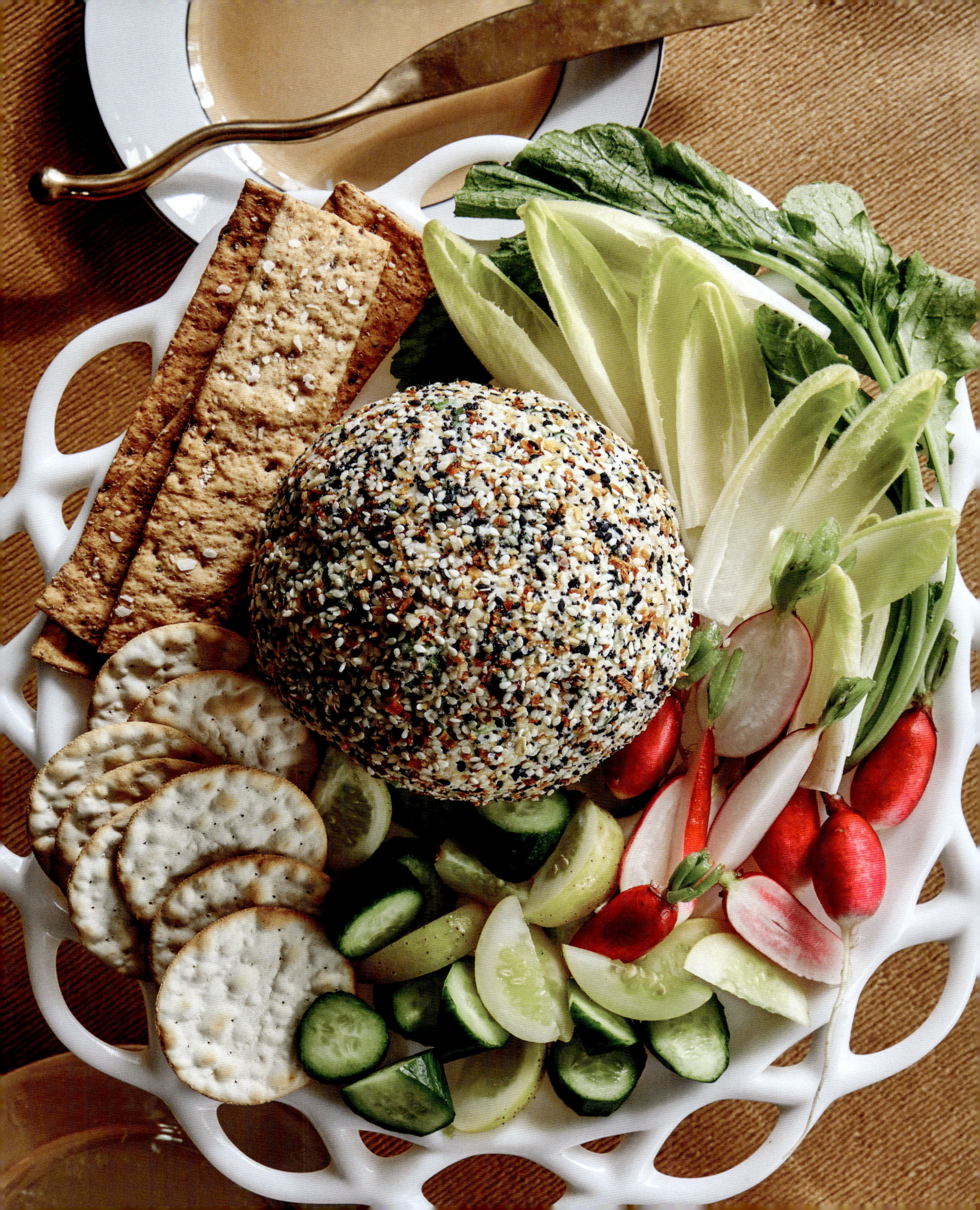

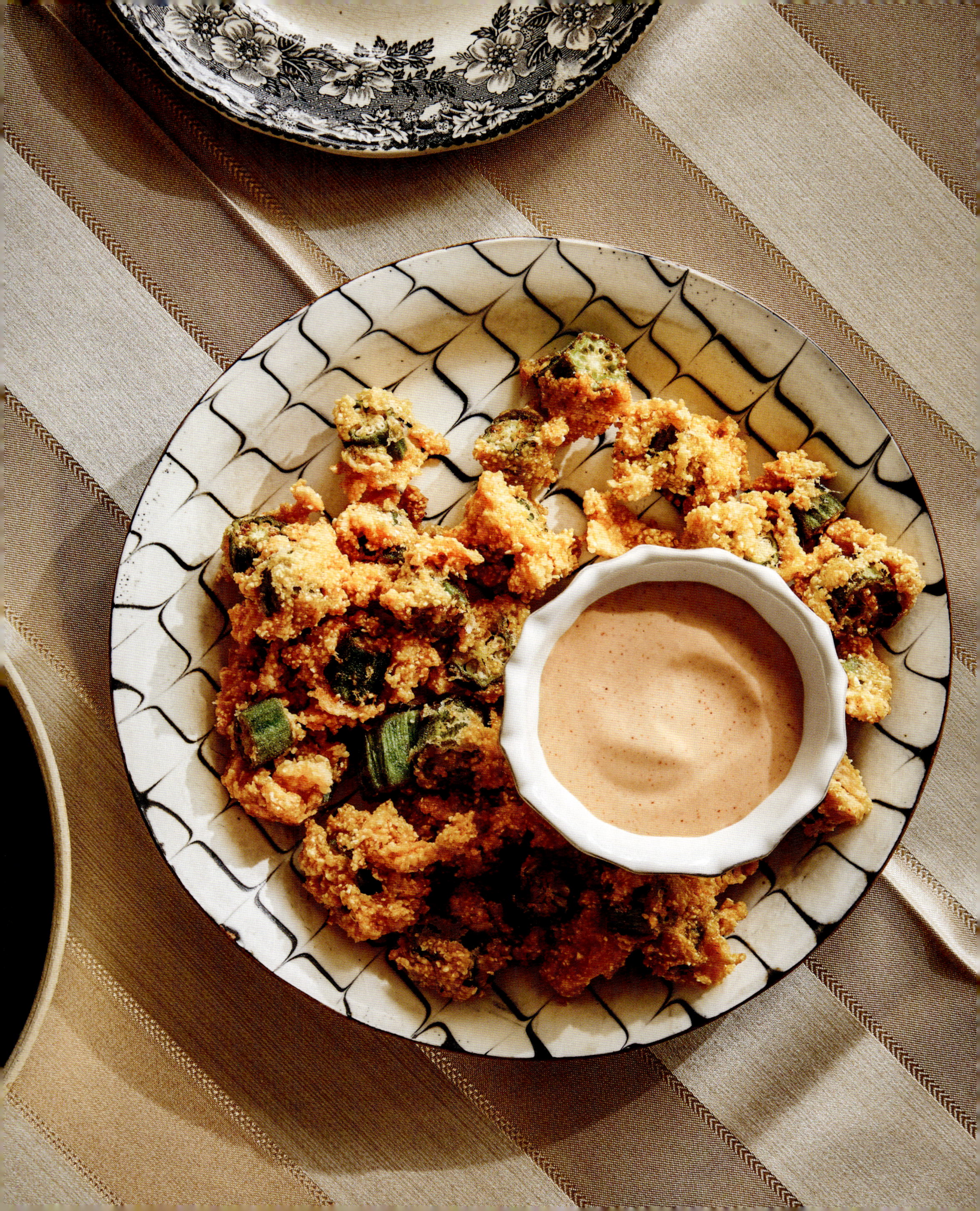

Cornmeal Fried Okra with Special Sauce

This is a recipe inspired by my husband's family (see page 76 for another Kentucky favorite, Summer Squash Casserole). Growing up in upstate New York and spending most of my adulthood in Los Angeles, I didn't have much experience with okra as an ingredient. I did know that it sometimes got a bad rap for being, ahem, slimy. But when I coated it in cornmeal and then fried it until golden brown, I was a quick convert to this crispy, salty snack.

NOTES: The sauce can be made up to 3 days in advance and stored in an airtight container in the refrigerator. Fried okra is best eaten immediately and will lose its crispy exterior if refrigerated.

Serves a crowd

SPECIAL SAUCE
¾ cup mayonnaise
¼ cup ketchup
1 tablespoon champagne vinegar
1 teaspoon Dijon mustard
½ teaspoon sweet paprika

OKRA
2 cups buttermilk
1½ teaspoons kosher salt, plus more to taste
1 teaspoon sweet paprika
1½ pounds okra, ends trimmed, cut into ½-inch pieces
1½ cups cornmeal
1 cup all-purpose flour
Vegetable oil, for frying

1. **Make the sauce:** Whisk together the mayonnaise, ketchup, vinegar, mustard, and paprika in a small bowl.

2. **Make the fried okra:** Pour the buttermilk into a large bowl and add the salt and paprika; whisk to combine. Add the okra and stir until well coated. Use a slotted spoon to transfer the okra to a separate large bowl. Add the cornmeal and flour and toss well.

3. Pour about ½ inch of vegetable oil into a large pot, Dutch oven, or high-sided skillet and heat over high heat. When the oil begins to shimmer, working in batches, add the okra in a single layer and fry, flipping occasionally, until golden brown on all sides, 7 to 8 minutes. Transfer the okra to a paper towel–lined baking sheet and season with salt. Repeat until all the okra is fried.

4. Serve the okra immediately with the sauce on the side for dipping.

Antipasti Skewers

In June, it suddenly feels like everyone on Instagram is jetting off to Europe. Amongst the images of craggy Mediterranean shorelines and winding cobblestone streets, there's a parade of photos showing what they're all eating and drinking abroad. If you too are sitting home dreaming of a European getaway, might I suggest a spread of antipasti skewers to ease the jealousy? I love serving an assortment of these at a party, since there's truly a flavor profile for everyone. You'll notice there are no proportions included here; the proportions will depend on how many people you're feeding. A good rule of thumb is to plan on four skewers per person.

NOTES: Antipasti skewers can be made up to 1 day in advance and stored in an airtight container in the refrigerator.

Place a melon cube, prosciutto slice, and a mozzarella ball on a toothpick or skewer. Place a peppadew pepper, marinated artichoke, and a Fontina cube on a toothpick or skewer. Place an olive, guindilla pepper, and an anchovy on a toothpick or skewer. Repeat with the remaining skewers.

Serves a crowd

Cantaloupe or melon of choice, cut into ½-inch cubes

Prosciutto slices

Mozzarella pearls

Peppadew peppers

Marinated artichokes

Fontina cubes

Pitted Castelvetrano olives

Guindilla peppers

Anchovies

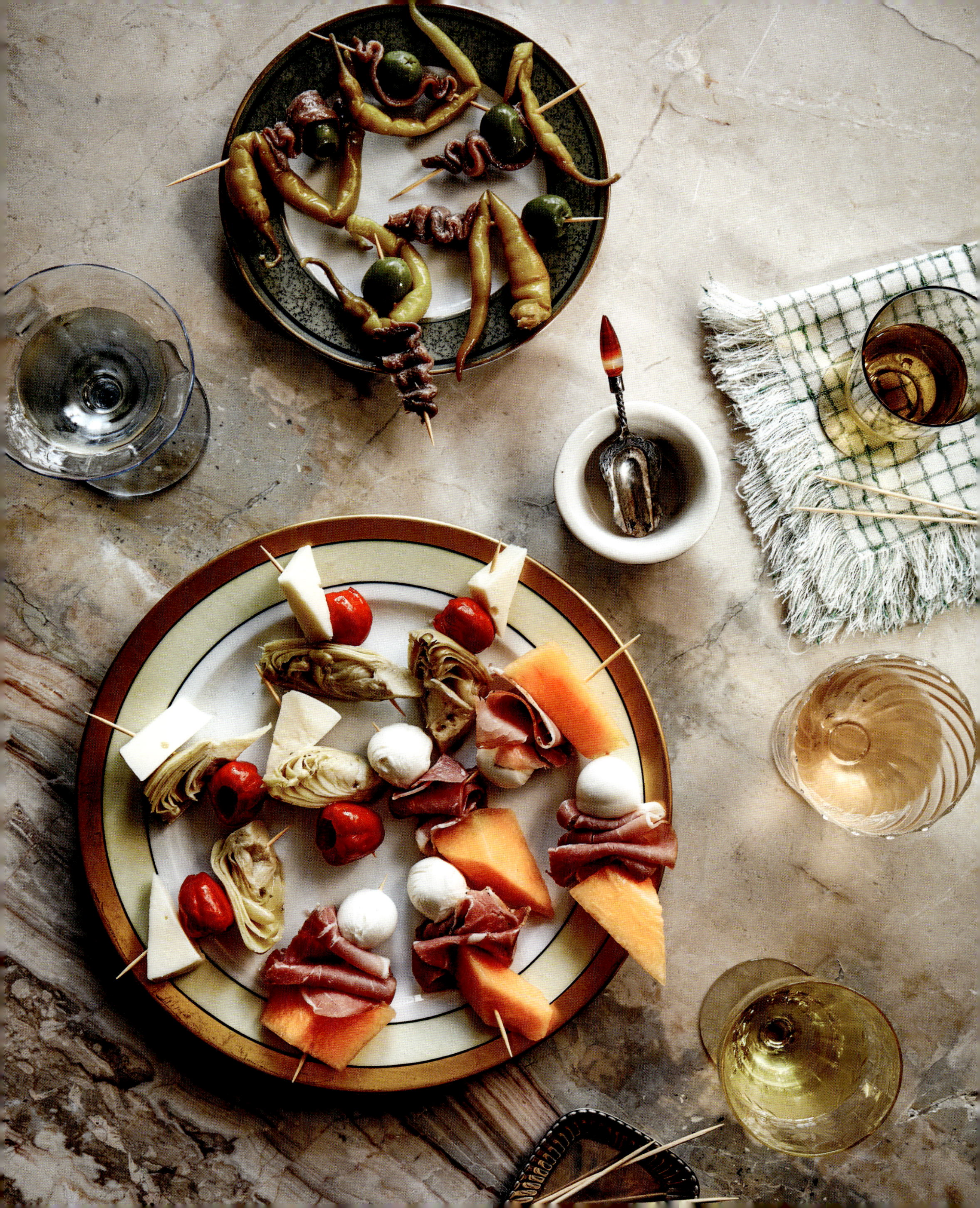

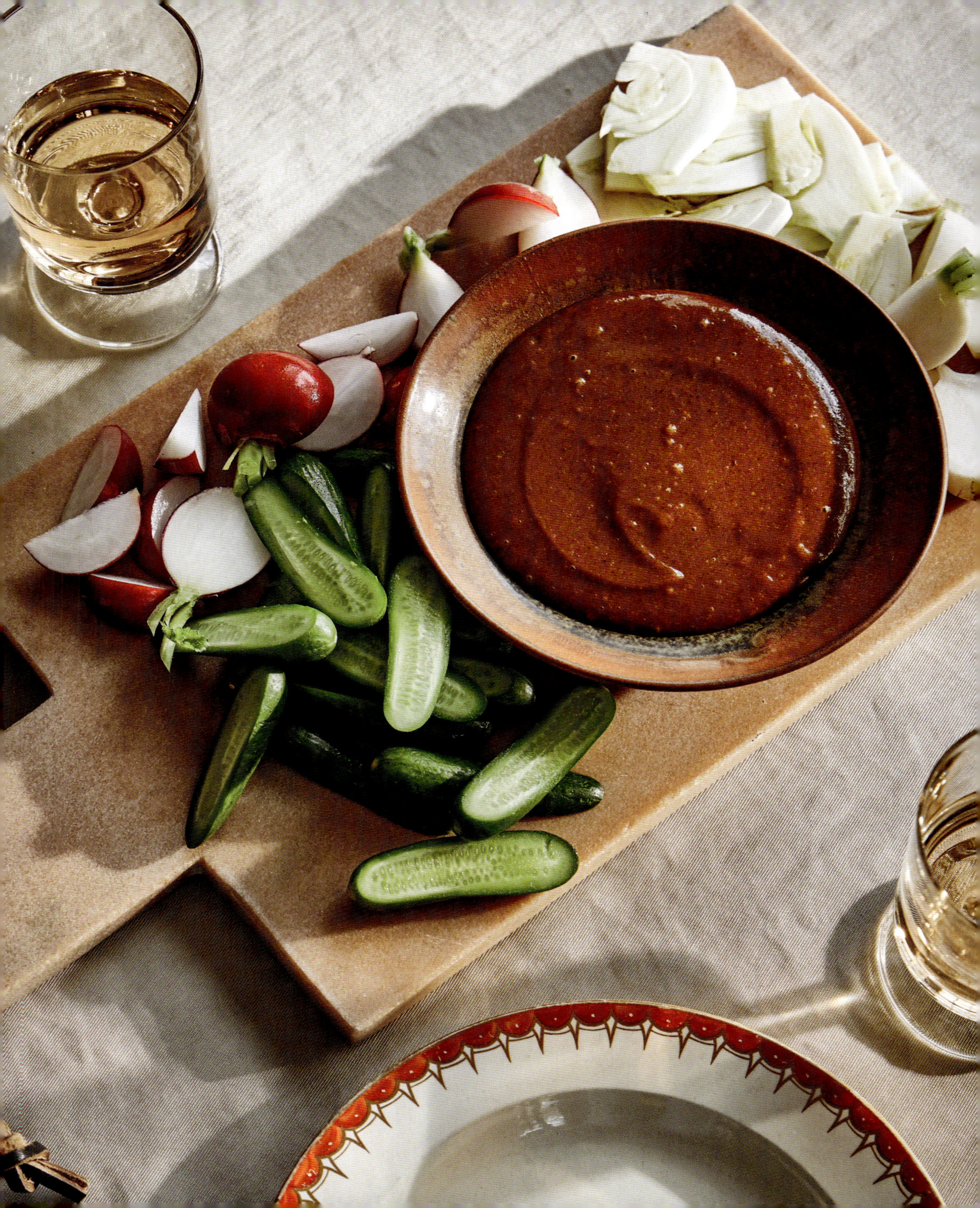

Gochujang Almond Butter Dip

This recipe is a riff on a dip my friend Hannah makes. At first glance it doesn't look like anything special, but after your first bite, you'll be flooded with a curious wave of umami. It's a bit salty, creamy, and punchy all at the same time. It's the kind of dip that begs you to come back for more, and suddenly you'll find yourself firmly planted next to it, eating your weight in cucumbers. While you may think the above story is exaggerated, I've never met anyone who's had a different experience when they tried this.

NOTES: I find that mini food processors are rarely handy, but this is a time to make use of one if you have it. Leftover dip can be stored in an airtight container in the refrigerator for up to 5 days.

1. Combine the almond butter, soy sauce, gochujang, lime juice, garlic, and 2 tablespoons water in a food processor and process until smooth.

2. Serve the dip with assorted cut vegetables or crackers.

Serves 6 to 8

½ cup almond butter

¼ cup soy sauce

2 tablespoons gochujang

Juice of 1 lime (about 2 tablespoons)

1 garlic clove, grated

Cut vegetables or crackers, for serving

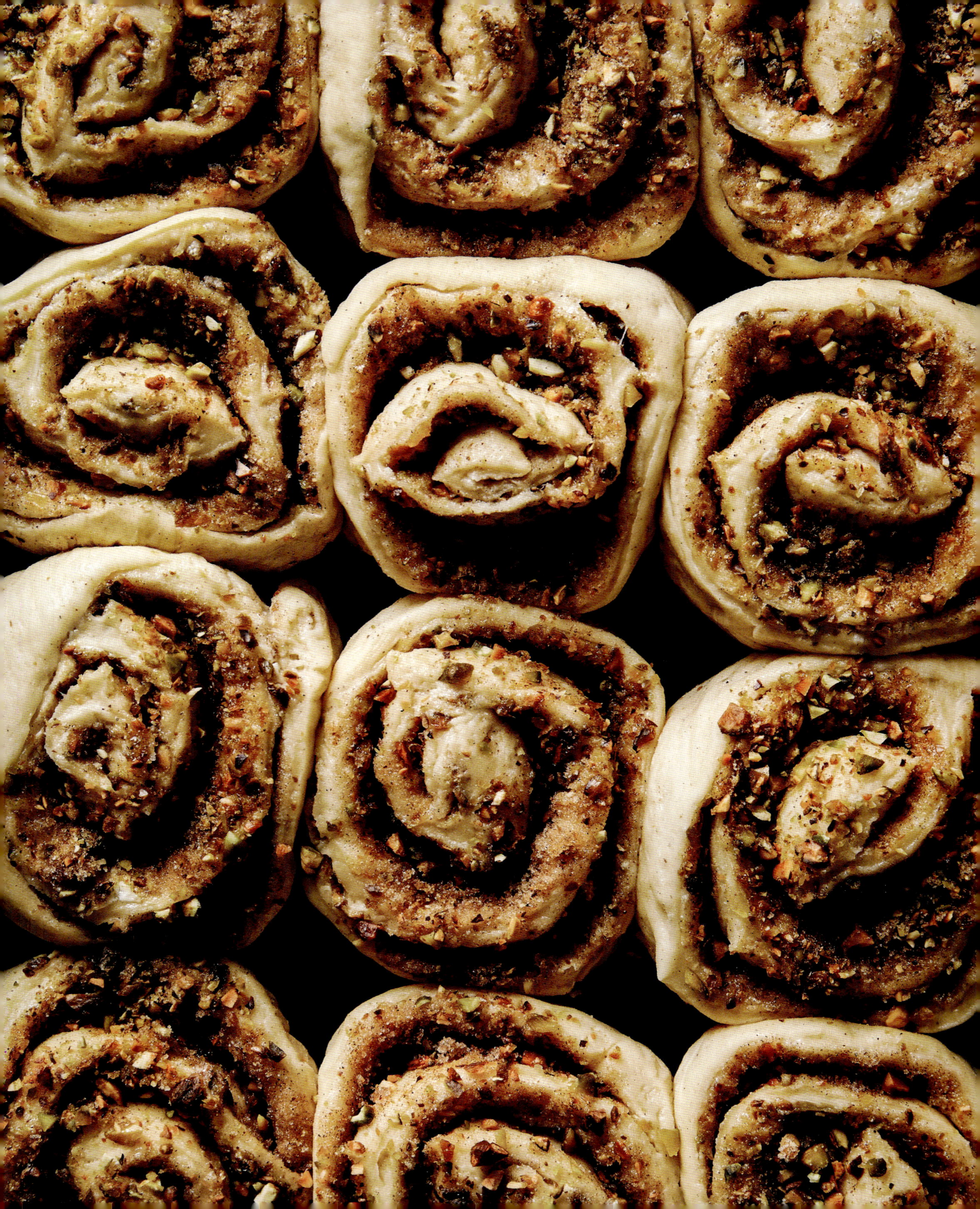

WEEKENDS

BRUNCH

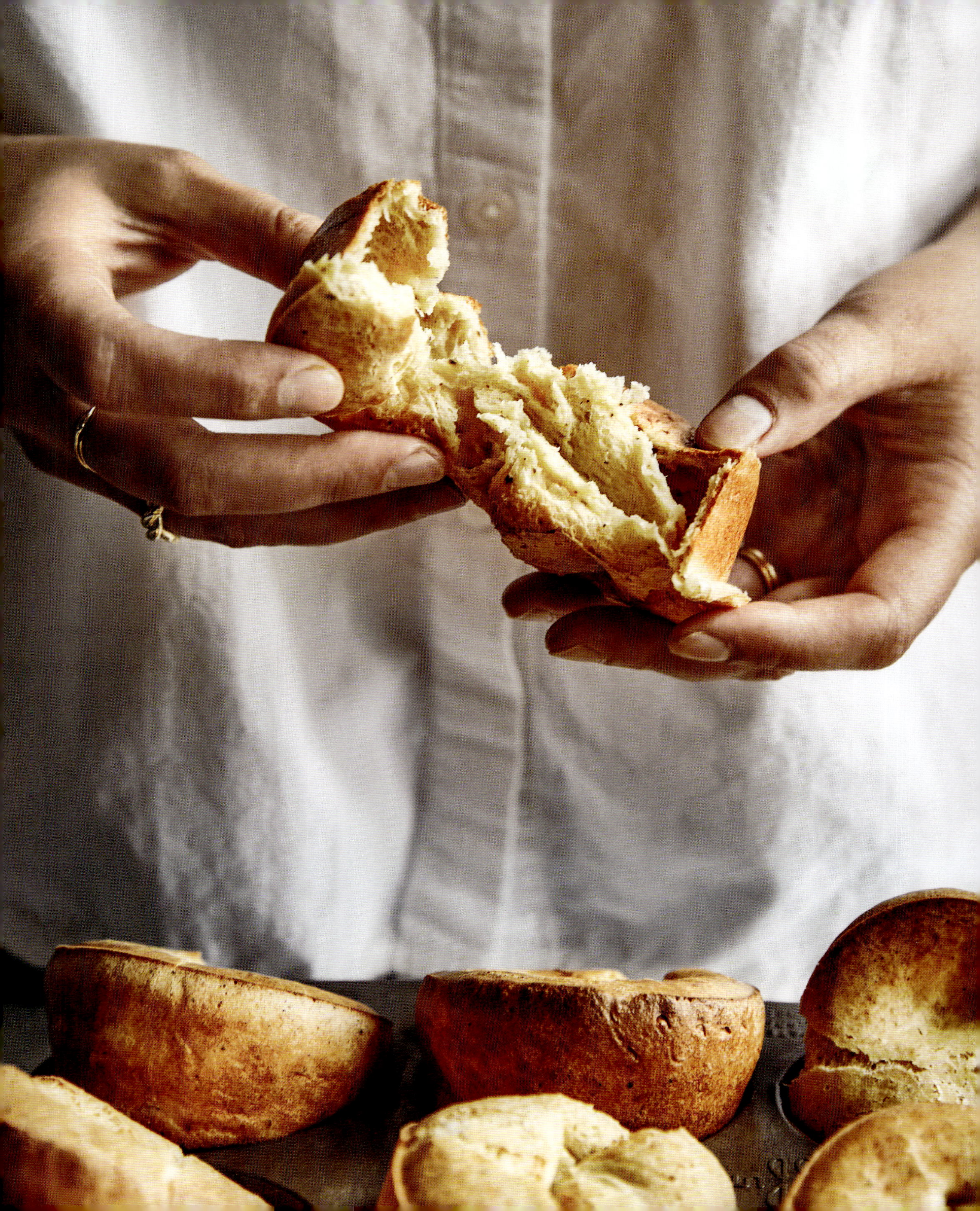

Cacio e Pepe Popovers

As a teenager I had little to no cooking skills but a whole lot of enthusiasm. Flipping through my mom's battered copy of *The Joy of Cooking*, I came across a recipe for popovers, which looked easy enough. Imagine my joy when out of the oven came a tray of perfectly puffed golden treats. Maybe it's because it was one of the first dishes I successfully made on my own, or maybe it's because they're exceptionally delicious, but whenever I'm in the mood for festive brunch, popovers are the first thing to come to mind. This version takes a cue from cacio e pepe, with a showering of Parm and a generous amount of pepper in the batter.

NOTES: To get picture-perfect puffy popovers, make sure the milk and eggs are at room temperature before you begin. If not, the popovers won't rise. To quickly get eggs to room temperature, let them sit in a bowl of room-temperature water for 5 minutes. I use a blender to make the batter, but you can do it in a large bowl using a whisk or even a handheld mixer; just be sure to mix it thoroughly. Popovers start to deflate as soon as they come out of the oven. This won't affect the flavor, but it means they're best eaten immediately, while they're still hot.

Serves 4 to 6

- Unsalted butter or cooking spray, for greasing
- 3 large eggs, at room temperature
- 1½ cups whole milk, at room temperature
- ½ cup freshly grated Parmigiano Reggiano cheese
- 1 tablespoon freshly ground black pepper
- 1 teaspoon kosher salt
- 1½ cups all-purpose flour
- 2 tablespoons unsalted butter, melted, plus more butter for serving

1. Preheat the oven to 450°F. Generously grease a 12-hole muffin tin with butter or cooking spray.

2. Combine the eggs, milk, Parmigiano Reggiano, pepper, and salt in a blender and blend on high until combined, about 15 seconds. Add the flour and blend on high until incorporated, about 15 seconds. Add the melted butter and once again blend on high until the mixture is smooth and combined, about 15 seconds.

3. Divide the batter evenly between cups in the muffin tin. Bake for 15 minutes, then, without opening the oven, reduce the oven temperature to 350°F and bake until the popovers are puffed and golden brown, 18 to 20 minutes.

4. Serve the popovers immediately, with butter.

Prosciutto and Brie Frittata

One of the joys of frittatas is that they're the perfect blank slate, a way to use up whatever odds and ends of food you might have tucked away in the crisper drawer—and you should do this. But they also deserve a moment in the spotlight, where the ingredients are really considered. Here, thin slices of prosciutto are buried under puddles of melted Brie. I've snuck whole-grain mustard into the batter, which adds a hint of acidity without overpowering the other flavors.

NOTES: If you don't have heavy cream, you can use milk, sour cream, or even yogurt in its place. If you don't have prosciutto, sliced ham will work. Leftover frittata can be stored in an airtight container in the refrigerator for up to 5 days.

Serves 2 to 4

Butter, for greasing

6 large eggs

¼ cup heavy cream

1 tablespoon whole-grain mustard

¼ teaspoon kosher salt

½ teaspoon freshly ground black pepper

3 slices prosciutto

3½ ounces Brie cheese, sliced

Cornichons, for serving

1. Preheat the oven to 350°F. Grease a 10- or 12-inch cast-iron or stainless-steel pan with butter.

2. Combine the eggs, heavy cream, mustard, salt, and pepper in a medium bowl and whisk until smooth. Transfer the egg mixture to the greased pan and top with the prosciutto and Brie.

3. Bake until the frittata is just set and has turned golden brown, about 25 minutes. Let cool for 5 minutes. Serve with cornichons.

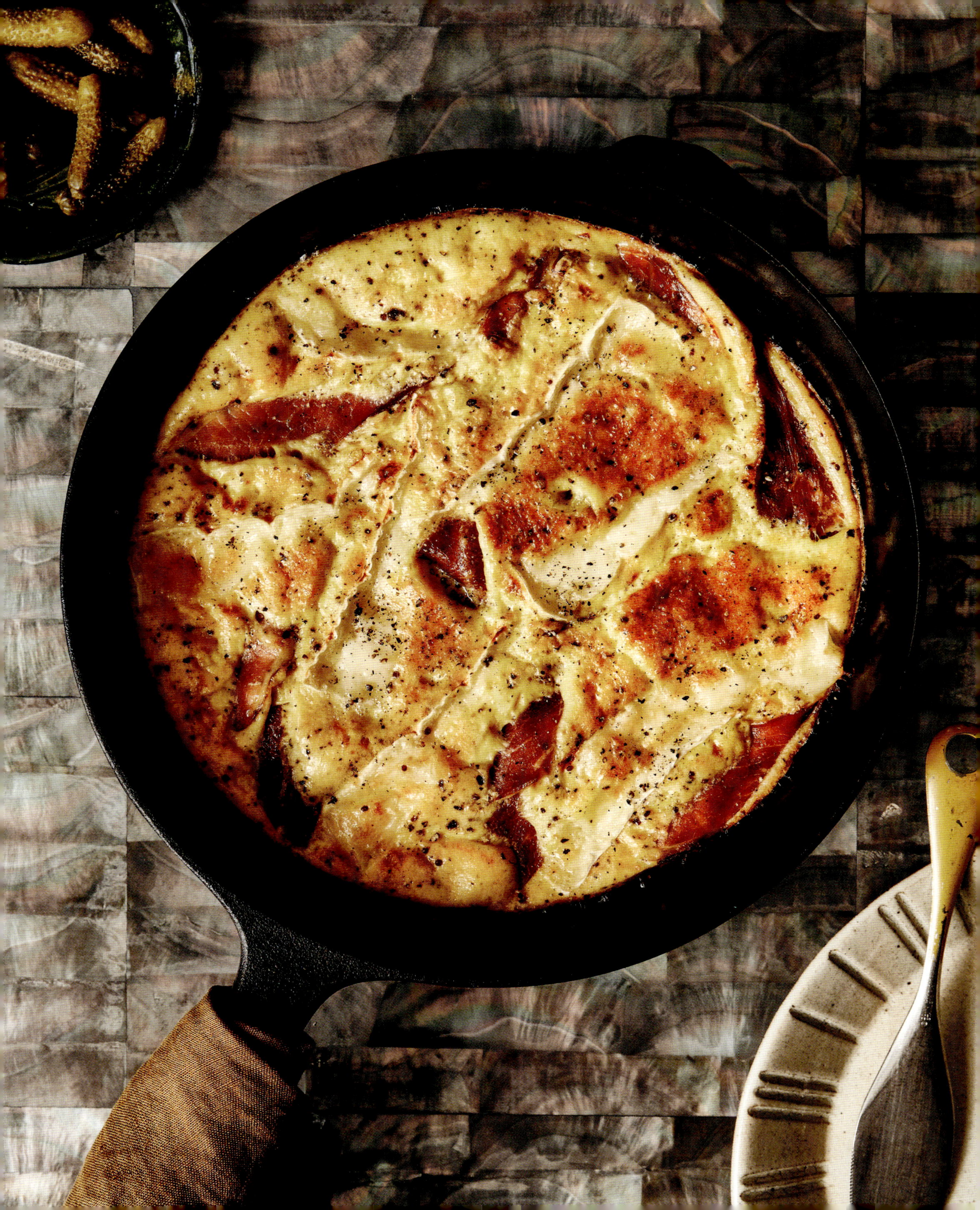

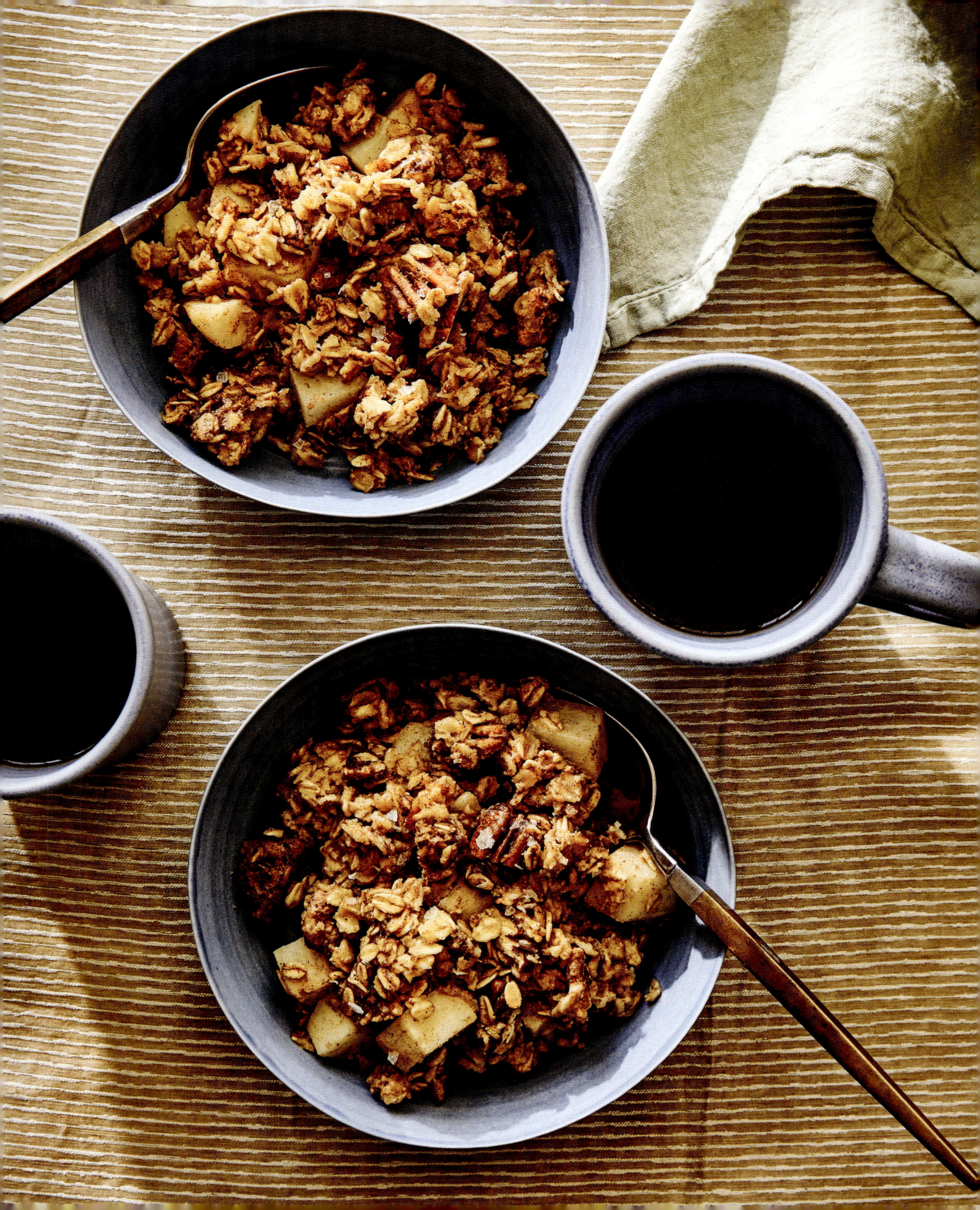

Pear and Pecan Baked Oatmeal

While a piping-hot bowl of steel-cut oats is my ideal breakfast, I'll admit that for a long time the prospect of baked oatmeal never interested me. But with the right balance of ingredients, the baked oatmeal takes on an almost cakey texture that's very appealing. This not-too-sweet version is studded with hunks of pears, which add acidity, and pecans for crunchiness. Really, though, it's a blank slate to experiment with whatever assortment of fruit and nuts you have on hand. Berries, apples, bananas, walnuts, and chocolate chips would all be great additions here.

NOTE: Leftover baked oatmeal can be stored in an airtight container in the refrigerator for up to 3 days.

Serves 8

- Cooking spray, for greasing
- 2 cups old-fashioned rolled oats
- 2 medium pears, peeled, cored, and cut into ½-inch pieces
- 1 cup pecans, coarsely chopped
- 1 teaspoon baking powder
- 1 teaspoon ground cinnamon
- 1 teaspoon kosher salt
- 1 (15-ounce) can unsweetened coconut milk
- 1 large egg, beaten
- ⅓ cup maple syrup
- 1 teaspoon pure vanilla extract
- Flaky salt, for serving

1. Preheat the oven to 375°F. Grease a 9-inch square baking dish.

2. Combine the oats, pears, pecans, baking powder, cinnamon, and salt in a large bowl and stir.

3. Add the coconut milk, egg, maple syrup, and vanilla and stir until well combined. Transfer the mixture to the greased baking dish.

4. Bake until the oats are lightly golden and puffed, about 25 minutes. Sprinkle with flaky salt and serve immediately.

Stone Fruit Salad

I love the idea of fruit salad, but I find that most versions combine out-of-season fruit in a way that I just can't get behind. Here, an assortment of stone fruit is tossed in a honey lime vinaigrette that enhances the sweetness of the fruit. You can use any combination of peaches, nectarines, apricots, plums, and cherries—just make sure the total amount comes out to six pounds. I love serving it as a side during summer brunches, but it's also an easy dessert with a scoop of whipped cream (or ice cream!).

NOTE: The stone fruit salad can be stored in an airtight container in the refrigerator for up to 1 day; after that, the fruit will begin to discolor.

1. Whisk together the lime zest, lime juice, olive oil, honey, and salt in a large bowl to combine well.

2. Add the fruit to the bowl and stir to combine. Serve immediately.

Serves 6

Zest and juice of 2 limes (about ¼ cup juice)

2 tablespoons extra-virgin olive oil

2 tablespoon honey

½ teaspoon kosher salt

6 pounds assorted stone fruit, pitted and thinly sliced

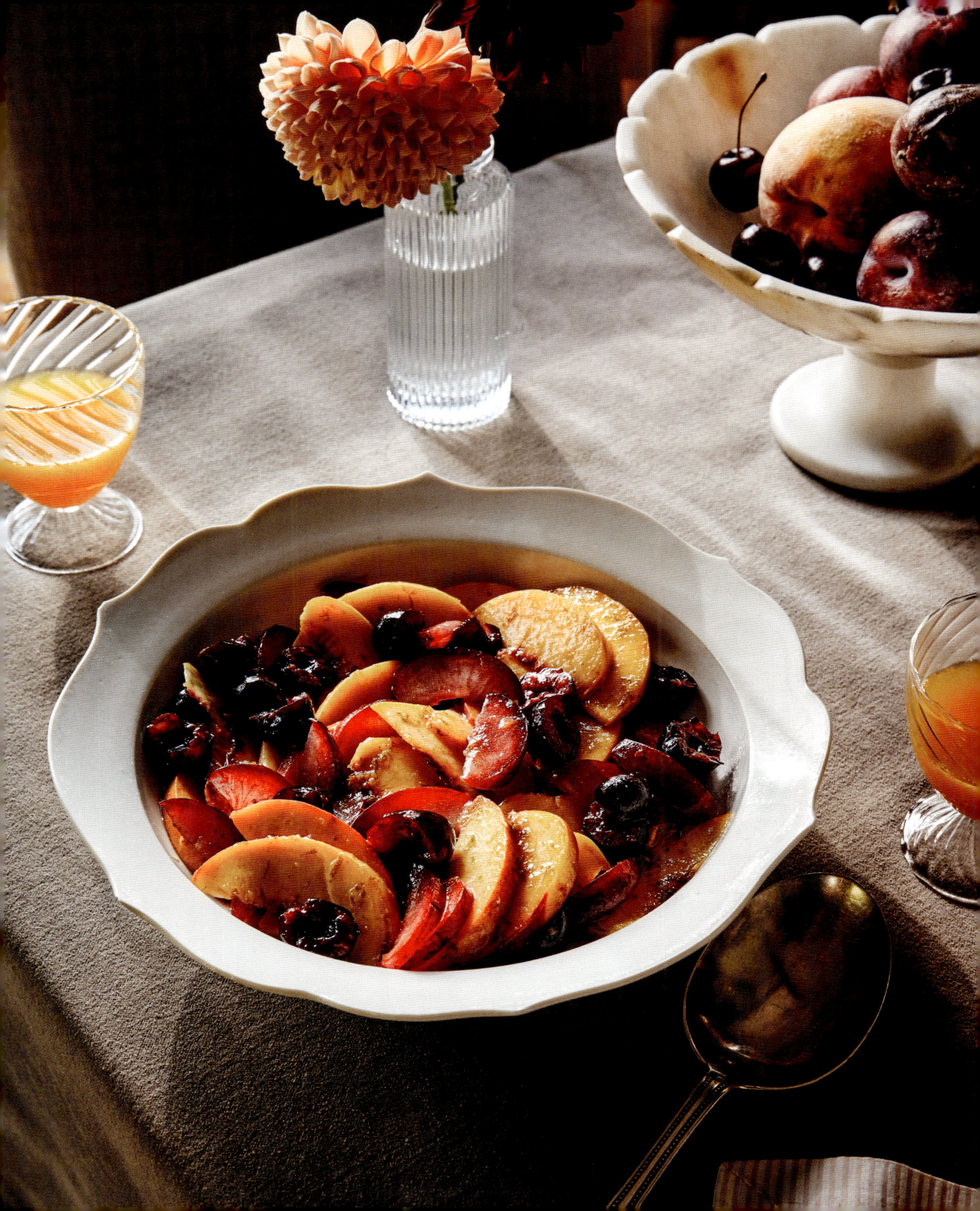

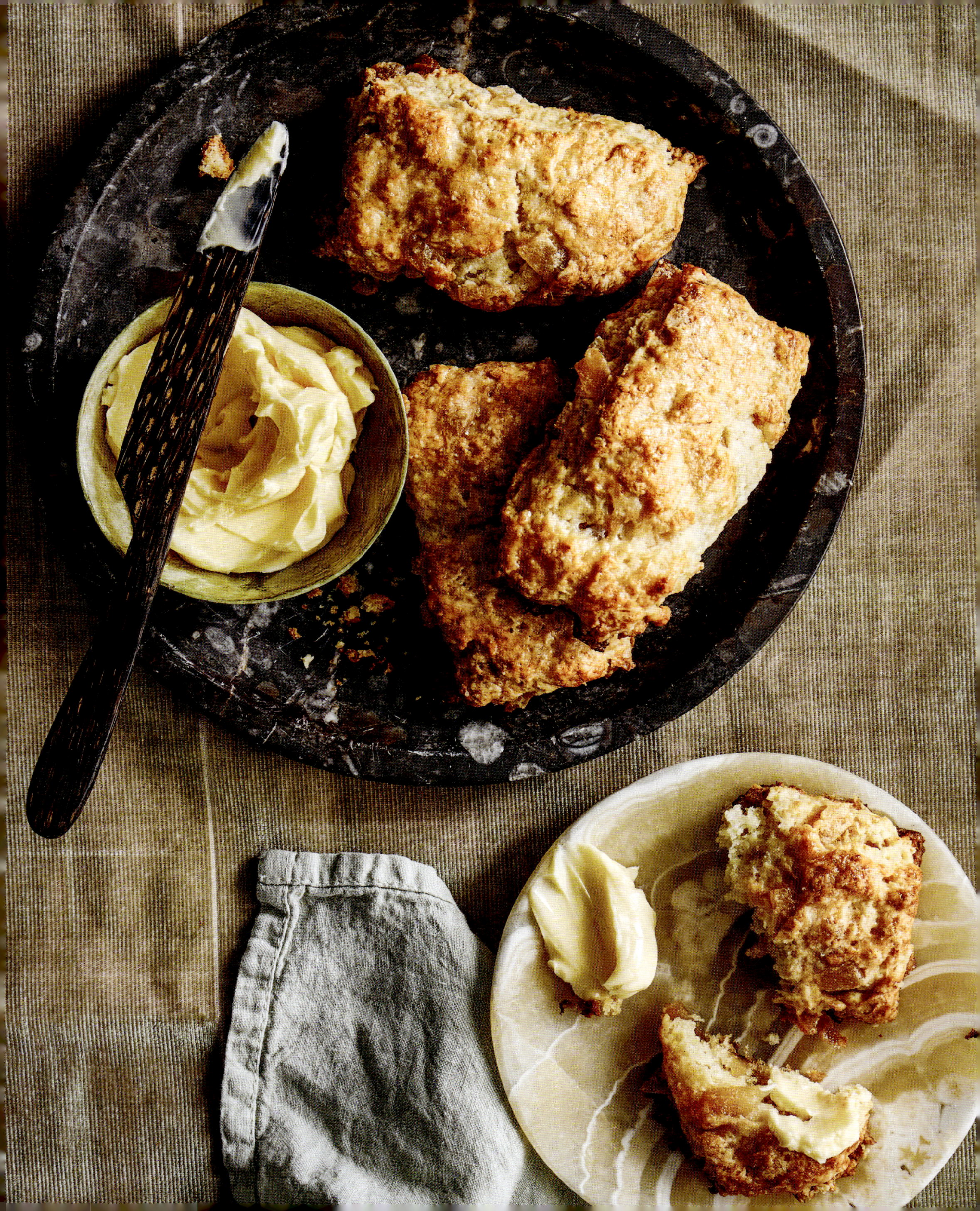

Buttermilk Ginger Scones

When my husband and I first moved in together, we were welcomed with a batch of scones fresh out of the oven from our neighbor Brian across the street. After our excessive praise, Brian began delivering weekly drop-offs of scones studded with everything from cherries and blueberries to poppyseeds and lemon zest. The scones were always perfectly tender, with just enough flakiness and a craggy golden topping. It was impossible to eat just one. When we moved back to the Catskills, this same neighbor gave me his recipe as a parting gift. I've since made a few tweaks and worked on my own flavor combinations, like my favorite here with candied ginger. I'm paying Brian's generosity forward, because these scones really do deserve a spot on your brunch rotation.

NOTES: Scones can be stored in an airtight container at room temperature for up to 3 days. They're best heated and slathered in butter before serving.

Makes 6 scones

¾ cup plus 1 tablespoon buttermilk

Zest of 2 lemons

2 cups all-purpose flour

3 tablespoons sugar, plus more for sprinkling

1½ teaspoons baking powder

1½ teaspoons ground ginger

1 teaspoon kosher salt

½ teaspoon baking soda

½ cup (1 stick) unsalted butter, cubed and chilled

1 cup candied ginger, chopped into pea-size pieces

1. Preheat the oven to 400°F.

2. Whisk ¾ cup of the buttermilk and the lemon zest together in a measuring cup.

3. Whisk together the flour, sugar, baking powder, ground ginger, salt, and baking soda in a medium bowl to combine. Add the butter to the bowl and use your fingers to combine the mixture until it forms pea-size pieces. Add the buttermilk mixture and use your hands to combine until a shaggy dough forms. Add the candied ginger and fold until just incorporated into the dough.

4. Transfer the dough to a clean work surface and briefly knead once or twice until it just comes together. Shape the dough into a 6×8-inch rectangle and cut it into 8 equal rectangles.

5. Transfer the scones to an ungreased baking sheet. Brush with the remaining 1 tablespoon buttermilk and sprinkle with sugar. Bake until the tops are golden brown, 14 to 16 minutes. Serve immediately.

Savory Breakfast Bowl

While I love making a big brunch dish for a crowd (this chapter is evidence of that), when it comes to the type of meal I make for my family on the weekends, most often it's some version of a savory breakfast bowl. The joy of this type of dish is leaning on the ingredients you already have in the refrigerator, whether that's leftovers from the night before or pantry staples.

❖ Every breakfast bowl needs a starchy element as the base to soak up all the eggs and toppings. Leftover grains like rice, farro, or quinoa work well here—a roasted sweet potato as well. My go-to is to use crispy rice, which I think makes everything better. To prepare it, heat a thin layer of neutral oil in a large pan over medium-high heat. When the oil begins to shimmer, add leftover cooked rice in an even layer; you may need to use a spatula to break up any clumps. Cook, without stirring the rice, until it becomes lightly golden and starts to crisp, 2 to 3 minutes. Use a spatula to flip the rice until all sides are crispy. The key to getting really crispy rice is to make sure it's as dried out as possible, which means at minimum two-day-old rice is preferable, but you can use up to five-day-old rice.

❖ To me, the only other requirement of a breakfast bowl is some form of eggs. Fried, poached, softly scrambled, or a perfectly jammy egg (see page 167) are all great contenders. I tend to opt for olive oil–fried eggs with a soft yolk and crispy, crackly edges. To make it, add a thin layer of olive oil to a cold pan. Crack the egg into the pan, then set it over medium-high heat. Cook, without moving until the white begins to set. Tilt the pan and use a spoon to baste the egg (white and yolk) in olive oil until it reaches your desired doneness.

❖ If you'd like to add in more protein, flaked salmon (page 223), thinly sliced steak (page 113), or even shredded pot roast (page 233) or crumbled sausage all work well.

❖ As you might have noticed, I try to tuck vegetables into recipes whenever I can, and a breakfast bowl is no different. Roasted vegetables like cauliflower, broccolini, zucchini, and squash are easy additions. If you have leftover sautéed greens from the night before, add them right to the bowl. You can even make use of canned artichokes or jarred peppers here.

❖ When it comes to toppings, I find it best to let everyone add their own in. I personally love a creamy element, like some type of crumbled soft cheese, a drizzle of tahini, or a dollop of labneh. To add some acidity to balance the bowl, think about ingredients like pickled red onions and cucumbers, kimchi, or a squeeze of lemon. Finish it off with a shower of herbs, thinly sliced scallions or avocado, hot sauce, chile crisp, furikake, or sesame seeds.

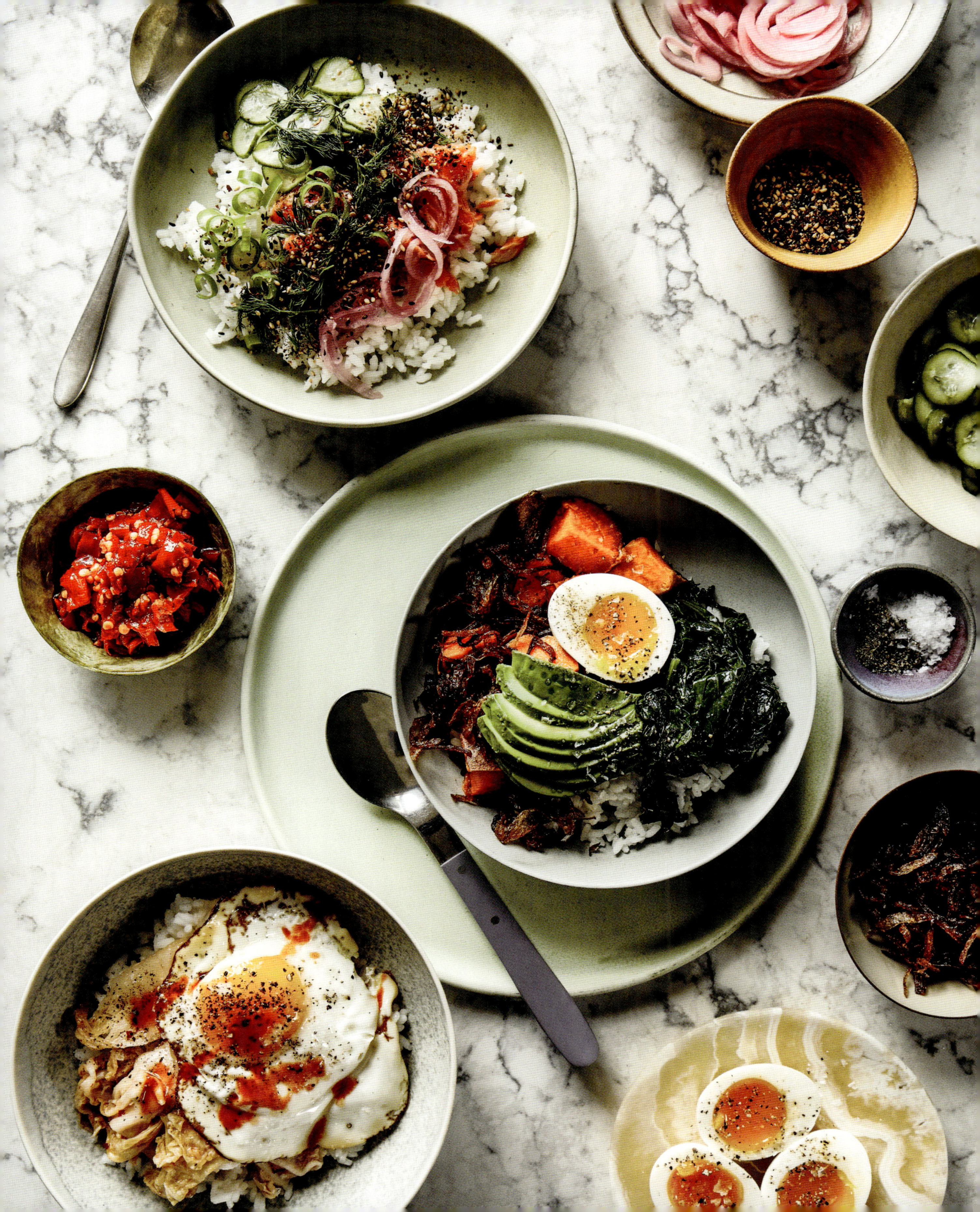

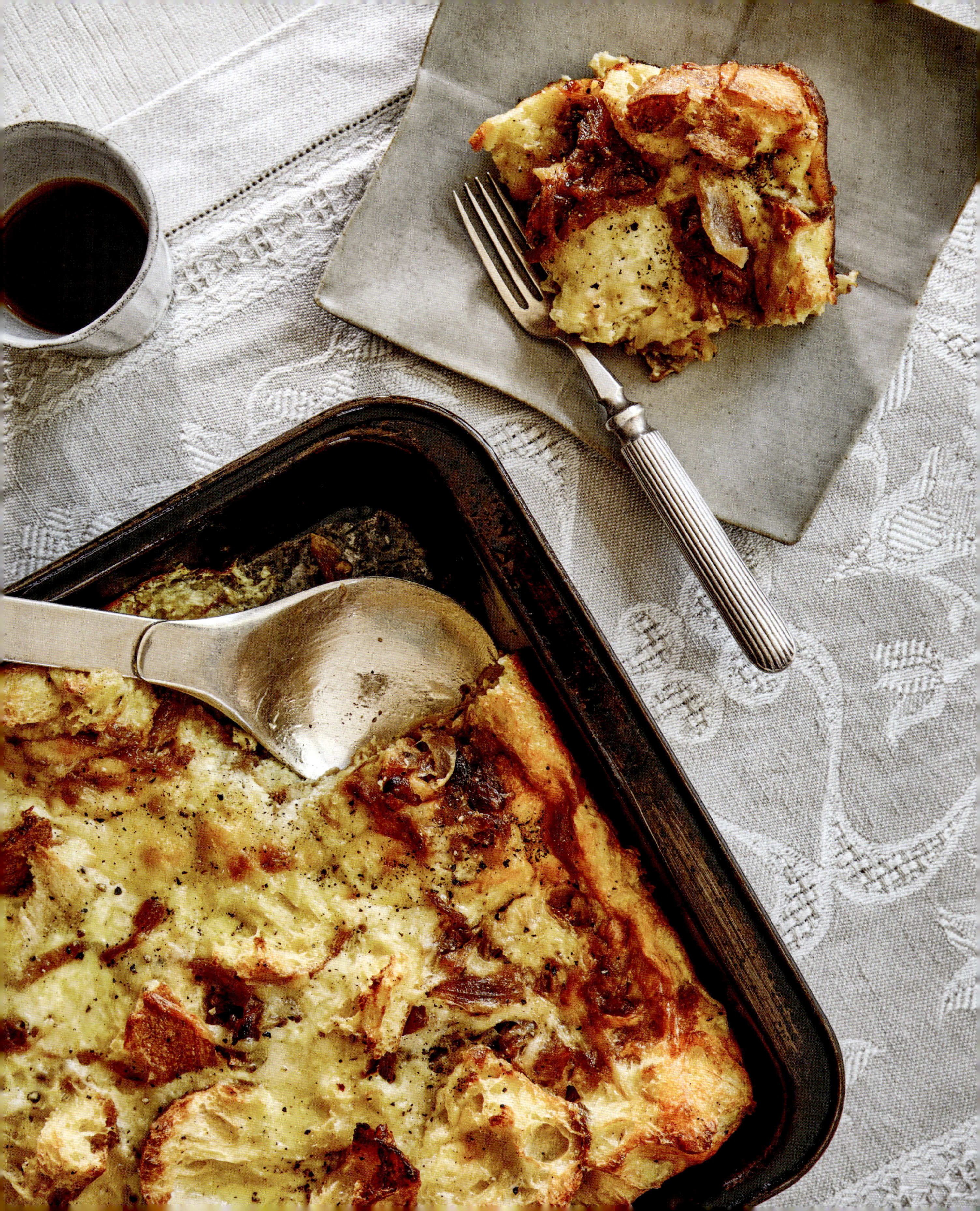

French Onion Soup Strata

Strata, an egg-based dish studded with hunks of roughly torn bread, is one of my brunch go-tos when I'm feeding a crowd. Despite its size, strata is decidedly low-lift. Here I've deconstructed the flavors of French onion soup for the strata, using caramelized onions, Gruyère, and fresh thyme. While traditional French onion soup requires deeply caramelized onions (to the point they're almost burnt), I've opted for keeping them a little lighter for this dish. To cut down on time, caramelize the onions a day or two before making the strata so that all you have to do is assemble the dish.

NOTES: You'll need about 1 medium loaf of bread for this—if it's going stale, that's even better. The caramelized onions can be made up to 5 days in advance and stored in an airtight container in the refrigerator. Leftover strata can be stored in an airtight container in the refrigerator for up to 3 days.

Serves 8

CARAMELIZED ONIONS

3 tablespoons unsalted butter

2 tablespoons extra-virgin olive oil

4 medium yellow onions, thinly sliced

2 tablespoons sherry vinegar

1 heaping tablespoon fresh thyme, finely chopped

½ teaspoon kosher salt

STRATA

Unsalted butter, for greasing

9 large eggs

2¾ cups whole milk

1½ teaspoons kosher salt

1 teaspoon freshly ground black pepper

8 cups roughly torn ciabatta

7 ounces Gruyère cheese, coarsely grated (about 3 cups)

1. **Make the caramelized onions:** Heat the butter and olive oil in a large pan over medium-high heat. When the butter has melted, add the onions and cook, stirring occasionally, for 5 minutes. Reduce the heat to medium-low and cook, stirring occasionally, until the onions are deeply golden brown and beginning to caramelize, about 20 minutes. Add the vinegar, thyme, and salt and stir, scraping up any brown bits from the bottom of the pan, for 1 minute.

2. **Make the strata:** Grease a 9×13-inch baking dish with butter.

3. Whisk the eggs, milk, salt, and pepper in a large bowl until smooth. Add the caramelized onions, bread, and Gruyère, and stir to combine. Pour the mixture into the greased baking dish and transfer it to the refrigerator to chill for 1 to 2 hours—any longer and the strata gets mushy. If you're short on time, you can go ahead and bake right away, but chilling helps keep the strata custardy.

4. Preheat the oven to 350°F.

5. Bake until the custard is set and the bread is golden brown and crisp wherever it peeks out, about 45 minutes. Let the strata cool for 10 minutes before serving.

Sticky Rolls with Pistachios and Caramel

Toeing the line between sticky buns and cinnamon rolls, these plush rolls are filled with a spiced pistachio and brown sugar mixture. As soon as they come out of the oven, they're draped in a blanket of caramel, ensuring every bite balances that sweet, crunchy stickiness. Yes, they take some time to put together—you need to get started the day before you plan to serve them—and yes, it's totally worth it.

NOTES: For a more uniform look, pulse the pistachios in the food processor until finely chopped. Rolls are best eaten immediately, although they can be stored in an airtight container in the refrigerator for up to 2 days. Before eating, I recommend reheating them until the caramel is warmed through.

Serves 12

DOUGH

1 cup whole milk

½ cup (1 stick) unsalted butter, melted, plus more for greasing

3 large eggs, at room temperature

⅓ cup plus 1 teaspoon sugar

1 (¼-ounce) packet active dry yeast

4 cups all-purpose flour

1 teaspoon ground cardamom

1 teaspoon kosher salt

FILLING

¾ cup packed light brown sugar

Zest of 2 lemons

1 teaspoon ground cardamom

½ teaspoon ground cinnamon

½ cup (1 stick) unsalted butter, at room temperature

1 cup lightly salted shelled pistachios, finely chopped

CARAMEL

½ cup sugar

3 tablespoons unsalted butter

¼ cup heavy cream

½ teaspoon pure vanilla extract

½ teaspoon kosher salt

1. **Make the dough:** Pour the milk into a large glass measuring cup or microwave-safe bowl and microwave on high until warm to the touch, about 45 seconds. (Alternatively, warm it in a small pot over medium heat.)

2. Add the melted butter and eggs to the bowl with the milk and whisk until smooth. Sprinkle 1 teaspoon of sugar and the yeast over the milk mixture and let sit until bubbly and frothy, 5 to 7 minutes.

3. Combine the remaining ⅓ cup sugar, the flour, cardamom, and salt in the bowl of a stand mixer fitted with the dough hook. Mix on low speed until combined, about 1 minute.

4. Increase the speed to medium and add the milk mixture, mixing until the dough comes together in a smooth and elastic ball, 8 to 10 minutes.

5. Grease a large bowl with butter and transfer the dough from the mixer into it. Cover with a kitchen towel and let rise in a warm place until doubled in size, about 1½ hours. Grease a 9×13-inch baking dish with butter.

6. **Meanwhile, make the filling:** Combine the brown sugar, lemon zest, cardamom, and cinnamon in a medium bowl and stir.

7. Punch the dough down in the bowl to deflate, and transfer it to a clean work surface. Roll the dough out to a 16×22-inch rectangle, with the long side facing toward you.

Recipe continues

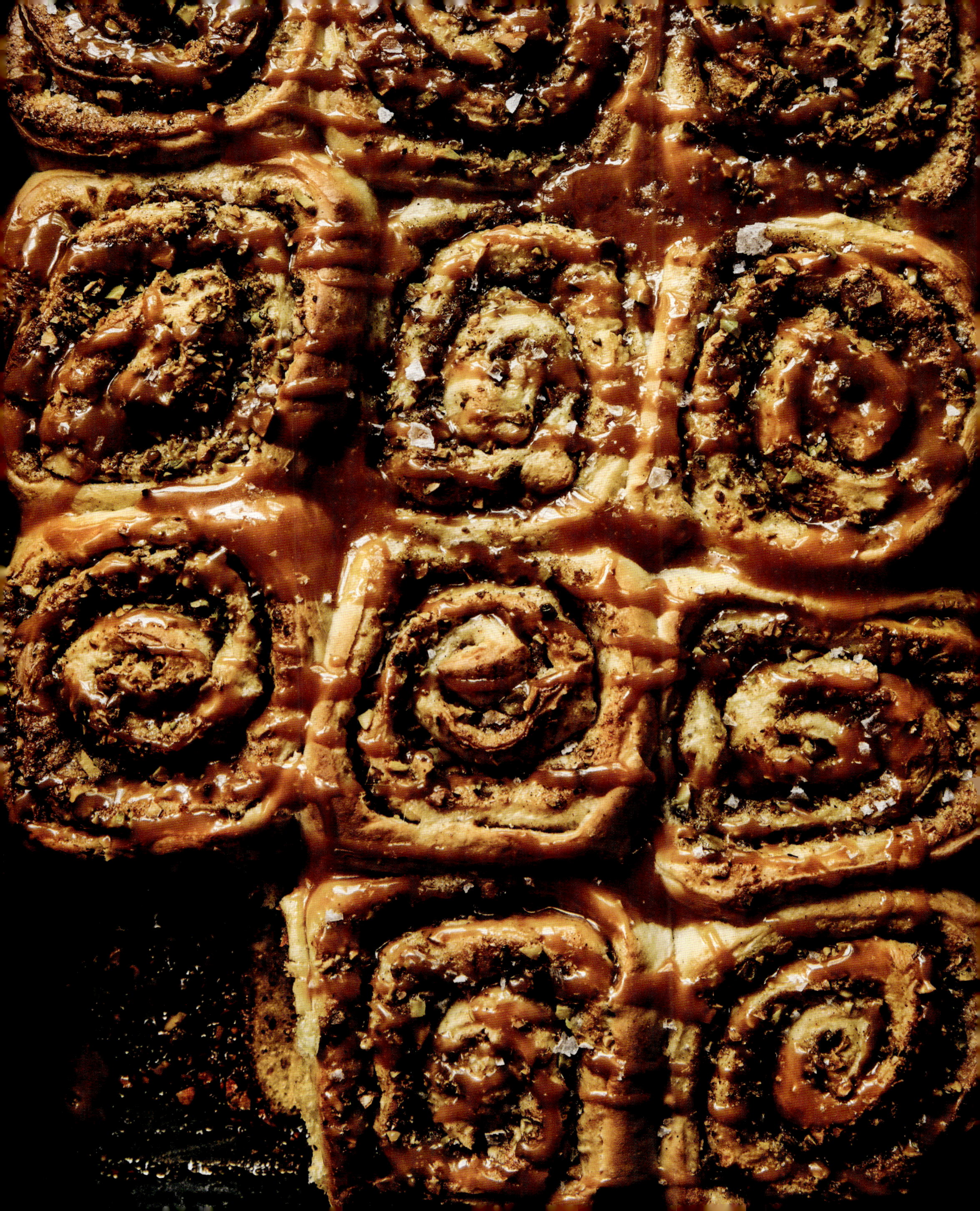

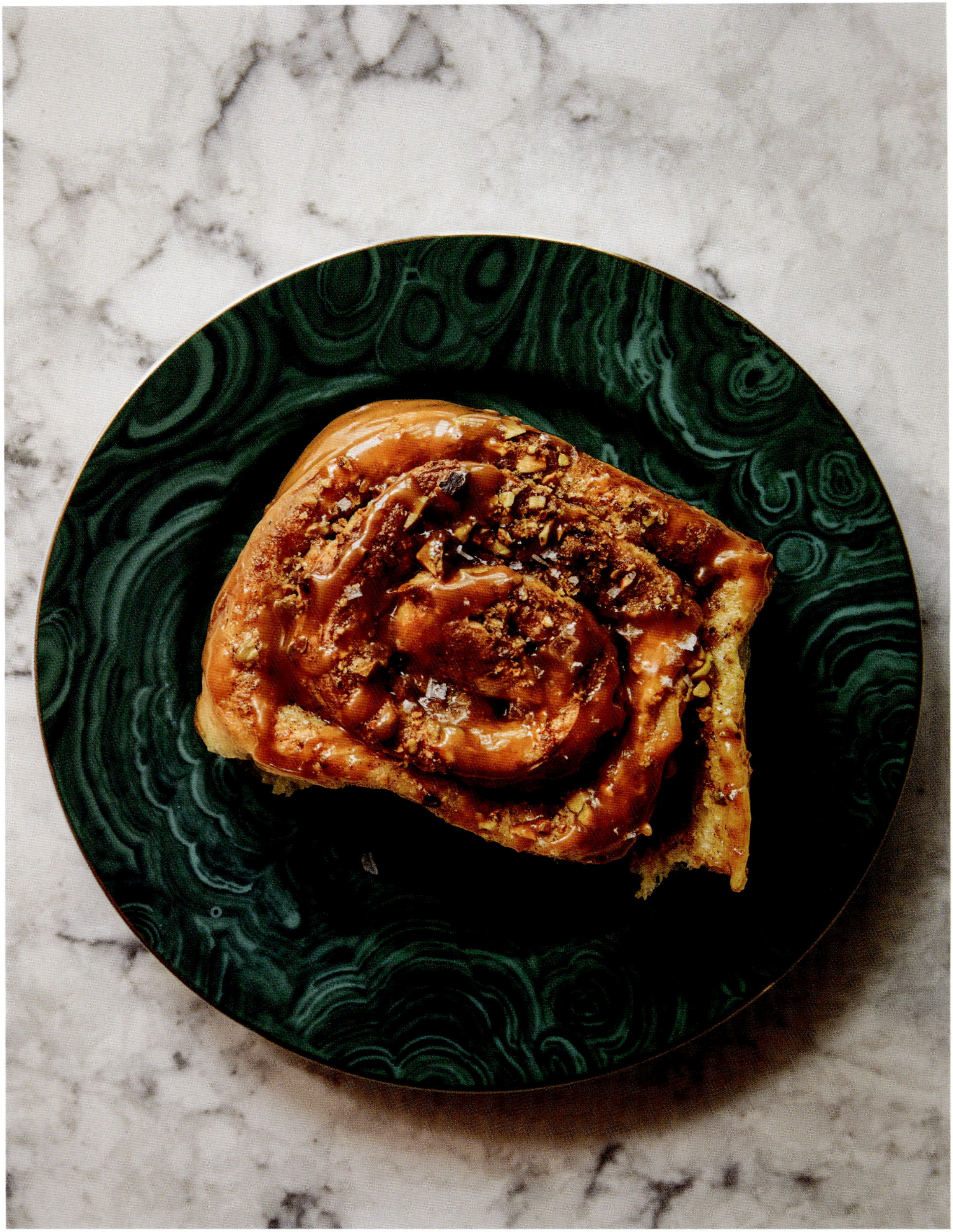

8. Spread the room-temperature butter all over the dough in an even layer. Sprinkle the brown sugar mixture over the butter. Sprinkle the pistachios in an even layer over the brown sugar. Starting at the long edge of the dough closest to you, carefully roll the dough up into a log. Cut the log into 12 equal rounds and transfer to the greased baking dish so that the swirl is visible. There will be space between the rolls, but they'll expand with rising. Cover the baking dish in plastic wrap and transfer to the refrigerator overnight.

9. When ready to bake, remove the rolls from the refrigerator and let sit out in a warm place for at least 1 hour.

10. Preheat the oven to 350°F. Bake the rolls until puffed and golden brown, about 25 minutes.

11. **Meanwhile, make the caramel:** Place the sugar in a small pot over medium-low heat and let melt, without stirring, but occasionally tilting the pan off the heat, until the sugar is the color of amber, 4 to 5 minutes. Add the butter and stir until melted—note that the mixture may bubble, so take care. Add the heavy cream and whisk until smooth. Let the caramel come to a low boil, about 1 minute. Remove the pot from the heat, add the vanilla and salt, and stir to combine.

12. When the rolls come out of the oven, immediately pour the caramel mixture over top in an even layer. Sticky rolls are best served within 30 minutes.

Olive Oil Banana Bread with Chocolate Chunks

After 2020 and the wave of banana bread recipes that followed, the only way I could justify including a recipe here was if it was exceptionally good. This one is based on a carrot cake loaf recipe from my best friend, Meagan. Meagan is one of those home bakers who can do no wrong in the kitchen. She's the kind of person who regularly whips up macarons like it's no big deal (I can assure you it is), can make a three-tiered cake in her sleep, and somehow nails every baking experiment she tries.

So, how does all this get me to banana bread? I figured if a loaf is a loaf is a loaf (kind of), then a similar recipe would work just as well swapping out the carrots for bananas. I made a few other tweaks to the recipe, like cutting down on the amount of oil since bananas have more moisture, as well as the amount of sugar. Adding the chocolate in chunks makes it not too overtly chocolatey but feels celebratory enough to serve for brunch or dessert, as well as for an afternoon snack. Don't skip the dusting of sugar before baking, which renders a delightful crackly crust.

NOTE: Banana bread can be wrapped in plastic wrap or transferred to an airtight container and stored at room temperature for up to 4 days.

Makes 1 loaf

Unsalted butter, for greasing

1⅔ cups all-purpose flour

1½ teaspoons baking powder

1 teaspoon baking soda

1 teaspoon ground cinnamon

½ teaspoon kosher salt

3 very ripe bananas

4 large eggs, beaten

¾ cup plus 1 teaspoon granulated sugar

½ cup packed light brown sugar

½ cup extra-virgin olive oil

1 teaspoon pure vanilla extract

4 ounces semisweet chocolate, coarsely chopped

1. Preheat the oven to 350°F. Grease a standard loaf pan with butter.

2. Combine the flour, baking powder, baking soda, cinnamon, and salt in a medium bowl and whisk.

3. Place the bananas in a large bowl and use a fork or potato masher to mash the bananas until clumpy. Add the eggs, ¾ cup of the granulated sugar, the brown sugar, olive oil, and vanilla and whisk to combine.

4. Add the flour mixture to the banana mixture and use a spatula to fold until just combined. Add the chocolate and fold once more until the chunks are just incorporated into the batter.

5. Pour the batter into the greased loaf pan. Sprinkle the top with the remaining 1 teaspoon granulated sugar. Bake until the top is deeply golden brown and a toothpick comes out of the center clean, about 1 hour. Let cool in the pan for at least 30 minutes before removing it.

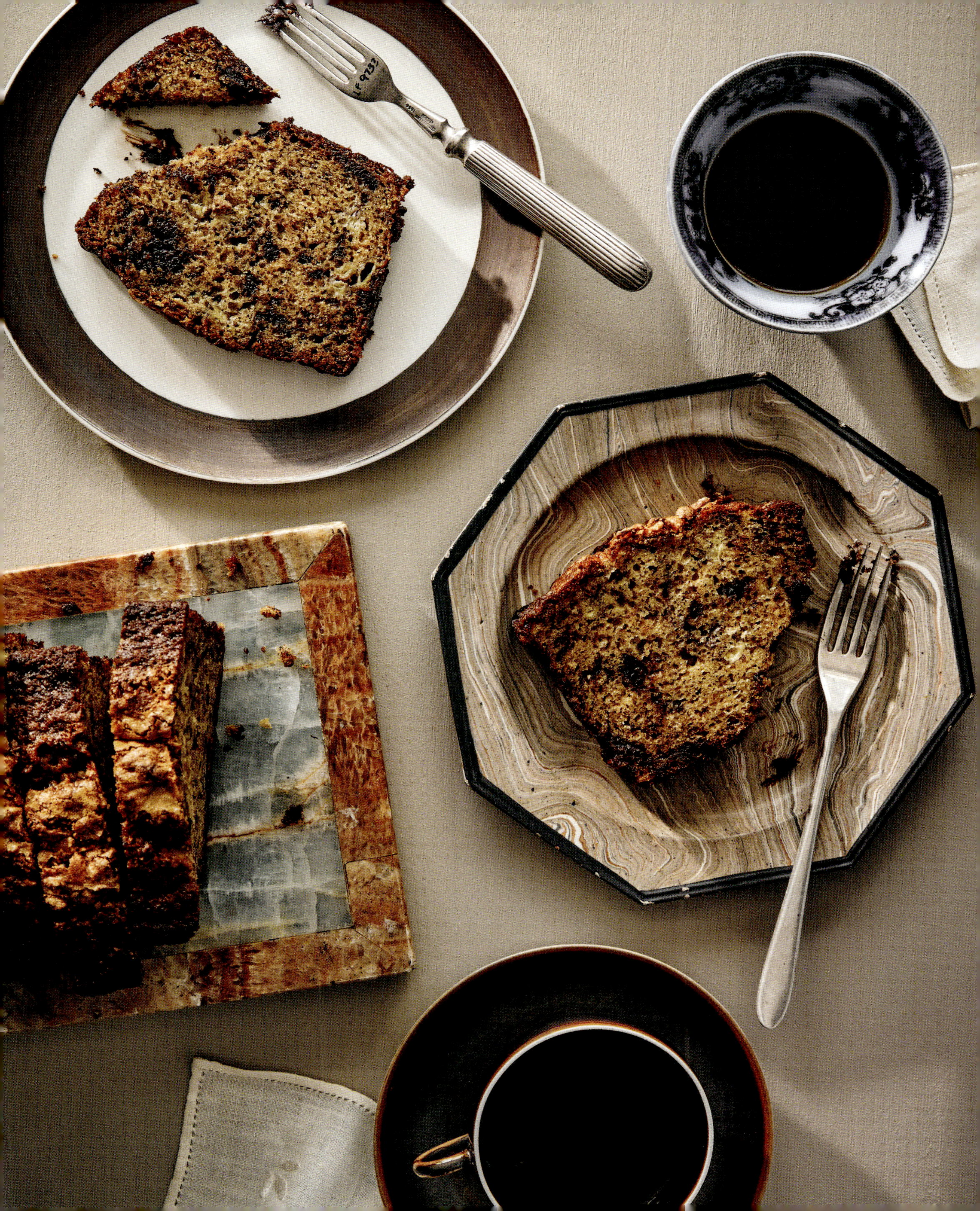

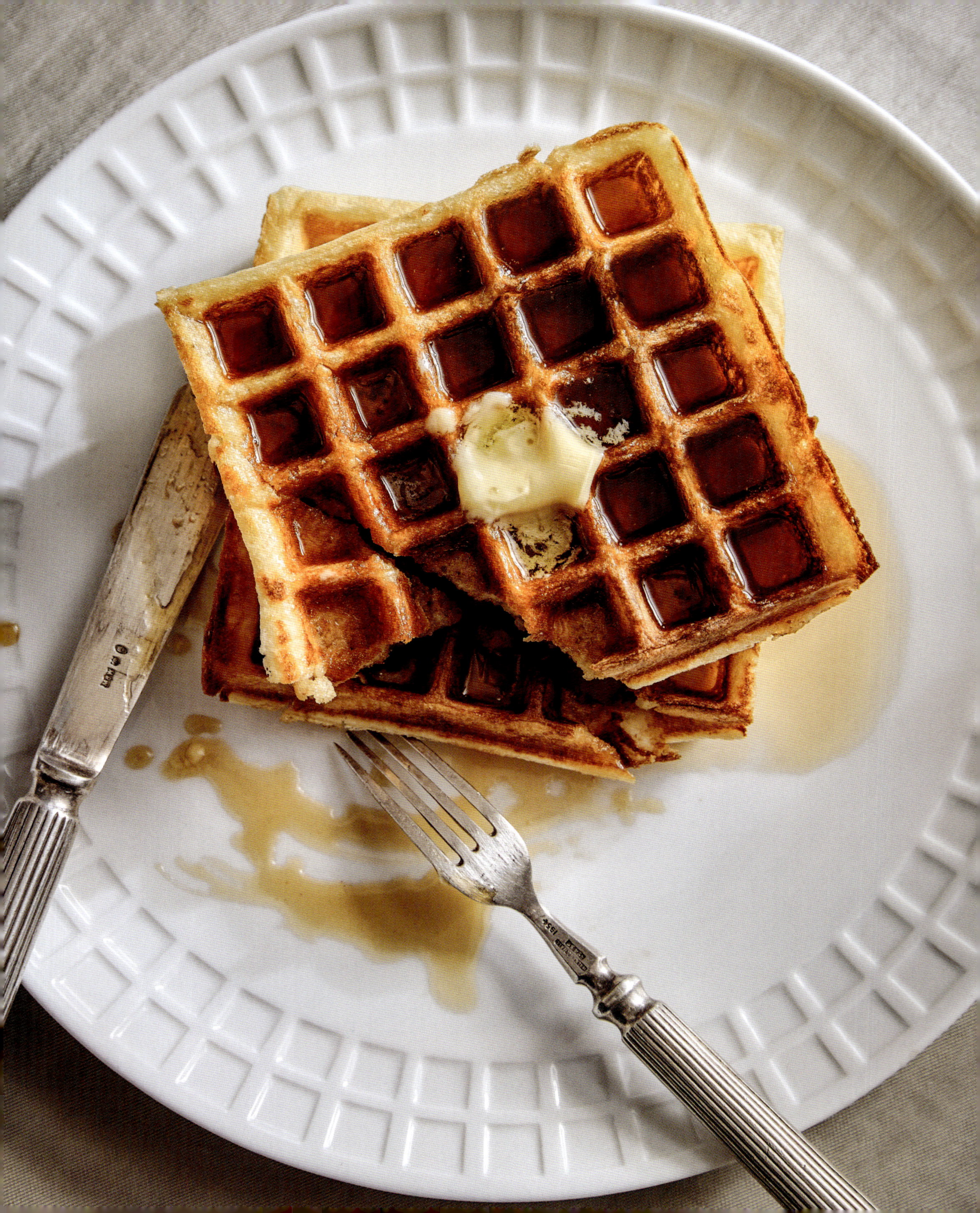

Sour Cream Waffles

I try to stay away from single-use gadgets, but a waffle maker is my one exception. I grew up eating Eggo waffles every morning before school for about ten years, and they just hit a nostalgic nerve for me. This recipe comes from my husband's grandmother, and I swear they're the best waffles I've ever had (sorry, Kellogg's). The batter is made with both sour cream and buttermilk, which keeps the interior of the waffle light and tender, while also adding some tanginess.

NOTE: Waffles can be kept in an airtight bag in the freezer for up to 1 month and reheated as desired. Heating them in a toaster or oven works equally well.

Serves 4

- 2 cups all-purpose flour
- 1 tablespoon sugar
- 1 teaspoon baking powder
- ½ teaspoon baking soda
- 1 teaspoon kosher salt
- 4 tablespoons (½ stick) unsalted butter, melted, plus more for the waffle iron
- 1 cup full-fat sour cream
- 1 cup buttermilk
- 2 large eggs
- Pure maple syrup or other toppings of choice, for serving

1. Combine the flour, sugar, baking powder, baking soda, and salt in a large bowl and whisk well.

2. Whisk together the melted butter, sour cream, buttermilk, and eggs in a medium bowl until smooth. Gently pour the wet ingredients into the dry ingredients and use a spatula to fold until just combined. The batter should be slightly lumpy—do not overmix.

3. Heat a waffle iron. When it is hot, grease it with butter, add between ⅓ and ½ cup of the batter (every waffle maker holds a different amount of batter), and cook until golden brown. Transfer the waffle to a plate and repeat with the remaining batter, greasing the waffle iron with butter between batches.

4. Serve the waffles immediately, with maple syrup or your toppings of choice.

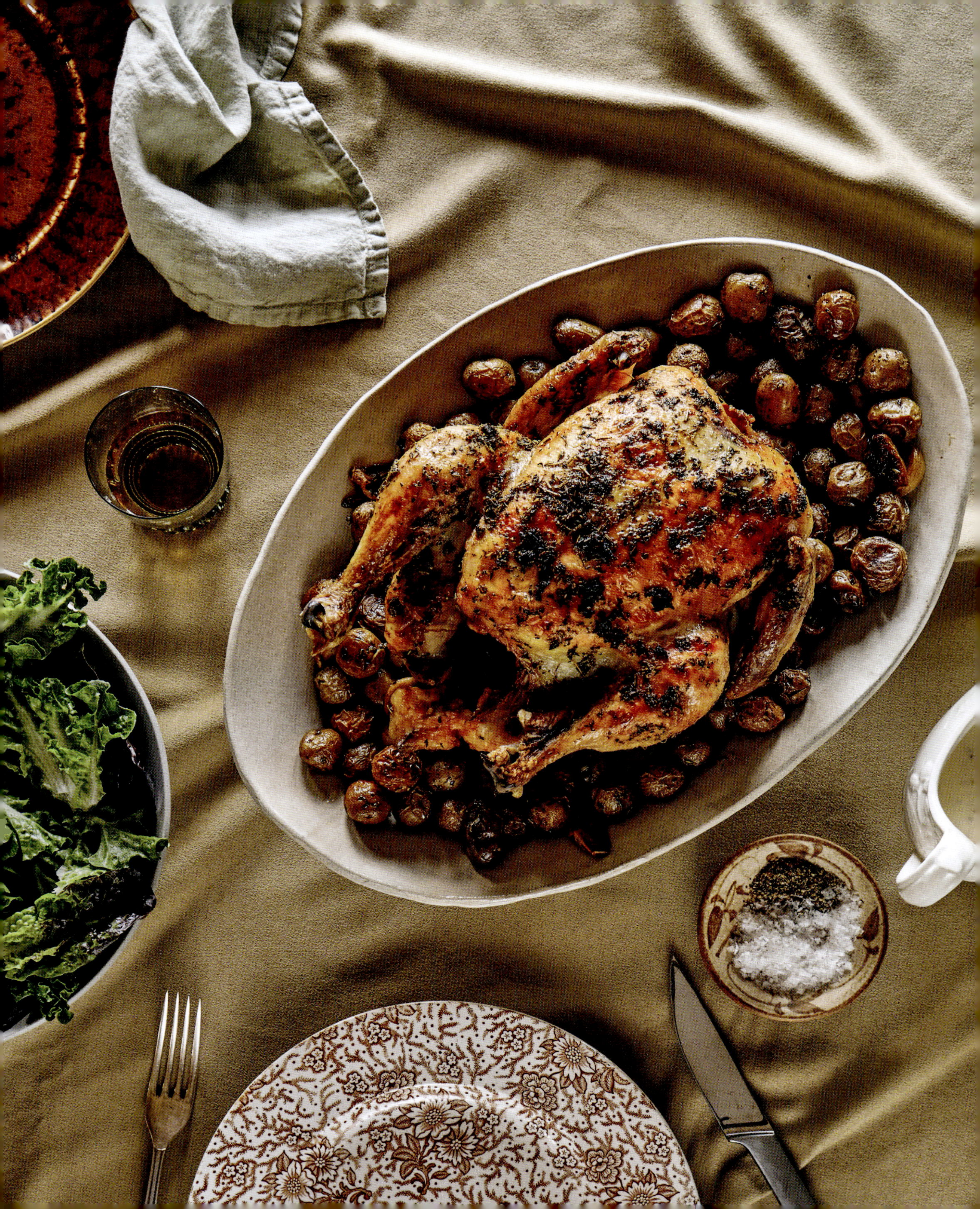

WEEKENDS

DINNER

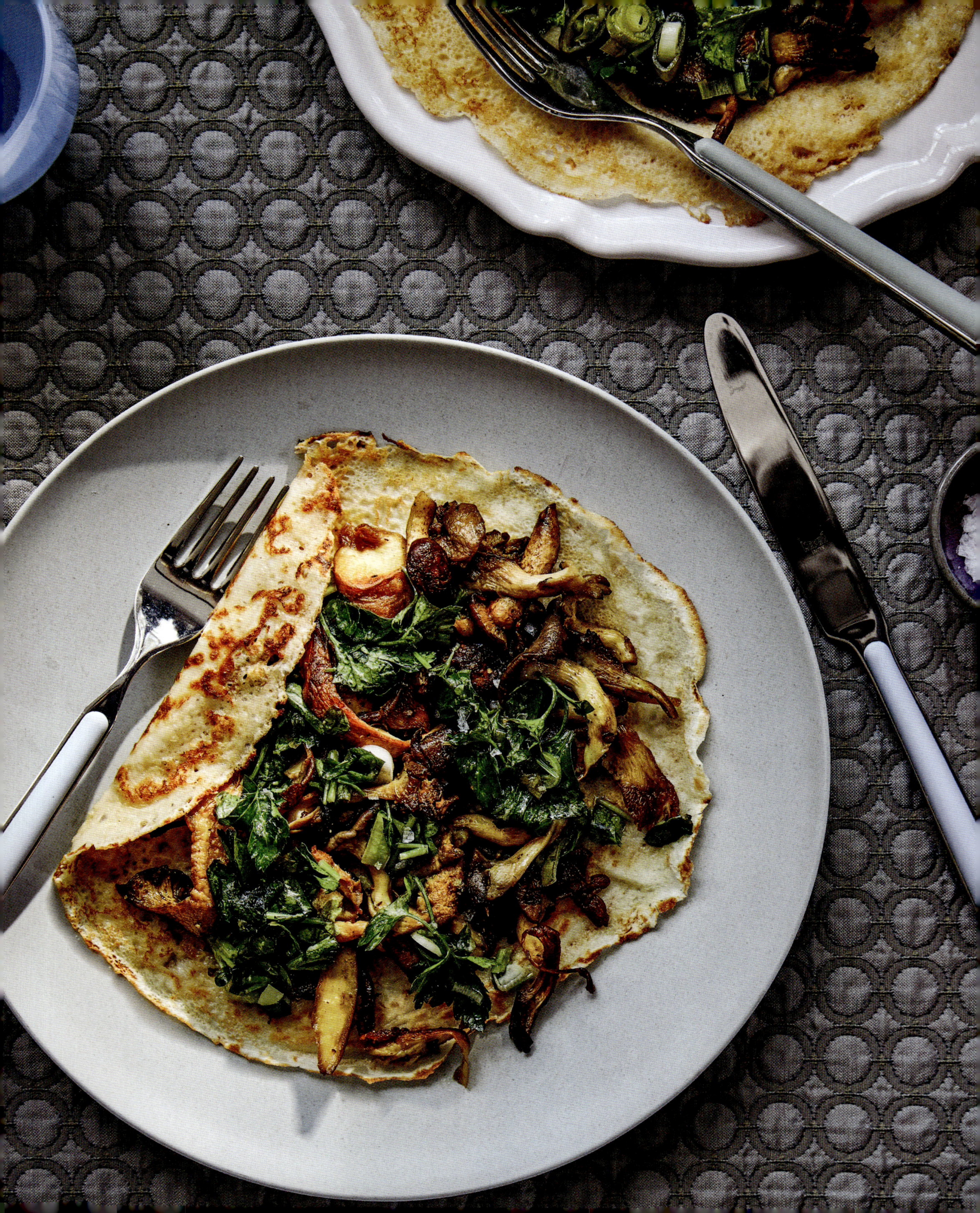

Crêpes with Mushrooms and Gremolata

I'll take any excuse to eat pancakes—or in this case, crêpes—for dinner. These are not the anemic street crêpes you may have come across on study abroad. Fried in ample butter, the crêpes take on the look of a dappled moon with swaths of brown spots and the occasional crispy edge. Of course, you could also serve crêpes for brunch with a pat of butter and dusting of sugar or maple syrup.

NOTES: Mushrooms and gremolata can be stored in an airtight container in the refrigerator for up to 3 days. To store crêpes, place wax paper between the crêpes and place in a large zip-top bag in the refrigerator for up to 4 days.

1. **Make the gremolata:** Stir together the parsley, scallions, lemon zest, lemon juice, garlic, olive oil, and salt in a small bowl to combine.

2. **Make the mushrooms:** Heat the olive oil in a large pan over medium-high heat. When the oil begins to shimmer, add the mushrooms and cook, stirring occasionally, until they are golden brown, about 10 minutes. Add the salt, pepper, fennel, turmeric, and cumin and stir to combine. Remove the pan from the heat.

3. **Make the crêpes:** Crack the egg into a large bowl and beat with a whisk. Add a few tablespoons of the flour and whisk to combine. Add a few tablespoons of the milk and whisk to combine. Continue alternating adding flour and milk and whisking until they have all been incorporated and the batter is smooth. Add the salt and whisk to combine once more.

4. Melt ½ tablespoon of butter in a large pan over medium-high heat. When the butter has melted, reduce the heat to medium. Add ¼ to ½ cup of batter to the pan and tilt the pan making sure the batter fills the entire surface, creating a circle. Cook for 1 to 2 minutes, until the edges of the crêpe begin to curl up and you no longer see raw batter in the center. Flip the crêpe over with a spatula and cook for 1 minute. Transfer the crêpe to a plate and repeat with the remaining batter, adding thin slices of unsalted butter with every addition.

5. Serve the crêpes immediately with a spoonful of mushrooms and a drizzle of gremolata.

Serves 4

GREMOLATA

Leaves and tender stems from ½ bunch flat-leaf parsley, coarsely chopped (about 1 cup)

1 bunch scallions, thinly sliced

Zest and juice of 1 lemon (about 2 tablespoons juice)

1 garlic clove, grated

3 tablespoons extra-virgin olive oil

½ teaspoon kosher salt

MUSHROOMS

2 tablespoons extra-virgin olive oil

2 pounds assorted whole mushrooms, roughly torn

1 teaspoon kosher salt

1 teaspoon freshly ground black pepper

1 teaspoon fennel seeds, crushed with a mortar and pestle

½ teaspoon ground turmeric

½ teaspoon ground cumin

CRÊPES

1 large egg

1½ cups all-purpose flour

2 cups whole milk

1 teaspoon kosher salt

Unsalted butter, for frying

Rib Eyes with a Party Wedge Salad

There is nothing new or inventive about this recipe, except to say that it's my perfect meal. When you live 163 miles from the nearest worthwhile steak house, you take matters into your own hands. Rib eyes are my cut of choice, and here I sear them to get a deeply browned crust before finishing them in the oven. A wedge salad is obligatory. To bookend the meal, start with shrimp cocktail and oysters and end with an ice cream sundae or, better yet, spumoni (page 259).

NOTES: Blue cheese dressing can be made up to 3 days in advance and stored in an airtight container in the refrigerator. Leftover steak can be stored in an airtight container in the refrigerator for up to 3 days.

1. **Start the rib eyes:** Pat the rib eyes dry on both sides with a paper towel. Generously season them with salt and place on a rimmed baking sheet, uncovered, in the refrigerator for at least 8 hours or up to 48 hours. Take the rib eyes out of the refrigerator 1 hour before cooking.

2. Preheat the oven to 450°F.

3. **Make the salad:** Heat a large pan over medium-high heat. When the pan is warm, add the bacon and cook, stirring occasionally, until crispy, 8 to 10 minutes. Transfer the bacon to a paper towel–lined plate.

4. Combine the sour cream, mayonnaise, lemon juice, garlic, pepper, and salt in a medium bowl and whisk until smooth. Stir in the blue cheese.

5. **Make the steaks:** Heat the oil in large cast-iron or stainless-steel pan over medium-high heat (use two pans if needed). When the oil begins to shimmer, add the rib eyes and cook, undisturbed, until a crust forms, about 4 minutes. Add the butter and thyme and flip the rib eyes. Cook, basting the steaks continuously with the butter, until golden brown, about 4 minutes.

6. Transfer the pan to the oven until the internal temperature reaches 140°F (for medium-rare—adjust the time as needed for your desired doneness), 5 to 6 minutes. Let the rib eyes rest on a cutting board at room temperature for 10 minutes. Slice and place on a serving platter.

7. Place the iceberg on a serving platter and spoon the dressing over the top. Sprinkle with the tomatoes, bacon, chives, and black pepper. Serve with the steak alongside.

Serves 6

RIB EYE STEAKS

4 (1-inch-thick) rib eye steaks (2½ to 3 pounds total)

Kosher salt, to taste

Freshly ground black pepper, to taste

1 teaspoon neutral oil

3 tablespoons unsalted butter

3 thyme sprigs

SALAD

10 slices thick-cut bacon, cut crosswise into ½-inch pieces

½ cup full-fat sour cream

¼ cup mayonnaise

Juice of 1 lemon (about 2 tablespoons)

1 garlic clove, grated

1 teaspoon freshly ground black pepper, plus more for serving

½ teaspoon kosher salt

3 ounces blue cheese, finely crumbled

1 medium head iceberg lettuce, cut into eighths

2 cups cherry tomatoes, halved

¼ cup finely chopped fresh chives, for serving

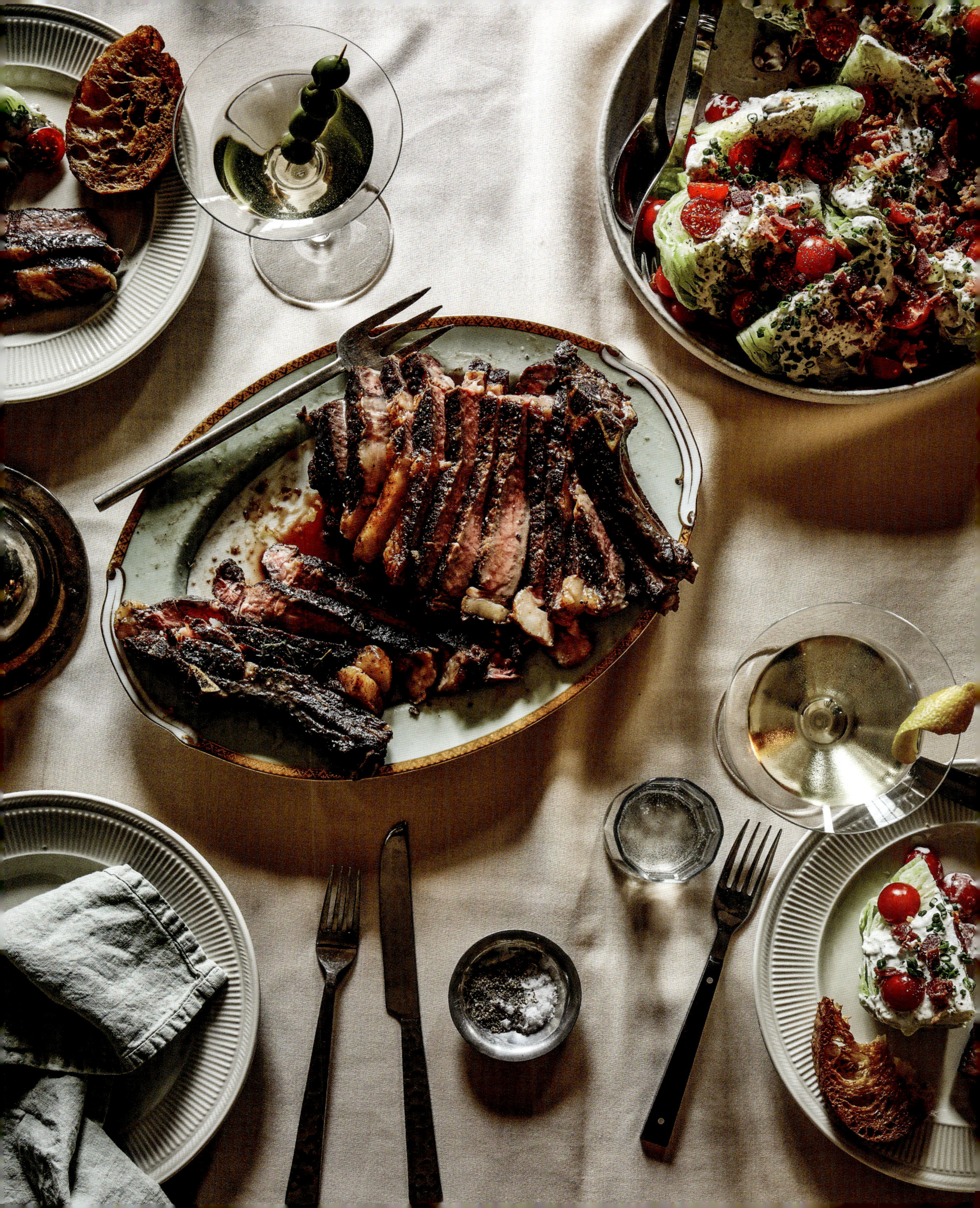

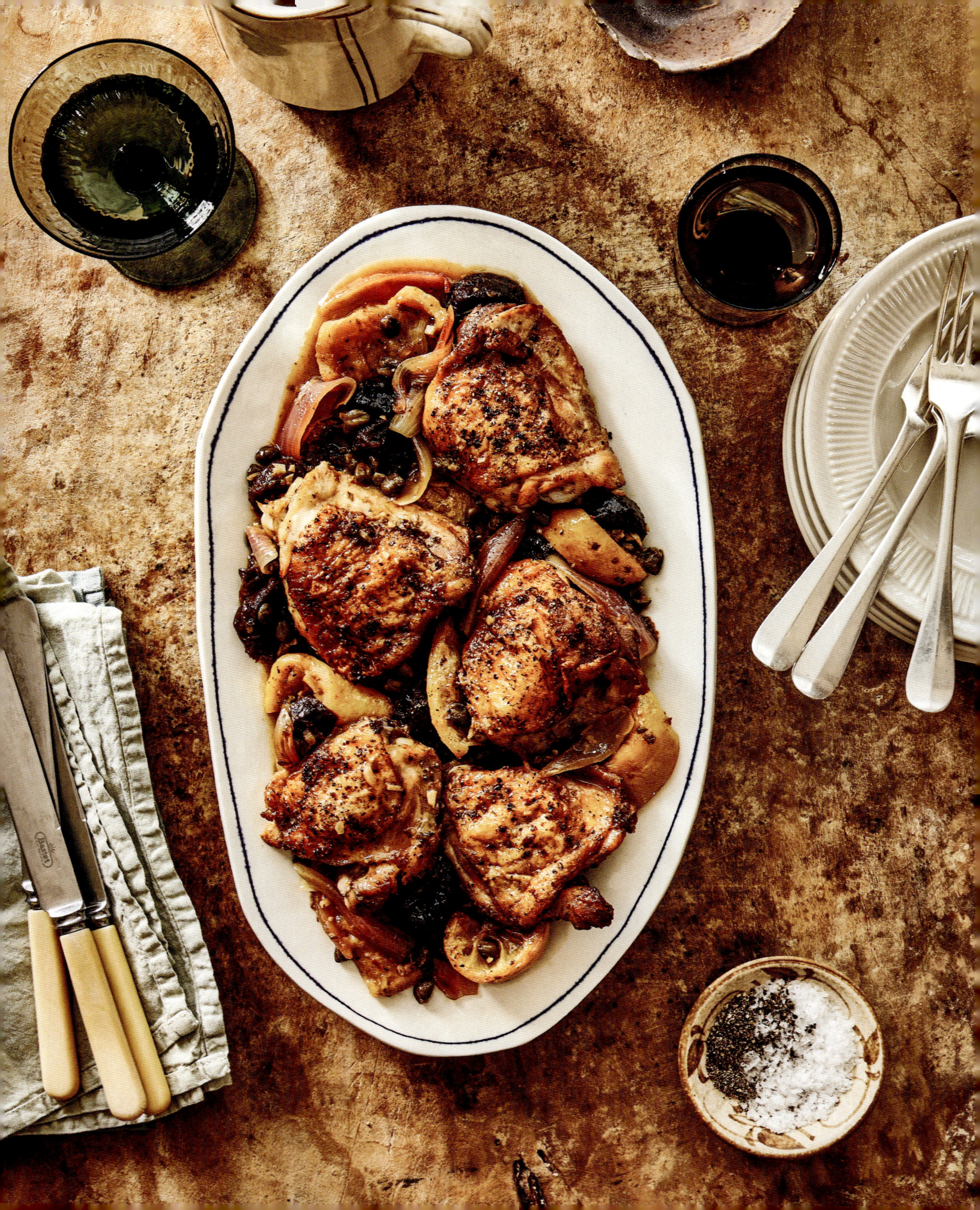

Braised Chicken Thighs with Prunes and Lemons

I rarely use other people's recipes, but one that I keep coming back to is the chicken marbella from *The Silver Palate Cookbook*. This cookbook truly changed the game for home cooks in the '80s, and the recipes still hold up decades later. My take on this recipe keeps a few elements the same, like the prunes and capers, while making some tweaks (one-pot, no overnight marinating, charred lemons). The result might be one of my favorite recipes ever. This chicken is extra saucy, so serving it with something to sop it up, like crusty bread, rice, or pasta, is a must.

NOTE: Leftover chicken can be stored in an airtight container in the refrigerator for up to 3 days.

Serves 6

- 8 to 10 bone-in, skin-on chicken thighs
- 2 teaspoons kosher salt
- 2 teaspoons freshly ground black pepper
- 1 tablespoon extra-virgin olive oil
- 1 medium red onion, cut into eighths
- 2 lemons, quartered
- 1 (8-ounce) package pitted prunes (1½ cups)
- 6 garlic cloves, minced
- 2 tablespoons capers, drained and rinsed
- 2 tablespoons light brown sugar
- 2 teaspoons dried oregano
- ½ teaspoon red pepper flakes
- ¾ cup dry white wine, such as sauvignon blanc or pinot grigio
- ¾ cup chicken stock

1. Preheat the oven to 350°F.
2. Pat the chicken thighs dry with paper towels. Season them on both sides with the salt and pepper.
3. Heat the olive oil in a large oven-safe pan or Dutch oven over medium-high heat. When the oil begins to shimmer, add half the chicken thighs skin-side down and cook, undisturbed, until the skin is golden brown, 7 to 9 minutes. Flip the chicken thighs over and cook until golden brown on the other side, about 4 minutes more. Transfer the chicken thighs to a paper towel–lined plate. Repeat with the remaining chicken thighs, searing them for 2 minutes less per side, since the pan will be hotter. Drain all but 3 tablespoons of the chicken fat from the pan.
4. Add the onion and lemons to the pot and cook, stirring occasionally, until both are lightly browned, about 3 minutes. Add in the prunes, garlic, capers, brown sugar, oregano, and red pepper flakes and cook, stirring, until deeply aromatic, about 1 minute.
5. Add the wine and stock and cook, scraping up any brown bits on the bottom of the pan, until the alcohol has burned off and the liquid is simmering, about 2 minutes.
6. Nestle the chicken thighs back into the pot and place the lid on. Transfer the pot to the oven and braise for 1 hour.
7. Transfer the chicken to a serving platter and spoon the sauce over it.

Butternut Squash and Ricotta Lasagna

Winter's favorite flavors come together in this vegetarian take on lasagna with butternut squash, roasted garlic, and sage. I like alternating the noodles so they creep out of the edge of the dish, becoming crispy in the oven.

NOTE: Leftover lasagna can be stored in an airtight container in the refrigerator for up to 3 days.

1. **Make the sauce:** Preheat the oven to 425°F.

2. Place the squash, onion, and garlic on a rimmed baking sheet, drizzle with olive oil, and sprinkle with 1 teaspoon salt, then use your hands to mix until well coated. Bake until the squash is easily pierced with a knife, 35 to 45 minutes.

3. Transfer the squash mixture to a blender or food processor. Add the stock, sage, 1 teaspoon salt, the black pepper, and the red pepper flakes and blend on high until smooth. Add the lemon juice and blend once more.

4. Bring a large pot of salted water to a boil over high heat. Add the noodles and cook according to the package instructions until 2 minutes shy of al dente. (The noodles should still have a bite and be just pliable enough to bend but not to break.) Drain the noodles in a colander, then run them under cool water to prevent sticking.

5. Stir together the ricotta and lemon zest in a small bowl to combine.

6. **Make the topping:** Stir together the panko, melted butter, sage, salt, and pepper in a small bowl.

7. **Assemble the lasagna:** Spread 1 cup of the squash mixture on the bottom of a 3-quart baking dish. Layer 4 noodles, slightly overlapping, over the squash. Spread ½ cup of the squash mixture on top of the noodles, then top with ¼ cup of the ricotta mixture and spread in an even layer. Repeat with the remaining noodles, filling, and ricotta. Sprinkle the panko mixture over the mozzarella and ricotta in an even layer.

8. Bake until the cheese has melted and the edges of the lasagna are crispy, 25 to 30 minutes. Let cool for 5 minutes before serving.

Serves 4 to 6

LASAGNA

1 (2-pound) butternut squash, peeled, seeded, and cut into 1-inch cubes

1 medium yellow onion, cut into ¼-inch slices

4 garlic cloves, smashed

1 tablespoon extra-virgin olive oil

Kosher salt

2 cups vegetable stock

1 tablespoon finely chopped fresh sage

1 teaspoon freshly ground black pepper

¼ teaspoon red pepper flakes

Juice of 1 lemon (about 2 tablespoons)

1 (16-ounce) box lasagna noodles

1 (16-ounce) container whole-milk ricotta

Zest of 2 lemons

TOPPING

½ cup panko breadcrumbs

3 tablespoons unsalted butter, melted

1 tablespoon finely chopped fresh sage

½ teaspoon kosher salt

½ teaspoon freshly ground black pepper

1 (8-ounce) ball fresh mozzarella, roughly torn

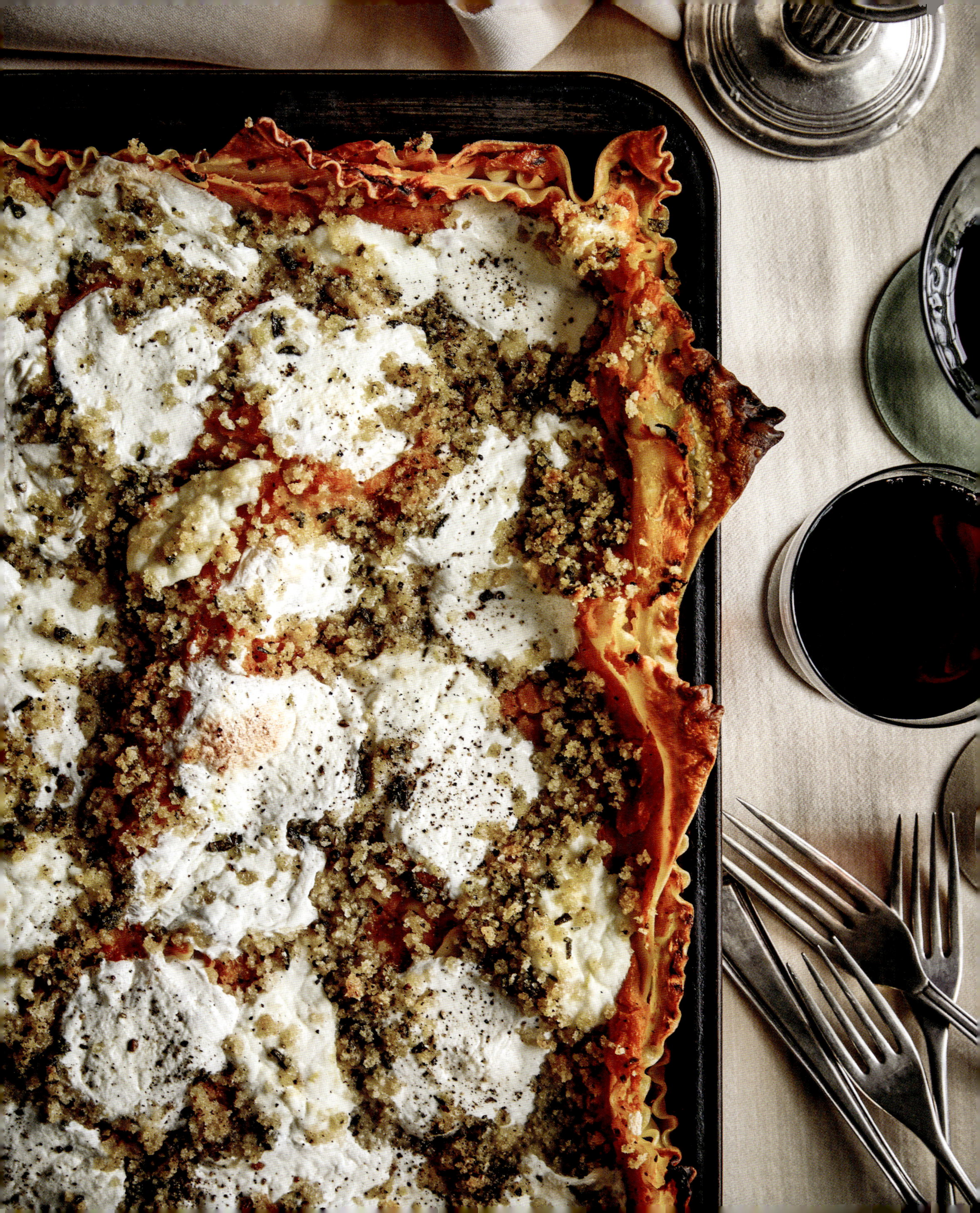

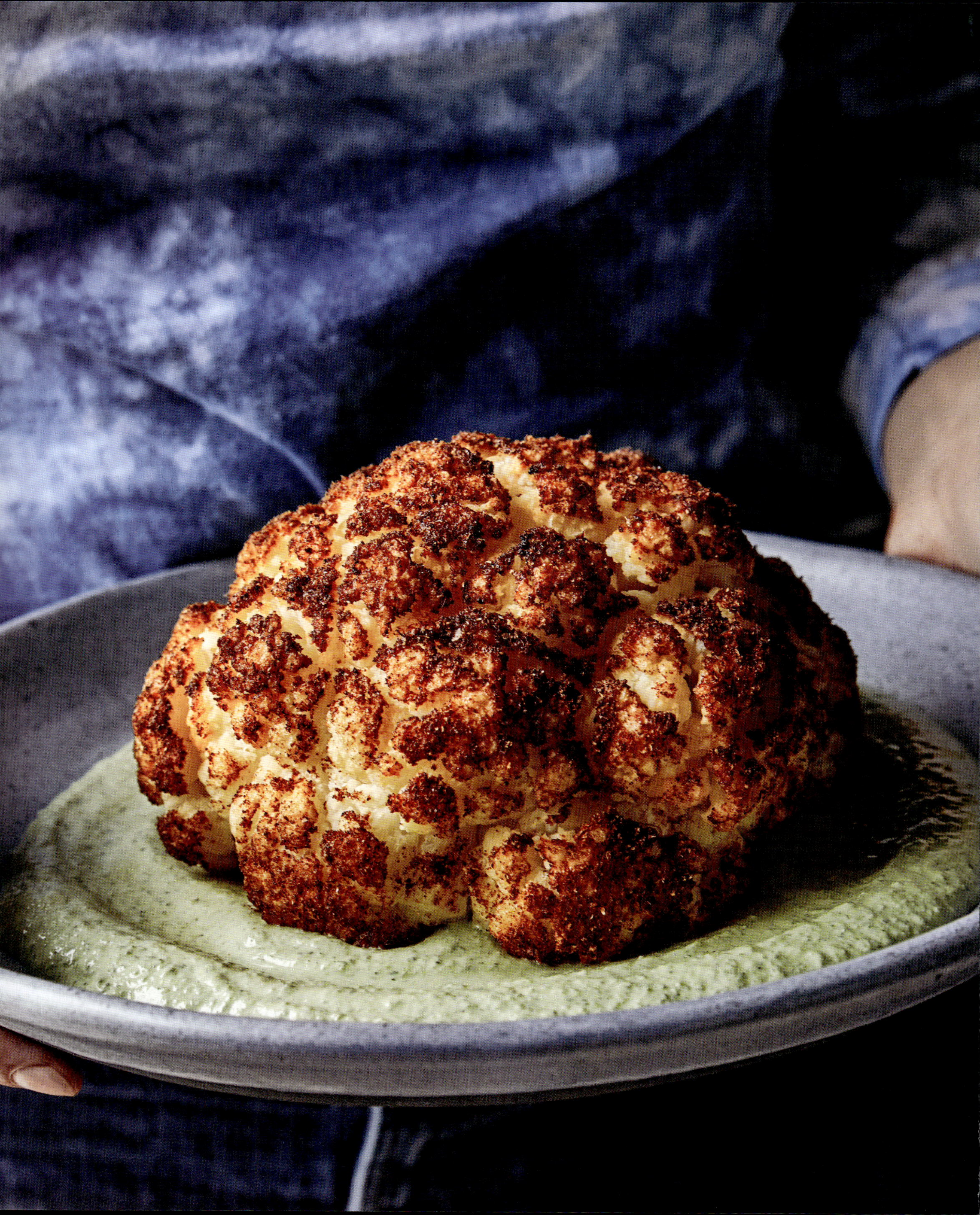

Whole Roasted Spiced Cauliflower with Herby Yogurt Sauce

While at first cauliflower may seem like a humble vegetable, it's really the ideal blank slate to take on so many different flavor profiles. Here, it's rubbed in a mix of spices and roasted whole until slightly charred before being served on a bed of herby yogurt. Boiling the cauliflower first, in this case in vegetable stock, imparts flavor from the inside out while keeping the cauliflower tender. My vision is that you serve it almost like a pie, or big roast, with a knife on the side that encourages everyone at the table to take a slice, getting some sauce along the way.

NOTES: The cauliflower can be boiled in the stock up to 24 hours in advance and stored, covered, in the refrigerator. The herby yogurt sauce can be stored in an airtight container in the refrigerator for up to 5 days.

Serves 6 to 8

CAULIFLOWER

12 cups vegetable stock

1 tablespoon plus 1 teaspoon kosher salt

1 large head cauliflower (about 2 pounds), stem and leaves trimmed

2 tablespoons extra-virgin olive oil

1 teaspoon sweet paprika

1 teaspoon ground cumin

1 teaspoon ground coriander

HERBY YOGURT SAUCE

2 cups plain full-fat Greek yogurt

½ bunch cilantro, coarsely chopped (about 1 cup)

½ bunch flat-leaf parsley, coarsely chopped (about 1 cup)

1 cup coarsely chopped fresh mint leaves

Zest and juice of 3 limes (about 6 tablespoons juice)

¼ cup extra-virgin olive oil

1 medium jalapeño, coarsely chopped

2 garlic cloves, grated

1 teaspoon kosher salt

1. **Make the cauliflower:** Pour the stock into a large pot, add 1 tablespoon of the salt, and bring to a boil over high heat. When the stock begins to boil, carefully add the cauliflower, stem-side up. Boil the cauliflower until a knife easily pierces the inside stem, about 12 minutes. Transfer the cauliflower to a colander and let drain.

2. Preheat the oven to 425°F.

3. Place the cauliflower on a rimmed baking sheet, stem-side down, and drizzle it with olive oil. Season with the paprika, cumin, coriander, and remaining 1 teaspoon salt, rubbing them all over the cauliflower. Roast until the cauliflower is browned, about 45 minutes.

4. **Meanwhile, make the herby yogurt sauce:** Combine the yogurt, cilantro, parsley, mint, lime zest, lime juice, olive oil, jalapeño, garlic, and salt in a food processor and process until smooth.

5. Spread the yogurt sauce on a serving platter. Place the cauliflower directly on top of it. Serve the cauliflower with a chef's knife at the table and let guests cut wedges out as they pass it.

Soy-Braised Cumin Lamb

On cold nights all I want is something to wake up the senses. Something sticky and caramelized, that balances big flavors and texture. Something like this, where hunks of lamb are braised in orange juice and soy sauce with a bevy of aromatics, including more cumin than you think is acceptable. I should warn you there's nothing traditional about this recipe. The final dish lands somewhere around Chinese cumin lamb married with Korean bo ssam in the way it's served, tucked into lettuce wraps with rice.

NOTES: You can swap in lamb stew meat for the boneless lamb shoulder. Leftover lamb can be stored in an airtight container in the refrigerator for up to 3 days.

Serves 4 to 6

- 3 pounds lamb stew meat
- Kosher salt and freshly ground black pepper
- 1 tablespoon extra-virgin olive oil, plus more if needed
- 2 medium yellow onions, thinly sliced
- 1 (1½-inch) knob fresh ginger, thinly sliced into strips
- 4 garlic cloves, thinly sliced
- 1 tablespoon ground cumin
- 1 teaspoon sugar
- ½ teaspoon red pepper flakes
- Juice of 2 navel oranges (about ½ cup)
- ¼ cup soy sauce
- Leaves and tender stems from 1 bunch cilantro, finely chopped (about 2 cups)
- Boston lettuce leaves, for serving
- Cooked white rice, for serving

1. Pat the lamb dry with a paper towel. Season with salt and pepper on all sides. Heat the olive oil in a large pot or Dutch oven over medium-high heat. When the oil begins to shimmer, add the lamb and cook, stirring occasionally, until golden brown on all sides, about 10 minutes. Depending on the size of your pot, you may need to add the lamb in batches. Use a slotted spoon to transfer the lamb to a paper towel–lined bowl.

2. Add the onions to the pot with the remaining lamb fat and cook, stirring occasionally, until golden, 3 to 4 minutes. If the pan is too dry, add a drizzle of olive oil.

3. Add the ginger, garlic, cumin, sugar, and red pepper flakes and stir until well combined and aromatic, about 1 minute. Add the orange juice and soy sauce and bring to a simmer. Add the lamb back to the pot and place the lid on. Reduce the heat to medium-low and simmer until the lamb is tender and caramelized, about 1 hour.

4. Add the cilantro and stir to combine. Serve the lamb in lettuce cups with rice.

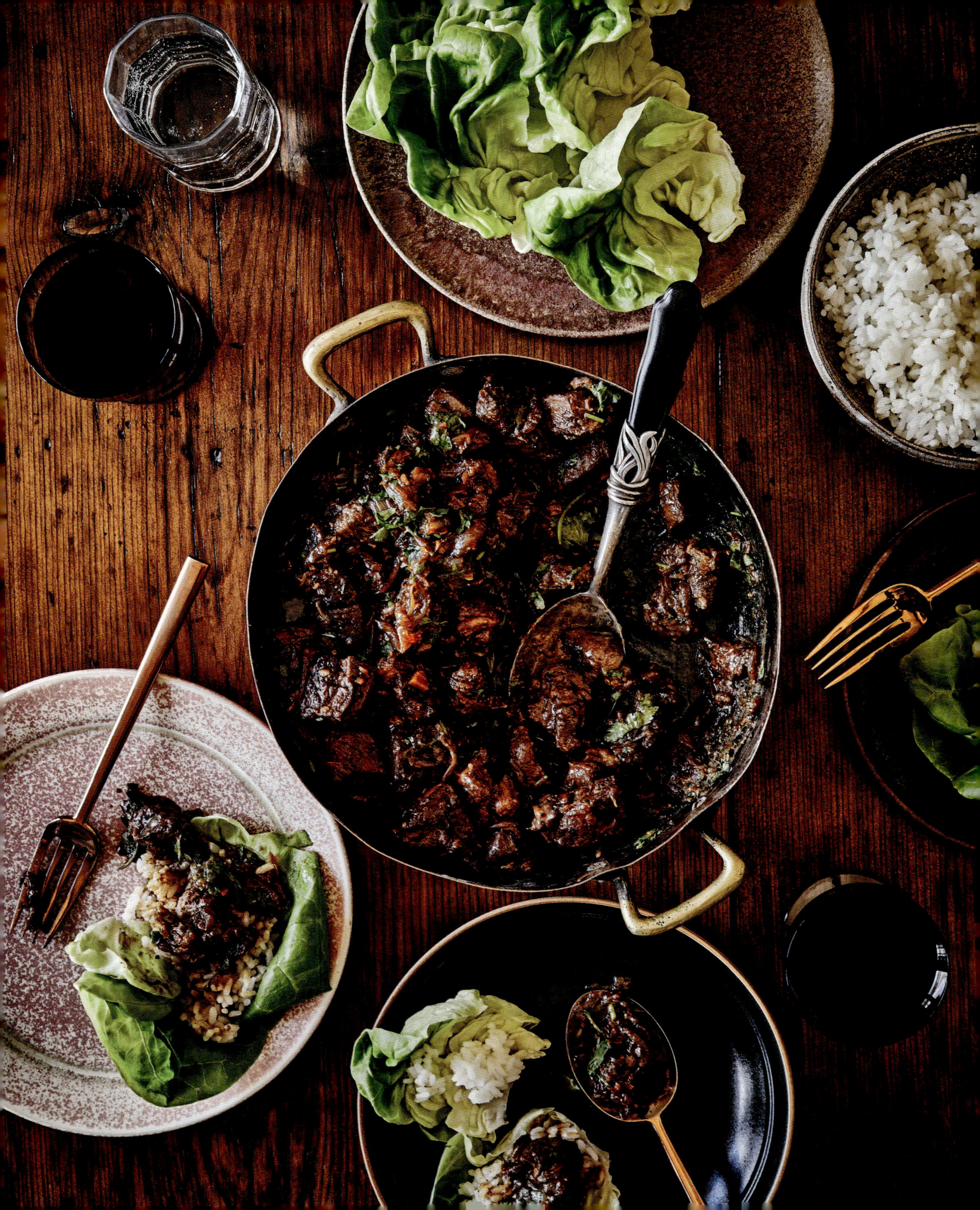

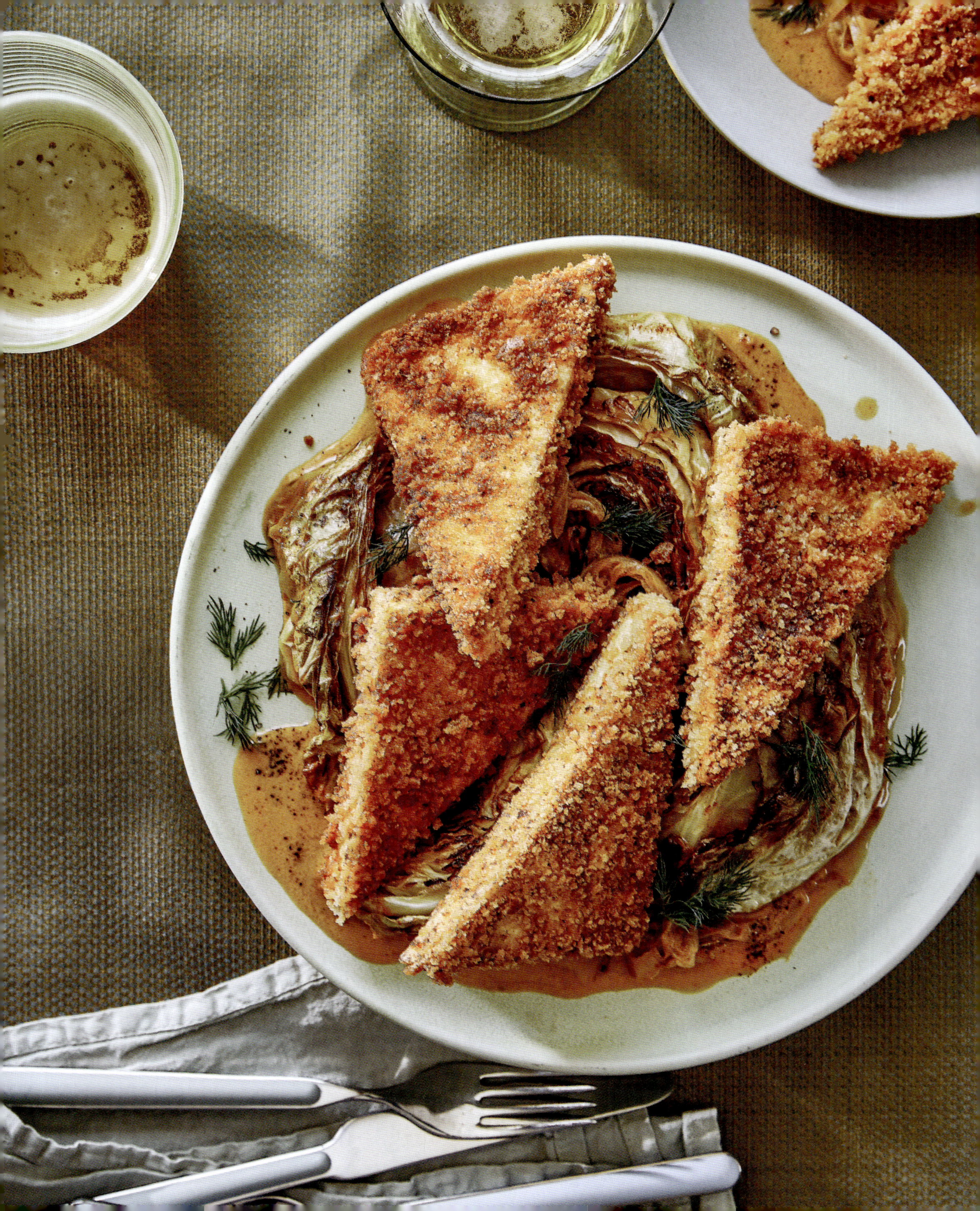

Tofu Schnitzel with Braised Cabbage

I'm not usually a fan of making vegetarian versions of meat-centric dishes, but this dish is an exception. Here, tofu gets the schnitzel treatment. Thin triangles of tofu are breaded and shallow-fried until golden brown and crispy to mimic a traditional thinly pounded pork tenderloin or chicken breast. While the tofu delivers all the crunch of traditional thinly pounded pork tenderloin or chicken schnitzel, the sleeper hit of this recipe is the braised cabbage. Cooked down in heavy cream, mustard, and aromatics, it takes on that melt-in-your-mouth quality while adding a welcome sauciness to the tofu.

NOTES: Cabbage and tofu can be stored in an airtight container in the refrigerator for up to 3 days. For optimal freshness, store them separately. Note that the tofu will lose its crunch after sitting in the refrigerator.

1. **Make the braised cabbage:** Preheat the oven to 400°F.

2. Cut the cabbage through the core into 8 wedges. Heat 1 tablespoon of the olive oil in a wide Dutch oven or large high-sided pan over medium-high heat. When the oil begins to shimmer, add 4 cabbage wedges to the pan in a single layer and cook, undisturbed, until charred, about 7 minutes. Flip the cabbage over and repeat, cooking until the other side is charred, about 5 minutes. Transfer the cabbage to a plate. Continue with the remaining cabbage wedges, adding an additional 1 tablespoon of olive oil before charring each batch.

3. In the same pan, cook the onions until lightly golden, about 3 minutes. Add the stock, heavy cream, mustard, garlic, salt, pepper, and paprika to the pot and stir to combine. Bring the mixture to a simmer, then nestle the charred cabbage wedges into the pan.

4. Transfer the mixture, uncovered, to the oven and braise until the cabbage is easily pierced with a knife, about 50 minutes. Drizzle the lemon juice and sprinkle the dill on top of the cabbage before serving.

5. **Make the tofu schnitzel:** To remove moisture, place the tofu

Recipe continues

Serves 6

BRAISED CABBAGE

1 medium green cabbage

4 tablespoons extra-virgin olive oil

2 medium yellow onions, thinly sliced

2 cups vegetable stock

1 cup heavy cream

2 tablespoons Dijon mustard

6 garlic cloves, peeled

1 teaspoon kosher salt

1 teaspoon freshly ground black pepper

1 teaspoon sweet paprika

Juice of 1 lemon

¼ cup fresh dill, finely chopped

TOFU SCHNITZEL

2 (16-ounce) packages extra-firm tofu

⅓ cup all-purpose flour

1 tablespoon freshly ground black pepper

2 teaspoons kosher salt, plus more to taste

2 teaspoons sweet paprika

1 teaspoon cayenne pepper

2 large eggs

2 cups panko breadcrumbs

2 cups neutral oil

Dijon mustard, for serving

WEEKENDS | DINNER

blocks on paper towels, top with more paper towels, and place a weight on top, such as a rimmed baking sheet topped with a cast-iron pan. Let stand for at least 1 hour. Remove the weight and paper towels. Stand the tofu blocks on a cutting board and cut them into thirds, creating 3 thinner squares. Cut each square on the diagonal to create a triangle.

6. Whisk together the flour, black pepper, salt, paprika, and cayenne in a shallow bowl. In a separate shallow bowl, whisk the eggs. Place the panko in a third shallow bowl.

7. Dip the tofu triangles in the flour, shaking off any excess. Next dip them in the egg, then lastly dip in the panko.

8. Heat the oil in a large pan with tall sides over medium-high heat. When the oil is very hot and shimmering, add half the tofu triangles and cook, undisturbed, until golden brown, about 5 minutes. Carefully flip the tofu over and cook until golden brown, about 5 minutes more. Transfer the tofu to a paper towel–lined baking sheet and season with salt. Repeat with the remaining tofu triangles.

9. Serve the tofu with a wedge or two of cabbage, along with the sauce and a dollop of mustard.

Slow-Roasted Salmon with Grapefruit and Crispy Shallots

I'll come right out and say that this method for cooking salmon should put it squarely in the weeknight dinner camp. Here's the thing, though: What makes this dish particularly festive is the shower of crispy shallots that gets sprinkled on top before serving. Since slowly stirring shallots until golden is decidedly a weekend activity, here we are. The salmon is rubbed in a simple spice mixture with crushed fennel seeds and coriander and cooked with a glug of olive oil and sliced grapefruit. The olive oil insulates the fish from overcooking while the grapefruit's flavor mellows. The idea here is to have salmon, grapefruit, and shallots in every bite.

NOTES: If you can find store-bought crispy shallots, this is a great time to use them, although homemade is hard to beat. Crispy shallots can be stored in a paper towel–lined airtight container at room temperature for up to 5 days. Leftover salmon can be stored in an airtight container in the refrigerator for up to 3 days.

Serves 6 to 8

CRISPY SHALLOTS
¾ cup neutral oil
8 medium shallots, thinly sliced
½ teaspoon kosher salt

SALMON
¼ cup extra-virgin olive oil, plus more for greasing
1 grapefruit
1 tablespoon light brown sugar
2 teaspoons kosher salt
1 teaspoon freshly ground black pepper
1 teaspoon ground coriander
1 teaspoon fennel seeds, crushed with a mortar and pestle
1 (2-pound) center-cut salmon fillet

1. **Make the crispy shallots:** Heat the oil in a large pan over medium heat. When the oil begins to shimmer, add the shallots and stir to combine. Reduce the heat to medium-low and cook, stirring every few minutes, until the shallots are deeply golden brown and crispy, 30 to 40 minutes, depending on your stove. The shallots will look like they're almost melting before they begin to crisp. Trust me, and keep going. Transfer the shallots to a paper towel–lined plate and season with salt.

2. **Make the salmon:** Preheat the oven to 300°F. Grease a rimmed baking sheet with olive oil.

3. Zest the grapefruit and put the zest into a small bowl. Add the brown sugar, salt, pepper, coriander, and fennel seeds and stir to combine.

4. Remove the rind and pith of the grapefruit. To do this, place the grapefruit on a cutting board and use a chef's knife or paring knife to carve downward in small sections, removing the pith of the grapefruit while keeping the fruit intact. Continue working your way around the grapefruit until the rind is completely removed, without any

Recipe continues

WEEKENDS | DINNER 223

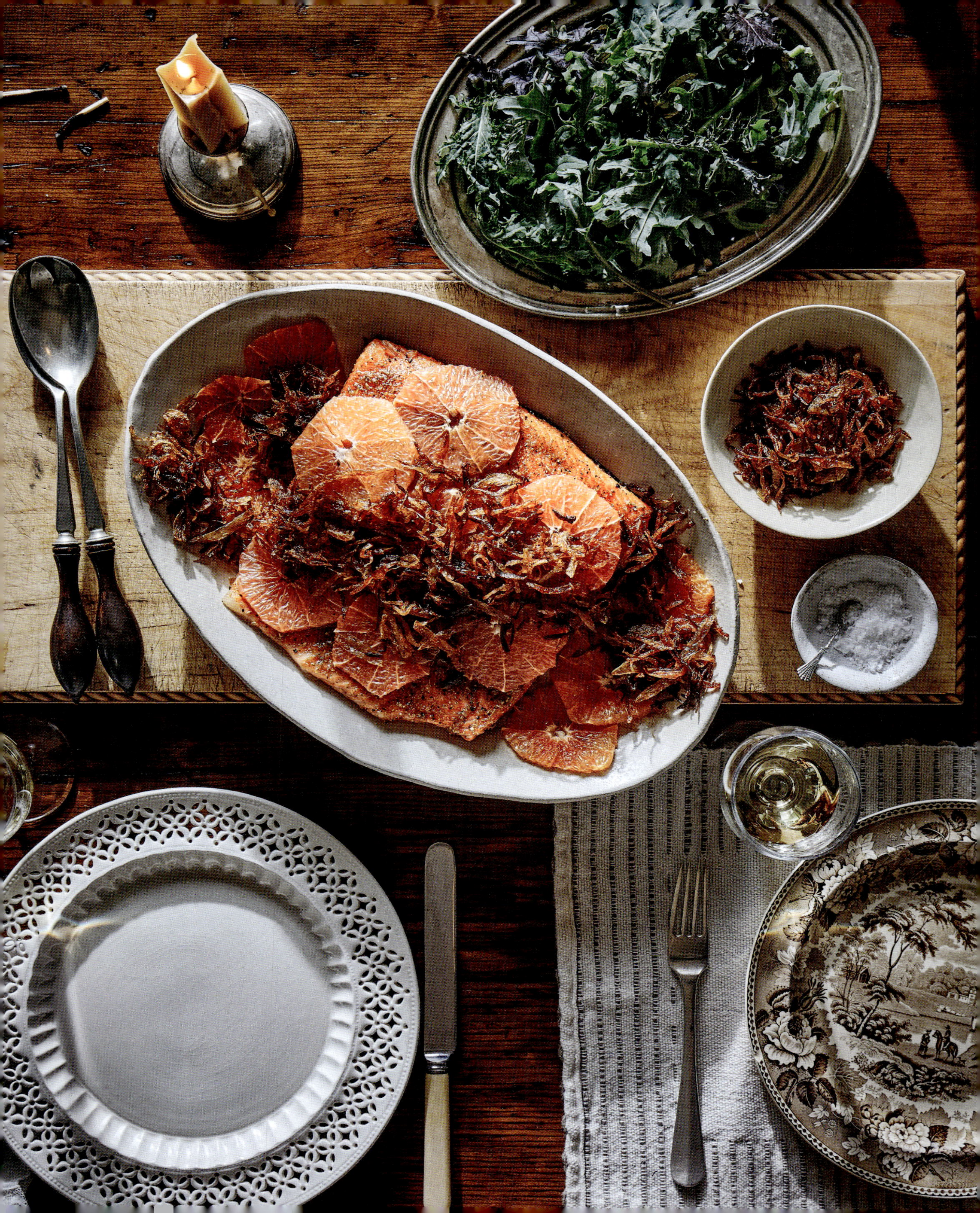

remaining pith. Cut the grapefruit crosswise into ¼-inch-thick slices.

5 Place the salmon skin-side down on the greased baking sheet and drizzle with the olive oil. Rub the brown sugar mixture over the salmon. Place the thinly sliced grapefruit over the salmon and bake until the edges of the salmon are opaque and the fish easily flakes, about 25 minutes. The salmon will still look very pink, but don't worry, it's cooked.

6 Serve the salmon, taking care to include some grapefruit with each portion, and top with the crispy shallots.

French Market Chicken with Schmaltzy Potatoes

If you've had the pleasure of wandering through a market in France, you've crossed paths with a very well-known market fare, poulet rôti. Poulet rôti is a simply prepared French-style roast chicken, often cooked on a rotisserie in the market, and served with schmaltz-drenched potatoes. Beneath a papery golden brown skin, the meat pulls away from the bone, offering hunks of perfectly cooked chicken. I wanted to achieve the same flavor and texture, but with a method that was more feasible for home cooks—since, let's be real, how many of us have rotisseries? The key here is cooking the chicken low and slow for a whopping three hours. To ensure an even juicier chicken, I start by roasting the bird breast-side down, then flip it halfway through the cooking time. I like pretending I'm in France when I make this and serve it with a doctored-up side of mayonnaise and a simply dressed green salad.

NOTE: The chicken and potatoes can be stored in an airtight container in the refrigerator for up to 3 days.

Serves 4

- 1 (4-pound) whole chicken, giblets removed
- 2 pounds new potatoes, halved
- 1 head garlic, cloves separated and peeled
- 2½ teaspoons kosher salt
- 4 tablespoons (½ stick) unsalted butter, at room temperature
- 2 tablespoons herbes de Provence
- 2 teaspoons freshly ground black pepper
- ¾ cup mayonnaise
- 2 tablespoons whole-grain mustard
- Juice of 1 lemon (about 2 tablespoons)

1. An hour before cooking, remove the chicken from the refrigerator. Blot it dry with paper towels on all sides, including the cavity, and let rest at room temperature.

2. Preheat the oven to 300°F.

3. Place the potatoes and garlic in a 9×13-inch baking dish and sprinkle with ½ teaspoon of the salt.

4. Combine the butter, herbes de Provence, pepper, and remaining 2 teaspoons salt in a small bowl and stir well. Rub the chicken with the butter mixture on all sides. Place the chicken breast-side down on top of the potatoes and roast for 1 hour 30 minutes.

5. Transfer the chicken to a cutting board. Stir to coat the potatoes in the chicken juices and spread them evenly in the pan. Place the chicken breast-side up on the potatoes and roast for 1 hour 30 minutes more. For more color, broil on high for 2 minutes until the skin is deeply golden brown.

6. While the chicken is in the oven, stir together the mayonnaise, mustard, and lemon juice in a small bowl.

7. Transfer the chicken to a cutting board and let it rest for at least 10 minutes before carving. Serve the chicken over the potatoes with the mayo mixture on the side.

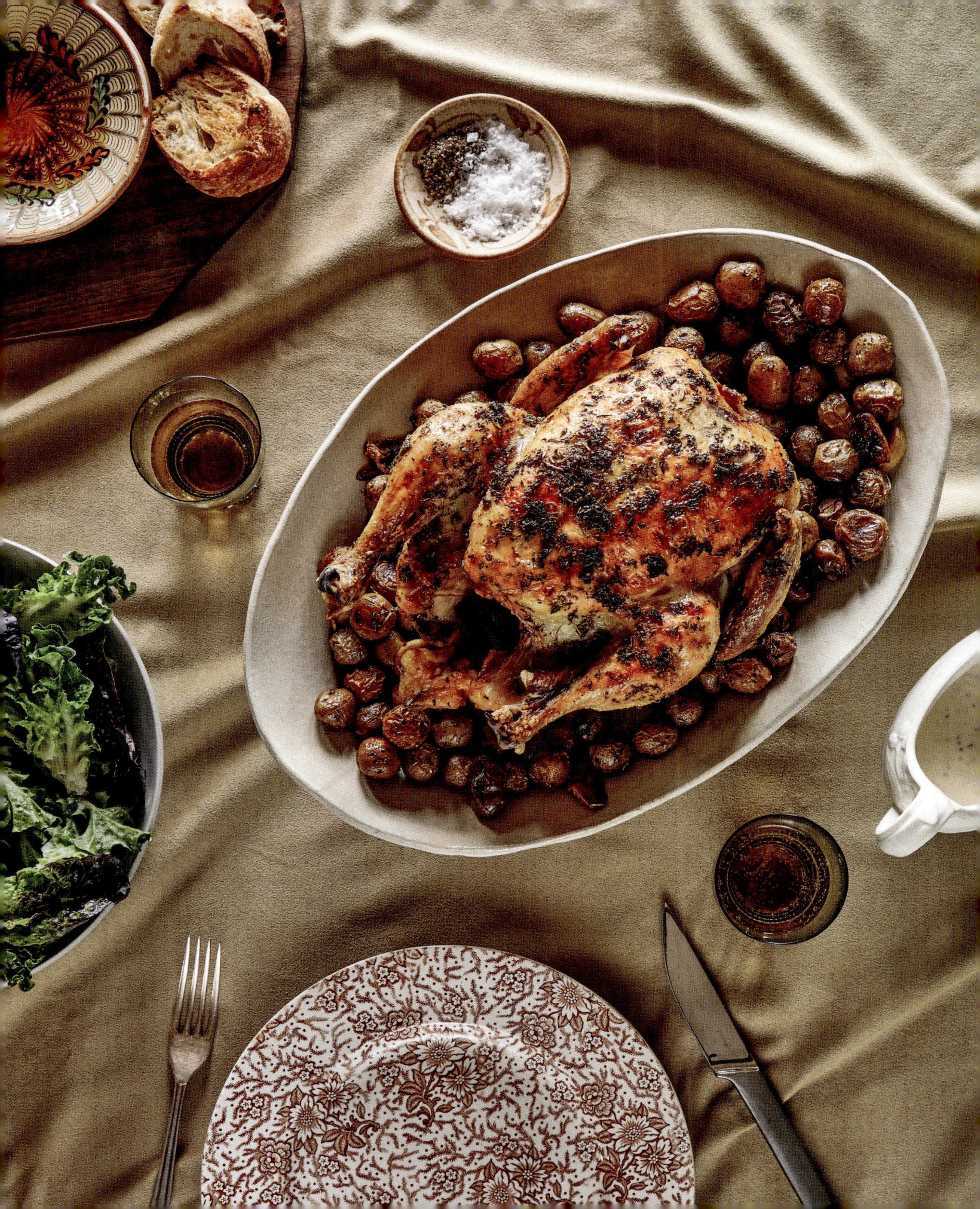

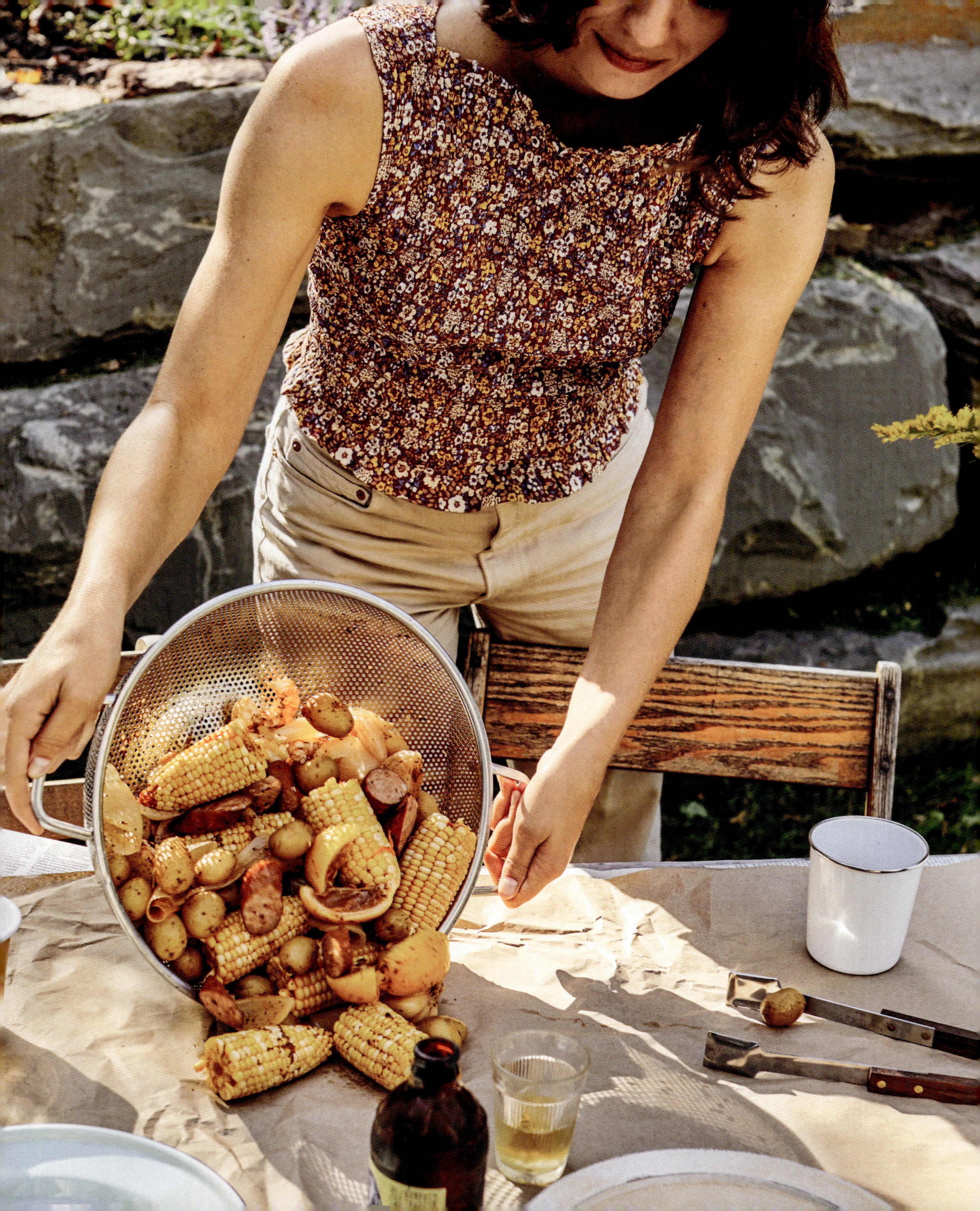

Shrimp Boil with Garlicky Old Bay Butter

Whenever I think of seafood or shrimp boils, I imagine those long tables in Louisiana where an assortment of seafood is poured onto sheets of newspaper. Despite living 1,500 miles from the Pelican State, somewhere along the way I developed an affinity for this Cajun classic. While a shrimp boil might seem daunting, it couldn't be easier to make. Each ingredient is added to a pot of boiling water until cooked through, so all it takes is keeping an eye on the timer. To me, the best part is drenching everything in the garlicky, Old Bay–spiked butter.

NOTES: I like to serve shrimp boils on a layer of newspaper covering an outdoor dining table; I love the communal feel, and it makes cleaning up a breeze. If you're serving a bigger crowd, you can easily double or even triple this recipe—just make sure to use a bigger pot. If you have leftovers, store them in an airtight container in the refrigerator for up to 3 days.

Serves 4

- 1 head plus 3 large cloves garlic
- ½ cup plus 1 tablespoon Old Bay seasoning
- 2 tablespoons kosher salt
- 1 tablespoon freshly ground black pepper
- 2 lemons, quartered
- 1 pound new potatoes
- 2 yellow onions, quartered
- 1 (1-pound) smoked kielbasa, sliced into 1-inch pieces
- 4 ears corn, shucked and halved
- 1 pound shrimp, peeled and deveined
- ½ cup (1 stick) unsalted butter
- ½ bunch flat-leaf parsley, coarsely chopped (about 1 cup)

1. Peel the 3 large garlic cloves; grate them and set them aside. Separate the head of garlic and peel the cloves.

2. Combine ½ cup of the Old Bay with the salt and pepper in a large pot. Squeeze the lemons into the pot, then drop in the rinds. Drop in the whole garlic cloves. Fill the pot with cold water and bring to a boil over high heat. Add the potatoes and onions and cook until the potatoes are just fork-tender, about 10 minutes. Add the kielbasa and cook for 5 minutes. Add the corn and cook for 5 minutes. Add the shrimp and cook until they turn pink and opaque, about 2 minutes. Drain the shrimp boil in a colander and let cool for 5 minutes.

3. Meanwhile, melt the butter in a small pan over medium heat, then add the remaining 1 tablespoon Old Bay and the grated garlic. Cook, stirring, until deeply aromatic, about 1 minute. Remove the butter from the heat and stir in the parsley.

4. Pour the Old Bay butter sauce over the shrimp boil and serve immediately.

Curried Chicken and Cauliflower Phyllo Pie

This recipe riffs on chicken potpie, with a few swaps to transform the dish into something more interesting than the classic. Instead of puff pastry or pie dough, I opted for the even easier route of scrunching up phyllo dough to make a crispy topping. The coconut milk–based roux is heavily perfumed with garlic, ginger, and spices, which gives the dish an added savory quality. In theory, this should serve six, but be forewarned that in my experience, people always go back for seconds, or even thirds.

NOTE: Leftover pie can be stored in an airtight container in the refrigerator for up to 3 days.

Serves 4 to 6

- 2 pounds boneless, skinless chicken thighs
- 2½ teaspoons kosher salt
- 1 teaspoon freshly ground black pepper
- 4 tablespoons extra-virgin olive oil
- 1 small head cauliflower, separated into florets (about 5 cups)
- 1 medium yellow onion, thinly sliced
- 4 garlic cloves, minced
- 1 (1-inch) knob fresh ginger, minced
- 2 teaspoons curry powder
- 1 teaspoon ground cumin
- 1 teaspoon ground coriander
- ¼ cup all-purpose flour
- 1 (15-ounce) can unsweetened full-fat coconut milk
- 2 cups vegetable stock or chicken stock
- 12 sheets phyllo pastry

1. Preheat the oven to 400°F.

2. Pat the chicken thighs dry with paper towels. Season them with 1½ teaspoons of the salt and the pepper. Heat 1 tablespoon of the olive oil in a Dutch oven or large pan over medium-high heat. When the oil begins to shimmer, add the chicken and cook, without moving it, until golden brown, 8 to 10 minutes. Flip the chicken over and cook until golden brown and cooked through, 7 to 9 minutes. Transfer the chicken to a plate and let cool for 10 minutes, then use your hands to shred.

3. Add 1 tablespoon of the olive oil to the pan along with the cauliflower and cook, stirring occasionally, until a knife easily pierces the stem of a floret, about 8 minutes. Add the onion and cook until it is lightly golden, about 3 minutes. Add the shredded chicken, garlic, ginger, curry powder, cumin, coriander, and remaining 1 teaspoon salt and stir for 1 minute until aromatic.

4. Add the flour and cook, stirring frequently, for 2 minutes. Add the coconut milk and stock and reduce the heat to medium. Cook, scraping up any brown bits on the bottom of the pan, until the mixture has thickened, about 10 minutes. Transfer the mixture to a 9×13-inch baking dish.

5. Scrunch each piece of phyllo with your hand until it resembles a frilly flower and place them side by side on top of the chicken filling until the entire top is covered. Use a pastry brush to brush the phyllo with the remaining 2 tablespoons olive oil.

6. Bake the pie until the phyllo is golden brown, about 25 minutes. Serve immediately.

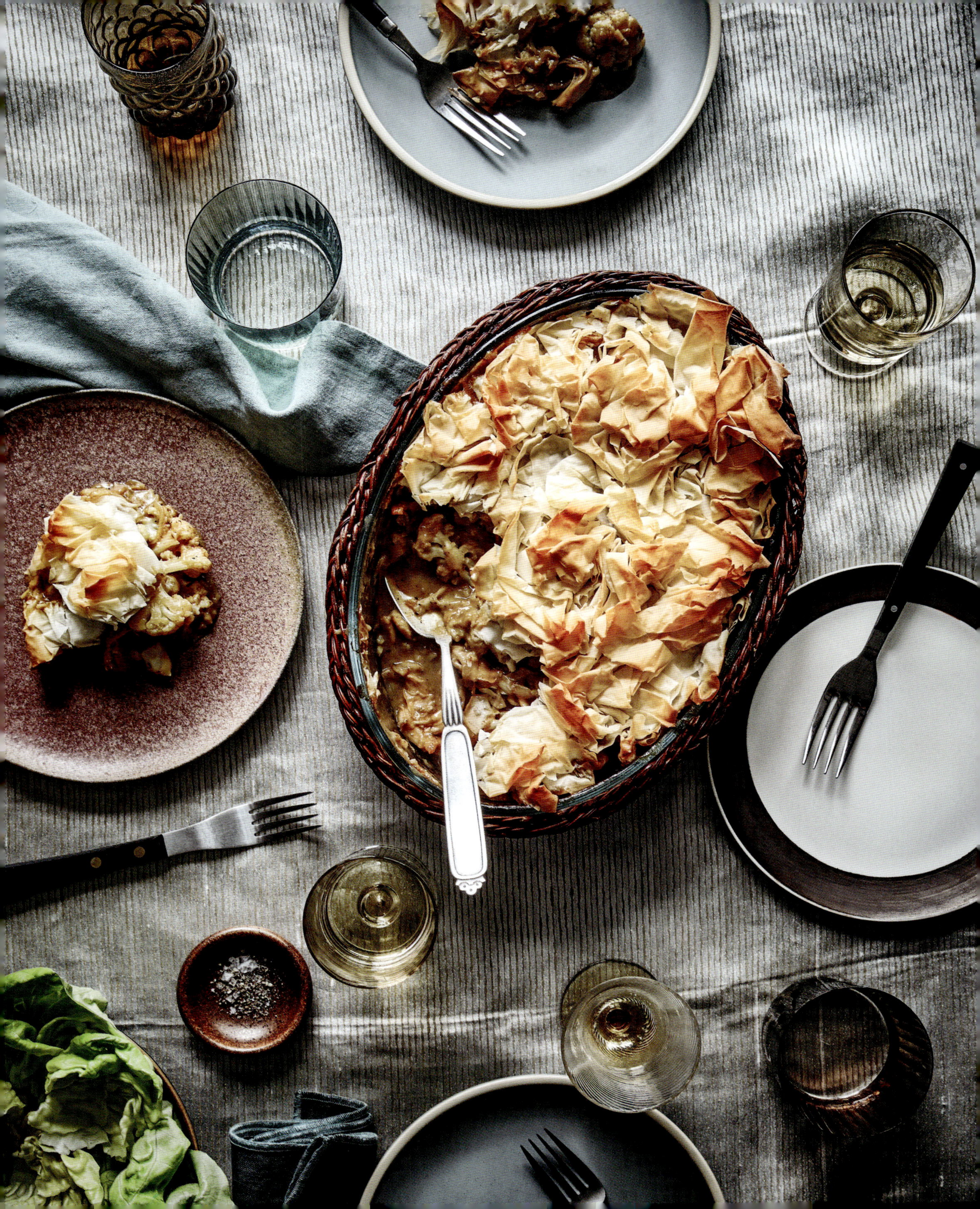

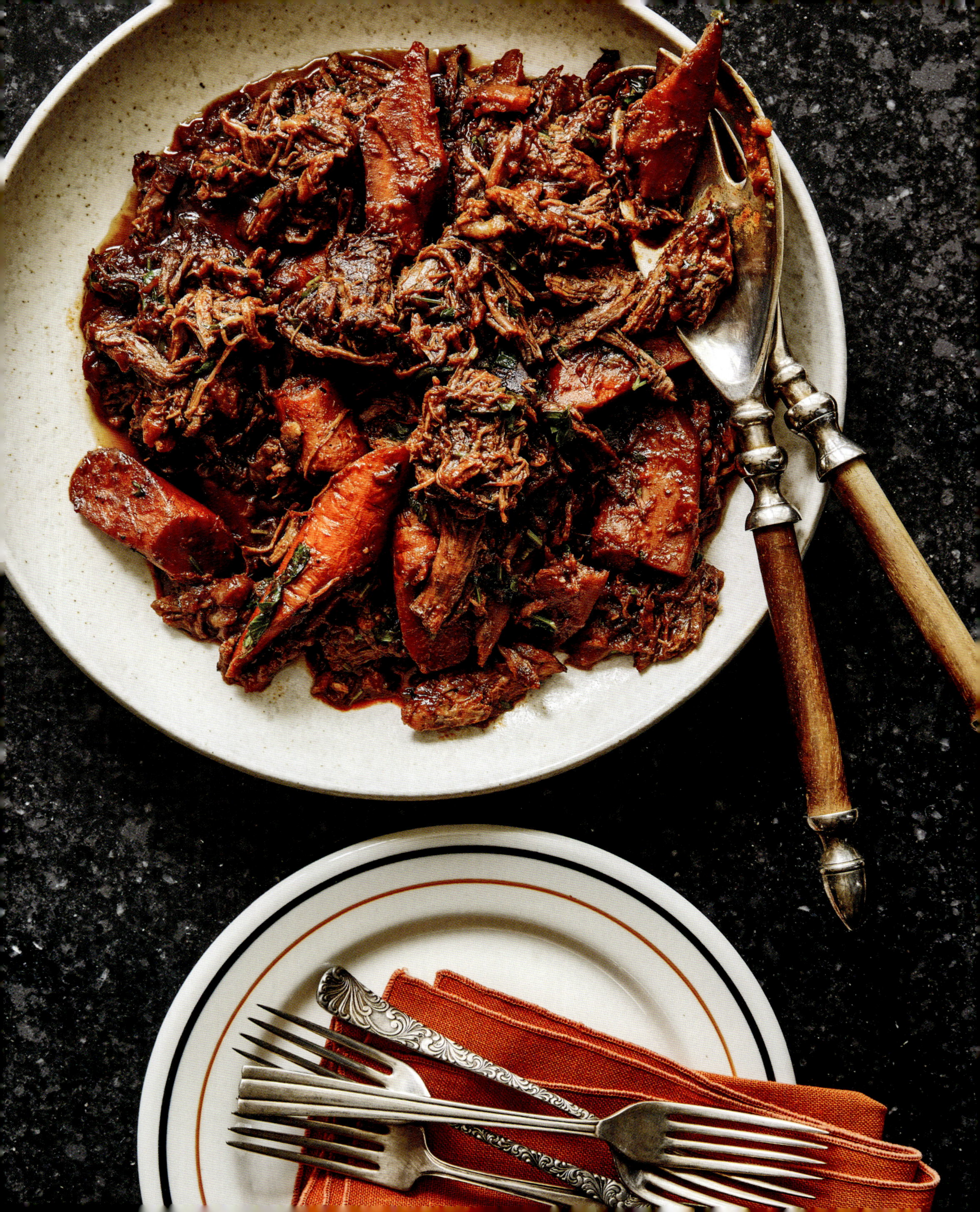

Vinegary Pot Roast with Parsnips and Carrots

It wasn't until fairly recently that pot roast entered my recipe rotation. This all-American dish never graced my table growing up, and my only associations with it came from recipes I'd seen that looked, well, boring. One night, my husband was determined to change my mind. After sitting around the table long after the meal was through, using the heel of a loaf of bread to sop up every last drop of sauce, I changed my tune—it's exactly the kind of thing I'd want to make on a blustery winter day. The key to turning this typically tough cut of beef into something tender and succulent is to cook it low and slow. I like serving pot roast with egg noodles, but you could also serve it with bread, rice, or regular ol' pasta.

NOTES: If you're abstaining from alcohol, you can swap in beef or chicken stock for the red wine. If you can't find parsnips, use more carrots, potatoes, or any other root vegetable of choice. Leftover pot roast can be stored in an airtight container in the refrigerator for up to 3 days or in the freezer for up to 3 months.

Serves 6 to 8

1 (3½-pound) boneless chuck roast

2 teaspoons freshly ground black pepper

1 tablespoon plus 1½ teaspoons kosher salt

2 teaspoons grapeseed oil

2 medium yellow onions, sliced

5 medium carrots, cut into 2-inch pieces on an angle

5 medium parsnips, cut into 2-inch pieces on an angle

4 anchovies

1 head garlic, cloves separated and peeled (about 10 cloves)

1 (6-ounce) can tomato paste

1 (750-ml) bottle dry red wine

Leaves and tender stems from ½ bunch flat-leaf parsley, finely chopped (about 1 cup)

2 tablespoons sherry vinegar

1. Preheat the oven to 250°F.

2. Pat the chuck roast dry with paper towels. Generously season it on all sides with the pepper and 1 tablespoon of the salt.

3. Heat the grapeseed oil in a Dutch oven or large pot over medium-high heat. When the oil begins to shimmer, add the chuck roast and cook, without moving it, until deeply golden brown, about 8 minutes. Brown each side of the chuck roast, about 5 minutes per side. Transfer the chuck roast to a cutting board or plate, leaving the pot on the heat.

4. Cook the onions, carrots, parsnips, and anchovies in the pot, stirring occasionally, until the onions are softened and golden brown, about 8 minutes.

5. Add the garlic and tomato paste and stir until well combined. Cook, stirring often, until the tomato paste turns to a deep brick-red color, about 2 minutes.

Recipe continues

6. Add the red wine and scrape up any brown bits on the bottom of the pan. Cook until the smell of alcohol subsides and the wine is at a low boil, 4 to 5 minutes.

7. Return the chuck roast to the pot and place the lid on. Transfer the pot to the oven and braise until the meat is fork-tender and easily shreds, about 3½ hours.

8. Transfer the chuck roast to a large bowl and shred with two forks. Meanwhile, set the pot over medium heat and simmer, stirring often, until reduced by half, about 10 minutes.

9. Add the shredded chuck roast, parsley, sherry vinegar, and remaining 1½ teaspoons salt to the pot and stir to combine. Serve immediately.

Tomato Pie with Buttermilk Biscuit Crust

There are a few words that always pique my interest in a recipe: "Tomatoes," "buttermilk," "biscuits," and "pie" are at the top of the list. Put them together, and you've got one of my favorite recipes ever: tomato pie. To me, it's a love letter to summer, to be made only when tomatoes are at their peak. I wasn't familiar with tomato pie until my friend Hannah introduced me to her family's recipe (and subsequently made it every summer for me going forward). While the exact history is a bit murky, tomato pie is a Southern dish that gained popularity in the 1970s. The only requirements for tomato pie are that it includes tomatoes, mayonnaise, and cheese. While any pie crust will do, I think Hannah's buttermilk biscuit version is hard to beat.

NOTES: Salting the tomatoes and letting them rest to release excess liquid is crucial for the success of tomato pie. If you skip this step, you'll get a watery pie that won't set and will be impossible to slice. Leftover tomato pie can be stored in an airtight container in the refrigerator for up to 3 days.

1. **Make the crust:** Combine the flour, baking powder, baking soda, and salt in a medium bowl and whisk well. Add the butter and use your fingers to combine until a coarse meal forms and some small pea-size lumps of butter remain. Add the buttermilk and knead gently with your hands until a dough forms. Wrap in plastic wrap and chill in the refrigerator for at least 1 hour or up to 12 hours.

2. **Meanwhile, make the filling:** Lay the tomato slices in a single layer on a paper towel–lined rimmed baking sheet. Sprinkle with salt and place more paper towels on top. Let the tomatoes stand at room temperature for at least 1 hour or up to 8 hours.

3. Position a rack in the center of the oven. Preheat the oven to 425°F.

4. Dust a clean work surface with flour. Place the dough on the flour and use a rolling pin to roll the dough into a 14-inch circle. Transfer the dough to a deep-dish pie plate and trim the excess dough hanging off the sides. Crimp the edges of the dough as desired. Whisk together the egg and 1 tablespoon

Recipe continues

Serves 4

BUTTERMILK BISCUIT CRUST

2 cups all-purpose flour, plus more for dusting

½ teaspoon baking powder

½ teaspoon baking soda

½ teaspoon kosher salt

6 tablespoons (¾ stick) unsalted butter, cubed and chilled

¾ cup buttermilk

1 large egg, beaten

1 tablespoon cornmeal

FILLING

2 pounds heirloom or beefsteak tomatoes, cored and cut into ¼-inch slices

Kosher salt, to taste

2 cups coarsely grated extra-sharp cheddar cheese

1 cup freshly grated Parmigiano Reggiano cheese

½ cup mayonnaise

1 bunch scallions, white and light green parts only, thinly sliced

1 cup loosely packed fresh basil leaves, finely chopped

1 tablespoon champagne vinegar

½ teaspoon freshly ground black pepper

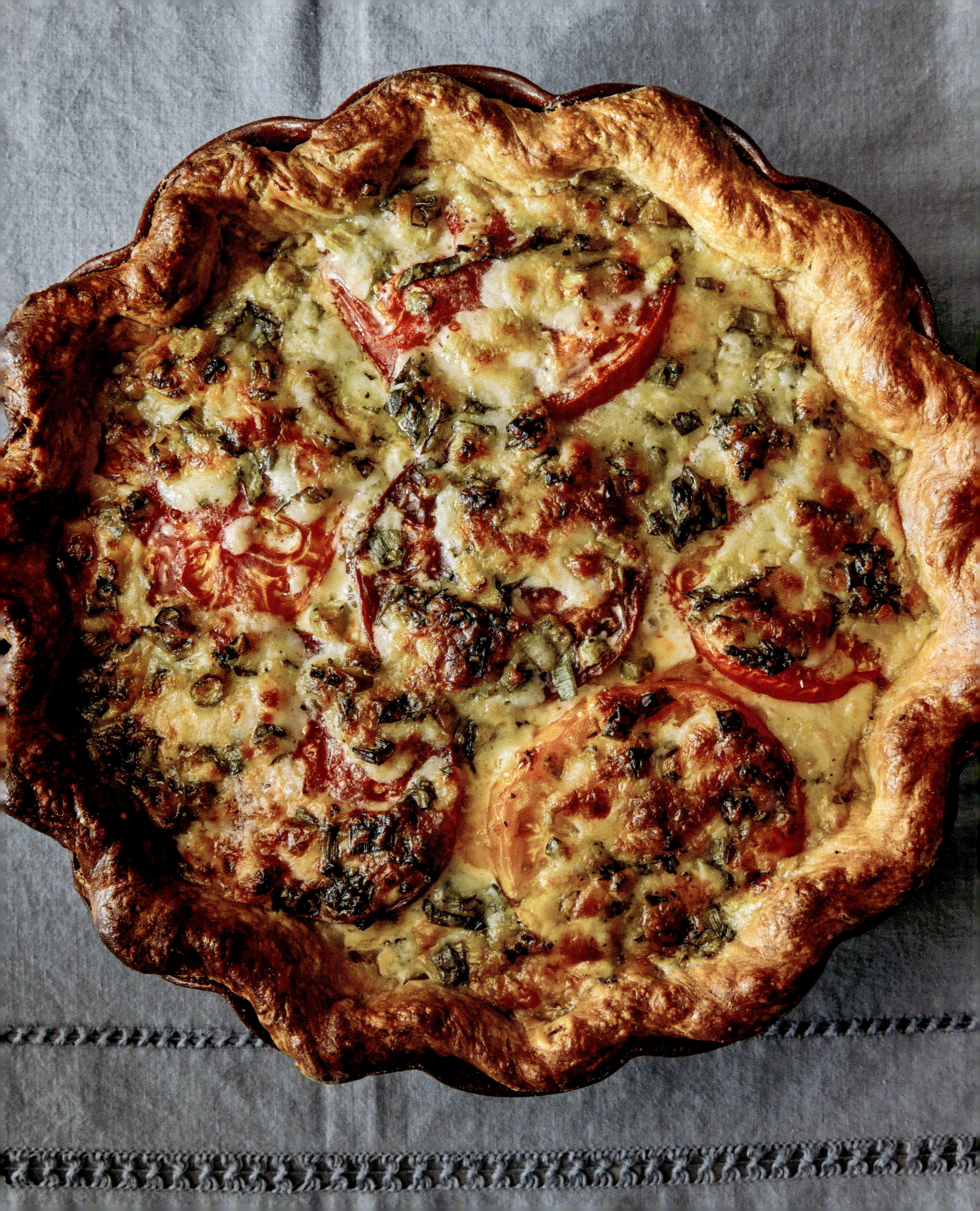

water in a bowl. Brush the dough with the egg wash and sprinkle the cornmeal evenly over the bottom.

5. Stir together the cheddar and Parmigiano Reggiano in a medium bowl to combine. In a separate small bowl, stir together the mayonnaise, scallions, basil, vinegar, pepper, and 1 teaspoon salt in a separate small bowl until well combined.

6. Spread ½ cup of the cheese mixture over the crust. Add one-third of the tomatoes over the cheese, overlapping as needed. Spread ⅓ cup of the mayonnaise mixture on the tomatoes. Repeat layering with the remaining ingredients, making sure the last layer is the cheese.

7. Bake the pie in the center of the oven rack until the crust and cheese is golden brown, 35 to 40 minutes.

8. Let the tomato pie cool for at least 1 hour before slicing.

Greekish Whole Fish

Technically this recipe could be in the weeknight section of the book—it's made on a sheet pan! You can have dinner on the table in thirty-five minutes!—but I know cooking whole fish can feel daunting. I'm here to tell you to push those fears aside. Cooking a whole fish in the oven requires little besides a sheet pan and salt, although aromatics are always welcome to add flavor. All it takes is seasoning the fish on all sides, cavity included, and baking until the fish is just cooked through. In this preparation, tomatoes, olives, and feta get baked alongside the fish and then stirred into couscous for a Greek-inspired meal that comes together quickly.

NOTES: The only whole fish available in my tiny town in the Catskills is trout, so that's what I used while testing. However, this recipe would work well with branzino, sea bass, or red snapper. If the fish you're using weigh more than 1½ pounds, be sure to add a few minutes to the cooking time. Fish and couscous can be stored in an airtight container in the refrigerator for up to 3 days.

Serves 4

ROASTED WHOLE FISH

3 cups cherry tomatoes

1 cup pitted Kalamata olives

1 medium red onion, thinly sliced

1 (6-ounce) block feta cheese

1 tablespoon extra-virgin olive oil, plus more to taste

2 (1½-pound) whole fish, scaled and gutted

Kosher salt and freshly ground black pepper

1 bunch oregano

1 lemon, thinly sliced

ISRAELI COUSCOUS

2¼ cups vegetable stock

1½ cups Israeli couscous

2 tablespoons extra-virgin olive oil

Zest and juice of 2 lemons (about ¼ cup juice)

1 teaspoon kosher salt

1 teaspoon freshly ground black pepper

1 bunch flat-leaf parsley, coarsely chopped (about 2 cups)

1 bunch scallions, thinly sliced

1. **Make the fish:** Position a rack in the upper third of the oven. Preheat the oven to 400°F.

2. Place the tomatoes, olives, red onion, and feta on a rimmed baking sheet and drizzle with olive oil. Bake in the center of the oven rack for 20 minutes.

3. While the pan is in the oven, prepare the fish. Pat the fish dry with paper towels. Season it on both sides and in the cavity with salt and pepper. Insert the oregano into the cavity, spreading it evenly. Arrange the lemon slices in the cavity.

4. Place the fish on the baking sheet with the tomatoes, olives, onion, and feta and bake until the fish easily flakes with a fork. The timing will depend on the type of fish you have, but you can assume that 12 to 15 minutes is the approximate time needed for a 1½-pound fish.

5. **Meanwhile, make the couscous:** Bring the stock to a boil over high heat, then add the couscous. Reduce the heat to medium-low and simmer until the couscous is cooked through and the liquid has evaporated, 8 to 10 minutes.

6. Place the olive oil, lemon zest, lemon juice, salt, pepper, parsley, and scallions in a medium bowl. Add the roasted tomatoes, olives, red onion, and feta and stir to combine. Stir in the couscous.

7. Serve the fish with the couscous.

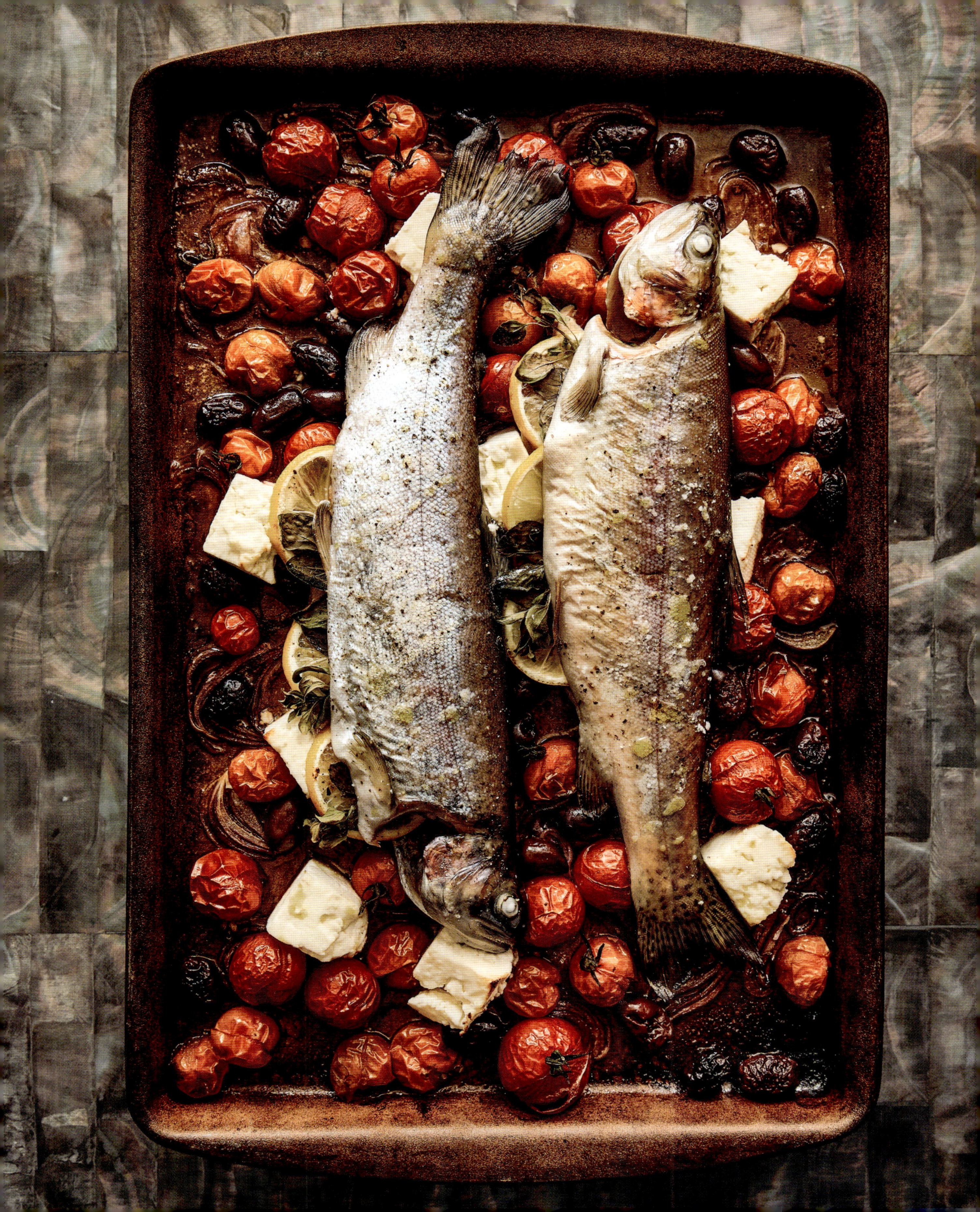

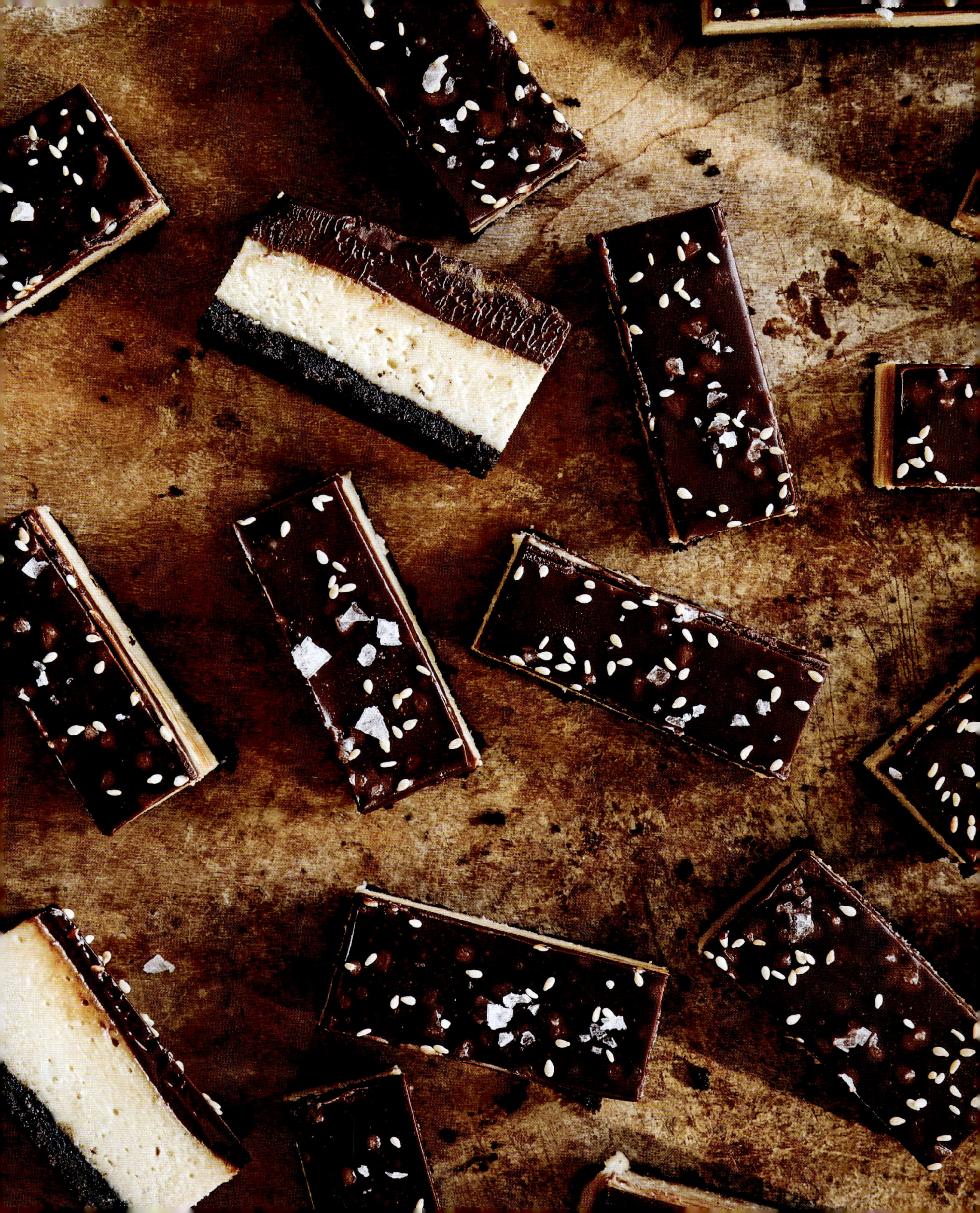

WEEKENDS

DESSERT

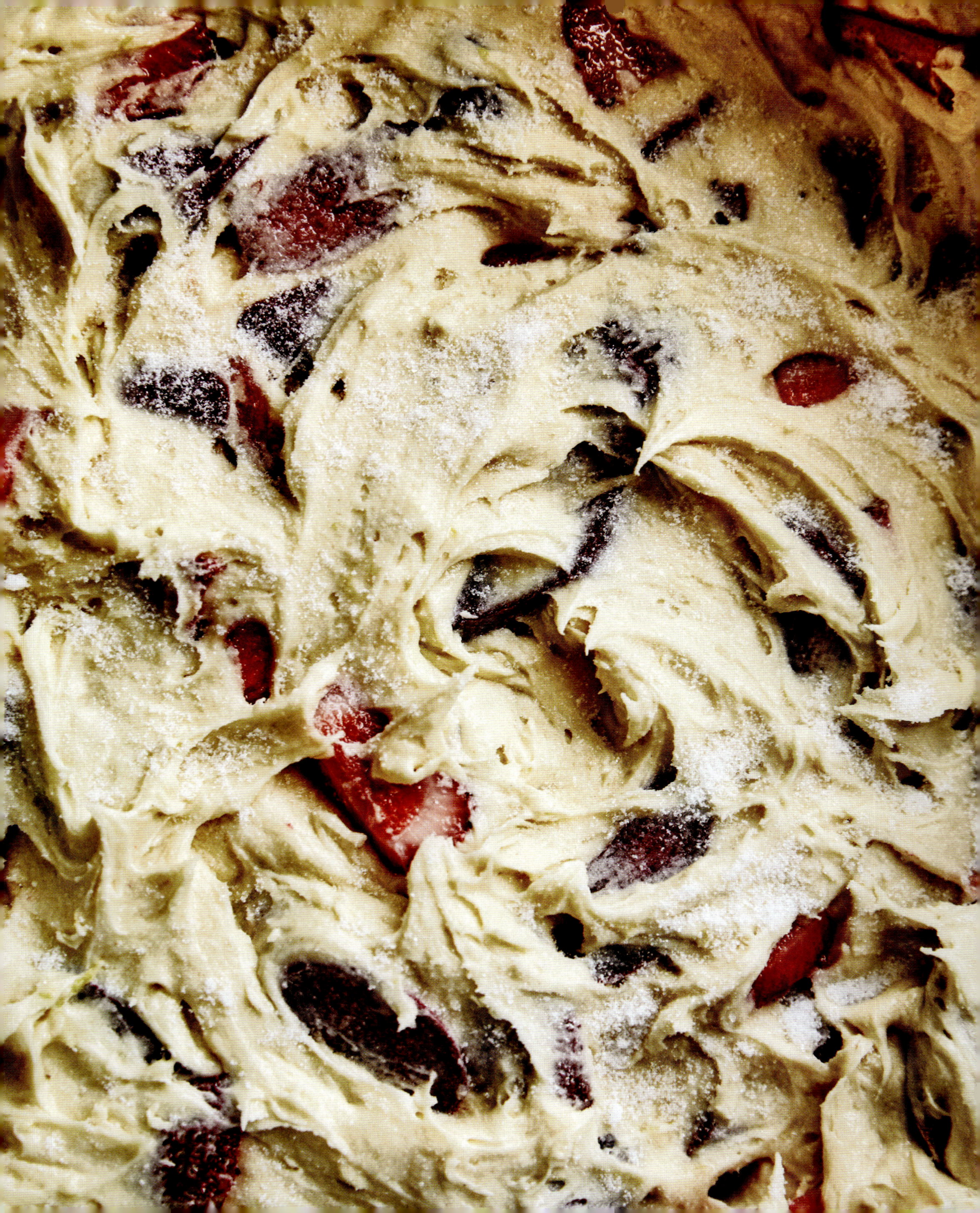

Strawberry Rhubarb Cake

I admit, I struggled with naming this recipe—it's really a marriage of a torte, a cake, and a tart. Whatever it is, it's a crowd-pleaser; I've never served it and had someone be satisfied with just one slice. You can serve it for dessert, of course, but I've also been known to eat it in the afternoon for a snack, and even for breakfast. It's shorter than most cakes, coming in at only 1½ inches tall, and has a tender, moist crumb with a crackly, crunchy, sugary top. Made in just one bowl and baked in under an hour, this is a great cake for new bakers. I love making this in spring when strawberries and rhubarb line the farmers' market stalls, but you could easily swap in your fruit of choice.

NOTES: If using other fruit, just make sure to keep the quantity to 2 cups. Cake can be wrapped in plastic and stored at room temperature for up to 3 days.

Serves 6 to 8

- ¾ cup (1½ sticks) unsalted butter, at room temperature, plus more for greasing
- 1 cup plus 2 teaspoons sugar
- 2 large eggs
- Zest of 1 lemon
- 1 teaspoon pure vanilla extract
- 1 cup all-purpose flour
- 1 teaspoon baking powder
- ½ teaspoon kosher salt
- 1 cup strawberries, hulled and quartered
- 2 medium stalks rhubarb, cut into ½-inch pieces (about 1 cup)

1. Position a rack in the upper third of the oven. Preheat the oven to 350°F. Grease a 9-inch springform pan with butter.

2. Combine the butter and 1 cup of the sugar in a medium bowl and use a handheld mixer to beat on medium speed until pale yellow and fluffy, about 2 minutes. Add the eggs and beat until combined. Add the lemon zest and vanilla and beat until just combined. Add the flour, baking powder, and salt and beat until combined. Add the strawberries and rhubarb and use a spatula to fold them in.

3. Transfer the batter to the prepared springform pan and sprinkle with the remaining 2 teaspoons sugar. Bake for about 40 minutes, until golden brown and puffy. Remove from the oven and let the cake cool to room temperature.

4. Run a knife between the pan and the cake, then release the springform ring and serve.

Classic Lemon Bars

There's a reason lemon bars are staples of potlucks and bake sales—yes, they're beloved, but they're also exceptionally easy to put together and only require a handful of ingredients, which I bet you already have in your pantry.

To me, a great lemon bar has a snappy shortbread crust with a smooth, tangy topping. Biting into one should release a burst of lemon tempered with sugar. It's crucial to pour the filling directly into the hot parbaked crust to ensure it fully sets in the oven. Rubbing the sugar with lemon zest when you make the crust perfumes it with lemon without being overpowering.

NOTES: For clean slices, dip the knife in hot water and wipe it dry between each cut. Lemon bars can be wrapped and stored in the refrigerator for up to 5 days. Just note that the powdered sugar will dissolve during storage; either hold off on dusting them or plan to dust them again before serving.

Makes 16 bars

CRUST

¼ cup granulated sugar

Zest of 1 lemon

¾ cup (1½ sticks) unsalted butter, at room temperature

½ teaspoon kosher salt

1¾ cups all-purpose flour

FILLING

4 large eggs, beaten

1½ cups granulated sugar

Zest of 1 lemon

¾ cup fresh lemon juice (from 5 to 6 lemons)

½ teaspoon kosher salt

⅓ cup all-purpose flour

Powdered sugar, for dusting

1. **Make the crust:** Preheat the oven to 350°F. Line the bottom and sides of a 9-inch square baking pan with parchment paper arranged so that it hangs over the sides by at least 2 inches.

2. Combine the sugar and lemon zest in a medium bowl and use your fingers to rub the zest into the sugar until fragrant. Add the butter and salt and beat with a hand mixer on medium until light and fluffy, about 2 minutes. Scrape down the sides of the bowl and add the flour. Beat on medium until a crumbly dough forms, about 30 seconds.

3. Transfer the dough to the prepared baking pan and use your hands to press it into an even layer. Bake until the crust is very lightly golden on the edges, about 15 minutes.

4. **Meanwhile, make the filling:** Combine the eggs, sugar, lemon zest, lemon juice, and salt in a medium bowl and whisk until smooth. Using a fine-mesh sieve, sift the flour into the filling mixture and whisk to combine.

5. When the crust is ready, immediately pour in the filling. Bake until the filling is just set, with a slight jiggle in the center, 18 to 20 minutes. Let cool on a wire rack to room temperature. Refrigerate for at least 2 hours or up to 24 hours before serving.

6. When ready to serve, use the parchment paper to lift the pastry out of the baking dish and transfer it to a cutting board. Cut it into 16 even pieces to create the bars. Pour the powdered sugar into a fine-mesh sieve and generously dust the tops before serving.

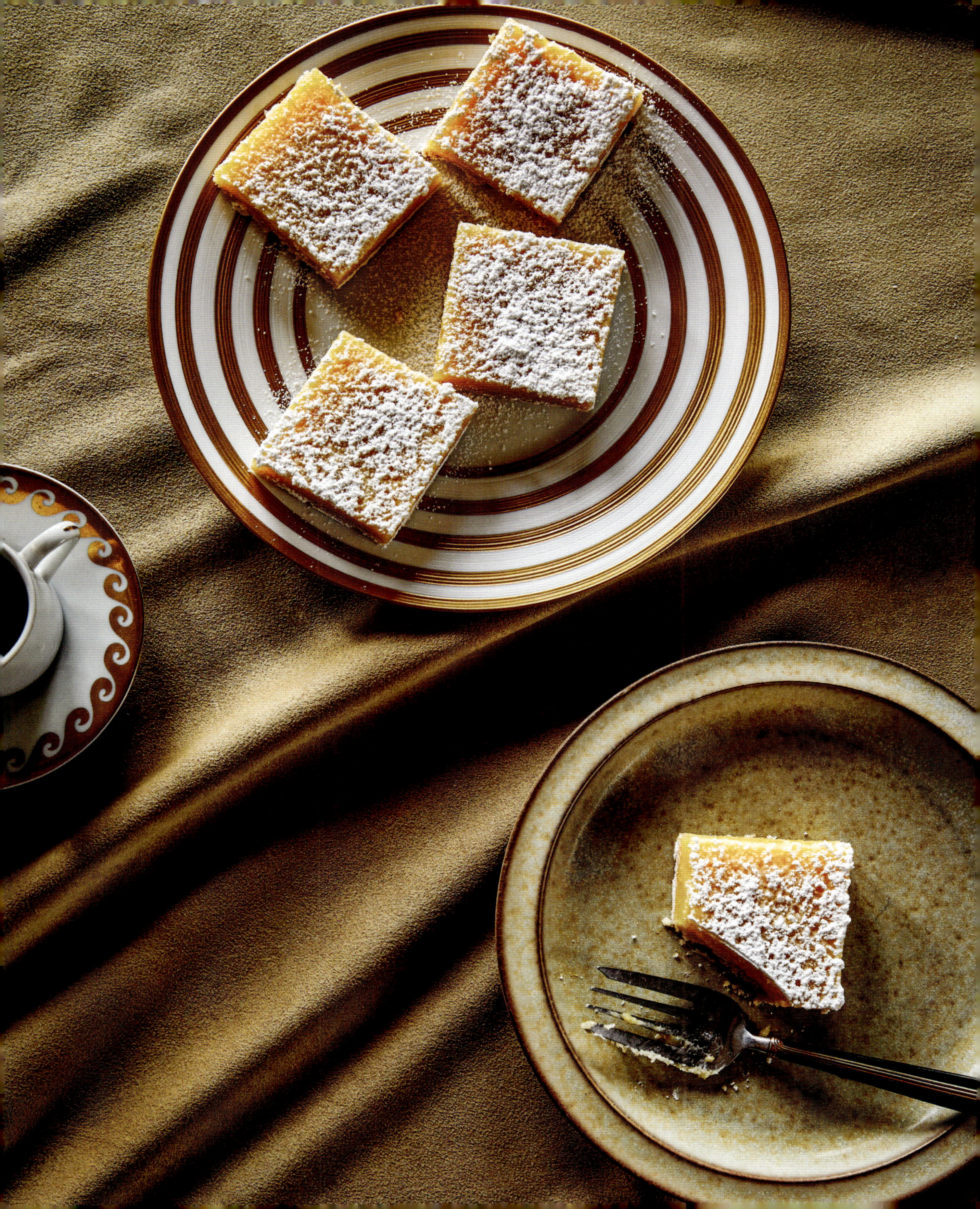

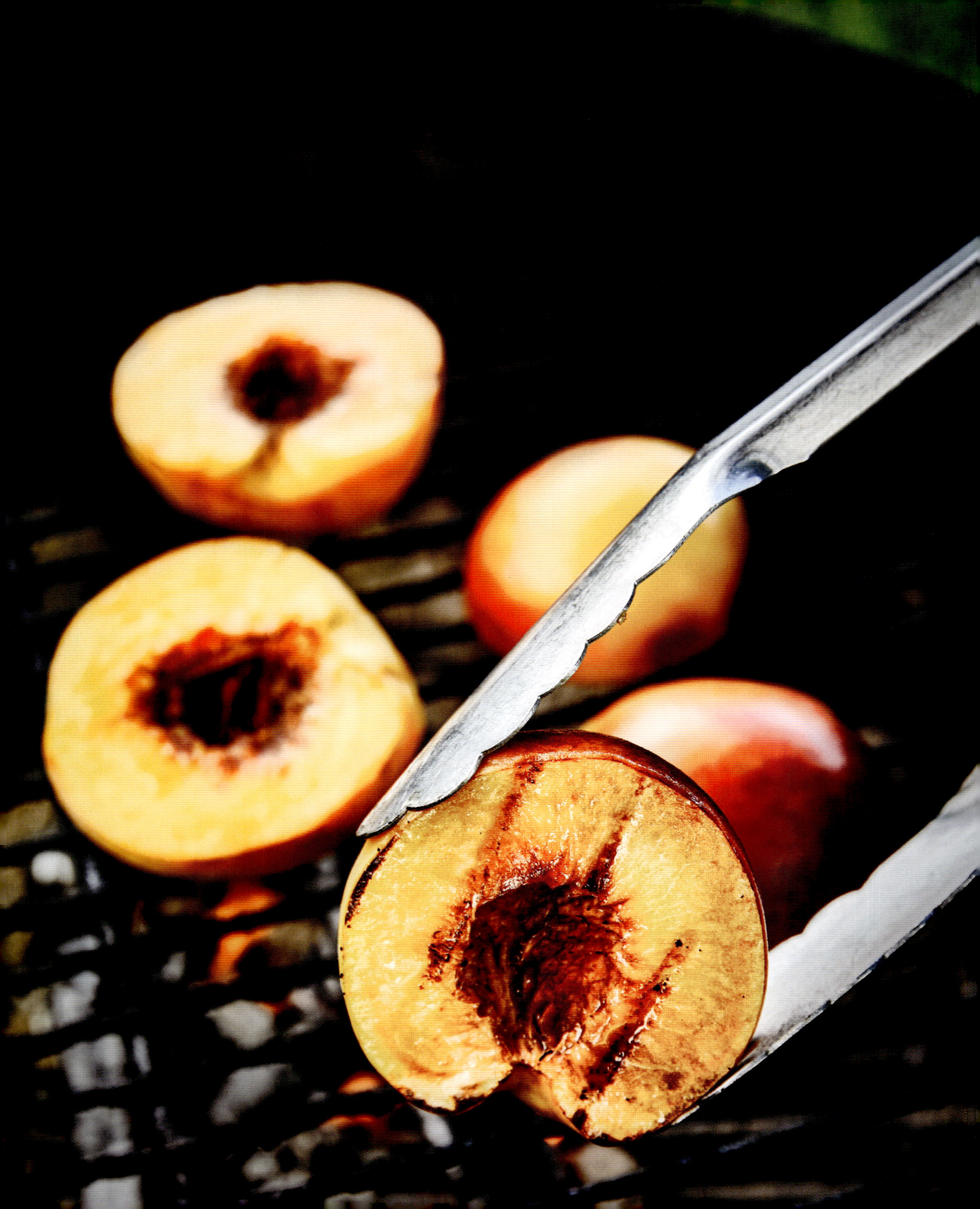

Grilled Peaches with Cardamom Honey Whipped Cream

Take advantage of peak-season peaches with this no-bake dessert. Peaches and cream are a classic combination, but to make it a little more interesting I've spiked whipped cream with ground cardamom and swapped out sugar for honey, for a warmer, earthier flavor. Some recipes call for dusting peaches in sugar before grilling, but if you're using ripe peaches, I've found that there's no need.

NOTES: This recipe is based on one peach per person, but you can easily double, triple, or even quadruple the amount depending on your appetite for peaches. Whipped cream can be made up to 3 days in advance and stored in an airtight container in the refrigerator. Peaches are best served hot off the grill, although they'll still be tasty for up to 3 days stored in an airtight container in the refrigerator.

Serves 4

- 1 cup heavy cream
- 3 tablespoons honey
- 1 teaspoon ground cardamom
- 4 ripe yellow peaches, halved and pitted
- Extra-virgin olive oil, for brushing and serving
- Flaky salt, for serving

1. Pour the cream into a medium bowl and use a handheld mixer to beat on medium-high speed until soft peaks form, about 3 minutes. (Alternatively, this can be done in the bowl of a stand mixer fitted with the whisk attachment.) Add the honey and cardamom and beat until just incorporated, about 30 seconds more.

2. Brush the peaches with olive oil.

3. Preheat a gas or charcoal grill to medium-high.

4. Place the peaches on the grill cut-side down and cook, undisturbed, until golden brown grill marks appear, about 3 minutes. Flip the peaches over and cook, undisturbed, until they have softened and developed golden brown grill marks, about 3 minutes more. (Alternatively, this can be done in a grill pan over medium-high heat.)

5. Serve the peaches topped with the whipped cream, a drizzle of olive oil, and a sprinkle of flaky salt.

Chocolate Frosting and Yellow Sour Cream Birthday Cake

I'm not a cake person, nor a chocolate person, and yet I can't get enough of this cake. For years I've been looking for an easy sheet cake recipe that could be whipped up with little preparation or special ingredients. This yellow cake has an impossibly tender crumb, thanks to both sour cream and buttermilk. I've cut down the sugar significantly compared to most buttercreams and added a pinch of salt so that it's not cloyingly sweet. There's also a touch of buttermilk in the frosting in place of heavy cream or milk, which adds a nice tang. I figure if you're buying buttermilk, you might as well use up as much as you can.

NOTES: If you don't have buttermilk, you can make a cheater version by adding 1 tablespoon of lemon juice to 1 cup of whole milk. Let it stand on the counter for 5 minutes until it looks slightly curdled and proceed with the recipe. The cake can be made up to 2 days in advance but must be thoroughly wrapped in plastic wrap and stored in an airtight container at room temperature to prevent it from drying out. The frosting can be made up to 3 days in advance and stored in an airtight container in the refrigerator—just give it a good stir before frosting the cake.

1. **Make the cake:** Position a rack in the upper third of the oven. Preheat the oven to 350°F. Grease a 9×13-inch baking dish with butter (or you could use cooking spray).

2. Place a fine-mesh sieve over a large bowl and use it to sift in the flour, baking powder, baking soda, and salt.

3. Combine the butter and sugar in the bowl of a stand mixer fitted with the paddle attachment. (Alternatively, use a large bowl and a handheld mixer.) Beat on medium-high speed until pale yellow and fluffy, about 3 minutes. Scrape down the sides of the bowl with a spatula. With the motor running, add the whole eggs and egg yolk, one at a time, until fully combined. Scrape down the sides of the bowl. Add the sour cream and vanilla and beat until just combined. Add the dry ingredients and buttermilk and mix until just combined, making sure not to overmix the batter.

4. Transfer the batter to the greased baking dish and smooth it into an even layer. Bake in the center of

Serves 16

CAKE

¾ cup (1½ sticks) unsalted butter, at room temperature, plus more for greasing

2½ cups cake flour

2 teaspoons baking powder

½ teaspoon baking soda

½ teaspoon kosher salt

1¾ cups sugar

2 large eggs, at room temperature

1 large egg yolk, at room temperature

¾ cup full-fat sour cream, at room temperature

2 teaspoons pure vanilla extract

¾ cup buttermilk, at room temperature

FROSTING

¾ cup (1½ sticks) unsalted butter, at room temperature

2 cups powdered sugar

½ cup unsweetened cocoa powder

1 teaspoon pure vanilla extract

½ teaspoon kosher salt

¼ cup buttermilk

2 tablespoons sprinkles (optional, but encouraged)

the oven rack until golden brown, or until a toothpick inserted into the center comes out clean, about 30 minutes. Let the cake cool in the pan to room temperature.

5 **Make the frosting:** Combine the butter, powdered sugar, and cocoa powder in the bowl of a stand mixer fitted with the whisk attachment. (Alternatively, use a medium bowl and a handheld mixer.) Beat on medium speed until well combined and fluffy, about 2 minutes. Add the vanilla, salt, and buttermilk and mix until combined and smooth, about 1 minute.

6 Spread the frosting over the top of the cooled cake in an even layer and top with sprinkles, if desired.

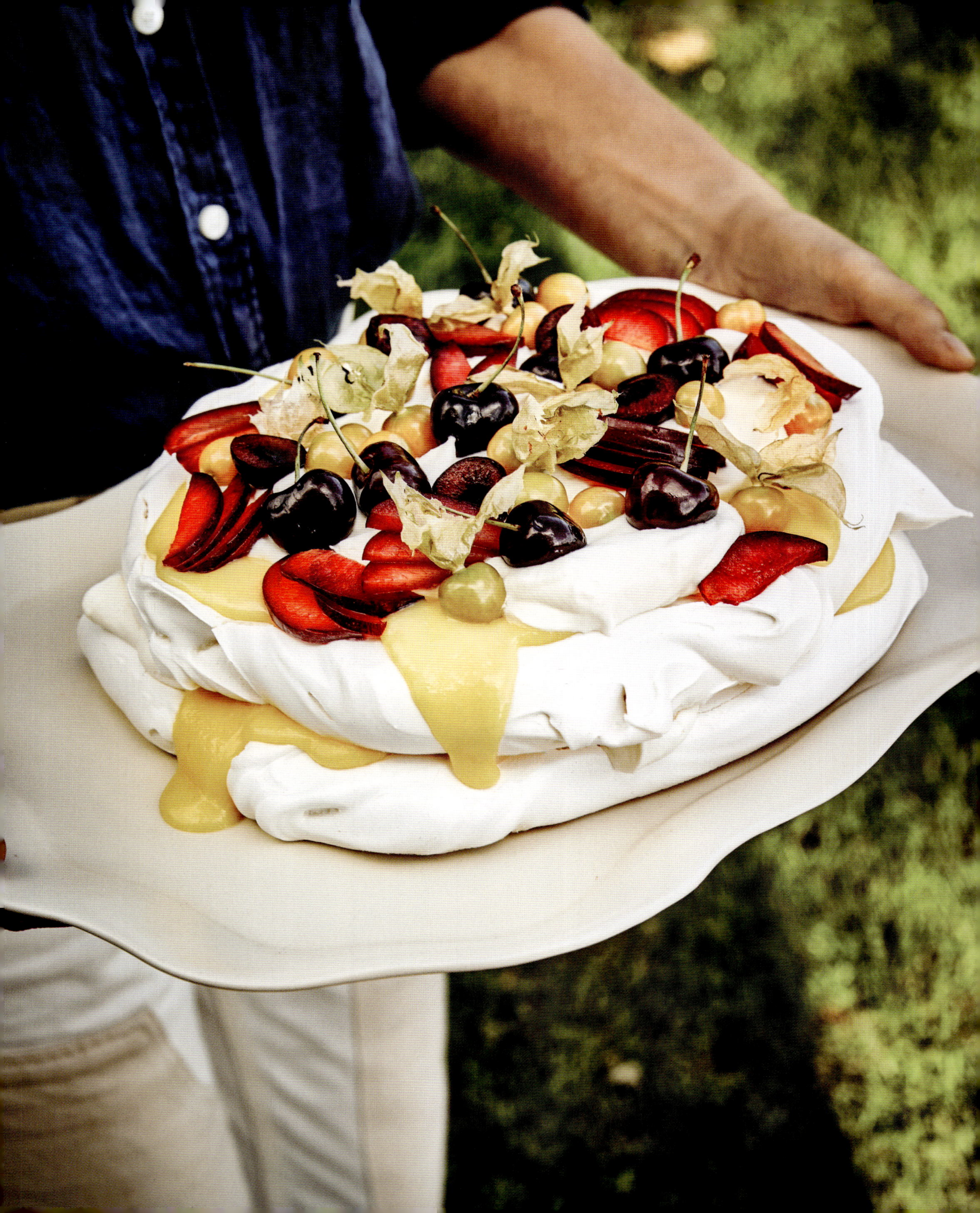

Party Pavlova

Of all the desserts, Pavlova is my absolute favorite. It's the ultimate showstopper: a crispy meringue piled high with whipped cream, punchy lemon curd to help cut the sweetness, and a crown of fruit decorating the top. To me, biting into Pavlova is what I'd imagine eating a piece of cloud would taste like—light, airy, a bit ethereal.

I will caveat this to say that I also understand that Pavlova can feel intimidating. The whipped cream and lemon curd elements are easy enough, but meringue can be temperamental. To avoid crises, do not try to make Pavlova on humid or rainy days. Humidity can cause the sugar in the meringue to absorb extra moisture from the air, causing the sugars to leak and making a crispy exterior impossible.

NOTES: It's easy to alter the size of Pavlova—just remember the golden ratio of 1 egg white to ¼ cup of sugar. If you don't have a vanilla bean, you can use 1 teaspoon vanilla extract. If you're not up for making your own lemon curd, store-bought is fine, or just leave it out. Pro tip: Pulsing sugar in a food processor until fine helps ensure an evenly incorporated Pavlova. Alternatively, you could use caster sugar, or just use the regular granulated sugar (it'll still work!). While Pavlova is best served immediately for its full effect, I actually love the flavor after it's been in the fridge—it transforms into a dessert akin to a giant marshmallow.

Serves 10 to 12

MERINGUE
6 large egg whites, at room temperature
1 teaspoon cream of tartar
½ teaspoon kosher salt
1½ cups sugar (see Notes)
Seeds scraped from 1 vanilla bean, pod discarded

LEMON CURD
3 large eggs
2 large egg yolks
Zest of 1 lemon
1 cup fresh lemon juice
½ cup sugar
⅛ teaspoon kosher salt
½ cup (1 stick) cold unsalted butter

WHIPPED CREAM
1½ cups heavy cream
2 tablespoons powdered sugar

Assorted fruit, for serving

1. **Make the meringue:** Preheat the oven to 200°F. Line two rimmed baking sheets with parchment paper.

2. In the bowl of a stand mixer fitted with the whisk attachment, combine the egg whites, cream of tartar, and salt and beat on medium speed until frothy, about 2 minutes. Raise the speed to high and add the sugar 1 tablespoon at a time, beating until stiff, glossy peaks form, 5 to 7 minutes. Add the vanilla bean seeds and beat the meringue for 1 minute more.

3. Use a silicone spatula to pile the meringue in the center of the prepared baking sheets, dividing it evenly, and spread it into a 10-inch circle with 4-inch-tall sides. Bake for 1½ hours, until the top is crisp and the meringue easily pulls away from the parchment paper. Turn

Recipe continues

WEEKENDS | DESSERT 251

the oven off and let the meringue rest in the oven for at least 4 hours or up to overnight.

4 **Make the lemon curd:** Combine the whole eggs, egg yolks, lemon zest, lemon juice, sugar, and salt in a large saucepan and whisk over medium heat until warmed through, about 2 minutes.

5 Add the butter 1 tablespoon at a time, whisking until fully incorporated. Continue cooking—it will feel like nothing is happening for about 7 minutes, when the curd slowly begins to thicken—about 10 minutes total.

6 Strain the curd through a fine-mesh sieve into a bowl. Let it cool to room temperature; it will continue to thicken as it cools.

7 **Make the whipped cream:** Pour the heavy cream into a medium bowl and use a handheld mixer to beat on medium-high speed until soft peaks form, about 3 minutes. (Alternatively, this can be done in the bowl of a stand mixer fitted with the whisk attachment.) Add the powdered sugar and beat until just incorporated, about 30 seconds more.

8 Transfer the meringue to a platter and top with the lemon curd and whipped cream. Place the second meringue on top and add more lemon curd and whipped cream. Arrange your fruit of choice on the whipped cream and serve immediately.

Maggie's Brown Butter Apple Crumble

Should you find yourself in Delaware County, New York, there's no better use of your time than seeking out a freshly baked pie from Magpies. Run by Maggie McDowell, an actress turned pie baker (and one of my dearest friends), Magpies has garnered a reputation for making the best pies, well, anywhere.

Maggie swears by an all-butter dough, which yields an impossibly flaky crust that makes the pies road-trip-worthy on their own. But what I think makes them so special is her ability to balance sweet, spice, and saltiness. Whatever pie I'm eating I swear is the best I've ever had, but her apple pie, piled high with a generously spiced brown butter crumble, really is my favorite. It's a staple at outdoor picnics on those sleepy nights when summer starts to fade into fall, on Thanksgiving, and for birthdays. I love this pie so much that Maggie baked a few for my wedding. She graciously allowed me to share the recipe with you, and I hope it brings you as much joy as it does all of us in this corner of the Catskills.

NOTES: Maggie has enough pie knowledge to write a whole book on the subject. Here are just a few of her helpful tips and tricks: Browning the butter in a stainless-steel pan will help it take on that classic caramelized color. The dusting of flour and sugar on the bottom of the pie crust will help prevent it from getting soggy. Starting the pie in the bottom of a hot oven will help the pie dough crisp up quickly and seal it against any potential leaks. If the crumble begins to burn, place a piece of foil on top until it's out of the oven. Apple pie can be wrapped and stored at room temperature for up to 2 days.

Serves 8

CRUST

1¼ cups all-purpose flour, plus more for dusting

1 teaspoon sugar

½ teaspoon kosher salt

½ cup (1 stick) unsalted butter, cubed and chilled

About ½ cup ice water

FILLING

6 tart baking apples, such as Granny Smith, Pink Lady, or Northern Spy (about 2 pounds), peeled, cored, seeded, and cut into ¼-inch slices

⅓ cup packed dark brown sugar

2 tablespoons all-purpose flour

Zest and juice of 1 lemon (about 2 tablespoons juice)

1 teaspoon ground cinnamon

¼ teaspoon ground nutmeg

¼ teaspoon ground cloves

¾ teaspoon kosher salt

1 (1-inch) knob fresh ginger, grated

1. **Make the crust:** Combine the flour, sugar, and salt in a food processor and pulse three times to combine. Add the cubed butter and pulse until the mixture forms lumps the size of lima beans.

2. Pulse the food processor and add the water, 1 tablespoon at a time, until the dough just holds together. You will have leftover ice water.

Recipe and ingredients continue

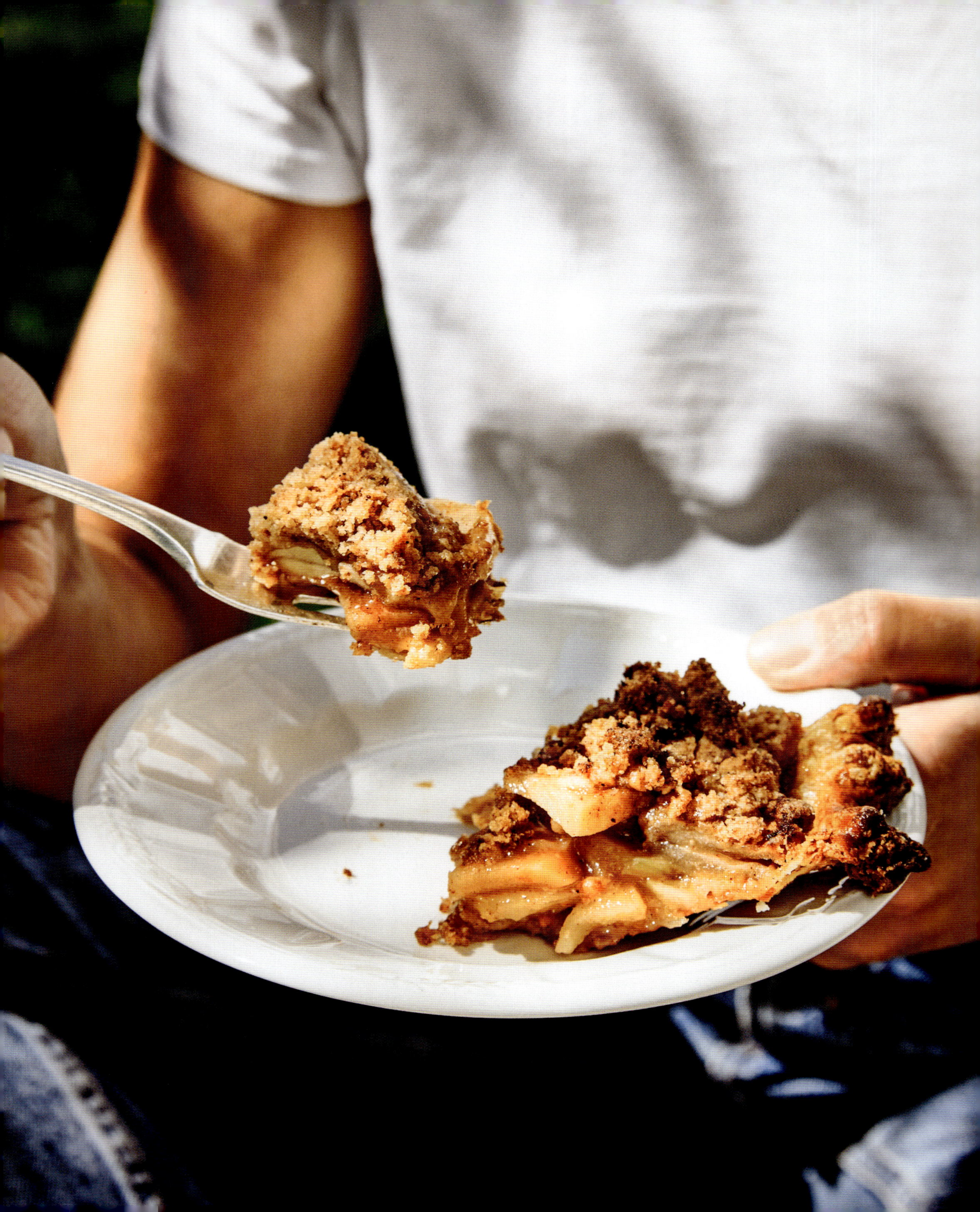

3. Turn the dough out onto a lightly floured work surface and form it into a 5-inch disk. Wrap in plastic wrap and refrigerate for at least 2 hours or up to 3 days. The longer it rests, the easier it'll be to roll out.

4. When ready to assemble, place the dough disk on a lightly floured surface, and roll it out to ¼ inch thick and at least 2 inches bigger than a deep-dish pie plate, flouring as needed to prevent sticking.

5. Place the chilled dough into a pie dish, making sure to tuck it so that it covers the contours of the dish. Let the excess dough hang over the edges. Crimp and dock the crust as desired, discarding any excess pie dough. Transfer the dish to the refrigerator to chill.

6. **Make the filling:** Combine the apples, brown sugar, flour, lemon zest, lemon juice, cinnamon, nutmeg, cloves, salt, and ginger in a large bowl and stir well.

7. **Make the crumble:** Whisk together the flour, brown sugar, granulated sugar, cinnamon, salt, and nutmeg in a medium bowl.

8. Melt the butter in a small pot over medium-high heat, swirling the pot occasionally. When the butter has become foamy, reduce the heat to medium-low and cook until the butter is lightly golden brown and smells nutty, 3 to 4 minutes. Immediately pour the browned butter over the crumble mixture, using a spatula to scrape the pan, and stir until well incorporated.

9. Beat the egg with 1 tablespoon water. Brush the egg wash over the rim of the chilled pie crust. Sprinkle the bottom of the crust with the flour and sugar. Stir the apples once more, then use your hands to layer them into the pie crust, making sure to leave the excess juice in the bowl. Drizzle half the leftover juices on top of the apples and discard the rest.

10. Position racks in the center and lower third of the oven. Preheat the oven to 425°F. Line a rimmed baking sheet with aluminum foil and place it on the lower rack.

11. Scatter the crumble over the apples in an even layer, taking care not to pile the center too high to prevent burning. Chill the fully assembled pie in the refrigerator for 15 minutes before baking.

12. Carefully place the pie on the preheated baking sheet on the bottom rack and bake for 25 minutes. After 25 minutes, carefully transfer the baking sheet and pie from the bottom rack to the middle rack. Reduce the oven temperature to 375°F and bake until the crumble is deeply brown, the crust golden brown, and the apples bubbling and aromatic, 25 to 35 minutes more.

13. Transfer the pie to a wire rack to cool completely, about 1 hour. Serve the pie at room temperature, or reheat it in a 300°F oven for 10 minutes before serving.

CRUMBLE

1 cup all-purpose flour

¼ cup packed dark brown sugar

¼ cup granulated sugar

½ teaspoon ground cinnamon

½ teaspoon kosher salt

Pinch ground nutmeg

7 tablespoons unsalted butter

ASSEMBLY

1 large egg, beaten

1 teaspoon all-purpose flour

½ teaspoon sugar

Gingersnap Cookies

December begs for holiday cookies, and while I always love seeing my fellow recipe developers' creativity, I like my cookies on the classic side. These are intentionally thin and crispy, which is the ideal texture for dunking into a cup of tea (my preferred method of cookie consumption). Heavily spiced with ground ginger, cinnamon, cardamom, cloves, and even a bit of black pepper, the cookies balance the molasses with the warmth of the spices. Rolling the cookies in sugar before baking ensures that signature crackled appearance, which isn't to be missed.

NOTE: Cookies can be stored in an airtight container at room temperature for up to 1 week.

Makes about 22 cookies

- 1½ cups all-purpose flour
- 1½ teaspoons baking soda
- 2 teaspoons ground ginger
- 1 teaspoon ground cinnamon
- 1 teaspoon ground cardamom
- ½ teaspoon ground cloves
- ½ teaspoon kosher salt
- ¼ teaspoon freshly ground black pepper
- ½ cup (1 stick) unsalted butter, at room temperature
- 1½ cups sugar
- 1 large egg
- ⅓ cup unsulfured molasses

1. Preheat the oven to 350°F.
2. Whisk together the flour, baking soda, ginger, cinnamon, cardamom, cloves, salt, and pepper in a medium bowl to combine.
3. Combine the butter and 1 cup of the sugar in a large bowl and use a handheld mixer to beat on medium speed until light and fluffy, about 2 minutes. Add the egg and molasses and beat until smooth.
4. Add half the flour mixture and beat until just incorporated. Add the remaining flour mixture and beat until completely incorporated.
5. Place the remaining ½ cup sugar in a small bowl. Use a 1-tablespoon measure to scoop out dough and roll it into a ball. Roll the balls in the sugar until fully coated.
6. Place 8 dough balls on a baking sheet, spacing them 3 inches apart, and bake until the cookies have spread out and are deeply aromatic, about 10 minutes.
7. Let the cookies cool on the baking sheet for 5 minutes before transferring to a wire rack to finish cooling. Repeat with the remaining cookie dough.

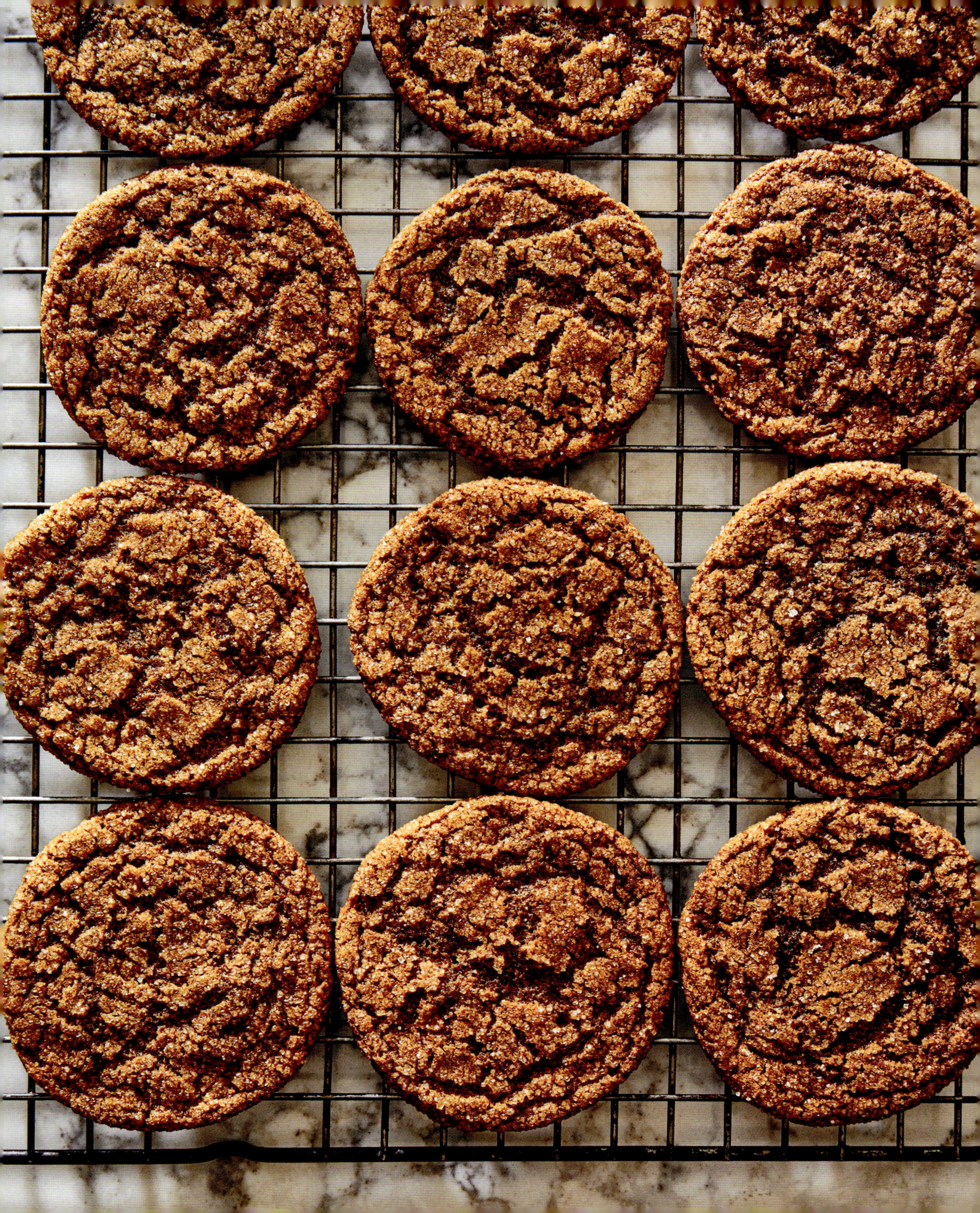

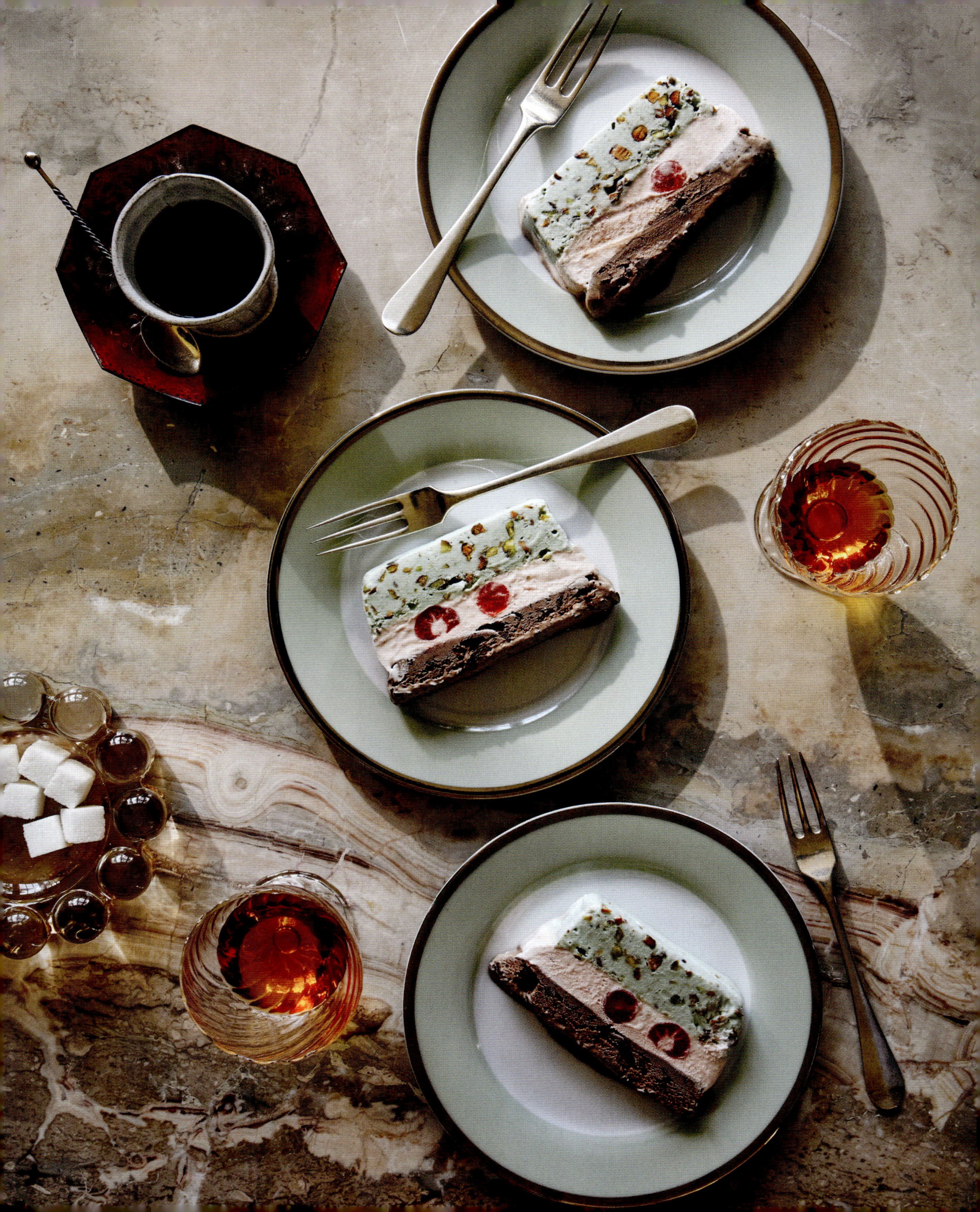

Spumoni

While I love an over-the-top dinner party dessert, sometimes simple is best. Enter spumoni. This Italian American dessert hits all the marks of being fun and festive, while being ridiculously easy to put together. Let's be real—it's basically a glorified ice cream cake with a fancy name. I've stayed in line with tradition and layered pistachio, cherry, and chocolate ice cream for an almost-Neapolitan look. I love how these flavors work together, but you can experiment with different combinations of ice cream flavors—just follow this recipe as a guideline.

NOTES: Spumoni can be prepared up to 1 month in advance, making it an ideal make-ahead dessert to prep for a dinner party. For clean slices, dip the knife under hot water before cutting.

Serves 10

- 1 pint pistachio ice cream (about 2 cups)
- ½ cup lightly salted shelled pistachios
- 1 pint vanilla ice cream (about 2 cups)
- ½ cup pitted maraschino cherries
- 1 pint chocolate ice cream (about 2 cups)
- 1½ ounces semisweet chocolate, thinly sliced (about ½ cup)

1. Cut a piece of parchment paper into two strips, one 18×3½ inches and another 18×7½ inches. Line a 9×5-inch loaf pan with the parchment paper so that at least 4 inches hang over the edges.

2. Let the pistachio, vanilla, and chocolate ice cream sit at room temperature until softened, 25 to 30 minutes.

3. Stir together the pistachio ice cream and pistachios in a medium bowl until combined. In a second medium bowl, stir together the vanilla ice cream and cherries until combined. In a third medium bowl, stir together the chocolate ice cream and chopped chocolate until combined.

4. Spread the pistachio ice cream in the bottom of the loaf pan in an even layer. Working quickly, add the vanilla ice cream and spread in an even layer. Finish by spreading the chocolate ice cream in an even layer.

5. Fold the parchment paper over the ice cream and transfer the pan to the freezer until frozen, at least 2 hours or up to 1 month.

6. To serve, invert the loaf pan on a cutting board and remove the parchment paper. Slice the ice cream loaf and serve immediately.

WEEKENDS | DESSERT

Tahini Chocolate Cheesecake Bars

If you're looking for all the joys of cheesecake in a more manageable form, these bars deliver the flavor of the classic dessert in a more refined manner. Here, the cheesecake batter is combined with tahini, which adds a subtle nuttiness without making the bars too sweet. They are draped in a layer of ganache, which does double duty by hiding any imperfections that might have appeared while the cheesecake baked and adds a snappy bite to contrast the creaminess of the filling. Waiting for these to set will feel next to impossible, but I can assure you it's worthwhile.

NOTE: Leftover bars can be stored in an airtight container in the refrigerator for up to 4 days.

Serves a crowd

CRUST

20 Oreo cookies

½ teaspoon kosher salt

5 tablespoons unsalted butter, melted

FILLING

2 (8-ounce) packages full-fat cream cheese, at room temperature

¾ cup sugar

1 cup tahini

½ cup full-fat sour cream, at room temperature

1 teaspoon pure vanilla extract

½ teaspoon kosher salt

2 large eggs, at room temperature

TOPPING

8 ounces semisweet chocolate chips

1 cup heavy cream

1 teaspoon toasted sesame seeds

¾ teaspoon flaky salt

1. **Make the crust:** Preheat the oven to 350°F. Line the bottom of a 9-inch square pan with a sheet of parchment paper long enough to hang over the sides by 1 inch.

2. Pulse the Oreos and salt in a food processor until finely ground. Add the melted butter and pulse until the mixture resembles wet sand.

3. Transfer the mixture to the baking pan, pressing it into an even layer (I like to use the bottom of a flat measuring cup for this). Bake until the crust is just set and fragrant, about 10 minutes.

4. **Make the filling:** Combine the cream cheese and sugar in the bowl of a stand mixer fitted with the paddle attachment. Beat on medium speed until smooth, about 1 minute. Scrape down the sides of the bowl, then add the tahini, sour cream, vanilla, and salt, and beat until just combined. Scrape down the sides of the bowl again. Add the eggs, one at a time, beating after each addition, until the mixture is smooth. Pour the filling into the crust and smooth into an even layer.

5. Bake until the filling is just set but has a slight jiggle in the center, 20 to 25 minutes. Place on a wire rack and let cool completely. Refrigerate for at least 4 hours or up to overnight.

6. **Make the ganache:** Place the chocolate chips in a medium heatproof bowl. Heat the heavy cream in a small pot over medium-high heat until it begins to simmer.

Pour the cream over the chocolate chips and let sit for 2 minutes, then whisk until smooth and glossy.

7. Pour the ganache over the cheesecake in an even layer. Let sit at room temperature until the chocolate begins to firm up, about 20 minutes. Sprinkle the chocolate ganache with sesame seeds and flaky salt. Refrigerate until set, at least 1 hour or up to overnight.

8. When ready to serve, use the overhanging parchment paper as handles to carefully lift the bars from the baking dish and set them on a cutting board. Cut into bars.

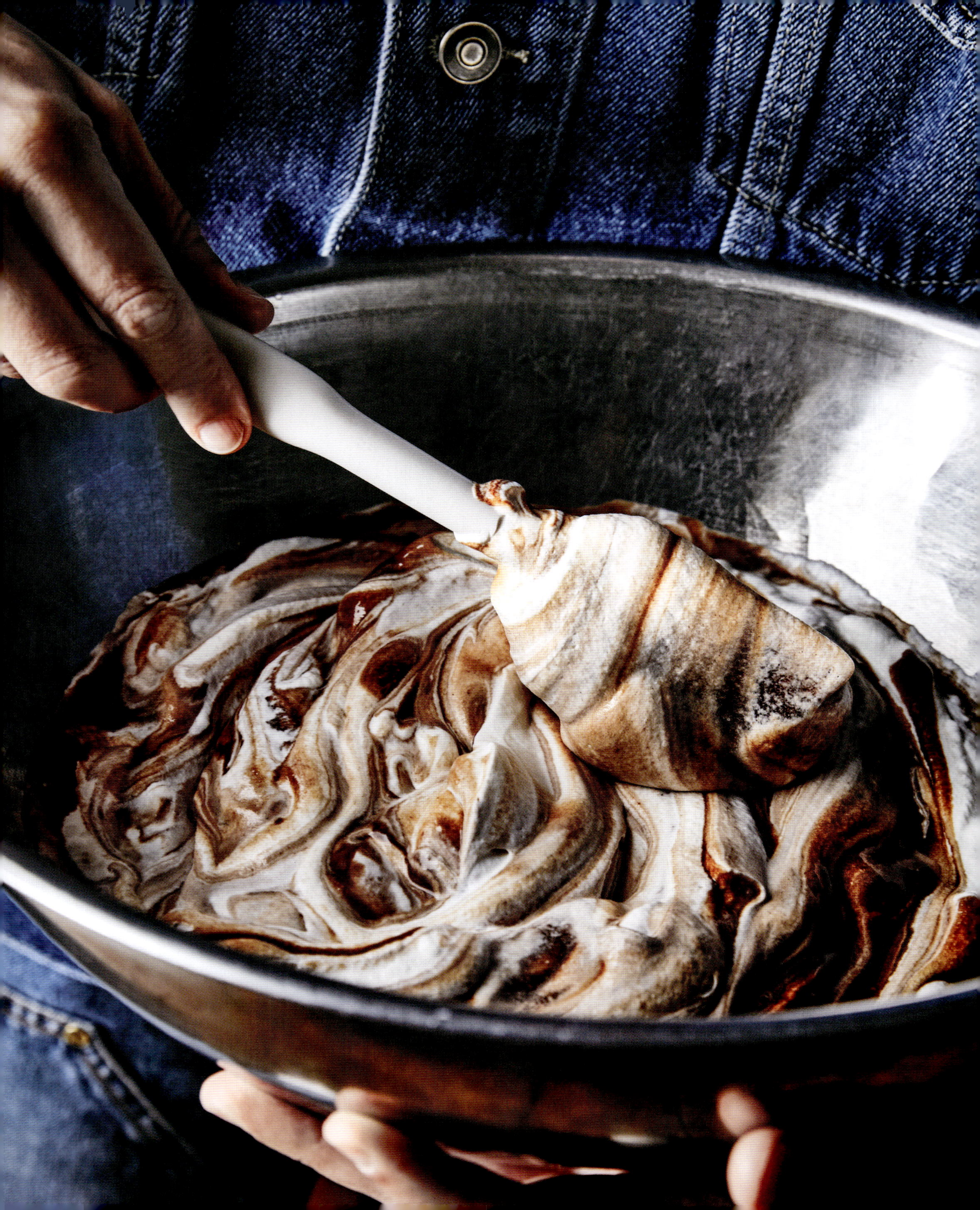

Dark Chocolate Mousse with Mascarpone Whipped Cream

I'm admittedly not a huge chocolate lover, but the dark chocolate in this mousse adds a nuanced depth of flavor that even I can get behind. While traditionally mousse is made by whipping egg whites until stiff, I've taken the easier route here and rely on whipped cream. Invest in a digital thermometer to ensure the egg yolk mixture reaches the appropriate temperature.

NOTE: Chocolate mousse can be stored in an airtight container in the refrigerator for up to 2 days.

Serves 4 to 6

- 4 large egg yolks
- ¼ cup granulated sugar
- ¼ teaspoon kosher salt
- 3¼ cups heavy cream
- 1½ teaspoons espresso powder
- 3½ ounces dark chocolate, finely chopped
- 1 teaspoon pure vanilla extract
- ½ cup mascarpone cheese
- ¼ cup powdered sugar
- Flaky salt, for serving

1. Place the egg yolks, sugar, and salt in a metal or heatproof bowl and whisk until smooth.

2. Combine ¾ cup of the cream and the espresso powder in a medium pot and whisk over medium heat until the espresso powder dissolves, about 1 minute. While whisking continuously, pour the hot cream into the egg yolk mixture in a thin stream and whisk to combine. Carefully pour the mixture back into the pot and cook over low heat, whisking continuously, until it coats the back of a spoon, becomes very foamy, and reaches 160°F, 4 to 5 minutes. Remove the pot from the heat and add the chocolate and vanilla, whisking until smooth. Let cool to room temperature.

3. Pour 1½ cups of the cream into a medium bowl and use a handheld mixer to beat on medium-high speed until stiff peaks form, making sure not to overmix, 4 to 5 minutes. (Alternatively, this can be done in the bowl of a stand mixer fitted with the whisk attachment.) Pour the cooled chocolate mixture over the whipped cream and use a spatula to fold until just combined.

4. Carefully pour the chocolate mousse into a serving bowl or individual serving bowls and refrigerate for at least 6 hours or up to overnight.

5. Pour the remaining 1 cup cream into a medium bowl and use a handheld mixer to beat on medium speed until soft peaks form, about 3 minutes. (Alternatively, this can be done in the bowl of a stand mixer fitted with the whisk attachment.) Add the mascarpone and powdered sugar and beat until stiff peaks form, about 1 minute more.

6. Top the chocolate mousse with the mascarpone whipped cream and flaky salt before serving.

Sticky Toffee Pudding

Sticky toffee pudding is one of those desserts that is effortlessly decadent without being cloying, toeing the line between celebratory and comforting. It's not a pudding in the American sense of the word, but an English take, which involves a sponge smothered in toffee sauce. Although it's thought of as a British classic, the dessert wasn't popularized in Britain until the 1970s. While the flavor isn't date-forward, they keep the cake moist with a tender crumb. Ice cream, custard, or a dollop of whipped cream is always welcome, although not required, for serving.

NOTES: Leftover cake can be stored in an airtight container in the refrigerator for up to 3 days. I recommend rewarming it before serving leftovers.

1. **Make the cake:** Preheat the oven to 350°F. Grease a 9-inch square baking dish with butter.

2. Place the dates and baking soda in a medium bowl. Pour the boiling water over the dates and let stand until softened, about 10 minutes. Transfer the date mixture to a food processor and process until smooth.

3. Whisk together the flour, baking powder, salt, cinnamon, cloves, and nutmeg in a medium bowl to combine.

4. Place the butter and brown sugar in the bowl of a stand mixer fitted with the paddle attachment. Beat on medium speed until combined, about 1 minute. Add the eggs one at a time, beating until just combined. Add the date puree and vanilla and beat until just combined. Scrape down the sides of the bowl, then add the flour mixture. Reduce the speed to low and beat until just combined.

5. Transfer the batter to the greased baking dish and use a spatula to smooth it into an even layer. Bake the cake until it is puffed and a toothpick comes out clean, 30 to 35 minutes. Remove the cake from the oven but leave the oven on. Immediately use the tines of a fork to poke holes all over the cake, poking all the way down to the bottom.

6. **Make the toffee sauce:** Melt the butter in a medium pot over medium-high heat. Add the brown sugar, cream, vanilla, and salt and cook, stirring, until smooth and glossy, about 1 minute.

7. Drizzle 1 cup of the toffee sauce all over the top of the cake. Return the cake to the oven and bake until the sauce bubbles, about 5 minutes.

8. Serve the cake immediately with the remaining toffee sauce on the side.

Serves 9

CAKE

6 tablespoons (¾ stick) unsalted butter, plus more for greasing, at room temperature

8 ounces pitted dates (about 1½ cups)

1 teaspoon baking soda

1 cup boiling water

1½ cups all-purpose flour

1½ teaspoons baking powder

½ teaspoon kosher salt

½ teaspoon ground cinnamon

¼ teaspoon ground cloves

⅛ teaspoon ground nutmeg

¾ cup packed dark brown sugar

2 large eggs, at room temperature

1½ teaspoons pure vanilla extract

TOFFEE SAUCE

½ cup (1 stick) unsalted butter

1¼ cups packed dark brown sugar

1 cup heavy cream

2 teaspoons pure vanilla extract

½ teaspoon kosher salt

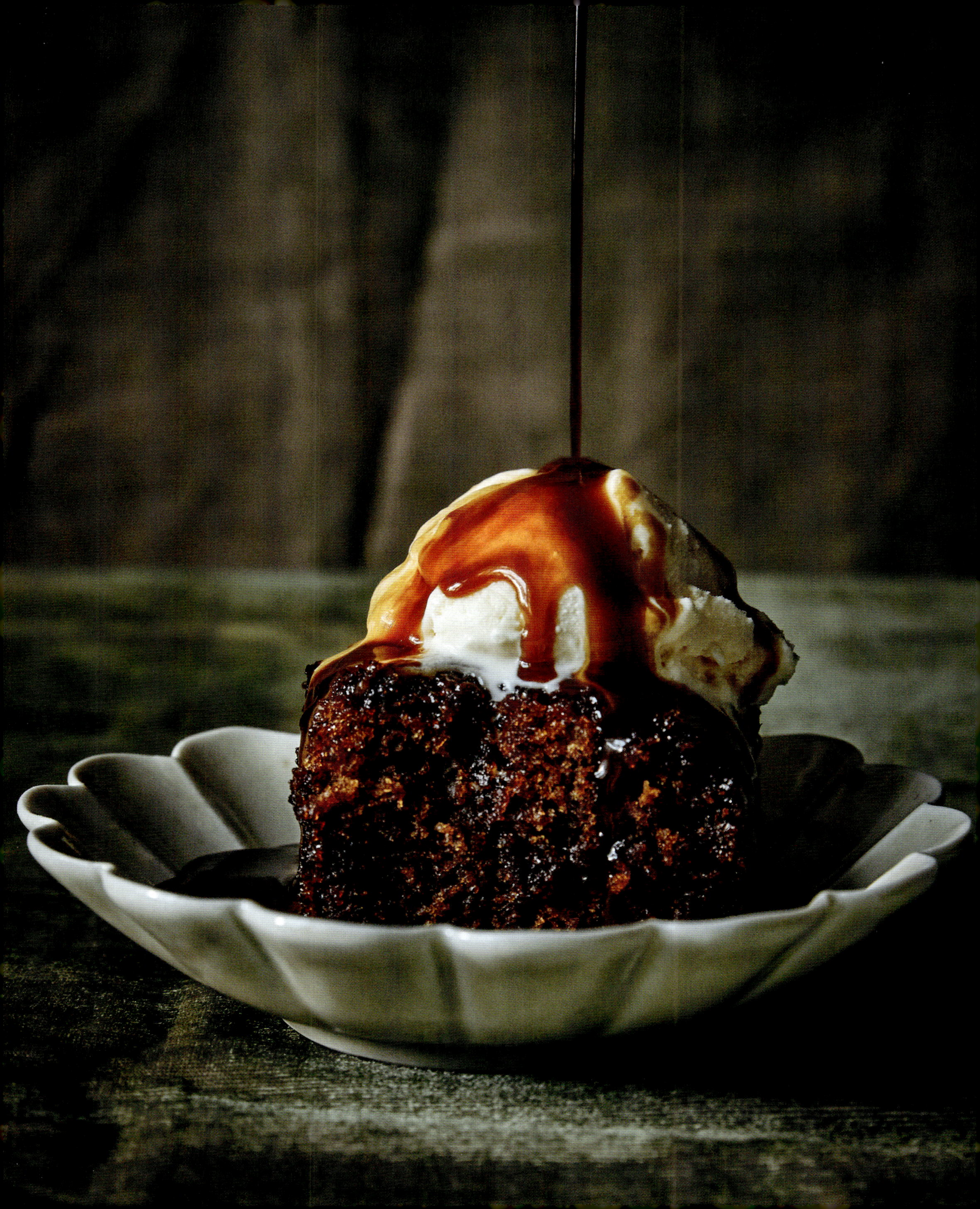

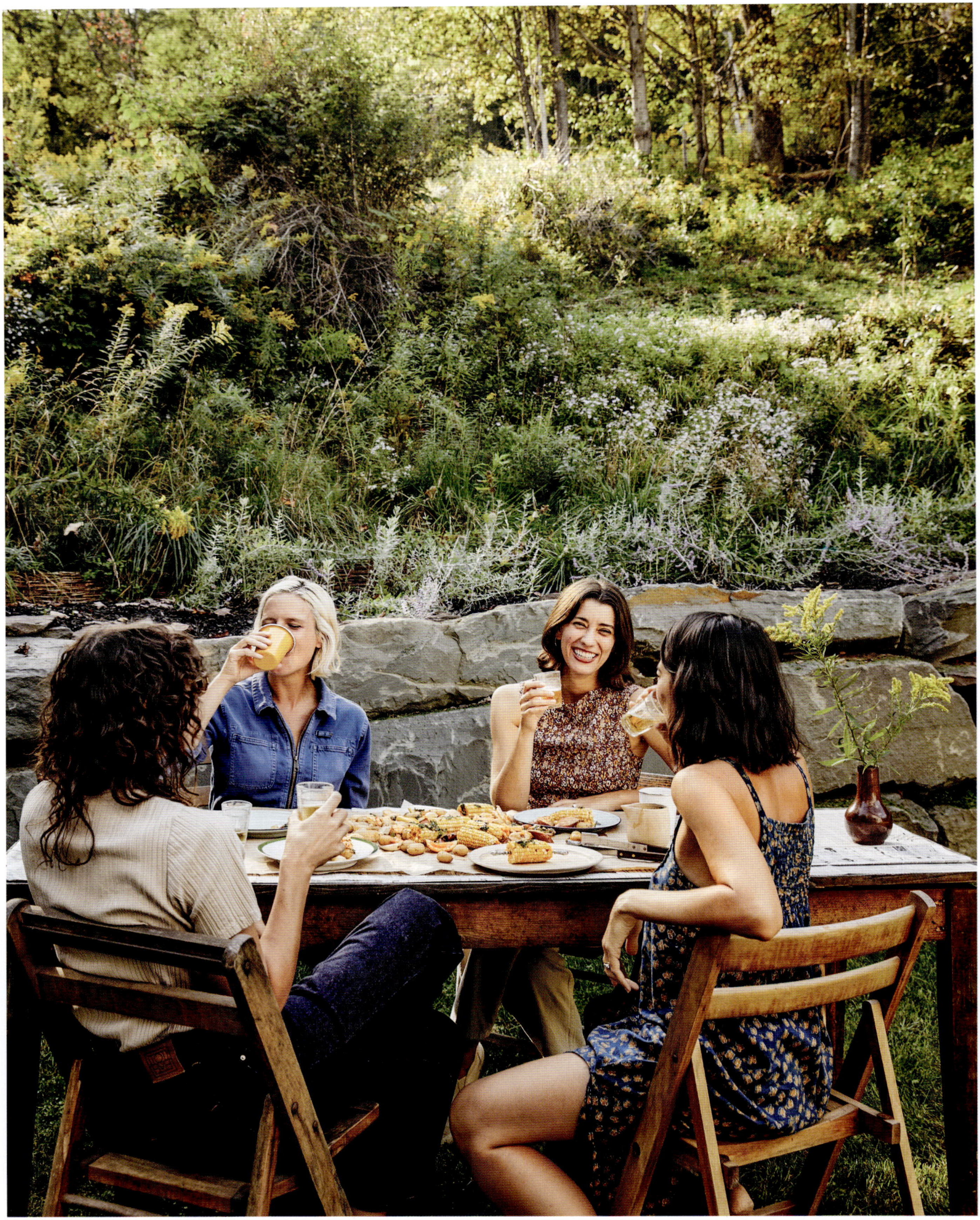

Acknowledgments

I'm so grateful to all the readers, cooks, and supporters who have made this career possible. I hope I can continue writing cookbooks for you for years to come.

It's not often that one gets to embark on a creative project surrounded by their favorite people, and I feel so lucky that I got to do just that. Christian Harder, you're not only one of my closest friends, but also the best collaborator. I can't wait for all the projects, family dinners, and adventures ahead of us. Thank you for always hearing out all my ideas, bringing my vision to life, and standing at the ready with a dirty martini after a long day. Rebekah Peppler, thank you for showing up for me in all the ways—especially in the middle of the biggest book tour of your life. There is no one who makes food look as good as you do. Rebecca Bartoshesky, your keen eye, calm presence, and appetite for everything I made was such a joy to have on set. I'm so glad that after all of this I can now call you a friend. Maggie McDowell, from hours rolling pie dough and peeling peaches, to days spent churning out recipe after recipe, there is nothing I love more than spending time in the kitchen with you. Thank you for being a constant bright spot and, of course, sharing your perfect apple pie recipe with me (and now the world!).

Caitlin Leffel, this book happened because of you. Thank you for your endless well of enthusiasm, patience, and thoughtful (sometimes laugh-out-loud) edits. You made me—and this book—better through this process. I'll make you a tomato panzanella whenever you want.

Thank you to the rest of the team at Union Square & Co., who put in countless hours to help create this book, including Lisa Forde, Renée Bollier, Amanda Englander, Ivy McFadden, and Terence Campo, and copyeditor Ana Deboo.

Eve Attermann, thank you for being one of my earliest champions, for taking endless calls, and for always being there for me with such thoughtful advice.

Monica Lee, I've never been so excited to get a DM before. Thank you for testing nearly every recipe in this book and for your boundless enthusiasm along the way. Your feedback made these recipes better.

So many friends helped throughout the process, from brainstorming, commiserating, and washing dishes to modeling and recipe testing and so much more. Thank you to Karlee Rotoly, Ryan Willison, Ben Mims, Ali Francis, Rebecca Firkser, Hannah Leighton, Sam Sullivan, Meagan Bennett, Lisa Pryzstup, Rose Annis, James Sprankle, Cliff Endo, Georgia Hilmer, Laila Said, Antonio Mora, Natalie Karic, Leah Wawro, Tania Hammond, Sophie Slotnick, Colu Henry, Phoebe Fry, Danny Newburg, and Rachel Watson.

Thank you to Illana Alpterstein, Cassandra Chamoun, and the rest of the team at Mona Creative, as well as Jennifer and Talia Sommer, for working tirelessly to share *Nights and Weekends* with the world.

Thank you to my mom, Heleen, for opening your home, inspiring me every day, and always thinking whatever I make is the best.

And to my husband, Ryan, who I dedicated this book to, thank you for your support, encouragement, brainstorming, and discerning palate. Your pursuit of betterment inspires me every day, and I'm so lucky to call you my partner in life. I love you!

Index

NOTE: Page references in *italics* refer to photos.

A

Almond Butter Dip, Gochujang, *180*, 181
Antipasti Skewers, *178*, 179
Apple Crumble, Maggie's Brown Butter, 253–255, *254*
artichokes
    Artichokes with Herb Aioli, *90*, 91
    Marinated White Beans and Artichokes, *82*, 83
    Roasted Tomatoes, Artichokes, and Leeks with Sardines, *146*, 147
Asparagus, Potato Salad with Pesto, Smoked Fish, and, *144*, 145

B

Baked Halibut with Pesto Rosso, *150*, 151
Banana Bread with Chocolate Chunks, Olive Oil, *202*, 203
beans. *See also* chickpeas
    Cheesy Potato and Pinto Bean Tacos, *88*, 89
    Marinated White Beans and Artichokes, *82*, 83
    One-Pot Rice and Beans, *74*, 75
    Saucy Shrimp with Beans and Greens, *142*, 143
    Tomato Sauce with Pancetta, White Beans, and Rosemary, *24*, 25
    White Turkey Chili, *54*, 55
beef
    One-Pot Gnocchi Ragù, *26*, 27
    Rib Eyes with a Party Wedge Salad, *210*, 211
    Skirt Steak with Scallion Butter and Slaw, *112*, 113
    Vinegary Pot Roast with Parsnips and Carrots, *232*, *233*–234

Big Green Seedy Salad, *108*, 109
Braised Chicken Thighs with Prunes and Lemons, *212*, 213
breads and rolls
    Buttermilk Ginger Scones, *192*, 193
    Cacio e Pepe Popovers, *184*, 185
    Olive Oil Banana Bread with Chocolate Chunks, *202*, 203
    Sticky Rolls with Pistachios and Caramel, *198–201*, *199–200*
broccoli, in Couscous with Merguez, Broccoli, and Halloumi, *126*, 127
Broccoli, Roasted, and Crispy Chickpeas with Tahini Dressing, *72*, 73
Broccolini, Roasted, and Banana Peppers over Ricotta, *96*, 97
brunch dishes, 183–208
Brussels Sprout Salad with Hazelnuts and Feta, *86*, 87
Buttermilk Ginger Scones, *192*, 193
Butternut Squash and Ricotta Lasagna, *214*, 215

C

Cabbage, Braised, Tofu Schnitzel with, *220*, *221*–222
Cacio e Pepe Popovers, *184*, 185
Cake, Strawberry Rhubarb, *242*, 243
Caprese, Crispy Gnocchi, *30*, 31
Caramelized Shallot Dip, *164*, 165
Cauliflower, Chickpeas, and Sweet Potatoes with Spiced Yogurt, Roasted, *102*, 103
Cauliflower Soup with Chile Crisp, Creamy, *62*, 63
Cauliflower with Herby Yogurt Sauce, Whole Roasted Spiced, *216*, 217
cheese. *See also* feta cheese
    Antipasti Skewers, *178*, 179
    Butternut Squash and Ricotta Lasagna, *214*, 215
    Cheesy Potato and Pinto Bean Tacos, *88*, 89
    Cheesy Potato Tart, *104*, 105
    Couscous with Merguez, Broccoli, and Halloumi, *126*, 127

    Crispy Gnocchi Caprese, *30*, 31
    Everything Bagel Spice Cheese Ball, *174*, 175
    French Onion Soup Strata, *196*, 197
    Halloumi Fattoush, *106*, 107
    Hot Cheesy Crab Dip, *170*, 171
    Prosciutto and Brie Frittata, *186*, *187*
    Stovetop Mac and Cheese, *28*, 29
    Summer Squash Casserole with Buttery Ritz Crackers, *76*, 77
    Tomato Pie with Buttermilk Biscuit Crust, 235–237, *236*
Cheesecake Bars, Tahini Chocolate, 260–261, *261*
chicken
    Braised Chicken Thighs with Prunes and Lemons, *212*, 213
    Chicken Thighs in Creamy Paprika Sauce, *114*, 115
    Curried Chicken and Cauliflower Phyllo Pie, *230*, 231
    French Market Chicken with Schmaltzy Potatoes, *226*, 227
    Grilled Chicken Sandwiches, *130*, 131
    Lemon Chicken Soup for Whatever Ails You, *42*, 43
    Rotisserie Chicken Salad with Snap Peas and Dilly Ranch, *118*, 119
chickpeas
    Chickpea Curry, *44*, 45
    Chopped Chicory Salad, *100*, *101*
    Couscous and Chickpea Salad, *66*, 67
    Pasta e Ceci, *52*, 53
    Roasted Broccoli and Crispy Chickpeas with Tahini Dressing, *72*, 73
    Roasted Cauliflower, Chickpeas, and Sweet Potatoes with Spiced Yogurt, *102*, 103
    Socca with Arugula Salad, *68*, 69
Chicory Salad, Chopped, *100*, *101*
Chili, White Turkey, *54*, 55

chocolate
- Chocolate Frosting and Yellow Sour Cream Birthday Cake, 248–249, 249
- Dark Chocolate Mousse with Mascarpone Whipped Cream, 262, 263
- Olive Oil Banana Bread with Chocolate Chunks, 202, 203
- Spumoni, 258, 259
- Tahini Chocolate Cheesecake Bars, 260–261, 261

Chopped Chicory Salad, 100, 101
Classic Lemon Bars, 244, 245
Cod in Green Sauce, 140, 141
Conserva Plate, 154, 155
Cookies, Gingersnap, 256, 257
corn
- Polenta with Saucy Sausage and Tomatoes, 124, 125
- Salmon, Potato, and Corn Chowder, 56, 57
- Sheet-Pan Sausage with Corn, Peach, and Cucumber Salad, 122, 123
- Shrimp Boil with Garlicky Old Bay Butter, 228, 229
- Tofu in Miso Butter Sauce with Corn, 78, 79

Cornmeal Fried Okra with Special Sauce, 176, 177
Couscous, Israeli, in Greekish Whole Fish, 238, 239
Couscous and Chickpea Salad, 66, 67
Couscous with Merguez, Broccoli, and Halloumi, 126, 127
Crab Dip, Hot Cheesy, 170, 171
Crab Pasta with Pistachios and Olives, 18, 19
Creamy Cauliflower Soup with Chile Crisp, 62, 63
Creamy Green Pasta, 38, 39
Crêpes with Mushrooms and Gremolata, 208, 209
Crispy Gnocchi Caprese, 30, 31

cucumbers
- Chile Crisp Salmon with Quick Pickle Salad, 138, 139
- Halloumi Fattoush, 106, 107
- Salmon Ceviche with Cucumber and Tajín, 162, 163
- Sheet-Pan Sausage with Corn, Peach, and Cucumber Salad, 122, 123

Curried Chicken and Cauliflower Phyllo Pie, 230, 231
Curry, Chickpea, 44, 45
Curry, Red Coconut, with Tofu, 60, 61

D

Dark Chocolate Mousse with Mascarpone Whipped Cream, 262, 263
desserts, 241–265
dinner dishes, 207–242
dips
- Caramelized Shallot Dip, 164, 165
- Gochujang Almond Butter Dip, 180, 181
- Hot Cheesy Crab Dip, 170, 171

Dumplings and Dill, Spring Vegetable Soup with, 46, 47

E

eggs
- French Onion Soup Strata, 196, 197
- Jammy Eggs with Mayo and Chile Oil, 167, 168
- Prosciutto and Brie Frittata, 186, 187
- Savory Breakfast Bowl, 194, 195
- Everything Bagel Spice Cheese Ball, 174, 175
- Everything Bagel Tomato Panzanella, 84, 85

F

fennel
- Chile Crisp Salmon with Quick Pickle Salad, 138, 139
- Chopped Chicory Salad, 100, 101
- Couscous and Chickpea Salad, 66, 67
- Everything Bagel Tomato Panzanella, 84, 85
- Skirt Steak with Scallion Butter and Slaw, 112, 113
- Socca with Arugula Salad, 68, 69

feta cheese
- Brussels Sprout Salad with Hazelnuts and Feta, 86, 87
- Feta Sauce for Spiced Lamb Flatbreads, 120, 121
- Not-Your-Mom's Pasta Salad, 20, 21

Fire Crackers, 172, 173
fish and seafood, 137–162
French Market Chicken with Schmaltzy Potatoes, 226, 227
French Onion Soup Strata, 196, 197
Frittata, Prosciutto and Brie, 186, 187
Frosting, Chocolate, and Yellow Sour Cream Birthday Cake, 248–249, 249
Fruit Salad, Stone, 190, 191

G

Gingersnap Cookies, 256, 257
Gnocchi Caprese, Crispy, 30, 31
Gnocchi Ragù, One-Pot, 26, 27
Gochujang Almond Butter Dip, 180, 181
Greekish Whole Fish, 238, 239
greens. *See also individual types of greens*
- Creamy Green Pasta, 38, 39
- Pasta with Brown Butter Wilted Greens and Walnuts, 22, 23
- Saucy Shrimp with Beans and Greens, 142, 143

Grilled Chicken Sandwiches, 130, 131
Grilled Peaches with Cardamom Honey Whipped Cream, 246, 247

H

Halibut with Pesto Rosso, Baked, 150, 151

Halloumi, Couscous with Merguez, Broccoli, and, 126, *127*
Halloumi Fattoush, *106*, 107
Hazelnuts and Feta, Brussels Sprout Salad with, *86*, 87
Herb Aioli, Artichokes with, *90*, 91
Horseradish Aioli Dressing, Shrimp Salad with, 148, *149*
Hot Butter Garlic Shrimp, 152, *153*
Hot Cheesy Crab Dip, 170, *171*

I
ice cream, in Spumoni, *258*, 259

J
Jammy Eggs with Mayo and Chile Oil, 167, *168*

K
Kale Salad with Roasted Grapes, 80, *81*

L
Lamb, Soy-Braised Cumin, 218, *219*
Lamb Flatbreads, Spiced, 120, *121*
Lasagna, Butternut Squash and Ricotta, 214, *215*
Lemon Bars, Classic, 244, *245*
Lemon Chicken Soup for Whatever Ails You, *42*, 43
Lemon Curd, in Party Pavlova, 250, 251–252
Lemons, Braised Chicken Thighs with Prunes and, *212*, 213
lettuce
    Big Green Seedy Salad, *108*, 109
    Halloumi Fattoush, *106*, 107
    Rotisserie Chicken Salad with Snap Peas and Dilly Ranch, 118, *119*

M
Mac and Cheese, Stovetop, *28*, 29
Maggie's Brown Butter Apple Crumble, 253–255, *254*

Marinated Olives in Citrus and Spices, *165*, 166
Marinated White Beans and Artichokes, *82*, 83
Meatballs, Turkey, with Puttanesca Sauce, 134, *135*
meat dishes, 111–138
Meringue, in Party Pavlova, *250*, 251–252
Miso Butter Sauce with Corn, Tofu in, *78*, 79
Miso Sesame Butter, Sweet Potatoes with, *94*, 95
Mousse, Dark Chocolate, with Mascarpone Whipped Cream, *262*, 263
Mushroom and Pea Toast, *70*, 71
Mushroom Larb, *98*, 99
Mushrooms and Gremolata, Crêpes with, *208*, 209

N
Not-Your-Mom's Pasta Salad, *20*, 21
nuts. *See individual types of nuts*

O
Oatmeal, Pear and Pecan Baked, *188*, 189
Okra with Special Sauce, Cornmeal Fried, *176*, 177
Olive Oil Banana Bread with Chocolate Chunks, 202, *203*
olives
    Antipasti Skewers, 178, *179*
    Chopped Chicory Salad, 100, *101*
    Crab Pasta with Pistachios and Olives, *18*, 19
    Marinated Olives in Citrus and Spices, *165*, 166
    Not-Your-Mom's Pasta Salad, *20*, 21
    Orzo with Leeks, Olives, and Golden Raisins, *34*, 35
One-Pot Gnocchi Ragù, *26*, 27
One-Pot Rice and Beans, *74*, 75
Orzo with Leeks, Olives, and Golden Raisins, *34*, 35

P
Panzanella, Everything Bagel Tomato, 84, *85*
Party Pavlova, *250*, 251–252
pasta
    full recipe section, 17–42
    Pasta e Ceci, 52, *53*
    Pasta with Bacon, Peas, Sour Cream, and Dill, *36*, 37
    Pasta with Brown Butter Wilted Greens and Walnuts, *22*, 23
Peaches, Grilled, with Cardamom Honey Whipped Cream, *246*, 247
peaches, in Sheet-Pan Sausage with Corn, Peach, and Cucumber Salad, 122, *123*
Peanut Sauce, Udon Noodles with, *32*, 33
Pear and Pecan Baked Oatmeal, *188*, 189
peas
    Mushroom and Pea Toast, *70*, 71
    Pasta with Bacon, Peas, Sour Cream, and Dill, *36*, 37
    Shrimp Salad with Horseradish Aioli Dressing, 148, *149*
    Spring Vegetable Soup with Dumplings and Dill, *46*, 47
Pecan Baked Oatmeal, Pear and, *188*, 189
Phyllo Pie, Curried Chicken and Cauliflower, 230, *231*
Pie, Tomato, with Buttermilk Biscuit Crust, 235–237, *236*
pistachios, in Spumoni, *258*, 259
Pistachios and Caramel, Sticky Rolls with, 198–201, *199–200*
Pistachios and Olives, Crab Pasta with, *18*, 19
Polenta with Saucy Sausage and Tomatoes, 124, *125*
pork
    Antipasti Skewers, 178, *179*
    bacon, in Rib Eyes with a Party Wedge Salad, 210, *211*
    Bacon, Peas, Sour Cream, and Dill, Pasta with, *36*, 37

Bacon and Croutons, Split Pea Soup with, 50, 51
Chopped Chicory Salad, 100, 101
Not-Your-Mom's Pasta Salad, 20, 21
Polenta with Saucy Sausage and Tomatoes, 124, 125
Pork Chops au Poivre, 132, 133
Pork Tenderloin with Pineapple and Peppers, 128, 129
Prosciutto and Brie Frittata, 186, 187
Sheet-Pan Sausage with Corn, Peach, and Cucumber Salad, 122, 123

potatoes
  Cheesy Potato and Pinto Bean Tacos, 88, 89
  Cheesy Potato Tart, 104, 105
  French Market Chicken with Schmaltzy Potatoes, 226, 227
  Potato Salad with Pesto, Smoked Fish, and Asparagus, 144, 145
  Salmon, Potato, and Corn Chowder, 56, 57
  Spring Vegetable Soup with Dumplings and Dill, 46, 47

Prosciutto and Brie Frittata, 186, 187
Pudding, Sticky Toffee, 264, 265
Puttanesca Sauce, Turkey Meatballs with, 134, 135

R

Red Coconut Curry with Tofu, 60, 61
Rhubarb Cake, Strawberry, 242, 243
Rib Eyes with a Party Wedge Salad, 210, 211

rice
  Chickpea Curry, 44, 45
  Chile Crisp Salmon with Quick Pickle Salad, 138, 139
  Cod in Green Sauce, 140, 141
  Mushroom Larb, 98, 99
  One-Pot Rice and Beans, 74, 75
  Red Coconut Curry with Tofu, 60, 61
  Tofu in Miso Butter Sauce with Corn, 78, 79

Tofu with Scallion Garlic Ginger Oil, 92, 93
Roasted Broccoli and Crispy Chickpeas with Tahini Dressing, 72, 73
Roasted Broccolini and Banana Peppers over Ricotta, 96, 97
Roasted Cauliflower, Chickpeas, and Sweet Potatoes with Spiced Yogurt, 102, 103
Roasted Tomato and Red Pepper Soup, 48, 49
Roasted Tomatoes, Artichokes, and Leeks with Sardines, 146, 147
Rotisserie Chicken Salad with Snap Peas and Dilly Ranch, 118, 119

S

salads
  Arugula Salad, Socca with, 68, 69
  Big Green Seedy Salad, 108, 109
  Brussels Sprout Salad with Hazelnuts and Feta, 86, 87
  Chopped Chicory Salad, 100, 101
  Couscous and Chickpea Salad, 66, 67
  Halloumi Fattoush, 106, 107
  Herb Salad, in Spiced Lamb Flatbreads, 120, 121
  Kale Salad with Roasted Grapes, 80, 81
  Not-Your-Mom's Pasta Salad, 20, 21
  Party Wedge Salad, Rib Eyes with a, 210, 211
  Potato Salad with Pesto, Smoked Fish, and Asparagus, 144, 145
  Quick Pickle Salad, Chile Crisp Salmon with, 138, 139
  Rotisserie Chicken Salad with Snap Peas and Dilly Ranch, 118, 119
  Sheet-Pan Sausage with Corn, Peach, and Cucumber Salad, 122, 123
  Shrimp Salad with Horseradish Aioli Dressing, 148, 149
  Slaw, Skirt Steak with Scallion Butter and, 112, 113

Salmon, Potato, and Corn Chowder, 56, 57
Salmon Ceviche with Cucumber and Tajín, 162, 163
Salmon with Grapefruit and Crispy Shallots, Slow-Roasted, 223–225, 224
Sandwiches, Grilled Chicken, 130, 131

sauces and dressings
  Aioli, Herb, Artichokes with, 90, 91
  for Chopped Chicory Salad, 100, 101
  Feta Sauce for Spiced Lamb Flatbreads, 120
  Green Sauce, Cod in, 140, 141
  Herby Yogurt Sauce, Whole Roasted Spiced Cauliflower with, 216, 217
  Horseradish Aioli Dressing, Shrimp Salad with, 148, 149
  Pesto Rosso, Baked Halibut with, 150, 151
  Potato Salad with Pesto, Smoked Fish, and Asparagus, 144, 145
  Puttanesca Sauce, Turkey Meatballs with, 134, 135
  Ranch Dressing, 118, 119
  Special Sauce, Cornmeal Fried Okra with, 176, 177
  Spiced Yogurt, Roasted Cauliflower, Chickpeas, and Sweet Potatoes with, 102, 103
  Tahini Dressing, Roasted Broccoli and Crispy Chickpeas with, 72, 73
  Tomato Sauce with Pancetta, White Beans, and Rosemary, 24, 25

Saucy Shrimp with Beans and Greens, 142, 143
Savory Breakfast Bowl, 194, 195
Scones, Buttermilk Ginger, 192, 193
Seedy Salad, Big Green, 108, 109
Sheet-Pan Sausage with Corn, Peach, and Cucumber Salad, 122, 123
Shrimp, Hot Butter Garlic, 152, 153
Shrimp, Saucy, with Beans and Greens, 142, 143

Shrimp Boil with Garlicky Old Bay Butter, 228, 229
Shrimp Salad with Horseradish Aioli Dressing, 148, 149
Skirt Steak with Scallion Butter and Slaw, 112, 113
Slow-Roasted Salmon with Grapefruit and Crispy Shallots, 223–225, 224
snacks, 161–184
Snap Peas and Dilly Ranch, Rotisserie Chicken Salad with, 118, 119
Socca with Arugula Salad, 68, 69
soups and stews, 41–66
Sour Cream Waffles, 204, 205
Soy-Blistered Shishitos, 168, 169
Soy-Braised Cumin Lamb, 218, 219
Spiced Lamb Flatbreads, 120, 121
Spiced Yogurt, Roasted Cauliflower, Chickpeas, and Sweet Potatoes with, 102, 103
spinach
    Cod in Green Sauce, 140, 141
    Creamy Green Pasta, 38, 39
    Lemon Chicken Soup for Whatever Ails You, 42, 43
    Split Pea Soup with Bacon and Croutons, 50, 51
    Spring Vegetable Soup with Dumplings and Dill, 46, 47
Spumoni, 258, 259
squash
    Butternut Squash and Ricotta Lasagna, 214, 215
    Summer Squash Casserole with Buttery Ritz Crackers, 76, 77
    Turkey and Butternut Squash Bowl, 116, 117
    Zucchini Soup, 58, 59
Sticky Rolls with Pistachios and Caramel, 198–201, 199–200
Sticky Toffee Pudding, 264, 265
Stone Fruit Salad, 190, 191
Stovetop Mac and Cheese, 28, 29
Strata, French Onion Soup, 196, 197
Strawberry Rhubarb Cake, 242, 243
Summer Squash Casserole with Buttery Ritz Crackers, 76, 77

Sweet Potatoes with Miso Sesame Butter, 94, 95
Sweet Potatoes with Spiced Yogurt, Roasted Cauliflower, Chickpeas, and, 102, 103

T

Tacos, Cheesy Potato and Pinto Bean, 88, 89
Tahini Chocolate Cheesecake Bars, 260–261, 261
Tart, Cheesy Potato, 104, 105
Toast, Mushroom and Pea, 70, 71
Toffee Pudding, Sticky, 264, 265
Tofu, Red Coconut Curry with, 60, 61
Tofu in Miso Butter Sauce with Corn, 78, 79
Tofu Schnitzel with Braised Cabbage, 220, 221–222
Tofu with Scallion Garlic Ginger Oil, 92, 93
tomatoes
    Baked Halibut with Pesto Rosso, 150, 151
    Chickpea Curry, 44, 45
    Crispy Gnocchi Caprese, 30, 31
    Everything Bagel Tomato Panzanella, 84, 85
    Halloumi Fattoush, 106, 107
    Not-Your-Mom's Pasta Salad, 20, 21
    Polenta with Saucy Sausage and Tomatoes, 124, 125
    Roasted Tomato and Red Pepper Soup, 48, 49
    Roasted Tomatoes, Artichokes, and Leeks with Sardines, 146, 147
    Tomato Pie with Buttermilk Biscuit Crust, 235–237, 236
    Tomato Sauce with Pancetta, White Beans, and Rosemary, 24, 25
Turkey and Butternut Squash Bowl, 116, 117
Turkey Chili, White, 54, 55
Turkey Meatballs with Puttanesca Sauce, 134, 135

U

Udon Noodles with Peanut Sauce, 32, 33

V

vegetables, mains, sides, and salads, 65–112. *see also* salads
Vegetable Soup with Dumplings and Dill, Spring, 46, 47
Vinegary Pot Roast with Parsnips and Carrots, 232, 233–234

W

Waffles, Sour Cream, 204, 205
Walnuts, Pasta with Brown Butter Wilted Greens and, 22, 23
weekend cooking, about, 159
weeknight cooking, about, 15
Whipped Cream, Cardamom Honey, Grilled Peaches with, 246, 247
Whipped Cream, in Party Pavlova, 250, 251–252
Whipped Cream, Mascarpone, Dark Chocolate Mousse with, 262, 263
White Turkey Chili, 54, 55
Whole Roasted Spiced Cauliflower with Herby Yogurt Sauce, 216, 217

Y

Yellow Sour Cream Birthday Cake, Chocolate Frosting and, 248–249, 249
Yogurt, Spiced, Roasted Cauliflower, Chickpeas, and Sweet Potatoes with, 102, 103

Z

Zucchini Soup, 58, 59